FROM HOMER TO TRAGEDY

FROM HOMER
TO TRAGEDY
The Art of Allusion in Greek Poetry

RICHARD GARNER

ROUTLEDGE
LONDON AND NEW YORK

First published 1990
by Routledge
11 New Fetter Lane, London EC4P 4EE

Simultaneously published in the USA and Canada
by Routledge
a division of Routledge, Chapman and Hall, Inc.
29 West 35th Street, New York, NY 10001

© 1990 Richard Garner

Printed in Great Britain by
TJ Press (Padstow) Ltd, Padstow, Cornwall

British Library Cataloguing in Publication Data

Garner, Richard, *1953–*
From Homer To Tragedy: The Art of Allusion in Greek Poetry.
I. Poetry in Greek. Critical studies
I. Title
881'.0.'09
ISBN 0–415–03599–6

Library of Congress Cataloging in Publication Data

Garner, Richard, 1953–
From Homer To Tragedy: The Art of Allusion in Greek Poetry/
Richard Garner.
p. cm.
Bibliography: p.
Includes indexes.
ISBN 0–415–03599–6
1. Greek drama (Tragedy)–History and Criticism. 2. Homer–Allusions.
3. Allusions. I. Title.
PA3136.G37 1989
882'.0109–dc20   89–6341

THIS BOOK IS DEDICATED TO

Sarah, Eadie, Phoebe, Sally, Sidnah, Lucy, Sarah
Selina, Martha, Mae, Myra, Nettie, Mildred, Verna,
Lois, Helen, and Vivian

the generations of women who, through three
centuries, have cared for and inspired their
family and without whose constant example
the book would never have been written.

οἵη περ φύλλων γενεὴ τοίη δὲ καὶ ἀνδρῶν.
φύλλα τὰ μέν τ' ἄνεμος χαμάδις χέει, ἄλλα δέ θ' ὕλη
τηλεθόωσα φύει, ἔαρος δ' ἐπιγίγνεται ὥρη·
ὡς ἀνδρῶν γενεὴ ἡ μὲν φύει ἡ δ' ἀπολήγει.

Iliad 6.146–9

ἡμεῖς δ', οἷά τε φύλλα φύει πολυάνθεμος ὥρη
ἔαρος, ὅτ' αἶψ' αὐγῆις αὔξεται ἠελίου,
τοῖς ἴκελοι πήχυιον ἐπὶ χρόνον ἄνθεσιν ἥβης
τερπόμεθα, πρὸς θεῶν εἰδότες οὔτε κακὸν
οὔτ' ἀγαθόν·

Mimnermus 2.1–5

ἐν δὲ τὸ κάλλιστον Χῖος ἔειπεν ἀνήρ·
"οἵη περ φύλλων γενεή, τοίη δὲ καὶ ἀνδρῶν"·

Simonides 8.1–2

ἔνθα δυστάνων βροτῶν
ψυχὰς ἐδάη παρὰ Κωκυτοῦ ῥεέθροις,
οἷά τε φύλλ' ἄνεμος
Ἴδας ἀνὰ μηλοβότους
πρῶνας ἀργηστὰς δονεῖ.

Bacchylides 5.63–67

Ἄγε δὴ φύσιν ἄνδρες ἀμαυρόβιοι, φύλλων γενεᾷ προσόμοιοι,
ὀλιγοδρανέες, πλάσματα πηλοῦ, σκιοειδέα φῦλ' ἀμενηνά,
ἀπτῆνες ἐφημέριοι, ταλαοὶ βροτοί, ἀνέρες εἰκελόνειροι . . .

Aristophanes, *Birds* 685–7

ἢ ὅσα φύλλα χαμᾶζε περικλαδέος πέσεν ὕλης
φυλλοχόῳ ἐνὶ μηνί (τίς ἂν τάδε τεκμήραιτο;)–
ὣς οἱ ἀπειρέσιοι ποταμοῦ παρεμέτρεον ὄχθας,
κλαγγῇ μαιμώοντες.
Apollonius of Rhodes, Argonautica 4.216–19

quam multa in siluis autumni frigore primo
lapsa cadunt folia, aut ad terram gurgite ab alto
quam multae glomerantur aues, ubi frigidus annus
trans pontum fugat et terris immittit apricis.
stabant orantes primi transmittere cursum
tendebantque manus ripae ulterioris amore.
Virgil, Aeneid 6.309–14

licuit semperque licebit
signatum praesente nota producere nomen.
ut silvae foliis pronos mutantur in annos,
prima cadunt: ita verborum vetus interit aetas,
et iuvenum ritu florent modo nata vigentque.
debemur morti nos nostraque.
Horace, Ars Poetica 58–63

Come d'autunno si levan le foglie
l'una appresso de l'altra, fin che 'l ramo
vede a la terra tutte sue spoglie,
similemente il mal seme d'Adamo
gittansi di quel lito ad una ad una
per cenni come augel per suo richiamo.
Dante, Inferno III.112–17

in number more than are the quivering leaves
Of Ida's forest.
Christopher Marlowe, Tamburlaine Pt. 2, III.5.5–6

His legions, angel forms, who lay entranced
Thick as autumnal leaves that strew the brooks
In Vallombrosa, where the Etrurian shades
High overarched embower, or scattered sedge
Afloat, when with fierce winds Orion armed
Hath vexed the Red Sea coast . . .
John Milton, Paradise Lost 1.301–6

CONTENTS

CONTENTS

ACKNOWLEDGMENTS

The author and publisher are grateful to the University of California Press for permission to reproduce the essay "Death and Victory in Euripides' *Alcestis*," which was originally published as an article in *Classical Antiquity*, 7, 1 (1988).

PREFACE

This is a study of the ways Aeschylus, Sophocles, and Euripides imitated and alluded to other poetry. For the most part, only instances in which the imitation or allusion could be to a specific passage have been considered. So, for example, repetitions or modifications of Homeric formulae are not included except when they occur in connection with a more specific reference or borrowing.

Chapter 1, the Introduction, begins with a few examples from Greek lyric poetry, for reasons explained there. The remaining chapters proceed more or less in chronological order with a few slight rearrangements to facilitate relevant comparisons. Thus Aeschylus is the subject of Chapter 2, and Chapters 3–5 follow the careers of Sophocles and Euripides up to their deaths. Euripides' *Cyclops* has been included even though it is a satyr play rather than a tragedy; it provides insight into Euripides' methods and perhaps Sophocles' as well. The *Rhesus* has been omitted. I do not know who wrote it or when it was written. As a small contribution to its study I direct readers to Appendix E, "Passages Used by Poets." There they will find that *Iliad* 10, on which *Rhesus* is based, is the only book of the *Iliad* alluded to nowhere in Greek tragedy. This may or may not have significance; it seems worthy of note.

Throughout the book there are references to passages which are frequently used, which the tragedians have used before or will use again. Rather than reminding the readers each time of all the instances considered so far, I rely on them to use Appendices E and F. By looking, for example, under *Iliad* 22 in Appendix E, "Passages Used by Poets," it is possible to find all the instances discussed in this book.

Chapter 1 begins with the metaphor of the dissection table and the anatomy of allusion. Appendices E and F at the end of this volume are the skeleton. There is something to be said for presenting the skeleton alone. It is the least whimsical, the most businesslike. I could not keep, however, from reconstructing a creature, as lifelike as I could make it, around this skeleton. At the same time, I am aware that many different reconstructions are possible. It is in fact one of my greatest hopes for this book that it will stimulate others to flesh out this skeleton in their own ways, and that the parallels which have languished in bare lists in the notes of learned commentaries will become a part of the life of the text they footnote.

The research for this book began while I was a Junior Fellow in the Society of Fellows at Harvard University. Those years have contributed in many ways to my work. My interest in allusion in Greek poetry was first aroused by an exciting course in Greek elegy with Arthur Adkins at the University of Chicago. I continued my research at the American School in Athens during the summer of 1986, aided by support from the Heyman Prize and the hospitality of Richard Burgi. A Morse Junior Faculty Fellowship at Yale made it possible to complete the book. For all this help I am deeply grateful. A word about the mechanics of this research is in order. A great deal of my work was done by reading, following references in seemingly countless commentaries, and trying out ideas with stacks of concordances. After much had been amassed, Yale acquired the Ibycus system for searching the *Thesaurus Linguae Graecae*. This made it possible to complete what remained much more quickly and to add to and refine my ideas in a way which would not have been possible otherwise.

Many generous readers have helped me with various forms of this manuscript over the years. One of the first was Julia Priest. Later, Emily Anhalt, David Konstan, Wilkins Poe, and Martin Bloomer read various sections. James Powell frequently helped with matters Homeric. Joe Solodow's suggestions improved the section on *Alcestis*. Heavier work at later stages was bravely undertaken by J.E. Lendon, E. Brian Roots, and Gordon Williams. Sarah Mace brought infinite patience and most welcome acuity to many drafts, early and late. The greatest number of improvements, large and small, came at the price of long effort contributed by two dear friends: Anne Burnett and Elizabeth Meyer. To this manuscript – at many stages – both women gave an amount of time and a quality of attention that had better been reserved for their own work, but which I was too selfish to refuse. Much that was awkward and unintelligible has been repaired by their stylish wit and clear intelligence.

Two other women have contributed profoundly to this work. Throughout the research and writing, Sarah Peirce provided support, encouragement, and joy without which it would have been difficult if not impossible to continue. Finally, my greatest and most happily owed debt is to Helen Aingworth. I first attended her college classes in botany and comparative anatomy thirty years ago. Over the next ten years our scientific work together ranged from field entomology to research into the nervous and respiratory systems of primitive fishes. From her I learned to compare, to analyze, and to trace the evolution of relationships. Through her, I first glimpsed the excitement of a life of teaching and learning informed by inspiration and love. She has been and continues to be an incomparable companion. Her example will always be my greatest guide.

Introduction: The Lyric Background

Poetic allusions – this is part of their power both to charm and to frustrate – cannot be proved or disproved. At first this elusiveness seems disastrous to the critic. Upon reflection, however, the problem seems less threatening: little that readers value in poetry responds reliably to the arid analysis of axiom and corollary, or even to the more pragmatic pins and tools of dissection that serve so well to examine the earthworm or affix the butterfly to the board once it can no longer fly. Metaphor, for example, illuminates its object with a light in which, but for the poet's rearrangement of our world, we would not have thought to place the familiar object. And once the new perception occurs, who will say how far the poet intended it to extend, where the boundaries are that should limit the insight the unexpected comparison provides?

Yet even metaphor has an anatomy; confronted with a new juxtaposition of this and that, one need not be simply reduced to ineffable aesthetic delight. In fact, the basic workings of metaphor can be explained fairly simply and with fair precision. And this is particularly fortunate, for they are very like the elements which operate in poetic allusion. Thus this introduction will make its initial explanation of poetic allusion in terms of the mechanics of metaphor – mechanics perhaps more familiar to the reader.

Though the ultimate subject of this book is Greek tragedy, this introduction takes its examples from Greek lyric. Such a course has several advantages. Lyric allusions tend to be simpler than tragic ones. Moreover, having been treated more thoroughly by other scholars in recent years, they provide immediate access to a range of recent opinion and method. Finally – and this ultimately makes it almost necessary to begin from lyric – during the classical age young Athenians were taught lyric poetry as part of their education, adults entertained themselves with it at dinner parties, and the tragedians, whose works are the basis for this book, had lyric poetry as part of their traditional and professional heritage. Playwrights may have learned the art of allusion from their predecessors working in smaller forms. May, perhaps, possibly . . .

What of certainty? To say that poetic allusions cannot be proved or disproved is to claim at once too much and too little. The reference to earlier poetry is beyond doubt in the following verses of an elegiac poet (it may have been Simonides):

ἐν δὲ τὸ κάλλιστον Χῖος ἔειπεν ἀνήρ·
"οἵη περ φύλλων γενεή, τοίη δὲ καὶ ἀνδρῶν"·

The man from Chios said one thing that is best:
Such as are the leaves' generations, so also are men's.

The elegist quotes, using in his next lines a single line that we recognize as a line from the *Iliad* (6.146). And even if the poet did not have *our Iliad*, he has selected the line as something unique from some body of verse and incorporated it into his own. The example is extreme – so much so, in fact, that it risks not being an example of allusion at all: it is plain and direct, not so much allusion as metrical citation.

Of course, whereas the memorable is often in some way unique, the unique is often not memorable at all. Many Homeric lines, for example, contain the sole Homeric occurrence of a given word. Yet a later poet could not expect words such as πλήν (*Od.* 8.207) or δίς (*Od.* 9.491), words which had become (or may well always have been) entirely common and part of everyday speech, to stimulate reflection in his audience. The frequency of non-allusive use has robbed words such as these of any power to suggest their original poetic context, unique though it may have been. This, then, is the other extreme, and although the occurrence of words such as πλήν and δίς has been called allusion by some, in this study, it will not.[1]

Between these two extremes – on the one hand, citation explicitly noted by the second poet and, on the other, words or phrases too common to arrest the attention of his audience – lie literary allusions. This in-between nature is part of their fundamental resemblance to metaphor. If they are to work, allusions must be sufficiently close to what they refer to, just as the metaphor must suggest some comprehensible resemblance in order to be effective. It will do the poet little good to write of the deep night of steamed asparagus if it is impossible to see why or how asparagus may be said to partake of evening. But the opposite is equally unsatisfactory: the reader's pleasure derives from juxtaposition across a distance worth leaping. To say that the wild strawberries were cherries in the grass is a metaphor of sorts; it may mean that the strawberries were as red as cherries – or perhaps as shiny? As edible? Attractive to birds? The problem is that one red fruit is so much like the other that in seeing the strawberry as cherry too little is gained.

All these aspects deserve more detailed explanation. And that had better be done with examples from Greek poetry. The following discussion makes use of terms and models developed by a great many scholars working on metaphor and allusion. My hope is that the multiplicity may be beneficial in two ways: first, readers may find those terms and explanations most agreeable and comprehensible to themselves; second, bringing the various approaches and terms together may help to clarify a similarity of process which all of them envision.

GENERATIONS OF LEAVES: MIMNERMUS

In the first Greek example above, the poet quoted a line from the *Iliad* on men and the generations of leaves. Mimnermus fr. 2, another elegiac poem, has always been recognized as depending on the same Homeric lines:

ἡμεῖς δ', οἷά τε φύλλα φύει πολυάνθεμος ὥρη
   ἔαρος, ὅτ' αἶψ' αὐγῆις αὔξεται ἠελίου,
τοῖς ἴκελοι πήχυιον ἐπὶ χρόνον ἄνθεσιν ἥβης
   τερπόμεθα, πρὸς θεῶν εἰδότες οὔτε κακὸν
οὔτ' ἀγαθόν· Κῆρες δὲ παρεστήκασι μέλαιναι,
   ἡ μὲν ἔχουσα τέλος γήραος ἀργαλέου,
ἡ δ' ἑτέρη θανάτοιο· μίνυνθα δὲ γίνεται ἥβης
   καρπός, ὅσον τ' ἐπὶ γῆν κίδναται ἠέλιος.

(vv. 1–8)

We – like leaves the many-flowered season brings forth
   in spring, when suddenly they grow in rays of sun –
for a small measure of time, in the flowers of our youth

take delight, knowing from the gods neither ill
nor good. But standing by us are black Fates,
  one with the end that is painful old age
the other – death. Brief is youth's
  ripeness, sunlight scattered across the ground.

Mimnermus' poem continues for eight more lines, cataloguing various horrors of old age, but this first half will be our main concern. Several times in the Homeric poems men are compared to leaves, but Mimnermus' opening lines have been modeled closely on the passage from which the elegiac poet cited above had quoted:[2]

οἵη περ φύλλων γενεή, τοίη δὲ καὶ ἀνδρῶν·
φύλλα τὰ μέν τ' ἄνεμος χαμάδις χέει, ἄλλα δέ
  θ' ὕλη
τηλεθόωσα φύει, ἔαρος δ' ἐπιγίγνεται ὥρη·

(*Iliad* 6.146–9)

Such as are the leaves' generations, so are men's.
Some leaves the wind casts down, others the forest
Brings forth in flourish, and the time of spring appears.

In the fifth line, however, Mimnermus' poem takes up a new Homeric parallel. Two fates stand by – one, old age; the other, death. The words echo Achilles' great speech in reply to the embassy in *Iliad* 9. He too has two fates, διχθαδίας κῆρας, with the end of death, θανάτοιο τέλος (*Il.* 9.411). But, having carefully designed his phrases to recall this key passage of the *Iliad*, Mimnermus has also made a significant change. For Achilles, each fate has some attraction: early death will bring noble fame, κλέος ἐσθλόν; the alternative is a long, albeit undistinguished, life amid the comforts of home, ἐπὶ δηρὸν δέ μοι αἰὼν (*Il.* 9.415). Mimnermus, by contrast, acknowledges nothing pleasant about either fate.

If, in fact, Mimnermus has made two allusions to the *Iliad*, how do they work? Like metaphor, we have said; so that must be explained.[3] (In the discussion which follows Mimnermus will, at times, drop from sight, but only so long as is necessary to provide new ways of analyzing his poem.) A metaphor breaks the flow of a statement with something which cannot be understood literally; it forces the audience to go outside the message to interpret it. If I

4

write, "the wild strawberries were in the grass" or "the strawberries were ripe," the reader can accept the facts and proceed. But "the wild strawberries were cherries in the grass" or "the strawberries were rubies against an emerald field" cannot be accepted at face value. Comprehension requires a decision as to why strawberries are like cherries or rubies. The literal object under consideration is frequently called the "tenor," the thing to which the metaphor suggests some comparison, the "vehicle." What the tenor and vehicle share in common has been called the "ground" or, with more precise limits, the "neutral term(s)."[4] In our example strawberries are the tenor, cherries or rubies the vehicle. The ground – and this will be very important throughout – is notoriously hard to specify completely and precisely. Here it at least includes being small, shiny, and red.

Tenor, vehicle, and ground describe static elements of the metaphor. But there are dynamic elements as well, for metaphor forces active interpretation. The failure of the message on a literal level, the puzzle which a metaphor presents to be solved, is often called the gap or a tension. The interpretation or solution, which explains how the image of the vehicle can be applied to the tenor, bridges that gap or releases the tension. The element which alerts the audience to the problem, whether it is simply a single seemingly inappropriate word or a more complicated product of words oddly combined, has been called an ungrammaticality, an impropriety, or a deviation from the norm. An ungrammaticality interrupts the narrative flow; sometimes, it is literally incorrect – cherries are *not* rubies; fruits are not gems. Such an intrusion invites interpretive thought; through reference to the vehicle, a new and more complex understanding is reached. The tenor has been enriched in the mind of the interpreter so that the ungrammaticality no longer seems ungrammatical, the impropriety no longer improper.[5]

The models for the elements and workings of metaphor apply equally well to allusion. The primary text will be the tenor; the text it alludes to, the vehicle; whatever the two texts share in common is the ground. Some ungrammaticality signals to the audience that an allusion is being made, thus creating a gap. Comparison of the two texts leads to an interpretation bringing tenor and vehicle into some relationship, just as in the solution of a metaphor.[6] There are many complexities in this process; more details will be added in due course.

We are now in a position to talk about Mimnermus 2 more precisely. The means, or ungrammaticalities, by which the reader is referred to Mimnermus' vehicle, the *Iliad*, are various. The second allusion, to the two fates of Achilles, is easier to analyze. The description of the two fates at first sounds familiar, but the blunt second alternative, death without any positive compensation, throws the expected contrast out of balance. Once attention is arrested, the similarity of the Mimnermus passage to Achilles' words in the *Iliad*, that is, the ground, directs the reader to associate the tenor with its vehicle. Moreover, an added pointer sending the reader to the *Iliad* for a reference which will bridge the gap is the first allusion itself, for that has already raised expectation for the theme of mortality as treated in the *Iliad*. Such pointers could be broadly considered ungrammaticalities; it may be more useful to have another term for instances in which something more general in the context (such as the previous allusion here) helps to precipitate or trigger the recognition of allusion: since the term "trigger" has already been similarly used in studying allusion in Greek poetry, it will be retained here.[7]

But what has been the ungrammaticality to signal the first allusion, the reference to the generations of leaves? Partly, the mere familiarity of the lines. We began with a direct quotation of *Iliad* 6.146 in an elegy which proclaimed the line the best, and a glance at either the beginning or end of this book, to the dedication or Appendices E and F, will confirm the popularity of the passage.[8] The near quotation of this passage, then, is a sort of ungrammaticality to alert the reader. It is somewhat like using quotation marks to label a borrowed phrase in the middle of one's sentence. The words are set apart as different from merely our own – they refer to language borrowed or used in some marked way. Moreover, Mimnermus' allusion is more likely to be identified because the conventions of Greek poetry lead the audience to have higher expectation of an allusion in the opening lines of a poem or a strophe than at other points in the verse. Thus, habit dictates that in first lines the audience will be particularly alert for anything out of the way which might suggest allusion. (Here I merely assert a convention which is demonstrated in some detail throughout the book. The passages I rely on as proof are collected in Appendix A.)

The real work – for the above has merely indicated how the allusions in Mimnermus are initially signaled, how the tension is set up – is to see how an allusion may be integrated interpretively. With metaphor, as with simile, it is up to the interpreter to decide how far the comparison goes, and much will depend on the context in which the metaphor or simile occurs.[9] Here is the difficulty of establishing the ground. What makes a comparison effective may depend not only on suggestive similarities, but also, sometimes, on pointed differences – even on the two together. In the *Iliad*, missiles hurled thick and fast in battle are compared to snowflakes. Some interpreters will limit their understanding to the shared speed and quantity of objects falling through the air; others will add to this the many contrasts – heavy and light, harmful and harmless, deadly clangor of war and peaceful silence of the snowstorm.

Textual allusions at once multiply possibilities and difficulties present in metaphor and simile, for the text of the tenor and the text of the vehicle both have contexts which must be examined for their interactions.[10] True, in the simplest instance, "allusion may be a mere cultural gesture in the direction of a generally admired predecessor."[11] A Homeric phrase may be used to lend a general air of respectable tradition. Often, however, things are less simple. Because each end, as it were, of the allusion may involve so many elements, it is useful to call the tenor and its context the primary field, the vehicle and its context the secondary field. In allusion, it is the interaction of the two fields, all their similarities and differences, and all the implications these have for the tenor, which are used by the audience to bridge the gap between the two texts.

The disruptive allusion, near but not exact quotation, with which Mimnermus begins his poem, excites the comparison of his tenor with the vehicle he has worked from. Both passages are concerned with the rapid passing of the leaves as an image for the relentless succession of the multitude of human lives. The secondary field, however, turns out to be quite different. In the epic simile one race is replaced by another, and each generation is known and remembered; Glaukos, the Homeric speaker, is a proud warrior from a famous line with every expectation of fame in the future. He will die, as all men die, but, in short, springtime comes again. How completely different is Mimnermus! Granted, the leaves of spring, just as in the *Iliad*, are what we are like. But in the primary field of the poem there is no consideration of the generations which came before, no thought of those to follow, no acknowledgement, even, that spring always returns. We take our pleasure in the blossoms of this brief abrupt burst of sunlight and that, for us, is all.

Actually it is not all. But what comes next is not cheerful. Immediately on the heels of ignorant youth come two black Fates. Again the similarity to Achilles' two fates in the *Iliad* and to the words he uses to describe them give rise to the allusive quotation marks around Mimnermus' phrases, pushing us to go to the secondary field to learn why the poet's message has strayed from simply his own words. The effect of the first allusion adds somber clarity to the changes Mimnermus has made for his second (noted above). For Achilles, brief youth and inescapable death are not the problem: each of his real choices affords some comfort. In the end, he will reject the pleasures of life at home for fame of unfading brilliance. For Mimnermus, by contrast, the choices, although formally expressed as such, are not choices at all. There is no pleasure of any sort past youth, no possibility of fame. Death seems preferable to life, but only because old age (as the poem goes on to describe it) is so unspeakably awful. Mimnermus, the allusions give us to understand, hasn't the luxury of a Homeric hero, and if only we think about it we will see that we do not either. However much we are all like leaves, we are not like Achilles and Glaukos.

Mimnermus' message could have been conveyed without allusion. Yet the forced integration of the epic world, the stark contrast with the consolations of Homeric greatness and immortal fame enrich Mimnermus' vision, transforming the quality of the sunlight he casts on his spring leaves with the power that is the property of great poetry. Recognition of the Homeric source leads to contemplation of our fate, and, at least while we are under the spell of Mimnerman elegy, our youthful rays of sun are collected, as if by a magnifying glass, into a briefer beam of burning intensity.

PARENTS AND SONS: TYRTAEUS

Hector, at the beginning of *Iliad* 22, is the sole Trojan before the walls of Troy. Achilles is in pursuit; Priam and Hecuba, Hector's parents, plead with him to come inside the walls lest Achilles kill him and rob the city of its greatest defender. Priam paints pathetic visions of the future; Hecuba holds out her breast as she pleads; Hector conducts a tragic debate with himself in what seems like a nightmare, comes at last to a tragic recognition, and meets his tragic end. This scene, more than any other in the Homeric poems, provided material for allusion: lyric poets, all three major tragedians, and Hellenistic poets drew on this climax of the struggle between Greeks and Trojans, Achilles and Hector.

The use Tyrtaeus found for the Homeric passage might seem paradoxical or even inept: Priam's plea to Hector to leave the fight and come inside to safety (*Il.* 22.66–76) has been reworked by Tyrtaeus to urge the youth of Sparta not to abandon the fight (fr. 10W).[12] Indeed, Tyrtaeus opens his poem with a paradoxical assertion which his verse must make persuasive if the young are to fight as he urges them to. "Dying is beautiful," he begins – τεθνάμεναι γὰρ καλὸν (10.1). This is no Mimnerman meditation theoretically weighing the diminished life of old age against the end of life altogether. The end of Tyrtaeus' first line immediately establishes that this is a concrete proposition: dying is beautiful when you fall in the front ranks of battle, ἐνὶ προμάχοισι πεσόντα (10.1). Tyrtaeus has set himself an unenviable task, and the allusion to *Iliad* 22 is the last and strongest of the propositions in the logic of his poetic argument.

Tyrtaeus leads into his conclusion with the following lines (10W.21–30):

αἰσχρὸν γὰρ δὴ τοῦτο, μετὰ προμάχοισι πεσόντα
  κεῖσθαι πρόσθε νέων ἄνδρα παλαιότερον,
ἤδη λευκὸν ἔχοντα κάρη πολιόν τε γένειον,
  θυμὸν ἀποπνείοντ' ἄλκιμον ἐν κονίηι,
αἱματόεντ' αἰδοῖα φίλαις ἐν χερσὶν ἔχοντα–
  αἰσχρὰ τά γ' ὀφθαλμοῖς καὶ νεμεσητὸν ἰδεῖν,
καὶ χρόα γυμνωθέντα· νέοισι δὲ πάντ' ἐπέοικεν,
  ὄφρ' ἐρατῆς ἥβης ἀγλαὸν ἄνθος ἔχηι,
ἀνδράσι μὲν θηητὸς ἰδεῖν, ἐρατὸς δὲ γυναιξὶ
  ζωὸς ἐών, καλὸς δ' ἐν προμάχοισι πεσών.

For this is shameful, when, having fallen in the front ranks,
  An older man lies in front of the young,
Hair already white and beard gray,
  Breathing out his brave spirit in the dust,
Holding his bloody genitals in his hands –
  Shameful to sight, a reproach to see –
His flesh bared. But for the young all is seemly,

9

As long as he has the bright flower of lovely youth,
A marvel to look on for men, for women an object of love,
While he lives, and fair when he falls in the front ranks.

Here are the Homeric lines they are based on (*Il.* 22.66–76):

αὐτὸν δ᾽ ἂν πύματόν με κύνες πρώτῃσι θύρῃσιν
ὠμησταὶ ἐρύουσιν, ἐπεί κέ τις ὀξέϊ χαλκῷ
τύψας ἠὲ βαλὼν ῥεθέων ἐκ θυμὸν ἕληται,
οὓς τρέφον ἐν μεγάροισι τραπεζῆας θυραωρούς,
οἵ κ᾽ ἐμὸν αἷμα πιόντες ἀλύσσοντες περὶ θυμῷ
κείσοντ᾽ ἐν προθύροισι. νέῳ δέ τε πάντ᾽ ἐπέοικεν
ἀρηϊκταμένῳ δεδαϊγμένῳ ὀξέϊ χαλκῷ
κεῖσθαι· πάντα δὲ καλὰ θανόντι περ ὅττι φανήῃ·
ἀλλ᾽ ὅτε δὴ πολιόν τε κάρη πολιόν τε γένειον
αἰδῶ τ᾽ αἰσχύνωσι κύνες κταμένοιο γέροντος,
τοῦτο δὴ οἴκτιστον πέλεται δειλοῖσι βροτοῖσιν.

In the end the savage dogs will tear me apart, in the
fore-doors, when someone, with sharp bronze,
wounds me and takes my spirit from my limbs –
the dogs I reared in the house to attend table and doors,
who will drink my blood and maddened in spirit
lie in the door-way. But for the young all is seemly,
war-slain, slashed with sharp bronze
lying there. All that shows is lovely, even in death.
But when gray hair and gray beard
and genitals of a slain old man are outraged by dogs,
this is the most pitiful thing for wretched mortals.

If Hector is killed the city will fall; so Priam envisions himself slain, eaten by his own dogs. And although the young are beautiful even in death, the old man, with his gray head and gray beard, will be a pitiable sight.

Tyrtaeus' use of the language from the Homeric lines begins with κεῖσθαι (v. 22), but this will not be noticed on a first hearing. His next line triggers the allusion: the last four words are a direct quotation of *Iliad* 22.74, the first three a slight variation. In Tyrtaeus' lines, the old man has died in battle because the young have fled and left him exposed. His bloody genitals (v. 25), like Priam's (22.75), are the focus of attention. In Tyrtaeus, what Priam called a pitiable sight (οἴκτιστον, 22.76) is described as

10

shameful or ugly (αἰσχρὸν, v. 21; αἰσχρὰ, v. 26). Then Tyrtaeus includes another near quotation as he too contrasts the ugliness of old age with youthful beauty (Tyrt. v. 27, *Il.* 22.71). Everything, Tyrtaeus says, befits the young man: men admire him, women desire him, and – it seems almost tautologous as presented – he is beautiful when he falls in battle – καλὸς δ' ἐν προμάχοισι πεσών (v. 30). And yet with this line Tyrtaeus comes full circle by nearly repeating the conclusion of his first line and at the same time makes what was so paradoxical thirty lines before – that dying in battle is beautiful – seem perfectly obvious now.

Tyrtaeus makes the Homeric allusion work for him several ways at once. First, repetition of the images of Priam's plea implies that between the vehicle of the battle for Troy and the tenor of Tyrtaeus' battle there is a common ground. Once the gap between the two texts is bridged, all the prestige of epic is lent to the fighting Tyrtaeus is commending at present. Tyrtaeus benefits from the moving quality of Priam's plea and the sobering fact that because Hector disregarded it, Priam, Hector, and Troy all perished; Priam's vision of the future was sadly accurate. Second, the comparison flatters Tyrtaeus' audience, for they must ultimately find themselves in the position of Hector. The application of the *Iliad* to the present shows that they are crucial to the defense of their city as that great hero was to his. Finally, Priam's speech has been touched up ever so slightly so as to make it lead toward the proof of Tyrtaeus' initial outrageous claim. Priam's emphasis on the pitiable nature of the fallen old man has been modified to become an elegiac insistence upon the ugliness of the scene. This makes the contrast, also borrowed from the *Iliad*, of the beauty of the younger fighter something which Tyrtaeus can elaborate a little further, and quite attractively. And it allows him to slide magically from the general declaration of the beauty of dying – which is hard to accept – to the beauty of the young – which is practically impossible to deny.

There is a last point to be noticed. Verse 30 of Tyrtaeus' poem begins with the words ζωὸς ἐών. They do not constitute an allusion as we have described that phenomenon, because the words seem too common to be noticed: they occur as a formula eight times in the Homeric poems, in six of these at the beginning of a line, as here. Nevertheless the phrase has been deployed

11

effectively to reinforce the flattering comparison that has been made with allusion; for it is regularly used to lament the passing of great warriors, figures of the greatest fame: four of the six line-initial uses are for Sarpedon, Patroclus, and Hector.[13] Tragedy makes a frequent practice of accompanying allusions with similar reinforcing effects. These are most often either mere imitations of specific passages which suggest no interpretive comparison between tenor and vehicle, or, as in these verses of Tyrtaeus, uses of more frequently found words and phrases which, despite the fact that they are not unique, have been suggestively applied.

APHRODITE IN BATTLE: SAPPHO

An echo – with an intentionally jarring change – of a Homeric formula serves as a trigger for Homeric allusion in Sappho 1 LP. Sappho describes one of Aphrodite's former visits when she yoked her divine chariot and was brought by swift – sparrows, ὦκεες στροῦθοι (v. 10). In the Homeric poems, of course, ὦκεες ἵπποι, swift horses, draw chariots. Sappho's playful deviation from the standard phrase alerts her audience to a more extensive allusive variation, and the unanimous verdict, since Page, has been that the scene which serves as Sappho's model is Diomedes' own encounter with female divinity in *Iliad* 5.[14]

Sappho calls on her old ally Aphrodite, Zeus' daughter (v. 2), to be her ally in battle (σύμμαχος v. 28) once again as she has been before (v. 5–8); in the past, the golden chariot was yoked (8–9); the goddess departed from Olympus (7) and flew through mid-air (11–12). Diomedes also calls on one of Zeus' daughters (*Il.* 5.115, cf. 5.733) with the prayer to help him now as before (5.115–17). When Athena does come to battle, there is mention of her dappled cloak (5.734–5, cf. Sappho 1.1); the golden chariot is yoked to its swift horses (5.729–32); there is departure from Olympus (5.749–50) and the same picturesque flight through mid-air (5.768–9).

If this were the extent of the allusion the integration of tenor and vehicle would be relatively simple. The ground would be a mortal in battle (military or erotic) seeking help from an ally-goddess. That Diomedes in this comparison is the vehicle for Sappho would either give her battle for love a more serious tone and lend it the splendor of Homeric combat, or, more likely, add a certain amount ironic perspective and humor to Sappho's own form of warfare. It might be difficult to balance the two effects. But Sappho's allusion is much more complex.

Between Diomedes' first call to Athena and her eventual appearance he has fought with and wounded Aphrodite herself (*Il.* 5.335–43). Thus part of the vehicle for Sappho's poem is directly involved with her tenor. Moreover, in the secondary field, the *Iliad*, the wounded Aphrodite flees from the scene in a chariot (5.363–9) drawn by horses which fly her back to Olympus, and she seeks comfort from the powerful goddess Dione who asks who has hurt her (5.373–4), just as in the primary field of Sappho's poem Aphrodite asks the disconsolate Sappho who has wronged her (v. 19–20). Thus the normal tension between tenor and vehicle has here been considerably complicated: Sappho to be helped by Aphrodite is like Diomedes to be helped by Athena, but Sappho to be consoled by Aphrodite is also like Aphrodite (wounded by Diomedes) to be consoled by Dione. Sappho draws simultaneously on two connected vehicles which are part of a continuous narrative in her secondary field. To appreciate Sappho's scene, the audience compares Diomedes' battle with Sappho's; the erotic struggle is different and calls for a sparrow-drawn rather than a horse-drawn chariot – and as if to make sure the audience sees the significance of the gap, there is Aphrodite herself in the secondary field trying to do military battle with Diomedes and failing miserably: she had better stick to the type of encounter where she is most skilled, leave bloody epic behind, and come to Sappho in lyric instead.

Forcing the audience to work from more than one viewpoint, to see comparisons in multiple ways which reveal the complications of the problem under consideration – this is Sappho's chosen method.[15] Elsewhere it is done by other means than literary allusion: in Sappho 16, for example, the paradigm of Helen and Menelaus and Paris must be applied to that of Sappho and Anaktoria and Anaktoria's new husband in more ways than one before the problem comes into focus. Within each triangle the relationships are tangled, and once the tenor and vehicle are superimposed, no one comparison will bring out all the similarities. The relationships are asymmetrical; if the ratios and proportions were neater, the stories of love would be happier, more mathematical – and less human.

The example of Sappho 1 is important in several respects. It combines allusion with imitation; in fact, the imitation of the common Homeric formula may even trigger the allusion. The use of *Iliad* 5 itself is quite complex; it requires integrating multiple incidents from a long narrative in order to get the full benefit of the interaction between the two fields. Finally, we may note here that the Diomedes passage continues without a break into *Iliad* 6 and the encounter with Glaukos and the discussion of the generations of leaves motivated by Diomedes' concern to avoid further theomachy. *Iliad* 5 and 6 will be important for allusions in tragedy as well: passages from the two books are repeatedly used, and the episode with Aphrodite combined with material from *Iliad* 6 will be considered again in relation to Sophocles' *Antigone*.

MEN AND BEASTS: STESICHORUS

The three examples considered so far each alluded to a different passage of the *Iliad*: Mimnermus to Glaukos' confrontation with Diomedes in *Iliad* 6, Tyrtaeus to Hector's scene with his parents in *Iliad* 22, and Sappho to Athena's and Aphrodite's involvement with Diomedes in *Iliad* 5, all epic passages to be used by the tragedians as well. The following incident in Stesichorus' poetry uses a simile from the *Iliad* which does not appear again until Virgil uses it. Nevertheless it is an instructive example: it combines the complicating power of metaphor and allusion to maximum advantage, thereby attesting to the early sophistication with which Greek poets elaborated their verse.

The papyrus text of Stesichorus' *Geryoneïs* (**P**. Oxy. 2617) offers a reasonably continuous description of Heracles' battle with the three-headed monster, Geryon. Damage deprives us of the beginning, but the account comes into focus as an arrow tipped with poison from one monster, the Hydra, pierces one of the heads of another, Geryon, making it droop like a poppy. Since Greek allows both the arrow and the poppy to have "heads," the weapon and the plant are linked to the two monsters by simple word-play. But Stesichorus has gone beyond banality and bound these four subjects together with three types of comparison – metaphor, simile, and Homeric allusion. The result is a three-headed rhetorical creature perfectly suited to the monster whose death it describes.[16]

Stesichorus gives the passage an initial focus by describing the tip of the arrow as its head (κεφαλά), but the metaphor is almost certainly already dead and is the least marked part of the opening, for the head is said to have death around it:

]ων στυγε[ρ]οῦ
θανάτοι]ο . .[ ]
κ]εφ[αλ]ᾶι πέρι [πότμον] ἔχων

(*Geryoneïs* S15 col. ii.1–3)

Since arrow heads do not properly have anything around them, much less something as abstract as death, this will seem to be the metaphor. This initial ungrammaticality is easily resolved, for a weapon – since it brings death – could be said to have death around it or to be clad in death. But this solution to the metaphor, although true, turns out to be only part of the truth, for Stesichorus immediately reveals that the arrow's head has been smeared with blood and bile. These physiological details begin to revive the metaphor of the arrow's head. And the metaphor comes fully to life when the origin of this death of blood and bile is revealed: these drops, says Stesichorus, *are* the pains of the speckle-necked hydra:

πεφορυ–
γ]μένος αἵματ[ι . . . . .] . . [. .]ι τε χολᾶι,
ant.
ὀλεσάνορος αἰολοδε[ίρ]ου
ὀδύναισιν Ὕδρας·

(*Geryoneïs* S15 col. ii.3–6)

With the addition of this image, the initial gap is seen to require a bridge very different from the one first supplied. The literal bloody death from the heads and necks of the hydra has been applied to the head of the arrow. As that arrow pushes silently into one of the heads of Geryon, it pierces flesh and bone so that Geryon's head and body become blood-smeared just like the head of the arrow which killed him. The Hydra's death pains, blood, and bile have produced more pain, blood, and death.

The pierced head flops over lifelessly to the side – a striking image – especially since the body will continue to fight under the direction of its two remaining heads.[17] Here Stesichorus introduces a simile used in the *Iliad* when, once Gorgythion has been killed by an arrow, his head flops, as does Geryon's, like a poppy.[18] Compare:

15

καὶ τοῦ μέν ῥ' ἀφάμαρθ', ὃ δ' ἀμύμονα Γοργυθίωνα
υἱὸν ἐῢν Πριάμοιο κατὰ στῆθος βάλεν ἰῷ,
τόν ῥ' ἐξ Αἰσύμηθεν ὀπυιομένη τέκε μήτηρ
καλὴ Καστιάνειρα δέμας ἐϊκυῖα θεῇσι.
μήκων δ' ὡς ἑτέρωσε κάρη βάλεν, ἥ τ' ἐνὶ κήπῳ
καρπῷ βριθομένη νοτίῃσί τε εἰαρινῇσιν,
ὣς ἑτέρωσ' ἤμυσε κάρη πήληκι βαρυνθέν.

Iliad 8.302–8

In fact he missed that man; instead he hit blameless
Gorgythion, Priam's good son, in the chest with his arrow
(his mother was a bride from Aisyme,
the beautiful Castianeira with a form like the goddesses').
He cast his head to one side – like a poppy which, in the
garden, is weighed down with ripeness and spring showers –
thus his head sank to one side, weighed down by his helmet.

ἀπέκλινε δ' ἄρ' αὐχενα Γαρ[υόνας
    ἐπικάρσιον, ὡς ὅκα μ[ά]κω[ν
ἄτε καταισχύνοισ' ἀπαλὸν [δέμας
    αἶψ' ἀπὸ φύλλα βαλοῖσα γ[

(*Geryoneïs* S15 col. ii.14–17)

So Geryon bent his neck
    to one side, as when a poppy
fouling its delicate form
    suddenly casts its petals . . .

Even though the Stesichorean fragment breaks off before the simile
is finished, several points are clear. In the *Iliad* it is specifically the
poppy's and warrior's heads which are mentioned. Stesichorus has
tied his image not only to the arrow by mentioning its head, but
also to the Hydra's neck by mentioning that Geryon has bent his
neck – a useful change since it recalls the Hydra's necks – and after
all Geryon has several himself. In Homer there is a stark contrast
between the poppy in the garden, damp from a spring shower, and
the blood-soaked warrior on the field of battle (we will likely
choose to see the similarity and the difference in their crimson
coloration as well even though it is not explicitly mentioned in the
Homeric tenor or vehicle). Stesichorus has pushed this contrast
further: even though he describes the poppy as battered, its petals
and delicate form – described as a body, δέμας – will only be

beautiful in comparison with Geryon. The monstrous contrast of the warrior and the poppy has been heightened by Stesichorus in several ways. First, Geryon has not been wounded in the chest, as had Gorgythion; instead he has an arrow all the way through his head, which means that the drooping flower will be moistened and dripping liquids horribly in contrast with pure spring moisture. Moreover, through the description of the arrow and particularly of the Hydra, monstrous both in life and in its poison-giving mangled death, Geryon's beastly necks and heads have been magically if illogically multiplied and have been bound through the logic of metaphor and image to a fate of fatal bloody disfigurement.

It has been said of the Homeric simile that after the poppy is mentioned "the simile goes its own way without regard for the context."[19] Even if this is true of the epic context, however, Stesichorus' adaptation gives added relevance to the details. The secondary field from which the simile is drawn must be brought into some relation with the primary field in which Stesichorus has placed it. It will be seen immediately that such synthesis involves a complex comparison which will always be required when a poet alludes to a simile or metaphor in an earlier text: the original passage itself contains both a tenor and a vehicle, a primary and a secondary field; so will the new passage; and the original passage, as a whole, serves as a vehicle or secondary field for the tenor or primary field represented by the new passage as a whole.

The resulting multiplicity of potentially dynamic relationships is sufficiently complex and potentially so important that it perhaps deserves one more description. When simile or metaphor is involved in allusion, both the main tenor or primary field and the main vehicle or secondary field can each be further subdivided into the tenor and vehicle contained *within* each field. The relationship between the main tenor and vehicle, that is, the two texts, will be partially, but not entirely, a result of the comparison and contrast of the dynamic relationship between the tenor and vehicle that each text contains. That is, although tenor may be compared to tenor and vehicle to vehicle, the final closing of the gap between the two texts may well require a comparison of how the gap is bridged between tenor and vehicle within each text. Such a use of two fields, each of which itself consists of two fields, is a device eventually exploited to the fullest by Sophocles. In our present example, the scene of heroic Homeric battle (the tenor in the secondary field) contrasts with this literally monstrous fight (the tenor in the primary field) in which Stesichorus' Heracles is involved. In the *Iliad*, the dying Gorgythion in his immobilized condition is comfortingly more like the unmoving flower of the simile than is this Geryon who, for all his likeness to a hero in Homer, is still capable of locomotion with his grotesque version of a red wilting flower draped alongside other still dangerous necks and heads. The Hydra's venom is *man*-destroying – but Heracles is using it against a monster. The original context of the simile helps to emphasize the contrast between man and monster, thereby heightening the dramatic tension in Stesichorus' account: what worked with human foe may well fail with a more outlandish opponent. Thus does allusive craft bring the dead metaphor of the arrow's head to life in the struggle to kill Geryon.

SOME FINAL CONSIDERATIONS

So much for the basic anatomy and mechanics of allusion. Some scholars would admit the logic of the model but reserve its application to Hellenistic and Roman poetry; Greek poetry of the archaic and classical periods is a product of a society more oral, less bookish. Furthermore, the above discussion with its host of modern terms is made necessary partly by the fact that there is practically no ancient discussion of allusion with terms that we can borrow.[20] Is this a sign that the phenomenon was not recognized in classical Athens or even – which is nearly the same thing, after all – that it did not exist? Probably not. There are few technical literary discussions of any sort from the ancient world; this has not discouraged the modern development of analyses, for example, of meter. Moreover, there is evidence from classical Athens that the importance of oral performance is only one side of the place of poetry in society. Euripides reflects an awareness, even assumption, that poetry, especially the poetry of the older poets, is written and known from writing (*Med.* 423, *Hipp.* 451–3, *IA* 794–800). In any case, recognition of allusions depends on the audience knowing that poetry, having it in their heads, regardless of how they learned it. And there is much evidence that a major part of Athenian education consisted in learning poetry. In fact, Aristophanes' *Clouds* suggests that at least by the late fifth century passages from Aeschylus formed a part of the curriculum to be learned by heart.[21]

Even, however, if the possibility of allusion is admitted, there are special problems facing those who would study allusions in fifth-century tragedy. Allusions to the Homeric poems are the most secure. Granted, a great deal of early epic has been lost, and that loss will figure – at least in speculative fashion – in following chapters. But the *Iliad* and *Odyssey* were always of great importance, and these two surviving poems repeatedly prove rewarding vehicles for allusion. Outside the Homeric poems, however, the problems are greater. Little of Greek lyric or tragedy has survived. There will always be the possibility that what looks like an allusion in tragedy to an earlier lyric or tragic passage may not be one at all. A full tradition might make it clear that each of the two surviving passages refers to a third which has been lost, or that in each surviving passage the tenor alludes to a different vehicle, both from passages now lost, or even that what looks like a reference from the primary field in one text to the secondary field in the other is merely the chance survival of two instances of what in fact was a commonplace. These are sobering difficulties but not crippling ones.[22] In fact, part of the justification for a large-scale study of allusion in tragedy is the need to establish as securely as possible as many patterns as possible. The following chapters should help to lay a foundation, as nothing has before, for helping to evaluate the possibility of such poetic allusion in the classical period.

One major limitation remains to be accepted: no matter how securely a body of allusions in tragedy can be established, the collection – assuming that allusion took place – will be incomplete in two respects. Whatever, for example, we find in Sophocles' seven plays, it represents only what he did in barely more than five percent of his work. It may, or may not, be representative of his general practice. More disturbing, perhaps, is that even for those seven plays, we can only have a partial picture. If Sophocles was a creator of allusions, the bulk of his allusions to lyric and tragedy will be impossible for us to identify: his sources, like his own works, no longer survive.

All this must not discourage the reader. The Homeric poems are a rich source for the tragedians, and even the small sample of tragedy we have to study suggests persistent patterns in allusion. Moreover, as this study will show, we have been fortunate more than once in what the chances of survival have passed on to us.

INTRODUCTION

In the following chapters I will not use the terms explained here in discussing every example: this would be both tedious and inefficient. But the model always underlies the discussion. More often than not, I classify examples as allusions, in which an audience might appreciate the relation of tenor and vehicle, or as imitations, which seem to borrow from a specific passage without suggesting any interaction. These classifications are merely suggestions; no two readers will react to every instance alike. Sometimes I have left it to the reader to decide what to make of the phenomena presented. My view is that, given our partial knowledge of Greek usage and the small fraction of Greek literature which has survived, secure distinctions between allusion and imitation are frequently impossible to make. Ultimately, the terms are of little importance. Furthermore, deciding whether one passage or another works in a given way means less than recognizing that somewhere beneath the surface of the poetry, allusive technique imparts an added richness. And, after all, the history of our science has shown that even in the most detailed examinations, the dissection of Greek poetry is merely a mirage of dismemberment, for as each student completes or abandons his task, the butterfly is released from the board and continues its poetic flight unharmed.

2

Slices from the Banquet: The Tragedies of Aeschylus

INTRODUCTION

Tragedy created new possibilities for allusion: suggestive echoes could be multiplied, dispersed, and made to resonate in a poetic space extended far beyond the usual limits of polished lyric and pointed elegiac. Hints could be followed up and reinforced, shaped, and modified just as could the imagery internal to the play or even trilogy. Thus, extended or multiple allusions might seem a natural means for Aeschylus to use; but perhaps engaged in the labor of bringing tragedy from some primitive form into what we recognize as its classic shape, his creative energy was consumed in other matters. In any case, the three earliest plays we have from Aeschylus, the *Persians*, *Seven Against Thebes*, and the *Suppliants*, seem to fall together into a group in which allusion was of relatively little importance. Perhaps if we had any respectable portion of Aeschylus' dramatic output we would see this as part of a general pattern. Certainly he was generally less given to borrowing Homeric phrases and formulae than Sophocles or Euripides.[1] However, with so few plays to judge by, we may simply be faced with coincidence. Very different from the early plays is the work which closes Aeschylus' career, the *Oresteia*; yet like so much in Aeschylus, it is a special case in multiple ways: besides being late, it is also our only extant trilogy, and, unlike his other extant plays, it is explicitly concerned with the story of Troy. Some or all of these circumstances may help explain why the Homeric past more frequently finds its way into the poetry of the trilogy than into that of the earlier plays. There is, of course, a seventh play, the *Prometheus Bound*, which here is reserved for separate treatment. The allusions in the play are so extensive, so closely related to each

21

other, and so important to the plot and themes of the play itself that they require more extensive examination.

THE EARLY PLAYS

The *Persians* is Aeschylus' first extant play, and its first line is as clear an echo as anything in Greek tragedy: τάδε μὲν Περσῶν τῶν οἰχομένων paraphrases the first line of Phrynichus' *Phoenissae*: τάδ' ἔστι Περσῶν τῶν πάλαι βεβηκότων. Since Phrynichus' play (probably produced in 476 B.C.) and Aeschylus' (produced in 472) told much the same story, the tension that arises from the introduction of another poet's words is quickly and easily resolved: primary field and secondary field are essentially the same. The authoritative position of both lines as the first in their respective plays helps trigger recognition, but one recognizes more a compliment than an allusion.[2] In one small point exact memory makes Phrynichus' line an effective foil for Aeschylus': the earlier play's neutral βεβηκότων, which simply means "go," has been replaced by οἰχομένων, with its idiomatic possibility of "go to destruction," hinting ominously at the coming disaster.[3]

Just as the examination of Aeschylus' use of earlier tragedy is severely limited by the scarcity of surviving material, so observations about his allusions to lyric are generally confined to a bare identification of his sources. Thus, for example, Fraenkel declared that at *Persae* 763 the phrase "sheep-feeding Asia" was an "unquestionable borrowing" from Archilochus who had used the identical phrase (227W); since no context for the lyric line survives, no application of the vehicle to the tenor can be made.[4] Similarly, a poem of Alcaeus' (6V) has been thought to lie behind Aeschylus' image of an army as a dangerous wave opposed by a worthy man (*Pers.* 87–92), and there are some striking verbal similarities between the two passages. In this case, both the fragmentary nature of the Alcaean song and the great frequency of nautical imagery in Greek poetry block further interpretation of the echo.

In contrast to tragic or lyric allusions and imitations, the Homeric material always includes a context so that the secondary field can be examined for relevance. In the *Persians* the Homeric echoes, few though they are, represent a typical range of Aeschylean use, at least for the plays we have. They also follow a pattern which seems to hold true for tragedy as a whole: there are about twice as many imitations or allusions to the *Iliad* as to the *Odyssey*, and the Iliadic references tend to be crisper and more suggestively allusive. For example, Aeschylus seems to have taken the phrase used for Odysseus' raft – "a stout-bound raft" (σχεδίης πολυδέσμου, *Od*. 5.33 and 7.264) – as the model for the description of the bridge the Persians build to cross into Greece – "a cable-bound raft . . . stout-clamped" (λίνοδέσμῳ σχεδίᾳ . . . πολύγομφον, 68–71).[5] A phrase from the *Odyssey* has been imitated, but no gain is to be had by identifying its origin. A subsequent use of language from the *Iliad* seems to work somewhat differently. Thus, when the Persian elders learn of the destruction of their army, they cry that many Persian women have been made bereft of children and husbands (ὡς πολλὰς Περσίδων μάταν ἔκτισαν εὔνιδας ἠδ' ἀνάνδρους, 288–9). The word εὖνις, which must here be translated as "bereft of children," is quite rare and properly seems to mean simply "bereft." It occurs in earlier Greek literature only twice, once in the *Iliad* (22.44) and once in the *Odyssey* (9.524), and there are a number of reasons to suspect that it is taken from that same speech of Priam's in *Iliad* 22 which Tyrtaeus had used to such effect.[6] First, as a general consideration, this scene in the *Iliad* is the most frequently echoed in all Greek literature, so heavily used that it seems likely to have been widely known in great detail – perhaps regularly learned by Athenian children – and so it seems a particularly likely candidate for a significant allusion. More specifically, the text of *Persians* has a small but puzzling ungrammaticality which may trigger an allusion to this Homeric passage in particular. Aeschylus has used the adjective "bereft" elliptically; in order for the lines to make sense, one must understand the complement "sons." If one goes to Priam's epic speech, the word is explicitly supplied. Moreover, like the Persian elders, Priam emphasizes the multiplicity of the loss (υἱῶν πολλῶν τε καὶ ἐσθλῶν εὖνιν ἔθηκε). Epic had concentrated the loss of so many sons in the grief of one father, Priam, and in the destructive agency of one enemy, Achilles; but Priam's cry translates well into the woe of the many in Aeschylus. Finally, since Priam is an Asian ruler whose destruction is being carried out by a heroic Greek warrior, integration of the Homeric secondary field brings welcome connotations of brilliant Greek achievement and complete Asian ruin.

But supposing even the odd use of εὖνιν combined with the popularity of the Homeric passage could not trigger an allusion. Many times in tragedy, even when the tenor is greatly enriched by the vehicle of another text, and the relationship seems too carefully created to ascribe to chance, it is nevertheless so difficult to specify a certain trigger that the poet's work seems liable to be lost on his audience. Such circumstances can be paralleled in Greek literature: modern readers of Pindar and the tragedians have become accustomed to the presence of complicated features of their works which it is difficult to imagine their audiences could have noticed. Moreover, as with imitations, such details in poetic composition are interesting both as a guide to the author's creative process and frequently as an index to accompanying allusions.[7] I will use a term – the only one introduced by this book – for such allusions which have no trigger or a very weak one: the poet's apparent play with another text in this way will be called *collusion*.

Aeschylus' other use of the *Iliad* in the *Persians* illustrates two trends common to all three tragedians in allusive and imitative practice. Homeric imagery has been incorporated into a battle report that is part of a messenger speech (*Pers.* 302–30). Such speeches, concentrating on eventful narrative, are rich in epic flavor and often contain specific allusions (see Appendix C). Here the focus is on a Homeric simile, and this choice as well is characteristic of Greek tragedy (see Appendix D). In this case, the simile comparing a blood-stain on Menelaus' thigh to the dye used for ivory ornaments (*Il.* 4.141–7) has been converted by Aeschylus to a metaphor: blood from the fatal wound which stains the Persian commander's beard is described as deep purple dye (314–17).[8] Perhaps the charioteer for whom the ivory is ornamented in the Homeric simile influenced Aeschylus to apply his metaphor to a cavalry commander. The nature of this writing is hard to classify: it is certainly less than allusion, perhaps not even precisely collusion. Yet it makes a more precise use – more related to the context of the vehicle – than an example such as Odysseus' raft and the bridge just discussed above. There will be more examples in tragedy where the Homeric simile imitated bears a similarly complex relationship to the tragedian's material.

Seven against Thebes enjoyed great popularity in antiquity and was alluded to repeatedly by Sophocles and Euripides; but although

Aeschylus famously made it Ἄρεως μεστόν (full of Ares), he chose not to achieve his warlike tone with extensive allusions to the *Iliad*.[9] Still, the range of technique represented in the scattering of Iliadic echoes bears examination. Three early passages in the play are often compared to specific models. First, the opening image of the helmsman keeping his eyes open through the night (vv. 2–3) has been likened to a similar passage in the *Odyssey* (5.270–1), but the scholiast saw a resemblance to *Iliad* 2.24, and nautical imagery in general is so common in Greek poetry that the lines may not even be a direct imitation.[10] Next, Eteocles' rebuke to the chorus of Theban women that they should tend to their domestic matters and leave public matters to men (200–1) has been seen at least since the scholiast as an echo of Hector's similar advice to Andromache (*Iliad* 6.490–3). Again, however, despite the popularity of the possible Iliadic source, this sentiment may well be more a commonplace than an imitation. Finally, Eteocles presents a proverb to which the chorus responds with the assurance that god often helps the helpless even when clouds threaten (226–9). It has been suggested that the image recalls the incident of Athena clearing the mist from the eyes of the Greeks (*Iliad* 15.668–70), but except for the mention of eyes the two passages share little.[11]

Three remaining passages in this play can be tied much more confidently to the *Iliad*. First, a unique Homeric phrase for a jagged rock – χερμαδίῳ . . . ὀκριόεντι (*Il.* 4.518) – has been borrowed from a battle in the *Iliad* and put into the chorus' fearful description of the battle for Thebes (χερμάδ' ὀκριόεσσαν, 300). This quotation from the *Iliad* may help serve as a trigger for the next one which in turn reinforces the effect of the trigger itself. The women fearfully envision their city cast to Hades, and their words Ἀΐδᾳ προϊάψαι (322) are an obvious echo of the opening of the *Iliad*, so often alluded to (Ἄϊδι προΐαψεν, *Il.* 1.3).[12] To add to the tension created by quotation, Aeschylus has placed the Homeric phrase at the beginning of a strophe where, by convention, a gap is easily created. Thebes is equated with Troy by means of this near quotation, with the effect that the ultimate doom the chorus envisions for its city acquires ominous and authoritative weight. Here the play, surprisingly sparing in its use of epic, draws the maximum effect from the very simple allusion to the helpless plight of Troy. Considered out of context, an allusion to the opening lines of the *Iliad* seems unlikely to have a powerful effect. But by giving these words to the frightened women of the city, Aeschylus suggests all the horror similarly foreseen by Troy's terrified inhabitants at the climactic moments of the *Iliad*, particularly during the exchanges Hector has with his wife and parents in Books 6 and 22. Great art has distilled much of the *Iliad*'s tragic power into two carefully placed words.[13]

The final possible allusion in the *Seven* is another of the chorus's lyric reflections – this one on the deaths of Polyneices and Eteocles at each other's hands (930–6). The chorus says, "Of the same blood they are totally destroyed, in hostile parting and through frenzied strife, in the end of their quarrel." The duel fought by Polyneices and Eteocles as leaders of their opposing forces is thematically reminiscent of that fought by Hector and Ajax in *Iliad* 7. At the conclusion of that conflict, however, Hector proposes that the two – one a Greek, the other Trojan – part with gifts of friendship. The statement he imagines will be typically made of their friendly parting has been pointedly inverted by Aeschylus in the chorus' description:

> ἠμὲν ἐμαρνάσθην ἔριδος πέρι θυμοβόροιο,
> ἠδ' αὖτ' ἐν φιλότητι διέτμαγεν ἀρθμήσαντε.
>
> (*Il.* 7.301–2)

> They battled in strife that eats at the heart
> and then parted having formed an alliance in friendship.

> ὁμόσποροι δῆτα καὶ πανώλεθροι, / διατομαῖς οὐ φίλαις,
> ἔριδι μαινομένα,/νέκεος ἐν τελευτᾷ.
>
> (*Septem* 933–6)

> Kin indeed and done to death, with severance not
> friendly and maddened strife, in the end of quarrel.

Ajax and Hector fought in strife and then parted in friendship. The identical words for strife and the similar words for friendship in the two passages are notable. But most striking is the vivid Homeric verb for parting – διατμήγω, to cut in two; Aeschylus converts it to an odd phrase for parting (διατομαῖς), thereby creating a trigger.[14] The Aeschylean rewriting of the Homeric passage emphasizes the savagery and irony of the two brothers ending their quarrel with mutual slaughter rather than with an exchange of gifts. The chorus's earlier premonition of the destruction of Thebes, ornamented with allusion to the proem of the *Iliad*, has turned out to be a false alarm. Those same opening epic lines mention another pair of opponents who are ultimately reconciled: what hurled so many men to Hades was the anger of Achilles when he and Agamemnon quarreled and "parted in strife" (*Il.* 1.6). Thus, the elements of the *Iliad* to which Aeschylus alludes are completely inverted in the *Seven*: Troy must perish, but antagonists – whether Achilles and Agamemnon or Hector and Ajax – may convert strife to cooperation or friendship; in Thebes the brothers can only end their strife in mutual annihilation, but the city is saved.

The *Iliad* also provides the material for the few identifiable imitations in the *Suppliants*.[15] Two derive from closely related similes; the third is another echo of the proem. When Danaus gives instructions to his daughters, who are in desperate flight, he likens them to doves (πελειάδων) fearing hawks (κίρκων) in pursuit (*Supp.* 223–4). The simile has been taken from the image for hopeless flight in the Greek poets' favorite Iliadic scene, Hector's and Achilles' final confrontation before the walls of Troy (22.139–40): the doomed son of Priam also flees like a dove (πέλειαν) before a hawk (κίρκος). This first image helps explain the second echo in which the Danaids, fearing the sons of Aegyptus, describe the ships bringing them as swift-winged (ὠκύπτερος, 734), an adjective which before this Aeschylean passage occurs only once, again in a Homeric simile in which a hawk pursues another bird (*Il.* 13.62). The simile's context, in turn, has also provided other material for the *Suppliants* passage. In the *Iliad*, the simile described the departure of Poseidon who had just urged the two Ajaxes to defend the ships which he called νηῶν ὠκυπόρων (*Il.* 13.57–8), a phrase oddly like the Danaids' νῆες . . . ὠκύπτεροι (*Supp.* 734). Moreover, Poseidon has spoken of things very dreadful (περιδείδια, *Il.* 13.52) which the Danaids also seem to echo with their strikingly similar περίφοβον (*Supp.* 736). Even if Aeschylus did not mean to allude to Poseidon's fear and concern for ships, the context of the simile from which he borrows his word has influenced his writing. As a result, since the language of the *Suppliants* draws on material both from within the simile itself and from the narrative around it, the primary Aeschylean field and the secondary Homeric one have multiple points of contact. Yet as with the Homeric simile of dying

27

ivory used in the *Persians*, the interaction between the passages remains less than allusive, the phenomenon more one of multiple imitation. The last direct Homeric echo in the *Suppliants* is the easiest to recognize: just as Aeschylus' women of Thebes echoed the opening lines of the *Iliad* in an anxious song in the *Septem*, so do the Danaids in *Suppliants*. Not only would they rather die than marry the sons of Aegyptus, they would even let their corpses be prey for the dogs and a feast for the birds: κυσὶν . . . ἕλωρα καὶ . . . ὄρνισι δεῖπνον (*Supp.* 800–1). So the corpses of the many souls which the wrath of Achilles hurls to Hades are ἑλώρια . . . κύνεσσιν οἰωνοῖσί τε δαῖτα (*Il.* 1.4–5).[16] However, whereas in the *Septem* the similar plights of Thebes and Troy added tension to the allusive gap, the situation in the *Suppliants* bears little resemblance to that in the epic. This time the attempt to relate tenor and vehicle brings smaller rewards; the relationship between the tragic and epic texts remains more imitative than allusive, anxious parallelism is replaced by a more general suggestion of solemnity.

To be sure, in the context of the entire trilogy the echo of the *Iliad*'s opening lines might read differently; the loss of the companion plays to *Suppliants* makes it impossible to know. Fortunately, one such trilogy escaped destruction: all but the satyr play and a few odd lines of the *Oresteia* survive, and there – especially in the *Agamemnon* – the poetry is tied more closely to Homeric material than it has been in any of the plays considered so far.

ORESTEIA

The lyric density of the poetry in the *Oresteia* is a product not only of the pervasive use of certain images but also of the ways in which Aeschylus deploys them. The literal elements of omens in the *Agamemnon*, for example, are reused as vehicles in simile and metaphor throughout the trilogy so that the literal and figurative elements look forward and backward, suggesting elaborate connections of event and image. Likewise, as the actions of the members of the House of Atreus fall into patterns, they are described in images which take on increasing significance, so that plot and image seem to ripen simultaneously into poetic fates which crush the various actors.

Such a resonant poetic labyrinth allows metaphorical language to echo allusively backward and forward through the trilogy. Scholars are thus encouraged to read these plays for the fullest significance with which a given phrase either echoes words that have come before or points to others that follow. They examine ominous language much as Calchas and Cassandra, within the text, examine the flight of birds or the deeds of humans to find pattern and meaning in action. Indeed, many scholarly seers have been able to make their interpretive visions of the *Oresteia* persuasive because of the cosmic order which informs its poetic beauty.

In a text which legitimately bears so much interpretive weight, an allusion to a related image could spread its implications through the text with particular range and depth. The recent debate over the possible use of Archilochean material in the parodos of the *Agamemnon* provides an excellent introduction to the importance and the difficulty of determining how Aeschylus alluded to or used earlier poetry in this trilogy. Archilochus, in an epode of which we may have ten fragments (172–81W), told a version of the fable of the fox and the eagle whose pact of friendship was broken when the eagle took the fox's cubs to feed its nestlings. Zeus' justice then visited the eagle when an ember clinging to meat taken from an altar set the eagle's nest on fire, tumbling the nestlings to the ground where the fox ate them. The parodos of the *Agamemnon* compares the Atreidae, from whom Helen has been taken, to vultures who have lost their young, a circumstance which attracts the notice and avenging action of Zeus. In a way which is characteristic of the *Oresteia* the imagery of the simile recurs almost immediately with the chorus' narration of the ominous literal appearance at Aulis of the eagles that devoured a pregnant hare – eagles connected by interpretation both to Zeus and to the sons of Atreus. In addition to the shared themes of the loss of young and Zeus' concern for the fates of animals, there are a number of notable verbal phenomena shared by the Archilochean epode and the Aeschylean parodos: the rare use of παῖδες for the young of animals (179W, *Ag.* 50); the contrast of two types of eagle (178W, *Ag.* 115); and the use of δεῖπνον for an animal's meal (179W, *Ag.* 137).[17] Moreover, when the image is repeated in the *Choephori*, the worry over the fate of the eagle's nestlings (246–63) – now Orestes and Electra – again seems reminiscent of specific

29

Archilochean phrases. There is mention of altar and sacrifice as there was in Archilochus' fable and, more specifically, there is an anaphoric invocation of Zeus (177W, *Cho.* 246) and the mention of Zeus' associates Kratos and Dikē (177W, *Cho.* 244).[18]

The case shows clearly the extended life often granted to images in the *Oresteia*, a situation which augments the potential effects of allusive imagery. Yet the similarities to Archilochus may be simply due to generic qualities in the animal fable – terms from human culture such as "children" and "meal" are likely to be used to help establish the instructive analogy; and Aeschylus seems to have used material from popular fables elsewhere in the trilogy as well.[19] Moreover, if the poetry of the *Oresteia* is to be maximally effective in this case, the relationship of Aeschylus' lines to Archilochus' can at most be imitative. For in allusion, the juxtaposition of tenor and vehicle should complicate or intensify the poet's passage. *Without* allusion, Aeschylus' image has just that type of ambiguity which so often charges the *Oresteia* with added power: the Atreidae-eagles both offend and are offended, the same people simultaneously have and do not have justice on their side. Reference to Archilochus' fable and an eagle entirely in the wrong would impoverish Aeschylus' text rather than enrich it.

Similarly, yet another set of passages from the *Agamemnon* and *Choephori* seem oddly close both in content and form to six lines in Pindar's *Pythia* 2 composed some fifteen years earlier. The opening verbal resemblance is just a jingle but a very striking one, even though the grammar and meaning of the phrases are quite different: Aeschylus' phrase for relentless wrath (ὀργὰς ἀτενεῖς, *Ag.* 71) sounds remarkably like Pindar's ὀργαῖς ἀτενὲς (*Pyth.* 2.77) – the same two words in different grammatical relation. The echo could be easily dismissed except that the content of the six Pindaric lines which follow turns up in two places in the *Choephori*, suggesting the possibility that Aeschylus worked extensively from one passage. First, Pindar compares himself to the cork which floats above the rest of the net in the ocean depths (*P.* 2.79–80), and Electra uses the same contrast between the sunken net and the corks to describe how children hold up the house (*Cho.* 505–7). Then Pindar closes this section by further comparing himself to a wolf (λύκοιο δίκαν) in contrast with the citizen who is like a fawning (σαίνων) dog (*P.* 2.82–4), another comparison which Electra makes in very similar language (σαίνειν and

λύκος . . . ὥστ', *Cho.* 420–2).[20] Nevertheless, just as
Archilochus above, Aeschylus might be imitating without
This could even be a case of complex imitation like that i
the Homeric similes considered in *Persae* and *Suppliants*. More
likely, however, both Archilochus and Pindar are using traditional
animal fables in the service of praise and blame, and in all the
Aeschylean passages the same commonplace material with its often
repeated similes from everyday life has been employed without
particular reference to Pindar or Archilochus.

The three other candidates for Aeschylean borrowing from lyric
are simpler and can be dispensed with quickly. Two, like the lyric
imitations in *Persians*, would require a more fully preserved vehicle
for proper evaluation. Fraenkel called *Choephori* 123, where the
chorus assumes that it is natural to wish harm upon one's enemies,
"unquestionable borrowing from Archilochus."[21] But even in the
fragments of Archilochus there are not one but two relevant
passages (13.14W and 126W), and this was surely a commonplace.
Similarly, although Aeschylus' "arms of the ocean" (*Cho.* 587) has
been called an imitation of Archilochus fr. 213, all that can be said
is that the same metaphor with similar wording ("arms of the
waves") occurred there as well.[22] The final possibility of imitation,
Aeschylus' picture of Helen's departure from Greece and arrival at
Troy, focuses on her graceful and obliviously light-hearted walk
(*Ag.* 403–8). Here the possible vehicle, Sappho's account of the
departure and step of Helen and Anactoria (16.9, 17), is reasonably well preserved. And even the military might which the
Aeschylean Helen leaves temporarily behind her may make its
appearance in these lines under the influence of the infantry and
cavalry Sappho amasses to dismiss in favor of more feminine
glitter.[23] Yet the two texts occupy points at once too near and too
far to admit of analysis as primary and secondary fields: whereas
the shared elements of Helen's description approach identity, the
broader themes of Aeschylus' narrative resist interpretive integration with Sappho's more intimate aims. Her brilliant lyric gem
cannot serve as a foil for the vast dark tapestry of tragedy: the
tenor would simply obliterate the vehicle.

An examination of Homeric borrowings, by contrast, is much
more fruitful. Of the surviving work of Aeschylus, the *Oresteia* –
beginning, as it does, from the sack of Troy and Agamemnon's
return home – most naturally would seem to promise allusion to

the *Iliad* and *Odyssey*: Agamemnon figures throughout the *Iliad*, and the *Odyssey* repeatedly focuses on Agamemnon's return and on his wife Clytemnestra and son Orestes as pointed foils for the return of Odysseus and for the nature of his wife Penelope and son Telemachus.[24] Thus, as a supplement to the tragedy of Agamemnon's departure and return, the epic material invites allusions not only to the *Iliad* and *Odyssey* but to the *Odyssey*'s allusive comparisons of the two families as well.

Since the parodos of the *Agamemnon* looks back to the beginning of the Trojan War, the content itself creates an expectation of epic reference. Indeed, the first sentence of the parodos echoes two epic similes. In setting the Greek war effort in motion, the outraged sons of Atreus shout out the war cry like vultures who have lost their young (*Ag.* 40–54). The simile with vultures crying for lost nestlings clearly comes from the *Odyssey* (16.216–19), but the wording for the war cry itself closely follows a model in the *Iliad* (16.428–9).[25] This could be simple borrowing, but the context of each epic passage suggests something more. First, the last words before the chorus begins to recite this sentence are the watchman's reflections on the return of his master Agamemnon after the long absence, and the striking vulture simile in the *Odyssey* describes the weeping of Odysseus and Telemachus when father and son are reunited after Odysseus' long absence at Troy. Second, in the *Iliad* passage Patroclus and Sarpedon are also likened to vultures making a great shriek (μεγάλα κλάζοντε, *Il.* 16.429) when fighting, which Aeschylus has turned into the Atreid vultures' μεγάλ' . . . κλάζοντες Ἄρη (*Ag.* 48). Both in the *Agamemnon* (56–62) and in the·*Iliad* (16.431) Zeus takes note of the human vulture-shriek; the action he takes in the *Agamemnon*, sending the expedition to Troy against Alexander, leads to the moment of the shriek in the *Iliad* when Zeus must lose his own son Sarpedon. Although neither poet explicitly likens Zeus to the distraught vulture parents of these epic and tragic similes, he weeps tears of blood for the loss of his son (*Il.* 16.459). This moment from the *Agamemnon*'s narrative past shares a suggestive common ground with the moment in the *Iliad*, and if Aeschylus has any characteristic method in the *Oresteia*, it is to take important moments of action separated by time and link them by using unusual images to suggest their comparable nature and fated interconnection.

The juxtaposition of such separate narrative moments is conveniently achieved in tragedy by allusion to epic or to other tragedies. The gap thus bridged between tragic tenor and tragic or epic vehicle results in the juxtaposition of two moments, sometimes from one life, sometimes separated by generations. Here in the parodos of the *Agamemnon*, the narrative of the old men makes the Trojan War (now, of course, over) begin with a war cry paradoxically sounded during the war itself, on the battlefield of the *Iliad*; the agony and death of ten years of war, even Zeus' tears of blood, it seems, are all contained in this one ominous allusive shriek. The rather Virgilian literary result is that for a retrospective description of the distant past, the chorus borrows a phrase from the recent past which then foreshadows itself.

Other Homeric echoes, perhaps prepared for by these early ones, follow immediately in the parodos. The third sentence of the parodos (*Ag.* 60–7), which describes the toils laid upon Greeks and Trojans for Helen's sake (πολυάνορος ἀμφὶ γυναικός, *Ag.* 62), also echoes a passage from each of the Homeric poems. First, in the tenor, many men are brought to their knees in battle for this woman (πολλὰ παλαίσματα καὶ γυιοβαρῆ, γόνατος κονίαισιν ἐρειδομένου, *Ag.* 63–4); this recalls the bitter description voiced by Odysseus' servant Eumaeus: he wishes Helen's family would perish, ἐπεὶ πολλῶν ἀνδρῶν ὑπὸ γούνατ' ἔλυσε (*Od.* 14.68–71). Moreover, just as the Aeschylean chorus of old men anxiously wonders about the return of Agamemnon, so the aged Eumaeus worries about the return of Odysseus. The next Aeschylean lines, looking forward to Zeus' creation of toil for Greeks and Trojans alike (Ζεὺς . . . θήσων Δαναοῖσιν Τρωσί θ' ὁμοίως, 66–7), are modeled on the explanation of the dream Zeus sends to Agamemnon early in the *Iliad*, making him believe that he will sack Troy the next day: Ζεὺς . . . θήσειν . . . ἄλγεα . . . Τρωσί τε καὶ Δαναοῖσι (*Il.* 2.38–40). Recognition of the sources invites a comparison of Odysseus' return to his household with Agamemnon's return, of Agamemnon's frustrated attempt (in the secondary field of the *Iliad*) to take Troy with the successful one in Aeschylus.

The next two passages in the *Agamemnon* which show Homeric influence both depend on the technique of juxtaposing two moments of a continuous narrative, one in the primary field and one in the secondary. Moreover, both involve omens and prophecy, a circumstance which makes the device at once more natural and more eerie. The first allusion looks forward to the Homeric lines which will fulfill it, whereas the second fulfills its Iliadic source. After an anapaestic entrance the chorus continues in more epic-sounding dactyls, establishing the new meter with a line of dactylic hexameter (104). They report the omen which cast its shadow over the beginning of the Greek expedition, the two differently marked eagles killing and feasting on the hare with its unborn young (108–20). It is a strange omen, and Calchas' reading of it is strange as well – it means that the Greeks will later take Troy, but that there will be trouble with Artemis now (122–55). Calchas knows that the eagles are the Atreidae, different in temperament (122–4), and that Artemis knows they are, and he and she are right: in the heat of battle at Troy, the Homeric Agamemnon will voice the wish to his brother that they destroy all the Trojans – even the ones yet in their mothers' wombs (*Il.* 6.57–60) – and then Agamemnon will shove away and slaughter the Trojan whose suppliant pleas Menelaus has been tempted to honor. Different in temperament indeed![26] The literary result is that the omen of the tragic text is fulfilled in the epic one to which it refers. Those who know the *Iliad* best will best understand the omen.

The next *Agamemnon* passage looks to a moment slightly earlier in the same Homeric battle, when Sarpedon rebukes Hector for not ordering the other Trojans properly and raises the possibility that Troy may be taken and sacked and the people caught as if in the meshes of an all-catching net (*Il.* 5.485–9). When the chorus of the *Agamemnon* learns that Troy finally has been captured, they sing to Zeus so that no one can escape the net of all-catching doom he has cast over the city (*Ag.* 357–61). Their newly coined adjective for "all-catching" – παναλῶτος – matches the Homeric hapax πάναγρος. The effect Aeschylus achieved was seen by Fraenkel, who said, "What in a particular emergency has been feared by the ally of the Trojans as a possible fate is now turned into a terrible reality by the sentence of Zeus."[27] Repeatedly in this overture to the *Oresteia* Aeschylus used the same method. First he made Zeus, upon hearing a war-shout like a vulture's cry, initiate an action which will lead eventually to an almost identical shout in the *Iliad* to which, in turn, Zeus reacts with tears at the inevitable loss of his son. Second, he created a vivid omen which is just as vividly fulfilled in the *Iliad*. And third, for the realization of a fear expressed in epic he used the same striking metaphor in which it was originally voiced.

If the rest of the trilogy continued in this manner, Aeschylus could certainly be deemed one of the most brilliant and consistent practitioners of the art of allusion. However, from this point until near the end of the *Choephori* the examples seem less significant and more difficult to evaluate.

Sometimes words occurring only once in Homer seem carefully, perhaps collusively, reused. When Agamemnon describes the taking of Troy he uses a verb found only in Aeschylus (διαμαθύνω, *Ag.* 824), one that is clearly influenced by the Homeric hapax (ἀμαθύνω) also used to describe the razing of a city (*Il.* 9.593).[28] Similarly, when the chorus tells Cassandra that she will at least die gloriously (εὐκλεῶς, 1304), she cries out for her father and brothers; their adverb "gloriously" is the Homeric hapax which her brother Hector had used to describe his possible death in his famous last scene before Troy (*Il.* 22.110), a scene Aeschylus had used in both the *Persians* and the *Suppliants*.

Clytemnestra's vivid, almost lyric language is more likely allusive. The simile describing Menelaus' satisfaction at Patroclus' funeral games (*Il.* 23.597–600) is used by Aeschylus' Clytemnestra to describe her delight in Agamemnon's death (1390–2).

> τοῖο δὲ θυμὸς
> ἰάνθη ὡς εἴ τε περὶ σταχύεσσιν ἐέρση
> ληΐου ἀλδήσκοντος, ὅτε φρίσσουσιν ἄρουραι·
> ὣς ἄρα σοὶ Μενέλαε μετὰ φρεσὶ θυμὸς ἰάνθη.

Il. 23.597–600

His anger
Turned to joy, as when dew gladdens the heads
Of the growing grain, when the fields shudder.
Thus, Menelaus, the anger in your heart turned to joy.

> βάλλει μ' ἐρεμνῇ ψακάδι φοινίας δρόσου,
> χαίρουσαν οὐδὲν ἧσσον ἢ διοσδότῳ
> γάνει σπορητὸς κάλυκος ἐν λοχεύμασιν.

(*Ag.* 1390–2)

He hits me with a dark shower of bloody dew,
So I rejoice no less than the crop in
The god-given rain, giving birth to the grain.

Her joy is much more perverted than that of the original model, and her poetry is far more effective, for the dew of her simile has a horrible equivalent in Agamemnon's blood, whereas the comparison in the vehicle was entirely general.[29] The result is so striking that Sophocles in turn reworked Aeschylus' lines for two of his own plays (*Aj.* 376, *Ant.* 1238). Clytemnestra's rebuke to the chorus a few lines later (*Ag.* 1401–6) for treating her like a senseless woman has been seen by some scholars as another possible Homeric reminiscence. If it could be heard as an allusion to Hector's similar reply to Ajax not to treat him like a feeble child (*Il.* 7.235–7), the vehicle would ominously fit its tenor: Hector boasts competence in man-killing, a chilling correspondence to the husband-killing Clytemnestra so proudly displays.[30]

The remaining echoes in the *Agamemnon* all point to the *Odyssey*. Of these, some, such as the description in both works of Agamemnon's murder as "something great" which someone schemes (*Ag.* 1101, *Od.* 3.261), are such close imitations that there is no gap to bridge. The same is true of the use of this passage in *Odyssey* 3 for the description of Aegisthus staying at home from the war (*Ag.* 1625–7, *Od.* 3.262–4). Twice Aeschylus draws on Odysseus' trip to the underworld in *Odyssey* 11. In the first instance, the chorus's lament for the death of Agamemnon at Clytemnestra's hands and the loss of life caused by Helen (*Ag.* 1453–7) imitates the same combination of topics at *Odyssey* 11.436–9, where Agamemnon himself tells his story to Odysseus.[31] Then when Clytemnestra fantasizes the meeting of Iphigeneia and Agamemnon in Hades, she sarcastically suggests that her daughter may throw her arms around the father who slaughtered her. Obviously Clytemnestra means that such an embrace could never take place, and the phrase she uses, περὶ χεῖρε βαλοῦσα (1559), is a nearly exact quotation from the meeting of Odysseus with the shade of his mother, where the phrase περὶ χεῖρε βαλόντε (*Od.* 11.211) also designates an embrace from a female relative, longed for, but not to be enjoyed.

In the last example, the implied contrast between Odysseus, who can and does return from Hades, and Agamemnon, who cannot, could only add to Clytemnestra's satisfaction. Other passages, however, suggest comparisons between the households of Odysseus and Agamemnon, comparisons less flattering to Clytemnestra. Menelaus creates the first extended simile in the *Odyssey* when he describes Penelope's suitors as cowards (ἀνάλκιδες, *Od.* 4.334) who are like fawns in a lion's bed or lair (εὐνήν). Aeschylus' Cassandra reworks the Homeric simile to describe Aegisthus as a cowardly lion staying at home and in the bed (*Ag.* 1224–5). As a tenor in the Aeschylean simile, Aegisthus greatly resembles the tenor of Menelaus' simile: both Aegisthus and the men of Ithaca are suitors to the wife of a hero who has left home to fight the Trojan War.[32] Unfortunately, the images and very likely the text are somewhat askew here, making it impossible to decide whether the relationship between primary and secondary fields encourages an additional unfavorable contrast between Clytemnestra, who has encouraged the intruder, and Penelope, who has remained faithful. Probably it does, for the contrast has already been suggested by a striking speech of Clytemnestra's which is related to an important speech of Penelope's. In her first speech to Agamemnon on his return, Clytemnestra tells of her worries for the house, her constant fears about her absent husband, and, notably, the sleepless nights with dreams broken by the thin wailing of a gnat (*Ag.* 889–94). Likewise Penelope, after Eurykleia has bathed Odysseus, tells her unrecognized husband of her constant grief and worry, and particularly of her inability to sleep at night, as she debates whether to wait for Odysseus or marry one of the suitors (*Od.* 19.509ff.). Her speech comes at a critical point in the epic: Eurykleia has just recognized Odysseus, and Penelope's speech includes her famous dream of the geese leading to the explanation of the gates of horn and ivory for dreams. Penelope likens her nighttime woe to that of the nightingale mourning for her slain child in a striking passage which Aeschylus soon uses for the chorus' description of Cassandra (*Ag.* 1141–8). Both Penelope's and Clytemnestra's speeches linger in the memory – it is a touching moment when after so many years the wives describe to their husbands (whether recognized or not) their sleepless, lonely nights. But Penelope is a sincere and faithful wife trying to come to a decision, talking with a man who is still hiding much from her, while Clytemnestra is guileful and faithless with all her decisions made and all the secrets in her own possession. Such are the echoes and allusions of the *Agamemnon*. The references to or borrowings from the *Odyssey*, clustered in the more domestic second half of the play as one would expect, to some extent encourage a comparison of the families and fates of Odysseus and Agamemnon in their returns from Troy.

The *Choephori* offers ample further opportunity for allusion to the *Odyssey*, but Aeschylus made little of it: most of the Homeric echoes in the trilogy's second play are quite general. As for the *Iliad*, Orestes' opening prayer to Zeus for vengeance (*Cho.* 18–19) may well be modeled on his uncle Menelaus' prayer (*Il.* 3.351), but there certainly seems to be no allusion to the earlier episode. Similarly, when Electra describes Orestes as filling the roles of many relatives for her (*Cho.* 238–43), her words may echo Andromache's plea to Hector (*Il.* 6.429–30), but they may also simply be a topos. The resemblances between the nurse's memories of rearing Orestes (*Cho.* 751–3) and Phoenix's of rearing Achilles (*Il.* 9.485–95) also seem suspiciously generic. The borrowings from the *Odyssey*, although similarly difficult to label as allusion, nevertheless have a certain thematic coherence, centering on preoccupation with the dead and so continuing the use of epic scenes in Hades. In the passage from Odysseus' trip to the underworld, the failed ghostly embrace which supplied Clytemnestra's taunt in the *Agamemnon* is followed immediately by a description of the various fates of body and soul after death which Aeschylus echoes in a choral address to Orestes (*Od.* 11.219–22, *Cho.* 324–6). Orestes responds a few lines later with an address to his father in Hades (*Cho.* 345–53) which is closely related to two passages from the *Odyssey*. One is from conversation among the dead, Achilles' speech to Agamemnon in Hades (*Od.* 24.30–4). Both Orestes and Achilles regret that Agamemnon did not meet a more honorable death, and the concern Achilles expresses for the child left behind is conveniently appropriate for Orestes to repeat. In a second *Odyssey* passage, Telemachus voices the same concerns for Odysseus as Orestes does for Agamemnon (*Od.* 1.235–44). The fates of the two father–son pairs are thus effectively contrasted if Aeschylus had these lines in mind, and there is evidence that he did: Electra seems to echo them again a little further on (363–6), especially with the use of μετά with the dative for those who died together at Troy (*Od.* 1.237, *Cho.* 365).[33] Moreover, there is an elegant variation of another line from this speech in the final play of the trilogy: οἴχετ' ἄϊστος ἄπυστος (*Od.* 1.242) becomes ὤλετ' ἄκλαυτος ἄστος (*Eum.* 565). Collusion may best describe all these examples.

There is one last echo of the *Odyssey* in this play. When Aegisthus is murdered, a servant rushes out with breathless and somewhat confusing – perhaps realistically confused – orders: open up, loosen the bolts, get a strong young man (*Cho.* 877–9). Lyric irony informs this concern with youthful men and the opening of women's gates, for what has been set in motion is the execution of the adulterer who got access to Clytemnestra's bedroom. The oddity of the orders, almost literally ungrammatical, may help trigger allusion to Odysseus' description of the bed which symbolizes Penelope's faithfulness to him – faithfulness so pointedly contrasted elsewhere with Clytemnestra's treachery.[34] "Not even a strong young man could pry it loose," Odysseus says (*Od.* 23.187–8), and the aptness of his image (in addition to the effective contrast in conjugal behavior) may well have struck Aeschylus. In neither passage are exertions of the strong young men actually a part of the events of the narrative; they are imagined in the first text, called for in the second. Each unreal in his own way, the young men nevertheless serve nearly identical thematic functions: in both cases the suggestively sexual images reinforce the poetry's primary concern with faithfulness and adultery. The lines of Odysseus' reply are in a sense the most important of the entire *Odyssey*: only here is he finally recognized by his wife. The passage must have been well known; yet even if the echoing tragic phrases, woven into the servant's excited iambic trimeters at a moment of quick and confusing action, passed unnoticed, Aeschylus is in collusion with his model.

If Clytemnestra contrasts unfavorably with Penelope as a wife, her treatment of Orestes and Electra shows her to be a very imperfect mother as well. When Clytemnestra the mother bares her breast and pleads with Orestes to pity her and spare her life (*Cho.* 896–8), she brings the action to an impasse which is resolved in a startling dramatic surprise: the mute Pylades speaks. Clytemnestra's request recalls that of Hecuba to Hector in more ways than one: the Trojan queen also holds out her breast and begs for the respect and pity owed by the child to the woman who suckled him (*Il.* 22.79–83). Aeschylus had probably used this pathetic scene as a model in the *Persians* (286–9), almost certainly in the *Suppliants* (223–4), and perhaps even in the *Agamemnon* (1304–5). Since the passage was so well known, Clytemnestra's gesture could the more readily trigger allusion to Hecuba's. Both mothers plead for a life; both fail to persuade their sons. One man, Hector, makes a brave last stand against the city's greatest enemy; the other,

Orestes, slaughters his own mother. A glance at the secondary epic field intensifies the horror of the primary tragic moment. If Clytemnestra is no Penelope, neither is Orestes a Hector.

At the doing of the deed the chorus sings an exquisitely crafted song of triumph. The trilogy's connections with epic material are kept explicit: the vengeance which came to the House of Priam is made metrically to respond exactly with that which has come to the House of Agamemnon (especially *Cho.* 935–41 = 946–52). This form of justice is said to be crafty-minded and interested in covert battle (*Cho.* 946–7). The rare adjective κρυπτάδιος (clandestine, illicit) occurs twice in Homer, once when a rather jealous Hera applies it to the type of justice her husband Zeus likes to render (*Il.* 1.542) and once to refer to clandestine adulterous sex (*Il.* 6.161). Both passages have φρονέοντα and the first has δολομῆτα, all of which seem to be picked up with the chorus's δολιόφρων (*Cho.* 947). (*Iliad* 6.161 had long ago been chosen for a vivid allusion by the poet Mimnermus in fr. 1.3.) An ingenious modern analysis of these lines makes this a double Homeric allusion which illuminates the fate of Clytemnestra, suggesting with its reference to justice and adultery "both the punishment and the crime."[35]

Again, collusion may best describe this last example. Time and again Aeschylus' epic references are either so delicate and complex, as here, or else so thoroughly reworked and seamlessly integrated into his own poetic universe that they would have functioned as allusions only for him and for others, poets or lovers of poetry, with time to study and consider the text at leisure. Moreover, the number even of these quiet echoes and imitations is generally small (the only two from the *Eumenides* were incorporated into the discussion of the first two plays of the trilogy). Both in the number and the nature of its allusions the *Prometheus Bound* stands apart from these six certainly Aeschylean plays.

PROMETHEUS BOUND

The mortal world, which poets expand through mere figurative language, is a concern in the *Prometheus*, but it is not its setting. Instead the play is removed to a chaotic corner of the cosmos where metaphor has become flesh, and immortal flesh, at that. Might and Force bind and impale Forethought right before the eyes of the audience; Ocean, with his winged transportation, and

Io, with her horns, are literal embodiments of what is normally limited to fantastic metaphor. Here in the *Prometheus*, for the first and last time in extant drama, Hesiod has provided the fabric from which the play is cut – at least on the surface. But even in the Hesiodic tale of divine struggle, the human world is constantly in view, and the author of the *Prometheus* has emphasized the story's implications for the world of mortals by employing a technique decidedly different from anything in the six Aeschylean plays considered so far.

Since the conflict between Prometheus and Zeus figures prominently in both the *Theogony* and the *Works and Days*, some Hesiodic echoes almost inevitably find their way into the tragedy. Still, they are few and, since the tragedian has created no important gap between his version and Hesiod's, these echoes are not made to work as allusions.[36] Instead, the Prometheus story has been enriched in this play by an emphasis on the Titan's power over Zeus – power that derives from knowledge shared by his prophetic and powerful mother Themis. Prometheus' secret, of course, is that marriage to Thetis would be disastrous for Zeus since the nymph is destined to bear a son greater than his father. In explaining that a marriage could end Zeus' rule, Prometheus twice echoes Pindar's description of this problem in *Isthmia* 8. As with the Hesiodic echoes, however, there is no gap between the original material and its echo, and so in both instances (*PV* 768: *I*. 8.35; *PV* 921–5: *I*. 8.34–5) there is more imitation than allusion.[37] Nevertheless the material creates a theme which, as we shall see, is crucial for other allusions.

Tales of the gods are ultimately tales about men, and a tragedy about gods must somehow be human in order to be a tragedy. Prometheus is, of course, as tied to mortals as any god – he has earned ill will from Zeus by exercising good will toward men. Prometheus' gifts to humanity figure prominently in the play, and his mistake in allying himself too closely with mortals is placed at the very center of the work (*PV* 544–5). In this regard, the Pindaric echoes do carry more than mere imitative weight, for the Pindaric text points even more specifically to the tension between man and god with which this story is concerned. *Isthmia* 8 tells the full story – that the marriage Prometheus knows about produces Achilles, the great hero of epic fame who is, nevertheless, doomed to die. In fact, the Homeric story of the grief of Achilles, his knowledge of the future, and his relationship to his mother is a doublet of the Prometheus story as it has been crafted and modified by the playwright. Prometheus' secret is ultimately about Achilles – their stories are connected both by the continuous mythological narrative and by paradigmatic parallel, and the author of the *Prometheus Bound* has carefully alluded to the Achilles of the *Iliad* throughout his work.

The first hint of the connection between Prometheus and Achilles comes in an early detail. In the opening lines Might (Kratos) directs Hephaistos to bind Prometheus to the rock with his hammer (ῥαιστήρ, v. 56). This rare word for hammer occurs nowhere else in Greek poetry or prose before the Hellenistic age – except once in the *Iliad* (18.477) where it names the hammer Hephaistos is using to forge the arms of Achilles which his mother Thetis has requested. We have seen that Thetis is thematically important in the *Prometheus* as the threat to Zeus. Furthermore, her connection with her son Achilles is also in the author's mind, as can be seen from a statement which Prometheus makes about *his* mother later in the play at the close of one of his big speeches. He knows the future, he explains, because his mother, Titan Themis, told him (μήτηρ ἐμοὶ διῆλθε Τιτανὶς Θέμις, v. 874). This is a very close paraphrase of Achilles' statement that he knows the future because his mother, divine Thetis, has told him (μήτηρ γάρ τέ μέ φησι θεὰ Θέτις ἀργυρόπεζα, 9.410).[38] The allusion should stand out boldly: Achilles' statement comes from a famous part of one of his most famous speeches. It is one of the passages used by Mimnermus in fragment 2, the impassioned rejection of the embassy with the reference to his undying fame (κλέος ἄφθιτον, 9.413).[39] That these are the only two figures in Greek literature to refer their insight into the future to their mothers would itself be striking. That the odd and dangerous female creature Prometheus has been told about is actually the very one who becomes Achilles' mother gives the allusion the eerie significance of a Delphic utterance. Here again is the tragic technique of bridging a gap simultaneously between two texts and two different points in a mythical narrative. The device was used by Aeschylus in the *Oresteia*, especially the *Agamemnon*, to make similarly complex, double allusive connections between the texts and the narrative chronologies of the *Iliad* and his own trilogy. In the *Prometheus*, however, the allusions are more extended

42

and have been placed at the thematic center of the play.

If we return to the mention of Hephaistos' hammer in the *Iliad* we find that it has an adjective as well – "mighty" (κρατερήν) – which also makes it the perfect word to come from the mouth of Might (Kratos) himself in *Prometheus*. And there is an ironic inversion here as well. In the *Iliad* Hephaistos is content to wield the mighty hammer for Thetis' son; in *Prometheus* Hephaistos must be urged by external Might to use the hammer against Themis' son – what was a coherent Olympian force in the epic has been split and put into conflict in this tragedy of fractured power.

Once one sees that the poet has fastened on the parallels between the immortal Prometheus and the mortal Achilles, a number of features of the play seem more natural. Achilles removed himself from the company of his peers by choice, whereas Prometheus is forced into isolation. But Prometheus will be no more inclined to accept embassies and attempts at peace-making than was – or rather, will be – Achilles: Ocean and Hermes will be dismissed as decisively as Ajax and Odysseus. Prometheus even predicts early in the play that the day will come when Zeus, the gods' leader who now maltreats him, will need his help (*PV* 167–76) and that neither sweet words nor threats will persuade him. The claim seems extravagant for someone in such a position, but it parallels the speech of Achilles at the opening of the *Iliad* (*Il.* 1.234–45) when he predicts that the Greeks will eventually long for his help and that Agamemnon, their leader, will be powerless.[40]

Despite their proud boasts, both god and man cry out in their grief, and the results are curiously similar. When Achilles makes his terrible groan, his mother, sitting at the bottom of the ocean next to her father, hears her son and rushes up to him along with the Nereids (*Il.* 18.35–64). This chorus of ocean creatures is given no lines to speak in epic, but it surely inspired the otherwise inexplicably odd chorus of Oceanids in *Prometheus*. These watery maidens, often and easily confused with the Nereids, also rush from the ocean caves where they have heard Prometheus' cries of pain.[41] They at once help trigger the allusion to Achilles and provide a charming variation on the silent nymphs who attend Achilles' sadness at the seashore (*Il.* 18.65–70). They learn the story of a god who is as ill fated (*PV* 119) as the stubborn mourning hero of the *Iliad* (*Il.* 1.417, 505; 18.96, 458). If the primary motivation for the Oceanid chorus is the Achilles theme, the author seems to have drawn secondary inspiration from Bacchylides' description of the Nereids in the poem on Theseus' dive (*PV* 127–35: Bacchyl. 17.96–111). The same poem seems to be echoed elsewhere in the play – the phrase πεπρωμένην αἶσαν occurs in classical Greek only at *Prometheus* 103–4 and Bacchylides 17.26–7. The nearby ποταίνιον seems part of the borrowing as well (*PV* 102 and Bacchyl. 17.51).[42]

The inflexibility of Achilles may inform Prometheus' attitude in the play, but it is by no means confined to him. In fact, Apollo's vivid description of Achilles' unbending mind (οὔτε νόημα γναμπτὸν, *Il.* 24.40–1) is here applied to Zeus (ἄγναμπτον νόον, *PV* 164). And two other characterizations of Achilles as made of stone or iron are combined to suggest the nature of anyone who would not sympathize with Prometheus (*PV* 242: *Il.* 16.33–5, 24.205). Thus Achilles gives shape not only to the play's protagonist, Prometheus, and to his major opponent, Zeus, but to hypothetical beings as well. Just as Prometheus hints at his secret, so the playwright keeps the figure of Achilles constantly just below the surface of the text, an allusive and pervasive subtext.[43]

At times the motives of this bookish author are difficult to pinpoint. Two Homeric words used only in the opening of *Iliad* 17, ἀδήριτος (17.42) and ἀκίχητα (17.75), have their only other appearances in classical poetry here (*PV* 105, 184), but there seems to be no particular allusion. The repetition of phrasing from the friendly parting of Hector and Ajax, when Prometheus imagines a friendly meeting between himself and Zeus (*Il.* 7.302: *PV* 191) also seems to be more imitative than allusive, despite the apparent notoriety of the incident.[44] It has been suggested that Prometheus' invocation of the elements (88–92) echoes Agamemnon's similar call at a sacrifice (*Il.* 3.276–8), but the frequency of invocations to the elements makes this unlikely. More obvious is the borrowing of a Homeric simile using the pursuit of doves by hawks (*Il.* 22.139–40). But here either the author is more directly borrowing from Aeschylus, or Aeschylus is borrowing from himself, for the Homeric simile was used in *Supplices* to describe the daughters of Danaus just as it is used to describe them in *Prometheus* (*Supp.* 223–4, *PV* 857).[45]

In addition to the uses of Pindar and Bacchylides already mentioned, there are echoes from other lyric poets as well. The play's closing allusion seems to point from its gods to the world of men. As earthquake from below and a furious storm from above boil the final scene into a violent mixture of earth, air, fire, and water, Prometheus describes the strife among the winds in political terms (ἀνέμων πνεύματα ... στάσιν ... ἀποδεικνύμενα, 1085–8) modeled on Alcaeus' vision of human civil strife using the same words (ἀνέμων στάσιν, 208V).

But it is the first allusion in the play which is the most clearly pointed use of lyric. As Hephaistus describes the punishment of Prometheus in the opening lines he mentions the deterioration of Prometheus' skin. "You will lose the bloom of your complexion," he says – χροιᾶς ἀμείψεις ἄνθος (PV 23) – and his phrase is a close imitation of Solon's χροιῆς ἄνθος ἀμειβομένης (27.6W), which describes the same phenomenon. This might seem simple imitation at first glance, but the contrasting contexts are crucial to the power of the play. Aging is a peculiarly – indeed definitively – mortal problem, and thus the allusion is like an initial emblem stitched to Prometheus, marking him as a god who suffers in appropriately mortal fashion for the human race. Just as Prometheus' power over Zeus derives from his knowledge of the danger of Thetis' child, his power as a dramatic figure derives from his resemblance to that child – the mortal Achilles, who in the *Iliad* stands for all mortals in their struggle against the limits of necessity and death.

In the *Iliad* the divine struggle for the control of Olympus is kept just below the surface of the poem. The mortal Achilles is the index to that tension, for through him we learn of Zeus' considerable obligations to Thetis.[46] In the *Prometheus* we have the reverse – the god is the pivot around which the overt divine struggle turns, while the plight of humanity and specifically the plight of the mortal Achilles provide the subterranean subject. When, at the center of the play, this secondary theme finds its most touching and open statement, it comes through an echo not of Achilles' story in the *Iliad*, but of Odysseus' in the *Odyssey*. Here the immortal Oceanids of *Prometheus* give a lyric description of the helpless human race:

οὐδ' ἐδέρχθης
ὀλιγοδρανίαν ἄκικυν,
ἰσόνειρον, ᾇ τὸ φωτῶν
ἀλαὸν γένος ἐμπεποδισμένον;

(PV 547–50)

45

Have you not seen that feebleness so powerless,
a mere dream, by which the blind race of humanity
is bound?[47]

The rare adjectives for "powerless" (ἄκικυν) and "blind"
(ἀλαὸν) derive from the speech of the anguished Cyclops
Polyphemus who describes the mortal who has blinded him:
νῦν δέ μ' ἐὼν ὀλίγος τε καὶ οὐτιδανὸς καὶ ἄκικυς
ὀφθαλμοῦ ἀλάωσεν ("But now, small, worthless, and
feeble though you are, you have blinded me," *Od.* 9.515–6). If the
echo is allusive, it suggests that men such as Odysseus, although
feeble, are not without resource, partly through the gifts of
Prometheus. Within the play, the power and significance of the
chorus's description of humanity is increased because it applies to
Prometheus as well. The power of tragedy partly lies in its ability
to make us feel our common liabilities and weaknesses. We
sympathize with this god because he is bound and powerless like us
and because in our moments of grief and distress we hope to have
resources hidden below the surface to which we can refer for solace
and even, sometimes, for salvation. The secret resource of
Prometheus is the story of Achilles, both hidden and revealed by
poetic allusion. In a sense, this is the secret tragic resource of this
play's author as well: when Prometheus and his epic double
Achilles share in our suffering, we are bound to them in a way
which frees us and allows us to share in their titanic grandeur.

CONCLUSIONS

In Aeschylus' earlier plays the reworking of other poetry seems a
private and internal matter: often intriguingly apt, the borrowings
seldom open outwardly, only infrequently drawing on or giving life
to the larger themes of the plays in which they are embedded. The
Oresteia, however, especially in its first two plays, makes more
forceful allusive use of Homeric material. Moreover, the allusions
mesh with the imagery and force of their epic sources in the same
way that the imagery of the trilogy has been interwoven so as to
give repeated patterns significance.

The *Agamemnon* and *Choephori* contain examples of two particularly important allusive techniques. Both are more than usually
complex – in one case this is because of peculiarities in the tenor

and vehicle themselves, in the other it is because of the nature of the relation between them. The first technique, introduced with Stesichorus' poetry in the previous chapter, imports a simile from the secondary field for use in the primary. Thus, establishing the relationship between the two fields may require a complicated comparison of the related comparisons contained in each. The attractiveness of the Homeric simile both naturally draws the poet's attention and also makes the simile promising material for effective allusion: it is likely to be recognized when reused. Even in the early plays Aeschylus shows a fondness for the Homeric simile, borrowing epic images of birds in pursuit and the dying of ivory – but without exploiting the potential advantages of alluding to a complex vehicle. The most involved Aeschylean use of a Homeric simile in the *Oresteia* may well have been the comparison of Aegisthus to a lion (*Ag.* 1224–5); it may even be that the difficulty of the passage contributed to the damage of the text which now frustrates analysis. The parodos of the *Agamemnon* also makes effective use of Homeric simile, but this is best considered in conjunction with yet another technique.

Inasmuch as the primary field in lyric poetry is seldom devoted to mythological narrative, the lyric poets had little occasion to use the second allusive technique that Aeschylus found so fruitful in the *Oresteia*, the suggestive comparison of two different moments in a continuous history by alluding to such events in a secondary poetic field. Since the *Agamemnon* is the immediate sequel to the Trojan War, a war in which Agamemnon played a large role, Aeschylus' allusions to the *Iliad* invite a consideration of material which is doubly suggestive because it literally contains his characters' past. This extra level of relation makes the use of Homeric similes in the parodos particularly convoluted: the cry of the vultures includes both the formal complexity of allusion to simile and the narrative connection that binds primary and secondary field in the common concern for events in the life of Agamemnon.

The *Prometheus Bound* also exploits the suggestiveness of the temporal poetic allusion, but it looks to the future rather than the past. The programmatic and organized allusions to the Achilles and Thetis of the *Iliad* have direct narrative relevance: the place of Thetis and her child in the future are the precious secret that Prometheus is withholding from Zeus. Moreover, just as this

47

allusive temporal collapse was combined in the *Oresteia* with another technique, so it is in *Prometheus*. Here however it is not simile or metaphor which complicates; rather, the chronological, historical connections between Prometheus and Achilles and the allusions which link the Titan and hero are enriched by a presentation which makes them thematically parallel as well and which places the parallelism at the heart of the play. Aeschylus' allusions make the proudly resistant and unfortunate Prometheus and Achilles, their mothers, and their relationship to the universal sufferings of humankind barely distinguishable variations of each other. In a play which alludes both more frequently and more noticeably to earlier poetry than do Aeschylus' other six plays, the central themes of Prometheus' fate are well served by the set of allusions made powerful by the chronological and paradigmatic connections to Achilles' story.

The *Prometheus* makes an excellent transition to the plays of Sophocles and Euripides from about 440 to 430 B.C. Either coincidence or fashion determined that the surviving plays from these two decades should, in the matter of allusion, form a group which seems set apart from the later plays and which the *Prometheus* seems to resemble much more than it resembles anything certainly written by Aeschylus. Thus, to the list of factors which have led many scholars to feel that the *Prometheus* dates from the third quarter of the century, one might add the allusive technique which connects the play's protagonist with Achilles.

3

Sophocles and Euripides:
The Early Plays

INTRODUCTION

As with Aeschylus, the single most important poetic resource for Sophocles and Euripides appears to have been the *Iliad*, but the *Odyssey*, the poems of Hesiod, and lyric poetry also found their way into the plays of the younger tragedians. They had, in addition, one rich resource for allusion not available to their great predecessor: the works of Aeschylus himself. If we had more than six or seven Aeschylean plays, his influence might emerge as even more pervasive, but the surviving works all made their mark, some more than others, and the *Agamemnon* most of all.

Sophocles' *Antigone* appeared fairly certainly in the late 440s, and *Ajax* seems most likely to have been written at about the same time. Euripides' *Alcestis* and *Medea* are dated securely to 438 and 431 respectively. Thus, these four plays, all written well after Aeschylus' death, are almost certainly the earliest we have from Sophocles and Euripides. (*Trachiniae* might be early, but its date is most uncertain, and it will be treated in the next chapter.) In a study of the art of allusion, the plays form a natural group, for they all make significant use of earlier poetry, and in three of them – *Alcestis*, *Antigone*, and *Medea* – appreciation of the allusions helps with aspects of the plays that have been found difficult and even baffling. *Ajax* and *Alcestis* each depend, among other things, on a series of related references to the *Iliad*, whereas in *Antigone* and *Medea* the sources are more varied and operate more exclusively in one or more of the plays' choral songs.

SWORD AND SHIELD: SOPHOCLES' *AJAX*

Sophocles was called the bee, for although many others imitated their contemporaries and predecessors, he alone plucked the brilliant bits from each one: such was the ancient verdict.[1] In the case of *Ajax*, Sophocles' debt to contemporary poets consists mainly in repeated use of Aeschylean material.[2] For example, in his grim farewell to life, Ajax calls on death (*Aj*. 854) imitating the invocation made by Aeschylus' Philoctetes (fr. 255R).[3] A long list of words and phrases which Sophocles could have borrowed from the *Persians* for the *Ajax* was collected long ago, and although most of the examples are uncertain, one is quite striking.[4] Ajax, in the famous speech on change and flexibility that misleads the chorus, describes how night gives way to "day with its white horses (λευκοπώλῳ . . . ἡμέρᾳ, 673) so it can kindle the light." Both *Ajax* and *Persians* (307) remind us that Salamis is the home of Ajax, and in the *Persians* another iambic speech sets the scene for the morning of the great battle there as follows: "Night gave way . . . And once day with its white horses (λευκόπωλος ἡμέρα, 386) covered the whole earth with brilliant kindled light to see . . ." True, the radically different dramatic contexts preclude any sort of allusion: the historic struggle of the *Persians* does not make an illuminating vehicle for the tenor of Ajax's philosophy. Nevertheless, phrase, rhythm, and thought have all been borrowed by Sophocles from this passage which describes the most famous event at his hero's home.

A number of times we can see the influence of *Agamemnon*. The vivid reports in Aeschylus' play of the discomfort of the Greeks in their long encampment at Troy, with details such as the unpleasantness of morning dew in their hair (559–62 and perhaps 983–6), have found their way into the words of Sophocles' chorus at least once (1206–10) and perhaps twice (600–5). And in both plays, characters involved in an attempt to persuade Agamemnon use very similar arguments in lines with similar and extremely distinctive rhythm. Clytemnestra assures her husband that for the fortunate even being defeated is becoming and then says, πιθοῦ· κρατεῖς μέντοι παρεὶς ἑκὼν ἐμοί ("Give in. The power is yours if you've yielded it to me willingly," *Ag*. 943). Odysseus' version is παῦσαι· κρατεῖς τοι τῶν φίλων νικώμενος ("Enough. The power is yours if you're defeated by your friends," *Aj*. 1353). In this latter example a tenor in *Ajax* would share so much common ground with a vehicle in *Agamemnon* that it is tempting to see an ominous or ironic allusion, one that would at once bridge a textual and chronological gap in the life of

Agamemnon. In the absence of a strong trigger – there is no unusual word or image, no particular impropriety in Odysseus' request – it is best to see this as a collusive collapse of time, one that draws a consistent picture of Agamemnon's character. Other Aeschylean echoes considered below are even more significant.[5]

Whatever Sophocles' debts to lyric and early tragedy were, the ancients were more concerned with his relationship to the Homeric poems: thus he was called both "the tragic Homer" and "the only student of Homer."[6] Of course, the material that gave rise to this reputation might have been concentrated in the more than one hundred lost plays rather than in the seven which survive. Nevertheless, even with only these seven to use, Eduard Fraenkel made the comment that the work he would like to write would be *On Sophocles the Student of Homer*, were it not for the fact that one life would not be enough.[7]

Of all the extant plays, the *Ajax* would seem to offer the most well-stocked grounds for the hunting of Homeric allusions: the setting, plot, and characters afforded abundant opportunity for a poet who wanted to use the *Iliad*. It is, in fact, the *Ajax* which, in the surviving Sophoclean corpus, provides the scene which has seemed far to surpass all the rest as Sophocles' most Homeric – the scene between Tecmessa and Ajax (*Aj.* 485–595). As a rule, the scholia to Sophocles use the Homeric poems to clarify meaning in a very general if not entirely random manner, but from lines 499 to 574 of the *Ajax* they refer six times to the scene in the *Iliad* with Hector, Andromache, and Astyanax (*Il.* 6.390–502) and to no other text at all. The scholiast, clearly assuming that the one scene is closely modeled on the other, has his gaze so firmly fixed that twice he even uses the Hector scene to explain something which could just as well – and probably even better – have been illustrated with other references.[8] But even if the scholiast is too zealous, he is in the main correct.

The general similarities in these scenes strike us at once. In both, a woman is pleading with the man she loves not to abandon her and their child – a son, in fact, who makes an appearance and whom the father holds and addresses. Both Tecmessa and Andromache describe their complete dependence on their mates due partly to the loss of their families (*Aj.* 514–19, *Il.* 6.415–30), and both fathers express hopes for their sons' futures (*Il.* 6.476–81, *Aj.* 550–1). Moreover, close Sophoclean echoes of Homeric wording tighten the connection. Both passages speak of inescapable necessity – ἀνάγκη (*Aj.* 485, *Il.* 6.458); both envision the future slavery of the woman and child and speak of it with the adjective δούλιος (*Aj.* 499, *Il.* 6.463); Astyanax's touching fear of his father's helmet (ταρβήσας, 6.469) is pointedly corrected to the assurance that Eurysakes will not fear Ajax (ταρβήσει γὰρ οὔ, 545); and in both scenes there is the vivid device of imagining what someone – some stranger – will say upon seeing the sad fate of the woman and child once attached to so great a warrior: ὥς ποτέ τις ἐρέει, it says in the *Iliad* (6.462); and Sophocles adheres almost exactly: τοιαῦτ' ἐρεῖ τις (504).[9]

Moreover, as has also been well pointed out, all the similarities help heighten the *differences* in ways which are useful for Sophocles. In the *Iliad* it is Hector who sees the sad future (6.448–65) – in Sophocles it is Tecmessa who is made to bring it up (497–505). Hector's tenderness with Astyanax is missing in Sophocles, as is the parents' laughter. And yet, quite recently it has been further suggested that even with these differences there is more suggestive similarity here than is usually recognized – that just as Hector is very moved by Andromache's appeal without necessarily being dissuaded from reentering the battle, so Ajax, although ultimately committed to suicide, is actually touched and softened by Tecmessa's words.[10]

Since Sophocles' attention was obviously focused so carefully on Hector, it is worth considering whether any of Hector's other famous moments in the *Iliad* might have found their way into the *Ajax*. The passage in the *Iliad* drawn on more frequently than any by Greek poets is Hector's second urgent family scene, when, before the walls of Troy, his mother and father, Priam and Hecuba, beg him to come inside and save his life (22.38–130). Earlier chapters have examined the uses Tyrtaeus and Aeschylus found for this passage.[11] Its popularity helped ensure its effectiveness as a source for allusive effect. Added to this, Sophocles' extensive use of the Hector and Andromache scene as a foil for Ajax and Tecmessa made it even easier to allude to the Homeric treatment of Hector and his fate. Thus, Tecmessa's pleas to Ajax to save his life, to honor his mother and father and not abandon them to a wretched old age without his help, to remember his familial bond (520–1) – all of these should recall the pleas of Priam and especially Hecuba to their son Hector.

Sophocles' use of Hector's two family scenes suggests that he might have used other Hector passages from the *Iliad* as well. After all, he has given direct prominence to Hector through the play's preoccupation with Hector's sword, the hateful gift with which Ajax commits suicide. In fact, although little attention has been given to the theme of Hector in this play, Sophocles' allusions are blood for his ghost from beginning to end.[12] When, in the first scene, Tecmessa describes Ajax's slaughter of the livestock, she notes especially – and one might think a bit superfluously – that the rams had white feet; furthermore this anatomical detail is conveyed with an extremely rare adjective – ἀργίποδας (237). This unexpected detail may be a trigger: the adjective occurs elsewhere only as the epithet which Hecuba uses for dogs when she begs Priam not to go to Achilles for Hector's corpse (*Il.* 24.211).[13] Hecuba began her speech with the exclamation ὤμοι – and so precisely does Tecmessa begin hers. Tecmessa has just described Ajax, who is outraging the corpses of the livestock, as ὠμοκρατής (205) – of savage strength – and Hecuba has just described Achilles who is outraging Hector's corpse as ὠμηστής – savage/raw flesh eating (24.207).[14]

Even if these echoes or borrowings from Hecuba's speech in *Iliad* 24 are merely imitation, they, like the allusions already considered, revolve around the inevitable death of Hector. Each successive reference connecting Ajax with Hector is like an omen making his own death more unavoidable. The images and reverberations gather in a manner reminiscent of Aeschylean artistry in the *Oresteia*, with the resemblances between the two warriors suggesting not that they are incidentally similar but rather that the larger pattern of fate which included Hector's defeat will only find its completion when Ajax is destroyed as well.

The remaining allusions to the Iliadic Hector also center on his death. Just before he falls on Hector's sword, Ajax says that when she hears of his death, his mother will let out a great wail – κωκυτός – throughout the whole city (851). And this is just what Cassandra did in the *Iliad* at Hector's death – κώκυσεν . . . πᾶν κατὰ ἄστυ (24.703). Now although women's lament in Greece was fixed by ritual, so that similar descriptions might be generic rather than allusive, there is other evidence that Sophocles had Cassandra in mind at this point. He has put a word into Ajax's mouth (ἀσφάδαστος, 833) which describes the way the hero hopes to die and which occurs in Greek elsewhere only on Cassandra's lips as she contemplates her death in Aeschylus' *Agamemnon* 1293.[15]

There is a final allusion to Hector's death and the fate of his corpse to be considered here, as striking and significant as the use of the scenes with his wife and parents. It is a fitting seal to the poetic connections which bind Hector and Ajax so closely, for it concerns the finality of the grave which draws them to their ultimate and permanent reunion. Hector's grave is named in *Iliad* 24.797 – the eighth line from the end of the poem as we have it – by a very rare word, χάπετον.[16] The word occurs only three times in the *Iliad* and only this once in the meaning "grave." At the close of the *Iliad* as the word for Hector's "grave" it is given the epithet κοίλην ("hollow"), and after this it is never used again by any classical author – with one exception. In the *Ajax* the grave of Ajax is referred to twice – at line 1165 and again at 1403, both times with the same noun-epithet phrase, κοίλην χάπετον. These allusions to Hector, then, form a systematic set of reflections on his death at once more organized and more extensive than any poetic references in the Aeschylean corpus with the possible exception of the preoccupation with Achilles in the *Prometheus Bound*.

There is another and larger body of epic allusions in the *Ajax*: even odder than the neglect of Iliadic Hector passages in studying Sophocles' *Ajax* has been the blindness to Sophocles' use of passages from the *Iliad* in which Ajax himself figures.[17] After all, Ajax appears at many critical points in the Homeric narrative; and although he suffers no Iliadic death to which Sophocles can allude, the poet has shaped his echoes of the epic Ajax so that they will culminate in a stunning allusion to Ajax and another fallen hero. We shall move toward that point, examining the Ajax allusions and echoes more or less in the order they occur in Sophocles' play.

When the chorus first begins to sing, it considers what drove Ajax to attack the cattle, which are called "herded cows" (βοῦς ἀγελαίας, 175). Elsewhere this phrase occurs only twice, once in the *Odyssey* and once in the *Iliad*, where it figures in Ajax's last appearance in the poem. In the latter passage it occurs in a simile describing the distance by which Ajax's opponent beat him in the shot-put (23.846). It is easy to see why Sophocles might have had the passage in mind, for it is certainly relevant to a play built around the dishonor Ajax incurs in his last, disastrous competitive

54

losses. Moreover, as will soon become clear, images of livestock from Homeric similes have found their way into significant non-metaphorical events of this play. Finally, another indication that Sophocles might have had his eye on this simile is that the next word after the phrase βοῦς ἀγελαίας in the *Iliad* is τόσσον, a form that makes one of its only two appearances in all Greek tragedy just ten lines after the herded cows (185).[18] This borrowing, albeit small, comes in the play's first lyric sentence. Moreover, there will be other reasons for thinking that Sophocles was making a significant reference to the funeral games of Patroclus.

Other *Ajax* passages from the *Iliad* seem to have contributed a number of words and phrases to the opening scenes of *Ajax*. So, for example, when the chorus enters in distress at the rumors of Ajax's madness, they speak of the blow of Zeus (πληγὴ Διός, 137) which has struck him, and their phrase can be found only once in the Homeric poems. Like the phrase the chorus echoed above, it comes from a simile, this time when Ajax has nearly succeeded in killing Hector, just after Hector failed to wound him (*Il.* 14.414). Just ten lines later the chorus uses a slightly more common Homeric phrase, αἴθωνι σιδήρῳ ("flashing iron," 147). One of its three occurences in the *Iliad* (4.485) is in a passage which features Ajax and Odysseus in battle and which also has the verb παπταίνειν ("to glance around," 4.496) which occurs in the opening lines of *Ajax* (11).[19] And although the word αἴθων occurs a number of times in the *Iliad*, it tends to crop up in Ajax passages, and it occurs again here at *Ajax* 222. Sophocles has carefully built these early choral lines with appropriate Iliadic diction taken from passages featuring not only Ajax but also his two greatest foes, Hector and Odysseus.

When Tecmessa responds to the chorus, she has added information, for she has witnessed the final stages of Ajax's delusion. She describes the lashing he gave to a poor bound beast with a whip she calls λιγυρᾷ μάστιγι ("shrill whip," 242), a phrase which occurs one other time in Greek literature – *Iliad* 11.532. This important *Ajax* passage begins with a direct address to Hector about Ajax, and besides the phrase μάστιγι λιγυρῇ, it has both παπτήνας (546) and αἴθωνα (548).[20] We will need the whole passage for reference:

Κεβριόνης δὲ Τρῶας ὀρινομένους ἐνόησεν   521
Ἕκτορι παρβεβαώς, καί μιν πρὸς μῦθον ἔειπεν·
Ἕκτορ νῶϊ μὲν ἐνθάδ' ὁμιλέομεν Δαναοῖσιν
ἐσχατιῇ πολέμοιο δυσηχέος· οἳ δὲ δὴ ἄλλοι
Τρῶες ὀρίνονται ἐπιμὶξ ἵπποι τε καὶ αὐτοί.   525
Αἴας δὲ κλονέει Τελαμώνιος· εὖ δέ μιν ἔγνων·
εὐρὺ γὰρ ἀμφ' ὤμοισιν ἔχει σάκος· ἀλλὰ καὶ ἡμεῖς
κεῖσ' ἵππους τε καὶ ἅρμ' ἰθύνομεν, ἔνθα μάλιστα
ἱππῆες πεζοί τε κακὴν ἔριδα προβαλόντες
ἀλλήλους ὀλέκουσι, βοὴ δ' ἄσβεστος ὄρωρεν.   530
Ὣς ἄρα φωνήσας ἵμασεν καλλίτριχας ἵππους
μάστιγι λιγυρῇ· τοὶ δὲ πληγῆς ἀΐοντες
ῥίμφ' ἔφερον θοὸν ἅρμα μετὰ Τρῶας καὶ Ἀχαιοὺς
στείβοντες νέκυάς τε καὶ ἀσπίδας· αἵματι δ' ἄξων
νέρθεν ἅπας πεπάλακτο καὶ ἄντυγες αἳ περὶ δίφρον   535
ἃς ἄρ' ἀφ' ἱππείων ὁπλέων ῥαθάμιγγες ἔβαλλον
αἵ τ' ἀπ' ἐπισσώτρων. ὃ δὲ ἵετο δῦναι ὅμιλον
ἀνδρόμεον ῥῆξαί τε μετάλμενος· ἐν δὲ κυδοιμὸν
ἧκε κακὸν Δαναοῖσι, μίνυνθα δὲ χάζετο δουρός.
αὐτὰρ ὃ τῶν ἄλλων ἐπεπωλεῖτο στίχας ἀνδρῶν   540
ἔγχεΐ τ' ἀορί τε μεγάλοισί τε χερμαδίοισιν,
Αἴαντος δ' ἀλέεινε μάχην Τελαμωνιάδαο.
Ζεὺς δὲ πατὴρ Αἴανθ' ὑψίζυγος ἐν φόβον ὦρσε·
στῆ δὲ ταφών, ὄπιθεν δὲ σάκος βάλεν ἑπταβόειον   545
τρέσσε δὲ παπτήνας ἐφ' ὁμίλου θηρὶ ἐοικὼς
ἐντροπαλιζόμενος ὀλίγον γόνυ γουνὸς ἀμείβων.
ὡς δ' αἴθωνα λέοντα βοῶν ἀπὸ μεσσαύλοιο
ἐσσεύαντο κύνες τε καὶ ἀνέρες ἀγροιῶται,
οἵ τέ μιν οὐκ εἰῶσι βοῶν ἐκ πῖαρ ἑλέσθαι   550
πάννυχοι ἐγρήσσοντες· ὃ δὲ κρειῶν ἐρατίζων
ἰθύει, ἀλλ' οὔ τι πρήσσει· θαμέες γὰρ ἄκοντες
ἀντίον ἀΐσσουσι θρασειάων ἀπὸ χειρῶν
καιόμεναί τε δεταί, τάς τε τρεῖ ἐσσύμενός περ·
ἠῶθεν δ' ἀπὸ νόσφιν ἔβη τετιηότι θυμῷ·   555
ὣς Αἴας τότ' ἀπὸ Τρώων τετιημένος ἦτορ
ἤϊε πόλλ' ἀέκων· περὶ γὰρ δίε νηυσὶν Ἀχαιῶν.
ὡς δ' ὅτ' ὄνος παρ' ἄρουραν ἰὼν ἐβήσατο παῖδας
νωθής, ᾧ δὴ πολλὰ περὶ ῥόπαλ' ἀμφὶς ἐάγη,
κείρει τ' εἰσελθὼν βαθὺ λήϊον· οἳ δέ τε παῖδες   560
τύπτουσιν ῥοπάλοισι· βίη δέ τε νηπίη αὐτῶν·
σπουδῇ τ' ἐξήλασσαν, ἐπεί τ' ἐκορέσσατο φορβῆς·
ὣς τότ' ἔπειτ' Αἴαντα μέγαν Τελαμώνιον υἱὸν

56

Τρῶες ὑπέρθυμοι πολυηγερέες τ' ἐπίκουροι
νύσσοντες ξυστοῖσι μέσον σάκος αἰὲν ἕποντο.   565

Kebriones saw the Trojans in trouble, and he stood by Hector
and said, "We two are fighting here with the Greeks at one end
of the raucous battle, but the rest are driven in confusion, horses
and all (525): Ajax is doing it – I know him well. He has his
broad shield shouldered. We should drive there too where most
all the men in chariot and on foot are killing each other in evil
strife and the cry is raised unstopping (530)." He spoke, and
with his whistling whip he lashed the fair-maned horses. They
felt the blow and lightly took the swift chariot toward the
Trojans and Greeks, trampling corpses and shields. The axle
underneath was all spattered with blood, and drops flew from
the horses' hooves to the rims of the carriage and the wheels
(537). He wanted to rush and enter the crowd of men and break
it. He threw terrible panic on the Greeks and briefly rested his
spear. Then he ranged among the other men with spear and
sword and great stones, but he avoided battle with Ajax (542).

Father Zeus on high put fear in Ajax. So he stood stunned,
threw back his seven-fold shield, and looking at the crowd he
was struck with fear, like a beast, turning back round, slowly,
step by step (547). Just as country men and dogs drive a tawny
lion away from the cows' pen and watch all night and don't let it
take the fat of the cattle. Wanting meat, it charges but gets
nothing, for many javelins greet it rushing from bold hands, and
lit torches which it fears despite its eagerness. At dawn it goes
away vexed (555). So then Ajax, vexed, went away from the
Trojans all unwilling, fearing for the Greeks' ships. As when a
lazy ass masters the boys in the field, though many a club is
broken over him he still goes in and ravages the tall grain. The
boys beat him with sticks, but their force is foolish (561). They
barely drive it out once it's sated. So then the spirited Trojans
with their various allies stabbing the middle of his shield with
their spears steadily drove great Ajax.

In this Homeric passage two memorable similes describe Ajax's
retreat. In the first Ajax is likened to a lion which attacks the
livestock at night and wants terribly to devour the animals – a lion

which is only driven away from that night attack with the greatest difficulty. Sophocles has taken the simile and used it both for the action and the imagery of his play.[21] The Trojans in this passage of the *Iliad* have Hector to drive Ajax back, but Ajax's problem in the *Ajax* is that there was no one to drive him back from the Greek livestock which he has attacked in non-metaphorical fashion. It is a scene of gruesome horror repeatedly described and referred to in *Ajax*[22] – a scene which is so horrible that even Odysseus begs not to be made to look even at its remnants. Yet it is just this spectacle which makes him realize the frailty of humanity in an entirely new way and which converts him ultimately from Ajax's opponent into his only effective defender. The recurrence of the imagery of hunting and livestock throughout the play and its ironic relation to Ajax's initial rampage has been noted.[23] What has not been seen is that both incident and imagery have their genesis in this Ajax passage from the *Iliad*: the simile has been realized and transformed with precisely what everyone has long been accustomed to call Sophoclean irony. The second simile, which likens Ajax to an ass which the children try to drive out of the grain field, may have appealed to Sophocles in a more general way, for it is a perfect image of the type of stubbornness and rigidity considered the hallmark of the Sophoclean hero.

When Ajax regains his sanity he too has a chance to examine the actions already described by the chorus and Tecmessa. He calls his madness a "frenzied disease" (λυσσώδη νόσον, 452). The adjective λυσσώδης is used earlier in Greek literature only by Poseidon when (in the form of Calchas) he describes Hector to Ajax (*Il.* 13.53).[24] Again, the echo illustrates one of the types of associations, sometimes collusions, which inextricably bind Ajax to Hector throughout the play.

Even when this scene develops into its repeatedly allusive variations on the parting of Hector and Andromache, there may be a nod to the Iliadic Ajax in a comparable situation. When Tecmessa pleads with Ajax she uses a very unusual imperative twice in two lines (506–7) – αἴδεσαι, she says, "Show the respect you should." The rare form occurs once in the Homeric poems when the embassy is sent to Achilles and Ajax himself begs Achilles to relent (*Il.* 9.640).[25] In the second half of the play there are further indications that the insult to Achilles' honor in general and the embassy scene in particular were in Sophocles' mind.[26]

58

Certainly here, as Tecmessa makes her vain request to the implacable hero whose pride is wounded, it is as if Ajax, having failed to win the arms of Achilles, has instead inevitably inherited the posture of the insulted warrior whose will he himself failed to bend.

When Tecmessa has finished her speech, Ajax asks for their son Eurysakes to be brought. Holding the boy, he makes a moving speech (545–82) which closes with the theme so pervasive in this play, the question of the hero's armor. None of Ajax's arms are to be passed on to or claimed by anyone, except for his famed broad shield, σάκος εὐρύ. This he bequeaths to his son, noting that it is responsible (ἐπώνυμον) for the boy's name, Eurysakes (574). The etymological importance of names was actually raised by Ajax in his previous speech (430–80), which also has bearing on Eurysakes and the shield. The speech contains a striking echo of Aeschylus' *Seven against Thebes*, a play Sophocles uses extensively elsewhere.[27] Here Ajax describes his enemy Odysseus as "a man capable of anything" – φωτὶ παντουργῷ φρένας (445), and the Aeschylean phrase, which describes Polyneices, is almost identical: φωτὶ παντόλμῳ φρένας (*Septem* 671). Both speakers have the same concern with weapons, the same perception of an outrageous absence of justice. But the most remarkable thing is that both times the striking phrase follows immediately on a reflection upon the etymological suitability of a name: Ajax opens his speech with an exclamation of grief which explains why his is ἐπώνυμον (430ff.); Eteocles explains why Polyneices' is (ἐπωνύμῳ, 658). Both times the adjective is the one used by Ajax in his farewell musings on Eurysakes and the broad shield he will inherit.

These, then, are the main allusions or echoes in the first half of the *Ajax*. They come from a large number of Iliadic Ajax passages, but so far there has been no apparent use of an episode in which Ajax figures most prominently, the struggle for possession of the corpse of Patroclus (*Il*. 17). Here Ajax is at his most stubborn, the bulwark formed by him and his shield are at their most useful. Moreover, the central plot of the *Iliad* hinges on the outcome of this struggle, making it one of the climaxes of the poem. If Sophocles were in fact drawing on many of the Ajax passages in the *Iliad*, it would seem rather odd for him not to use this one.[28]

He does: but instead of alluding to it while Ajax still lives, he reserves it for one of his greatest and most ironic allusive transformations. The second half of the play is an extended sardonic variation of the Homeric scene – instead of Ajax and other warriors struggling to do great deeds over the corpse of Patroclus, a powerless Teucer and an arrogant and offensive pair of generals conduct a squalid contest of words over a corpse which is of course that of Ajax. Although Teucer himself fails to defend the body, Sophocles has used him for a more subtle purpose: to make sure that the reversal of the Homeric scene, besides being embodied in the general dramatic action, is explicitly signaled by the poetry itself.

Almost immediately upon entering, Teucer triggers the allusion when he calls for Eurysakes to be brought. Ajax's earlier call for Eurysakes and his speech to him were highly allusive; Teucer's request for the child has, if anything, a greater complexity. He orders the boy to be brought lest he be snatched up by some enemy like a lion cub separated from its mother (*Aj.* 985–9). The image is drawn from a description of Ajax in *Iliad* 17 as he defends the corpse of Patroclus.

> Αἴας δ᾽ ἐγγύθεν ἦλθε φέρων σάκος ἠύτε πύργον·   128
> Ἕκτωρ δ᾽ ἂψ ἐς ὅμιλον ἰὼν ἀνεχάζεθ᾽ ἑταίρων,
> ἐς δίφρον δ᾽ ἀνόρουσε· δίδου δ᾽ ὅ γε τεύχεα καλὰ
> Τρωσὶ φέρειν προτὶ ἄστυ, μέγα κλέος ἔμμεναι αὐτῷ.
> Αἴας δ᾽ ἀμφὶ Μενοιτιάδῃ σάκος εὐρὺ καλύψας
> ἑστήκει ὥς τίς τε λέων περὶ οἷσι τέκεσσιν,
> ᾧ ῥά τε νήπι᾽ ἄγοντι συναντήσωνται ἐν ὕλῃ
> ἄνδρες ἐπακτῆρες· ὁ δέ τε σθένεϊ βλεμεαίνει,   135
> πᾶν δέ τ᾽ ἐπισκύνιον κάτω ἕλκεται ὄσσε καλύπτων·
> ὣς Αἴας περὶ Πατρόκλῳ ἥρωϊ βεβήκει.
> Ἀτρεΐδης δ᾽ ἑτέρωθεν ἀρηΐφιλος Μενέλαος
> ἑστήκει, μέγα πένθος ἐνὶ στήθεσσιν ἀέξων.

(17.128–39)

Ajax approached with his tower-shield, and Hector drew back into the crowd of companions and mounted his chariot quickly. He gave the fair armor to the Trojans to take to the city, great fame for himself. Ajax covered Patroclus with his broad shield and stood over him like a lion over its young, a lion which hunters meet in the woods leading its young, and it exults in its strength with a great fierce scowl. So Ajax took his stand over

60

the warrior Patroclus. And Menelaus, son of Atreus, dear to
Ares, stood opposite, with great grief in his heart.

The Homeric simile compares Ajax to a lion defending its cubs
from men who would snatch them away.[29] Just as important is the
non-metaphorical description of the defense: Ajax has protected the
corpse with his broad shield – that is, of course, σάκος εὐρύ
(*Il.* 17.132).

With the corpse of Ajax lying on stage and Teucer having
arrived to defend it, with all the stress laid on the etymology of
Eurysakes' name in this play, Teucer's call for the boy and use of
this lion simile should suddenly and surely trigger the allusion. The
man who defended a corpse with his shield has now become a
corpse and cannot even defend his own son, the shield's namesake.
It is tragic, pathetic, and ironic; it is profoundly Sophoclean – very
much in the manner of the blindness of Teiresias which Oedipus
ultimately inflicts on himself. Moreover, this intertextual allusion
has been made to gleam not simply so that its technical brilliance
will dazzle the observer, but so that it may serve as the perfect
spotlight for Sophocles' tragic stage: tragedy in general and the
Ajax in particular are about the reversal of fortune. The contrast
between Ajax the effective warrior and Ajax the helpless corpse,
which allusion to the Patroclus episode makes even more vivid, is
one of the main elements of this drama. And finally, this allusion
has been prepared for and its effectiveness ensured and enhanced
by all those allusions which came before, each acting as a small
trigger for this one.

Sophocles then has done what Aeschylus did not: the device of
Homeric allusion, already familiar in lyric poetry, has been raised
to a new level of complexity and sophistication. Sophocles has
created a thematically related series of allusions and spaced them
though the play to achieve a cumulative effect not available to the
lyric poet working with less scope. Once allusive force has been set
loose in this play, it moves with particular power, for the allusions
to the Homeric Ajax and Hector reinforce the explicit concern with
those heroes in Sophocles' text. This coherent effect is at its
greatest when the series of allusions culminates in the tragic
reversal, the heart of the genre into which Sophocles has brought
the device.

Having come as far as the death of Ajax and having seen the

ways Sophocles uses the *Iliad* to point up the plight of the fallen hero, we can now glance back profitably to the old problem surrounding Ajax when he is still on the boundary between life and death – that is the so-called deception-speech which makes the chorus think that he has renounced suicide when in fact he has not. This speech is immediately preceded and immediately followed by choral song. In each of these songs there is one and only one Homeric formula. In the song before Ajax's speech it is the phrase μέγα πένθος (615); in the song after, the phrase αἰνὸν ἄχος (706). This latter phrase is used nine times in the *Iliad* – and so its occurrence could not signal a specific context to any audience. But in that desperate and doubtful struggle in which Ajax defends the corpse of Patroclus, this phrase occurs right at the beginning where it is applied to Hector (17.83), the sight of whom makes Menelaos see the need for Ajax. The other phrase, μέγα πένθος, has the ring of a common Homeric formula, but it actually occurs only four times in the *Iliad*.[30] Granted, this is sufficiently often that, coming before Ajax's speech, it would not suggest a specific context. Nevertheless, we find that it closes off the last line of the Ajax–Patroclus passage, coming just five lines after the lion simile (17.139).

No audience could grasp this frame which Sophocles has placed around the deception speech. More than that, it is unquestionably important that the scene of the defense of the corpse *not* be called to mind until Teucer calls for Eurysakes after Ajax's death. The poet was writing for himself here, as Aeschylus sometimes did, taking a speech which makes the chorus ecstatic and surrounding it with the very phrases which enclose the scene from the *Iliad* which he will reverse to show the fall of his hero from his moment of greatest glory to that of his greatest shame. The Sophoclean irony of the joyful chorus with its allusion to the defense of Patroclus is eventually quite clear, but it is first and most subtly encoded in the poet's private ironic frame, his collusion surrounding the ode of joy.

Sophocles has worked very carefully and intricately toward this final allusion to the height of Ajax's glory, and there will be nothing in the *Ajax* after it to compare in power. The earlier references to the grave had quietly insisted on the deep connection between Ajax and Hector, lending to the cadence of *Ajax* all the weight of the end of the *Iliad*. There is another footnote, similar and yet more exquisite. Like the call for Eurysakes, it comes from Teucer after the corpse of Ajax is revealed. Teucer, horrified at the sight of Ajax impaled on the sword that came from Hector, asks how Ajax might be pulled off the "gleaming spike" (*Aj.* 1025). This is a highly marked phrase. The adjective I have translated as "gleaming" – αἰόλος – is used of a huge, bloody, gasping snake dropped from the sky; of annoying wasps; of the brilliant, immortal talking horse Xanthus just before the Furies silence him; and of the maggots Andromache imagines will eat Hector. It is always vivid; it is nowhere else in Greek used of a sword.[31] Once in the *Iliad* it is used of a whole set of armor (5.295). *Twice* it is used of a single piece of heroic equipment; and then, with the sole exception of Teucer's bitter description, it will never again be used of armor in Greek. Both the applications to a piece of armor in the *Iliad* come in Ajax passages – one in 16.107 and the other the passage in 7.222, on which Sophocles drew so extensively. Both times it describes the shield of Ajax. So by an intricate yet firmly insistent reference the sword of Hector and the shield of Ajax are brought together with one epithet. The application of αἰόλος to a heroic weapon marks the end of that usage in the Greek language, just as *Ajax* gives us the end of the heroic world where such weapons are used by such heroes in combat.

Ajax dies on Hector's sword; Teucer describes it as if it were Ajax's shield. This is more than just a precious poetic ploy. The fates of these two men have been linked throughout the play. That is what moved Sophocles to use the Hector and Andromache scene, which is the one allusion which has never gone unnoticed. And as soon as Teucer sees Ajax and the sword he is moved to reflect on their linked and mutually allusive fates:

> I ask you, consider the fortune of these two men: Hector, with
> the very belt that had been given to him by Ajax, was gripped to
> the chariot rail, and mangled until he gasped his last. It was
> from Hector that Ajax had this gift, by which he perished in this
> deadly fall. Was it not the Fury who forged this sword? And did
> not Hades, wild creator, make that belt? I, at least, would say
> that these things, and all things always, are devised by gods for
> men.
>
> (1028–37)

Just as Teucer believes that all the ties between Ajax and Hector have been forged by the creator gods, in this play they have been forged with patient, careful Homeric allusions by Sophocles, the creator of Teucer and his lines.

One of the reasons it seems likely that *Ajax* was produced sometime around 440 is that in the *Alcestis*, which appeared in 438, Euripides often seems to be following the technique Sophocles used in the *Ajax* – not only in the general manner of weaving allusions into a play but also, more importantly, in the choice of the specific passages from the *Iliad* to use for allusion. It is to *Alcestis*, then, that we turn next.

DEATH AND VICTORY IN EURIPIDES' *ALCESTIS*

The first part of Plato's *Symposium* culminates in Socrates' report of a speech delivered on an earlier occasion by Diotima. Although the audience seems not to notice, Plato has let Diotima's priestly prescience, or Socrates' narrative manipulation, produce an address prefigured in form and content by the much simpler one with which Phaedrus had begun the evening. Most strikingly, both speeches couple Alcestis and Patroclus, something not explicitly done anywhere else in Greek prose or poetry. Plato, however, had an equally ingenious predecessor in this association, for Euripides had already shaped his portrait of Alcestis with Patroclus in mind. Understanding the *Alcestis* requires recognition of this connection: it is one of the threads, exquisite but essential, by means of which Euripides tied his play to two non-dramatic genres, epic and epinician. An analysis of Euripides' allusions sets both the content and tone of *Alcestis* in a new and clearer light.

Light is needed, for the *Alcestis* is infamously obscure: even among Euripides' problem plays it has been called "the most baffling."[32] The riddle of *Alcestis* has given rise to a body of critical literature of which it has been said without exaggeration that to look at it is "to contemplate Chaos"; and this literature continues to grow steadily without becoming significantly more orderly.[33] The confusion stems at least partly from a peculiar external fact: this play is a tragedy which was put in place of a satyr play. This irregular substitution has encouraged scholars, in their internal examinations, to see the play's lighter, more comic, or even simply positive elements as problematic. The play is then found to have an ironic, corrosive nature – which, after all, scholars often find in tragedies of Euripides' that were not substitutes for satyr plays.[34] Another approach has been to take the positive at face value, to allow Admetus his victory as a good host, and to see the reclaiming of Alcestis as a deserved prize for his behavior.[35]

Victory and prize occasion joy and celebration, elements which have been analyzed as the proper close for a satyr play – indeed for a whole tetralogy; and so they are. From another point of view they will be seen to constitute a form of epinician. Normally, epinician brilliance requires a foil, and for this the first half of *Alcestis* serves perfectly: its darkness is as natural as it is deep, for it establishes the play's concentration on death. Alcestis sees death coming long before she succumbs; Admetus has barely escaped it; and Pheres has contemptuously rejected it, as if he could live forever. But both Apollo and the chorus remind us that Asclepius himself is dead, and the possibility of avoiding death has died with him. Indeed, dying holds such importance for the play that although death's essence is final silence and inevitable material disintegration, it has acquired voice and body: Death himself, a crude and coarse ogre, interrupts the beautiful Apollo's dignified prologue, asserts himself rudely, and drives the brighter, purer god from the stage. In this fashion, then, the death of Alcestis, foretold and foreseen, infects great stretches of the play in a way which is more reminiscent of the *Iliad* than it is of any tragedy. In the epic poem, Sarpedon, Hector, and Patroclus must die. So, eventually, must Achilles; and his consultations with his divine mother keep his mind on his choice: death soon or death later. Whether he converses consolingly with Priam or harshly with Lykaon, mortality is the issue. Ultimately, to come to terms with the inevitable eventual deaths of the protagonists is to wrestle with the mortality of humanity; and this is something which both the *Iliad* and the *Alcestis*, each in its own way, force us to do.[36] Moreover, Euripides has taken advantage of the strength of this theme in the *Iliad*, designing his presentation of the story of Admetus and Alcestis so as first to bring the *Iliad* to mind, and then to encourage the recollection of some of the problems the earlier poem addresses.

More than once reactions to Alcestis' death invite comparison with reactions to the deaths of Patroclus and Hector. When Alcestis is dying (193–5), and after she is gone (769–71), one of the servants notes how kind she always was, even to the humblest.

Now both Patroclus and Hector displayed such kindness, and, just as with Alcestis, this trait was mentioned at their deaths: Briseis notes the sweetness of Patroclus in the time of her distress (*Il.* 19.295–300), and Helen beautifully describes the exceptional kindness Hector extended to her when others were harsh (*Il.* 24.767–75). Similarly, before Alcestis is gone, Admetus speaks of the vision of her ghost which will come to him in his dreams (*Alc.* 354–6); this, combined with Alcestis' dying requests, recalls the sad ghost of Patroclus, which visits and pleads with Achilles as he sleeps (*Il.* 23.65–107). Such reminiscences, like phantoms in shadow, might seem to be of the sort which vanish in bright light, but they are surrounded by words and phrases drawn by Euripides from the *Iliad* so as to *suggest* that poem to his audience.

We have seen that the eulogy of Alcestis' kindness gives her a general link to Patroclus and Hector, whose deaths and funerals draw the characters and the themes of the *Iliad* together climactically in a great double closure.[37] At first glance, however, it might seem difficult to link Alcestis verbally with such figures. The armor of Achilles is neither lent to her nor captured by her: she has no need of weapons; for she is not a warrior but rather a woman and, above all, a wife. What is most emphatically noted of her, of course, is that she is the best, ἀρίστη, and the *Iliad* applies this term of highest commendation both to Hector and to Patroclus.[38] But ἄριστος is applied to other Greeks and Trojans as well, and a mere declaration of excellence will not be sufficient to suggest a comparison between Alcestis and the *Iliad*'s various ἄριστοι – particularly since a woman's excellence will normally be so different from a man's. Nevertheless, even though the Homeric hero and the faithful wife seem hardly susceptible of being linked, Euripides found some characteristically clever ways to make this connection.

Given the play's focus on death, the most obvious element to exploit for the purposes of allusion would seem to be the funerals of Patroclus and Hector, and in fact, Euripides concentrates on these moments. His Homeric allusions, considered in the order in which they occur in *Alcestis*, will each have consequences for our impressions of Alcestis and her husband.

After his wife has died and Admetus has declared the regulations for mourning which are to take effect, the chorus sings a song to Alcestis (435ff.) the opening of which, at least since Monk, has been seen to echo the address of Achilles to the deceased Patroclus (*Il.* 23.179–83). Dale has even suggested that this "remarkably close echo" may have resulted at least partly from the intrusion of a parallel quotation in the margin, but, as she admits, even a partial reduction of the passage (which in fact seems unnecessary) would still leave a clear reminiscence of Homer. Here are the two passages (the near-perfect parallelism disappears in translation):

χαῖρέ μοι ὦ Πάτροκλε καὶ εἰν Ἀΐδαο δόμοισι·

'(*Il.* 23.179)

I wish you joy, O Patroclus, even in Hades' halls.

Χο.   ὦ Πελίου θύγατερ,   str. a
χαίρουσά μοι εἰν Ἀΐδα δόμοισιν
τὸν ἀνάλιον οἶκον οἰκετεύοις.

(435–7)

O daughter of Pelias,
with the joy I wish you in Hades' halls
may you make the sunless house your home.

Is this echo actually an allusion which makes some significant connection between Alcestis and Patroclus? Notice that the allusion is followed almost immediately by a description of Alcestis as πολὺ δὴ πολὺ δὴ γυναῖκ' ἀρίσταν ("far, far the best of women," 442). Perhaps the epithet ἀρίστη functions as a trigger to help make a response to the Homeric language more likely. Moreover, this echo, placed at the very opening of the first strophe in the stasimon, will have all the benefits of eminence that that conventional placement confers.[39] The echo has thus been given two triggers, the epithet and conventional position, to encourage its recognition. The final and most reassuring clue to the significance of this allusion appears when we recognize the correct location of the Iliadic source. The passage traditionally named as parallel to Euripides' lines is the one cited above, but there is an identical line in a similar address to Patroclus earlier, at 23.19.[40] This first address follows immediately on Achilles' instructions to his men about mourning, just as the stasimon follows the similar orders of Admetus, and consequently the earlier statement must be Euripides' secondary field. Here the ground connecting tenor and vehicle includes not only the addresses but also their settings, at once distinctive and virtually identical.

The gains which come in bridging the allusive gaps are considerable. Patroclus dies for Achilles as Alcestis does for Admetus, and so Alcestis' stature is increased by the association which helps us see that she has matched the feat of a male hero. On the other hand, the consequences for Admetus in this comparison are mixed. Both he and Achilles, the men who have been left behind, are so miserable that they behave as if their lives were over. Indeed, whatever the ancient reception may have been, moderns have regularly condemned both of these men, first as culpable in the loss of their loved ones, and then as self-indulgent in their complaints and behavior while mourning. Probably reactions to Admetus will remain as varied as those to Achilles. The Homeric allusion and the comparisons it suggests do not dictate how one is to react to Alcestis and Admetus; rather they enrich the immediate emotions and judgments of the audience by tying the present tale to one of the best known stories of all.

The next allusion in *Alcestis* provides a connection with Hector, and again the Iliadic passage on which it depends has long been cited in the commentaries as a parallel.[41] The scene of Priam's lament in Book 22 is one of the climaxes of the poem, and it was used repeatedly by Greek poets both in lyric and drama for their allusions.[42] Most recently, the passage had figured in Sophocles' *Ajax*, providing some of the arguments for Tecmessa's plea. In *Alcestis* Admetus is describing the range of disasters to which a man married and with children is liable, while in the *Iliad* Priam is envisioning the disasters which the death of his son Hector would eventually bring:

παίδων δὲ νόσους καὶ νυμφιδίους
εὐνὰς θανάτοις κεραϊζομένας
οὐ τλητὸν ὁρᾶν, ἐξὸν ἀτέκνους
ἀγάμους τ' εἶναι διὰ παντός.

(Alc. 885–8)

It is unbearable to see the childrens' illnesses and the bridal bed ravaged by death when it is possible to remain childless and unwed forever.

δύσμορον, ὅν ῥα πατὴρ Κρονίδης ἐπὶ γήραος οὐδῷ
αἴσῃ ἐν ἀργαλέῃ φθίσει κακὰ πόλλ' ἐπιδόντα
υἷάς τ' ὀλλυμένους ἑλκηθείσας τε θύγατρας,

καὶ θαλάμους κεραϊζομένους, καὶ νήπια τέκνα
βαλλόμενα προτὶ γαίῃ ἐν αἰνῇ δηϊοτῆτι,

(*Il*. 22.60–4)

Wretched me, whom father Zeus will destroy at the threshold of old age with a painful fate of seeing many ills: sons destroyed and daughters dragged off, the bedroom ravaged, and tiny children thrown to the ground in terrible battle.

Both passages include a vision of house and children destroyed; both look to a theoretical scene of disaster; and both use an otherwise almost non-existent passive form of the verb κεραΐζω, "to ravage."

This part of Admetus' speech has been seen as not terribly relevant to its setting,[43] but Euripides has bought considerable advantage at the price of such apparent irrelevance. Moreover, as often, the slight disruption in the logic of the text helps attract attention so that the borrowing can have effect. An Admetus who echoes Priam by implication equates Alcestis with Hector, the second of the two great figures to die in the *Iliad*. The resemblances are strong: Apollo has tried, both for Hector and for Alcestis, to keep death away, but at this point the end has become inevitable for both mortal creatures. Soon Andromache will lament the death of her husband just as Admetus does that of his wife. Then, led appropriately by Hermes psychopomp, Priam will go to a sort of Hades to reclaim Hector's corpse from the figure responsible for his death, just as Heracles must go and reclaim Alcestis from Death himself. But whereas Priam will have to talk Achilles into releasing the dead, Heracles will have to talk Admetus into taking the body back. Once the similarity in the two situations is apprehended, such differences or variations take on added significance.

Fortunately, the apparent popularity of Priam's speech, along with the clarity of the reference to it, should spark the recognition which illuminates the contrast. Whereas Priam begs Hector to come inside the walls so that this son of his will not meet death, Admetus has just had a disagreement with his father, who resoundingly rejected the death which would have kept his son alive. This contrast is emphasized by Euripides, who not only makes the scene with Pheres shocking, but also gives it unexpected prominence within the plot of the play.[44] Moreover, this contrast between Admetus and Priam helps point to yet another inversion of Hector's family situation. Admetus' repeated requests to Alcestis not to abandon him and the children (250, 275, 380–91) place his wife in the position of Hector; for Hector listens to just such vain requests from his wife Andromache (*Il.* 6.407–39).[45]

The repeated association of Alcestis and Hector within the play establishes a variation which reverses the roles of husband and wife. External evidence, moreover, strengthens the likelihood that such close patterning is being undertaken, for just a few years before, Sophocles had used the same scene between Hector and Andromache for his own purposes of comparison and contrast in the *Ajax*, without, of course, inverting the family structure.[46] Thus two memorable scenes of Hector's, both used by Sophocles as foils for Ajax, figure here for Alcestis. Hector's critical moments in the *Iliad* might begin to seem almost traditional points for poetic reworking. However, since Sophocles' use of the Hector and Andromache meeting was noticed by the scholiasts, it may just as easily have been noticed by Euripides. (In later chapters we will see other instances of Euripides following closely in Sophocles' footsteps.) At any rate, there is one more echo of Hector left to consider which also has Sophoclean precedent.

Euripides next ties Alcestis' fate to Hector's with an even rarer phrase and perhaps an even more marked passage. When Admetus laments the fact that he was prevented from leaping into Alcestis' grave with her, his phrase for the grave is τύμβου τάφρον ἐς κοίλην (898). The similar Homeric phrase κοίλην κάπετον describes Hector's grave at the close of the *Iliad* (24.797). The word for the grave itself, κάπετον, occurs only three times in the *Iliad* and only this once in this sense. Euripides has slightly varied his borrowed phrase, substituting the two words τύμβου τάφρον for κάπετον, but the phrase is no less recognizable: this is the only passage in Greek where a τάφρος is κοίλη. Alcestis' hollow grave is associated with Hector's hollow grave, her death with his. Moreover, in addition to the rarity of this phrase there is yet another indication that Euripides wanted to emphasize this image of the hollow grave into which Admetus has not been able to leap: in just a few lines Admetus describes the empty bed, κοίτας ἐς ἐρήμνους, in which he will have to lie instead (925). Finally, just as Euripides coupled his first Homeric echo with ἀρίσταν (435, 442), so here too he has followed the hollow grave immediately with the description of Alcestis μετ' ἐκείνης τῆς μέγ' ἀρίστης (899–900). The rare and the typical are thus combined to link Alcestis with Homeric heroes, and specifically with the two whose deaths shape the end of the *Iliad*, Patroclus and Hector.

It is worth recalling, before going on, Sophocles' allusion to Hector's grave, both times with the exact Homeric phrase κοίλην κάπετον (*Aj.* 1165 and 1403). The phrase made an effective allusion which helped associate the fate of Ajax with Hector's. To find the same reference (probably only a few years later) in Euripides' *Alcestis* seems to indicate that the success of Sophocles' allusion encouraged Euripides to use it as well.

The last stasimon of *Alcestis* ends as the first one began – with a contrastive allusion to the *Iliad*. The end of the chorus's antistrophe is a direct quotation of a statement they imagine will be made at Alcestis' tomb: "This woman once died for her husband . . . " (1002–4). Formal framing devices introduce and follow this speech, giving it special prominence. "Someone stepping aside on the path will say the following," they say; and at the close of the speech they conclude the stanza with, "Such speeches will address her" (1005). Like the chorus, Hector (*Il.* 7.84–91) looks forward in time to the speech a future traveler will make when passing by a tomb – the tomb of a man Hector will have killed. And like the chorus he surrounds the stranger's words with rhetorical markers: καί ποτέ τις εἴπῃσι, he begins (7.87); and he closes with ὥς ποτέ τις ἐρέει (7.91).

Of course both the chorus and Hector present these speeches from an imagined future as proof of the fame Alcestis and Hector will enjoy. τὸ δ' ἐμὸν κλέος οὔ ποτ' ὀλεῖται, says Hector (7.91), and the chorus assures Admetus that all that was dear about Alcestis will survive as time passes (992). In both the *Iliad* and *Alcestis* this theme serves as a reminder of a possible compensation for the inevitability of death. Characters in the *Iliad* focus frequently on their future fame and reputation. Most notably, Achilles considers the alternatives of long life without a heritage of fame as opposed to a shorter life with undying fame – κλέος ἄφθιτον (*Il.* 9.413). In fact, the statements and opinions of future men are a regular topic in the *Iliad* (2.119, 3.287, 3.460, 6.358, 22.305 and 4.176–82, 6.462, 7.87–91, and 22.106–8). Just as Achilles sings the stories of famed men (9.189), his friends appeal to him on those same grounds (9.524). Helen imagines herself as the subject of song in times to come (6.358). And Euripides had sounded this theme early on with the chorus' assurance to Alcestis that her fame would survive in song as well: σε μουσοπόλοι μέλψουσι . . . κλέοντες ὕμνοις (445–7).

The similarity between these carefully framed speeches at the tomb, each with its concern for fame, is unlikely to be accident. To be sure, one could imagine a topos which incorporated epitaphs into narrative poetry in just this fashion. But against an attempt to reduce these lines to a generic statement there stand the earlier pointed references to the Hector of the *Iliad*, to the decisive moment before his death, and to the description of his grave. Once again, this association, which connects Alcestis with a heroic male and encourages comparison with him, points to suggestive differences between man and woman. Hector sees his fame as depending on his having killed the man in the tomb. Alcestis' fame will depend instead on her having died for a man – her husband. Just as Admetus and Alcestis have reversed the roles of Hector and Andromache elsewhere, so here gender suggests similarity tempered by a distinctive difference. The symmetry of such effects would seem to indicate that the allusions are legitimate. Fortunately, we have a further piece of evidence, small but compelling, that Euripides was considering the passages in the *Iliad* in which people imagine future speeches to be delivered at tombs. Earlier in the play Admetus envisions a future trip to Argos which he calls the διψίαν χθόνα (560). Now nowhere else in Greek lyric or tragedy are Argos and thirst associated so directly; but once in the *Iliad* when Menelaus has been wounded, Agamemnon contemplates how horrible it would be, if Menelaus actually died, to return to πολυδίψιον Ἄργος (4.171) – horrible, that is, for Agamemnon, because of the shame he would suffer and the things people would say at his brother's tomb. Here, too, an imagined speech is quoted, surrounded by the formal declaration that this is what someone will say (τις ὧδ' ἐρέει, *Il.* 4.176; ὥς ποτέ τις ἐρέει, *Il.* 4.182), indicating that Euripides had it in mind.[47]

Just after the imaginary address at the tomb of Alcestis comes the final Homeric reminiscence of Euripides' play, and it too has long been recognized by the commentators.[48] Heracles describes the imaginary games in which he claims to have won Alcestis (1026–34), and he gives a list of prizes patterned after those set by

Achilles for the games in the *Iliad* (23.257–70).[49] The allusion strengthens those which have come before, for once again the reference is to Patroclus, with whose death Alcestis' has been intimately linked. The games for Patroclus are emblematic contests marking his entry into Hades; these games which Heracles describes are a fictional version of the real contest he has just won in order to bring Alcestis back.

Such is the set of Homeric allusions in the *Alcestis*. The argument could be put forth that a certain amount of epic diction can be found in almost all Greek poetry. Yet all the main passages adduced center on the same two heroes, and no allusions or echoes have been intentionally omitted in this survey. Odysseus, Ajax, Diomedes, Paris, or Aeneas might have figured, but they do not. The focus is always on Hector and Patroclus, and Hector and Patroclus must die: death underlies one side of this tragedy. At the same time, however, the final Homeric allusion to athletic games brings us to the other side of the play, to the elements which connect it with the brilliance and joy of epinician poetry. The victory ode often used the dark side of man's life as a foil to the brilliance of his achievement,[50] and in much the same way Heracles (in the speech which provides the final epic allusion to death) turns blame and loss into praise and victory. Heracles himself begins by mentioning blame in what sounds very much like an epinician γνώμη·

φίλον πρὸς ἄνδρα χρὴ λέγειν ἐλευθέρως,
Ἄδμητε, μομφὰς δ' οὐχ ὑπὸ σπλάγχνοις ἔχειν
σιγῶντ'.

(1008–10)

Admetus, one ought to speak to a friend freely and not keep blame quietly in one's belly.

There is talk of hospitality, crowning, and libations at feast, all natural epinician themes. Then after more talk of blame (1017), Heracles moves to his description of the games and the prizes. This is followed by another passage which almost sounds as if it were lifted from Pindar, gnomic but for the specificity of τόδε:

ἐντυχόντι δὲ
αἰσχρὸν παρεῖναι κέρδος ἦν τόδ' εὐκλεές.

(1032–3)

73

Having chanced on it, it would be shameful to let go this profit
that carries good fame with it.

Athletic victors of course knew, but were told anyway, that fame
will come only with effort; glory comes only to those who do not let
the opportunity slip by (Pind. *Olymp.* 1.81–7, 6.9–12, *P.* 4.187–90,
12.27–8; Bacchyl. 1.71–4). The speech closes with a hopeful
description of the praise that the victor Heracles will soon receive
(1036). These lines bring epinician poetry more readily to mind
because Heracles is the paradigmatic athletic victor, the founder of
the Olympic games, as Pindar so often noted (*Ol.* 2, 3, 6, and 10).
The victory song written by Archilochus and used at Olympia
began with an address to this great victor (324W), and his
adventures often found a natural place in the more elaborate songs
commissioned for later performance. Each time Archilochus' song
hailed Heracles as victor, however, the immediate victory belonged
to some mortal, and so in the *Alcestis* Heracles' prize is not merely
his own. Soon the victory will be revealed as Admetus' as well, the
prize being his own wife. But before seeing how this is all done in
the final lines we must go back and see how Euripides has been
preparing for it.

The epinician character of *Alcestis* has been built into the very
center of the play, the ode for the House of Admetus (568–605).
Euripides has not decorated this stasimon with Homeric allusions:
it must do other work. The themes of the stasimon are hospitality,
wealth, and song and they are expressed in a remarkably Pindaric
manner. The first word of the ode, πολύξεινος, is notably
Pindaric (*Ol.* 1.93) and was used by him in an opening also (*N.*
3.2). The first order of business is Admetus' association with
Pythian Apollo, noted for his wonderful lyre. The sounds of this
lyre and the song which accompanies it thus logically occupy many
of the following lines. The description of Admetus' house,
πολυμηλοτάταν ἑστίαν, is striking in its resemblance to the
home of Hieron in *Olympia* 1 which also follows the mention of
song: ἑστίαν, . . . ἐν πολυμάλῳ Σικελίᾳ (11–13). Also, ὁ
Πύθιος ᾿Απόλλων of this stasimon (570) and the band of
animals he draws, especially the fawn βαίνουσ' . . . σφυρῷ
κούφῳ, χαίρουσ' εὔφρονι μολπᾷ (586–7), strongly resemble
the Πύθιον ᾿Απόλλωνα (11) of *Olympia* 14 with his associated
figures φιλησίμολπέ τ' Εὐφροσύνα . . . Θαλία τε

74

ἐρασίμολπε, ἰδοῖσα τόνδε κῶμον ἐπ' εὐμενεῖ τύχᾳ
κοῦφα βιβῶντα (14–17). I do not wish to claim that
Euripides is alluding to either of these Pindaric odes: other odes
could also be adduced with similar clusters of words. The point is
that in addition to the appropriate content, the diction is
inescapably epinician. Striking as they are, the above features pale
in comparison with the close of the stasimon, a series of gnomic
statements which have the unmistakable stamp of the victory ode
on them:

> τὸ γὰρ εὐγενὲς
> ἐκφέρεται πρὸς αἰδῶ.
> ἐν τοῖς ἀγαθοῖσι δὲ πάντ' ἔνεστιν σοφίας. ἄγαμαι·
> πρὸς δ' ἐμᾷ ψυχᾷ θάρσος ἧσται
> θεοσεβῆ φῶτα κεδνὰ πράξειν.

(600–5)

Nobility tends toward reverence.
Among good men no part of wisdom fails. I marvel.
In my heart sits confidence that the pious
man will profit.

First there is the predictably correct behavior of nobility, a topic
dear to Pindar (*Ol.* 2.10–11, 9.100–2, 13.13, *P.* 1.41–2, *Isthm.*
3.13–14, 7.22). Then there is the equally Pindaric closing hope
expressed as confidence that such a well-behaved man will enjoy
continued good fortune (*Ol.* 1 and 5). Finally these three
declarations, each one epinician in character, when strung together
as a group, and particularly as a group which closes the song,
inevitably suggest the close of a victory ode (Pind. *Ol.* 1 and 5, *P.* 1
and 12, *Nem.* 11 and especially Bacchyl. 1 and 10 all end with just
such series). Of course although the chorus cannot know it, all
these themes look forward to the end of their play, and all their
wisdom will in fact be applicable. Admetus' nobility and good
manners will ultimately win out and lead to his continued
happiness and prosperity.

But between this epinician stasimon and the speech of Heracles
in which he describes his imaginary athletic victory comes the
section which is the most closely linked to victory song of any in
the play, Heracles' drunken speech to the servant. Heracles

instructs the servant with gnomic wisdom in the way which is so rhetorically conventional in victory song, specifying that the teaching is directed at the wise or at least at those whose wisdom may be increased (779; cf. Pind. *Ol.* 8.59–60 and 2.83–5). His themes are the most famous lessons of epinician. Heracles first asks the servant if he knows the nature of human affairs (780) and eventually gives him a very particular answer:

ὄντας δὲ θνητοὺς θνητὰ καὶ φρονεῖν χρεών·

(799)

Mortals must think mortal thoughts.

Pindar once put it very similarly: θνατὰ θνατοῖσι πρέπει ("for mortals mortal things are fit," *Il.* 5.16), and the thought was common in victory poetry, since men who have approached divinity need to be reminded of human limits (*P.* 2.33–4, 52–3, *N.* 11.14–16, 41–3, *I.* 3.18). All men must die (782), Heracles explains, and his is also a typical reminder to the victor (*I.* 7.41–2). Of course, he continues, normally no one of mortals may see the future (783–4), again common wisdom in epinician (*Ol.* 2.30–2, 12.7–11, *P.* 10.62–4, *N.* 11.43–8, *I.* 8.13–14; Bacchyl. 10.45–7). That is, there is an unpredictable element of chance in affairs which learning and craft cannot control (785–6). Here the words ἀφανές, τύχης, and τέχνη all are echoed in a few Pindaric lines on a similar theme: ἀφάνεια τύχας . . . τέχνα (*I.* 4.33–7). The conclusion to be drawn from the facts of inevitable death and of blindness to the future is that one must take one's daily pleasure now (788–91), a sentiment presumably welcomed by Pindar's victors at celebrations which included the Heraclean pleasures of food, wine, and sex (*Ol.* 1.96–101, *P.* 3.102–9, *I.* 7.40–3).

It is an odd speech to deliver to a servant – but of course Heracles is drunk and a little unmindful of his audience. However, the real explanation of its inappropriateness is, first, that it has been borrowed and, second, that Euripides has left the edges of his allusion rough enough to trigger a response. In its original form the speech was composed not for Heracles but for Apollo, not by Euripides but by Bacchylides.[51] It is shorter in its original version:

θνατὸν εὖντα χρὴ διδύμους ἀέξειν
γνώμας, ὅτι τ᾽ αὔριον ὄψεαι

μοῦνον ἁλίου φάος,
χὤτι πεντήκοντ' ἔτεα
ζωὰν βαθύπλουτον τελεῖς.
ὅσια δρῶν εὔφραινε θυμόν· τοῦτο γὰρ
κερδέων ὑπέρτατον.

(3.78–84)

Being mortal you must cherish two views: that tomorrow you
will last see sunlight and that you will live in vast wealth for fifty
years. Be pious and have a cheerful heart: this is the greatest
gain.

Apollo delivers this address to Admetus. Moreover, it is preceded
and followed by words which echo in Heracles' speech. There are
ἐφάμερον (Bacchyl. 3.73), φρονέοντι (3.85), and ἀλαθείᾳ
(3.96) which can be matched by Heracles' καθ' ἡμέραν (788),
φρονεῖν (799), and ἀληθῶς (802).[52] Thus daily pleasures,
the wisdom to recognize them, and the truth of this message are
presented to Euripides' servant and Bacchylides' Admetus alike.
Apollo's opening, θνατὸν εὖντα χρή, has been used by
Euripides' Heracles as ὄντας δὲ θνητοὺς . . . χρέων (799).
The continued sentiment has been slightly reworded, but
αὔριον, which carries the main idea, is retained (784). Finally,
the phrase εὔφραινε θυμόν, with an imperative extremely rare
in Greek, finds an exact metrical match in Heracles' εὔφραινε
σαυτόν (788).

The lesson on living as one who must die may mean little to the
distraught servant, but it prepares us for Heracles' meeting with
Admetus in the final scene. There the epinician tone continues past
Heracles' "victory speech" into his conversation with Admetus.
Admetus fears blame (1057), but Heracles has nothing but praise
for him (1093, 1095); for χάρις, which has been mentioned so
frequently in the play (60, 70, 299, 544, 660, and 842), is finally
descending on Admetus (1074, 1101). He will share in the victory
with the victorious Heracles (1103) as a good Olympic victor
should, and he will in turn praise Heracles (1109). The play ends
with new orders which replace the former ones: mourning has been
turned into feasting and dance (1155–6), a conversion of what
might have been bad to what is certainly good, which is the ancient
function of much Greek poetry. The joy of the play's second half
has erased the grief of the first.

The two-part structure of this play has been noted before.[53] What has not been noted is just how this structure mirrors the play's content. In Bacchylides, Apollo tells Admetus that mortals should be of two minds (διδύμους γνώμας); this is because life has two crucial components, namely, the joy of life and, somewhat paradoxically, the grief in the face of certain eventual death. Euripides has expanded this teaching of Apollo and explored these two Bacchylidean γνῶμαι in great detail. Though, like Patroclus, Hector, Achilles, Alcestis, and Admetus, we all must die, our victory with Heracles is in taking the joy in life while we can – Admetus' victory celebration is our celebration. It is hard to be of two minds at once, and the joy Euripides has so skillfully created seems at odds with tragedy; this may be partly why the *Alcestis* has seemed so baffling. The emphasis here is not on the characters of Alcestis and Admetus nor on the unreality of their story. No Athenian audience would need an acidic Euripidean reminder that we cannot really come back from death or that merely remaining alive may not bring happiness. Euripides does not serve up bitter cynicism to the Athenians with the lesson of Admetus anymore than Bacchylides does to Hieron. Rather there is comfort – even delight – in the assurance that, as long as it lasts, life should be filled with pleasure and joy.

Plato's Phaedrus is interested in love for its own sake. But Diotima, Socrates, and Plato are interested in how, through love, human life may brought to its best form. So Euripides is interested in confronting death, not so that it can be escaped, but so that life can be lived in the best possible way. The traditional familiarity of his theme is harder for us to recognize because of the experimental nature of his methods. But then that is the sort of thing we have learned to expect from Euripides. Perhaps it is not so surprising after all that in the first glimpse of this playwright's work which the accidents of survival have granted to us, epic allusion and epinician echo have been so blended into an alien genre as to create of one of the least tragic – yet one of the most perfect – of Greek tragedies.

ANTIGONE, EROS, AND APHRODITE

The beginning of a poem by Ion of Chios so resembles part of the parodos of Sophocles' *Antigone* that one poet almost certainly was influenced by the other; more than that we cannot say, for Ion's poem cannot be dated.[54] That the two men met and talked about poetry is certain; we have Ion's own account of an evening the two poets spent together on Chios soon after the *Antigone* had been performed, when Sophocles, having been made a general, was on his way to Lesbos. The fire at the symposium put a glow in the cheeks of the boy who was pouring their wine, and a flirtatious compliment from Sophocles deepened the blush (Athen. 13.81). This in turn moved Sophocles to express his admiration for a phrase from the poetry of Phrynichus:

λάμπει δ' ἐπὶ πορφυρέαις παρῇσι φῶς ἔρωτος.

(fr. 13N)

The light of love shines on crimson cheeks.

The anecdote allows us a rare glimpse into a poet's workshop, practically into his notebook; for in looking at the *Antigone*, which Sophocles had finished so recently, we can see that he in fact did make use of this phrase in his ode on the power of love:

Ἔρως ἀνίκατε μάχαν, Ἔρως, ὃς ἐν κτήμασι πίπτεις,
ὃς ἐν μαλακαῖς παρειαῖς νεάνιδος ἐννυχεύεις . . .

(781–4)

Eros, unconquered in battle, who attacks possessions,
who spends the night in a young girl's soft cheeks . . .

Sophocles has replaced Phrynichus' shining light, which suggested no particular time of day, with a seductive evening eroticism; and, even though in Ion's anecdote he praises the color, in his own lines it has given way to the pleasures of touch.[55] Perhaps, when faced with just such lovely crimson cheeks, he was more likely to recall the detail he had so carefully altered.

Neither the topic nor the tone of these lines supplies what most readers would consider the key to *Antigone*, yet just what the proper interpretation of the play might be is far from established. Some of its passages are as famous and as much praised as any in surviving Greek literature; others have been found obscure, tasteless, or oddly disappointing. Some of the sharpest criticisms of *Antigone* can be refuted once Sophocles' borrowings and allusions, particularly in choral sections, are recognized and appreciated.[56] There is much to examine, for of Sophocles' extant plays, *Antigone* is without a doubt the one which allows us in greatest detail to see the poet transforming his sources into a new, magnificent work.

The opening words of the parodos (100) are identical to the words Pindar had used in 463 B.C. for the opening of his ninth *Paean*: ἀκτὶς ἀελίου. Pindar's dramatic motive is the threat Thebes had faced from the eclipse of the sun, whereas Sophocles' parodos celebrates the salvation of Thebes from the threat of destruction at the hands of Polyneices and his army. Any temptation to read significance into the echo has been discouraged on grounds that the paean is apotropaic whereas the parodos is a victory song.[57] Attempts to deny such a strong poetic connection seem somehow desperate: Pindar's problem was to see whether the τέρας at Thebes signified something bad or good.[58] Sophocles, then, begins the singing in *Antigone* with an apt poetic quotation, a tribute to an earlier song connected with the interpretation of a great and ominous event at Thebes.

The parodos moves on immediately to the first of the many echoes and borrowings from Aeschylus' *Seven against Thebes* which occur throughout *Antigone*. The material fits seamlessly into its new setting: the action of Sophocles' play follows immediately on that of Aeschylus, and the clatter of Ares which filled the first play makes an impressive opening for the sequel. The phrases Sophocles has selected from Aeschylus are vivid and very little changed. If the echoes were used to emphasize Sophoclean innovations or pointed contrasts with Aeschylus, they might be called allusions of a sort; but here they are simply echoes. Any ungrammaticality would be mischievous: there is no gap to bridge. The striking feature of the Sophoclean adaptation is that for one choral passage in his play (106–40) he has combined elements from two Aeschylean choral sections separated by hundreds of lines.[59]

The concentration of echoes from *Seven against Thebes* is greatest in the second stasimon of *Antigone*; but whereas the material for the parodos came from scattered passages, here Sophocles has used one stasimon of the *Seven* extensively. In fact, the extent to which the second stasimon of the *Seven* (especially 720–65) informs the first half of second stasimon of *Antigone* has no parallel in extant tragedy: Aeschylus' song contributes content, phrases, forms of expression, and even its simile. Again, since both songs treat the curse on the family of Laius in very similar manner and in plays treating the family at practically the same point in its accursed history, there is no real gap for an allusion to span. It is simply the fact that Sophocles takes over so very many details that is noteworthy.[60]

Far more interesting than these imitations of *Seven against Thebes* in the parodos and second stasimon is the way Aeschylus' *Oresteia* has been put to use in the *Antigone*. Sometimes it is merely an odd phrase which Sophocles reproduces: the "thirsty dust" of *Agamemnon* (495) has become a central element in *Antigone*, the means by which both symbolic burials of Polyneices are carried out (246–7, 429: διψίαν κόνιν). Similarly, the chorus' description of the transgression for which Antigone is being punished (*Ant.* 853–6) has been inspired by the occurrence both in *Agamemnon* (383–4) and *Eumenides* (539–42) of the image of kicking the altar of Justice. The recognition of Sophocles' debt even allows the text of *Antigone* 855 to be set in better order. The chorus points out to Antigone that in her daring she has fallen against Justice's high altar:

Προβᾶσ' ἐπ' ἔσχατον θράσους
ὑψηλὸν ἐς Δίκας βάθρον
προσέπεσες, ὦ τέκνον, πολύ·

(*Ant.* 853–5)

In Aeschylus, dishonoring Justice's altar with one's foot, ποδί, is discouraged (*Eum.* 541). So at *Antigone* 855 the bland πολύ can be replaced with the Aeschylean ποδί, resulting in a more vivid description of Antigone's offense.[61]

Arresting as these echoes are, a far more fundamental connection links *Antigone* and the *Oresteia*, coloring the readings of Sophocles' first, third, and fourth stasima, and ultimately affecting the interpretation of the entire play. The second stasimon of *Choephori* (585–651) has long been linked with the first stasimon in *Antigone* (332–75), often called the Ode to Man.[62] The famous Sophoclean opening, πολλὰ τὰ δεινὰ (332), inevitably suggests the opening of the earlier ode, πολλὰ μὲν γᾶ τρέφει δεινά . . . (*Cho.* 585–6). Yet in a way the connection seems limited and superficial, for the most awesome of earth's many awesome things which concern the Sophoclean chorus is the human race, whereas in Aeschylus' play the libation-bearers go on to sing of the destructive and terrifying force of female love.[63] It has been suggested that this Aeschylean theme of love has "crept" forward to Antigone's third stasimon, the Hymn to Eros, and even that the use of three exempla in the *Choephori* stasimon had a formal effect

81

on the fourth stasimon, the Danaë ode.[64] In fact the connections run deeper; demonstration of this first requires establishing the presence of the *Choephori* theme, the danger of love, in the Ode to Man itself.

Of all the topics in Greek poetry there is perhaps none which has a more conventional vocabulary and set of images than the description of love. At its first typical appearance in the *Hymn to Aphrodite* (vv.1–7), it controls all the beasts and birds that the sea and earth nourish: ὅσ' ἤπειρος πολλὰ τρέφει ἠδ' ὅσα πόντος (v.5). Aeschylus kept these elements in the *Choephori*, adhering especially closely to the *Hymn* with the words πολλὰ μὲν γᾶ τρέφει (585). Here the dangerous passion masters both beasts and mortals (*Cho.* 601), but the Aeschylean chorus is most concerned with the eros which controls women and drives them to deeds of great daring (594–601). The horror of Clytemnestra's adulterous passion which led her to murder her husband has suggested their theme, and they go on to sing of frightening examples of the destruction Eros has brought about. The close relationship between these passages and the Hymn to Eros in *Antigone* (781–801) is obvious. There too love controls beasts – both on land and sea – and mortals (*Ant.* 785–6); more specifically, the conquering verb which Aeschylus chose for "love" – παρανικᾷ (*Cho.* 600) – is echoed and made even more vivid in Sophocles' description of love's victory with the two verbs παρασπᾷς and νικᾷ (*Ant.* 792, 795).

This whole set of elements was repeated later by Euripides in his description of Eros and Cypris in *Hippolytos* (525–62, 1268–81). There again love crosses land and sea and controls all things the earth brings forth (*Hipp.* 1272–8). Nevertheless, the most intriguing parallels for this Euripidean hymn to love (noted without comment by the Oxford editor of *Hippolytus*) are not from the Eros hymn in *Antigone* (781–801), but rather from the Ode to Man (*Ant.* 332–75). And the reason the passages are so similar is that in his description of *human* power Sophocles has used all the conventions appropriate for describing the power of love: mankind (ἀνθρώπου) crosses the ocean (*Ant.* 335–8), rules its inhabitants (345–6), and controls birds and beasts as well (344–53). This remarkable "misapplication" of the commonplaces for the power of love encourages us to lend more weight to the opening echo – πολλὰ τὰ δεινὰ (*Ant.* 332) – of the *Choephoroi* stasimon. The content of the Aeschylean song is relevant; already in *Antigone*'s first stasimon, the ironic power of Sophocles' poetry is used to suggest the strength – or even danger – of women's love.

The danger of love, suggested by the allusion to Aeschylus' *Choephori*, is reinforced by the explicit content of the third stasimon (*Ant.* 781–801). In addition to the traditional elements just noted, the hymn's strophe describes the power of Eros to madden his victims (*Ant.* 790). The antistrophe declares that love moves mortals to unjust thoughts and deeds (791–2); desire in a maiden's eyes is victorious, for the game is played invincibly by – these are the chorus's closing words – "the goddess Aphrodite" (801). This vivid description of Aphrodite and the maiden is directly relevant to the next (fourth) stasimon and the Homeric allusion which informs it. Between the two stasima, however, comes Antigone's commos.

In the commos, Antigone laments her impending death and seeks sympathy in her loneliness. She is not much consoled by the chorus, but when it finally does sing, it presents her with a fourth stasimon consisting of tales of the sufferings of others. First they tell of Danaë, locked away in a grave-like room; next comes Lycurgus and the madness which sent him to a rocky prison; and finally they sing of Cleopatra and the sufferings of her sons (*Ant.* 944–87). This song, so different from the first and third stasima, is nevertheless related to the earlier two, and the connection depends partly on allusions related to the use of the *Choephori* ode and the theme of love. Establishing this will require a very detailed examination both of the fourth stasimon and of its setting.

Despite the considerable amount of comment the ode has generated, there is little agreement as to its aim or function and a good deal of puzzlement over some of its images. The basic approaches of those who have written on the ode are, like its mythological exempla, three. First, there are those for whom the chorus of Theban elders here (and sometimes in their other songs as well) violates the Aristotelian distinction between the integrated Sophoclean and detachable Euripidean chorus.[65] On this view, the ode becomes a "purely lyrical instrument" imaginatively used to provide "marvelous relief."[66] Less sympathetically expressed, the irrelevance of the chorus amounts to "tangential utterances" from "a company of poetic woolgatherers," not so much decorative as "feeble, mannered, useless."[67]

The second approach is to find in the images of the ode some particular and fairly specific relevance to the actions of the actors. Of such features, the two most readily identifiable are punishment by imprisonment and the high birth of the prisoner.[68] This relationship between image and action has been called contextual relevance, and has been viewed as choral commentary on what has happened and what may happen yet.[69] However, once one goes beyond the minimum point of relevance in this ode, the lessons of its lyrical commentary, like ambiguously positioned marginal scholia, prove susceptible of various application to various figures. Thus in mentioning Zeus' visit to Danaë, a Cassandra-like visionary chorus might be foreseeing Haemon's visit to Antigone.[70] Alternatively, clear-thinking analytic Theban elders will have realized that Zeus entrusted Antigone with a pious duty just as he committed the infant Perseus to the care of Danaë.[71] One popular interpretation makes the ode's sufferers – innocent females and guilty male – parallels respectively for Antigone and Creon.[72] The least didactic of these contextual readings treats the different tales of suffering in the ode like the alternatives in a long composite scholium separated by ἄλλως: the chorus, like the scholiast, makes no final declaration as to which is the appropriate gloss for Antigone and her fate.[73]

The third main approach, which may be either a companion or an alternative to the second, seeks what has been called thematic relevance and thus connects an ode to its play through "patterns of theme, image, or emotional tone" which recur particularly in other odes.[74] Treatments of this sort stress the importance of Eros/ Aphrodite and Dionysus in this ode and for the entire play.[75] What has remained the most puzzling problem for those who adopt this type of reading is Ares, who appears in two of the ode's three exempla.[76] It seems very possible that all these oddities are just the sort of deviations from the norm, ungrammaticalities, which frequently are to be normalized by recognizing and interpreting an allusion.

On top of everything else, the mere presence of these three exempla constitutes an oddity. Antigone's grief has inspired the only extant Sophoclean ode composed entirely of mythical parallels. Cautioning against detailed application of the examples, the scholiast explains that the chorus is "simply consoling (παραμυθεῖται) the girl by adducing similar misfortunes."[77]

For once, at least, one could hardly ask for a more precise and helpful piece of learning. The scholiast's παραμυθεῖται focuses our attention on the formal and conventional character of the song both by using the proper technical term for a consolation speech and also by echoing Creon's cruel and equally pointed refusal: οὐδὲν παραμυθοῦμαι (935).[78] In fact, the solution to the general problem of the function of this stasimon in the play and to the specific puzzle of Ares' presence in the exempla lies in pursuing this ancient comment and examining the genre of consolation and one notable poetic example of it.[79]

Now as the Greeks were no strangers to the idea that misery loves not only company, but particularly the company of the even more miserable, the common aim of many of the conventions of consolation was to assure the sufferer that he or she was not alone.[80] One commonplace was that various people suffer at various times – ἄλλοτε ἄλλως.[81] Stated negatively (and sometimes a little more sternly), this becomes "X is not the only or the first to suffer thus."[82] Sometimes combined with this, and very similar, is the assertion that many or even all suffer.[83] Other less standardized observations on the frequency or inevitability of human suffering seem to be related.[84] And finally, there is the method of consolation through specific examples, an approach which the chorus adopts in the fourth stasimon, but only after pointed suggestions and objections from Antigone herself. That is, the chorus's first response to Antigone's lament is to insist on the unique nature of her suffering – being buried alive (821–2). And this, far from providing comfort, is a blunt and tactless inversion of the requirements of consolation, highly marked in its contrast to all the expected rhetorical conventions.[85] However, not being one to collapse when others fail to cooperate, Antigone immediately takes up the task of consoling herself by adducing Niobe as an exemplum (824). The chorus's objection to the parallel on grounds of Niobe's divine ancestry (834) is as perverse in this context as their original assertion of Antigone's isolation, for extant consolation exempla are always either gods themselves, the children or grandchildren of gods, or men and women who have been made immortal.[86] It is no wonder that Antigone, faced with a chorus which twice presents her with the least appropriate rhetoric for consolation, cries out that she is mocked (839).

Such is the groundwork for the chorus's song. It is a painful introduction which in its handling of convention suggests that *Antigone*, in accordance with Creon's declaration, will receive no consolation speech at all. Nevertheless, when the chorus finally sings, it cites tales which, as a series of paraenetic exempla, lie squarely in the poetic tradition. Even then, the notably mortal status of Danaë and Lycurgus indicates that the Theban elders are still somewhat reluctant to make an entirely traditional speech. Moreover, these particularly mortal citations stand in contrast not only to common practice but also to a poetic passage which provided the model or prototype for this song – the consolation of Aphrodite in the *Iliad* (5.382–415).

The confrontation in which Diomedes wounds Aphrodite comes from a part of the *Iliad* used very frequently by Greek poets of the archaic and classical periods. Familiarity with the episode is essential for full appreciation of Sappho's prayer to Aphrodite (Sappho 1 LP), and that poem of Sappho's, placed first in her collected works in Alexandria, must have been appreciated by many. Moreover, Dione's reply to the distraught Aphrodite, whom Diomedes has just wounded in *Iliad* 5, was probably the most famous specimen of consolation through παραδείγματα in Greek poetry.[87] In this passage the goddess Dione binds together the exemplary sufferings of three gods with a crisp introductory echo: τλῆ μὲν . . . τλῆ δ' . . . τλῆ δ' . . . . The device certainly attracted Panyassis, who, in writing his *Herakleia*, may well have been drawn to the Homeric passage first by its content. After all, two of the gods in Dione's speech suffer at the hands of the theomachos Herakles. But Panyassis borrowed the passage and its rhetorical structure not, apparently, to rebuke his hero, but rather to console him on the occasion of his labors. Such, at any rate, seems the likely point of his expanded list of toiling gods whose works are joined by the τλῆ μὲν . . . τλῆ δὲ structure.[88] Further evidence for the popularity of the reply to Aphrodite is provided by its association with an even more famous scene. Even though the subject of theomachy is dropped after Dione's reply, its resumption is pointedly marked soon after when Diomedes echoes Dione's ominous words about theomachoi and cites a further example of disastrous battle against a god.[89] This speech (*Il.* 6.130–40) draws as an immediate response Glaukos' comparison of the generations of leaves and of men, which in turn leads to the exchange of armor. Again, Chapter 1 discussed Mimnermus' allusion to these lines and the poignant simile which western poets would, appropriately, pass on from generation to generation.[90]

While Dione's speech to Aphrodite is customarily cited as a parallel for the opening of *Antigone*'s fourth stasimon, the relationship of the two texts is never taken beyond the shared τλῆ/ἔτλα and the number (three) of ensuing anecdotes. Yet this is the third choral song in the play with a borrowed poetic tag at the opening of the first strophe; allusion can reasonably be expected. On the face of it, the exclusive concern of the Iliadic passage with the suffering of the gods and the contrasting concentration of the fourth stasimon on mortal woes would seem to limit the possibilities for connection between the two passages. But Sophocles, in a double move, has created a uniquely intricate framework for the allusion that connects his stasimon with the *Iliad*. On the one hand, the primary field itself in *Antigone* is split between Antigone and the exempla in the stasimon which act, as in metaphor, as vehicles to enrich our understanding of her situation. On the other hand, the literary vehicle for Sophocles' allusion, the secondary field, is split in exactly the same way: the *Iliad* passage includes both Aphrodite and Dione's exempla which provide comparisons. Within this symmetrical framework Sophocles takes advantage of a number of ways to connect the two fields.

Dione's speech and the chorus's address to Antigone are united by their occasions, or settings, which are not only remarkably similar but also, for consolation speeches, rare. That is, females, mortal and immortal, are crying out over their maltreatment at the hands of a man. The first exemplum of the stasimon is Danaë, whose inclusion is usually explained by the fact that she, like Antigone, is a noble woman unjustly imprisoned. Yet the common ground shared by Antigone and Danaë goes beyond that: both are imprisoned by men who would thwart the power of love (Acrisius and Creon). Furthermore, the relevance of this shared circumstance seems assured by the fact that in the *Iliad* Dione's speech is made to the goddess of love, who has herself just been violently opposed by a man.[91] Thus the ground linking Antigone (the tenor) to Danaë (the vehicle of the mythological allusion) is also shared by Aphrodite, the vehicle of the Homeric allusion. But why is Danaë sealed in a bronze room? And why does Sophocles' chorus mention Ares? Danaë's thwarted love is applicable both to Antigone's situation and to Aphrodite's (for she is love itself, even if she has momentarily engaged in non-erotic battle), but the details of the bronze room and Ares, ungrammatical puzzles in the mythological vehicles, must be solved not by reference to Antigone as their tenor, but rather by considering Antigone's literary vehicle, the secondary field of the Iliadic consolation and the exempla there. In *Iliad* 5, the first sufferer in Dione's reply is also bound up in a bronze container – in this case an urn. And this brass-bound victim is none other than Ares.

The second figure in the *Antigone* ode is Lycurgus; and even though the image of his prison helps connect him to Danaë, Antigone, and Ares, he seems, as a theomachos, a rather unlikely figure to make an appearance in a consolation speech. But the secondary field points the way to explanation again, for all three of Dione's examples are incidents of gods attacked by men. And although Lycurgus himself does not figure in her speech, she closes with a reflection on the brevity of the lives of theomachoi (*Il.* 5.406–9), the reflection neatly echoed by Diomedes in both opening and closing his companion speech (*Il.* 6.128–9, 140–1). He has but one example to add to Dione's list – the story of Lycurgus' attack on Dionysus and his nurses. Moreover, the reply to Diomedes, the speech on the generations of leaves, uses the phrase δεινὸν μένος (*Il.* 6.182) – a phrase which is virtually nonexistent elsewhere in Greek, but which also occurs here in the Lycurgus exemplum (*Ant.* 959–60).[92] Thus the second mortal example in the ode has an even more explicit antecedent in the Homeric lines than did the first. Furthermore, by the close of the first antistrophe there have been explicit references to Ares and Dionysus and an implication of Aphrodite, gods who all figure importantly in the Homeric speeches from which Sophocles has taken his striking phrases.

The second strophe and antistrophe of the fourth stasimon are entirely devoted to the third paradigm, and it is this third and final example which has proved most troublesome. In particular, why is the blinding of Cleopatra's sons described with such detail that we almost forget Cleopatra's misfortunes? That Ares witnesses the blinding of the brothers by their stepmother is the oddest detail of all, and thus it is the surest ungrammaticality or trigger requiring reference to the source of the images. Just as this one anecdote takes half the *Antigone* ode, so in Dione's speech in the *Iliad* one figure is treated at far greater length than the rest – Ares, who was maltreated by two brothers and saved through the intervention of their hostile stepmother. Now the joint occurrence of Ares and of imprisonment in bronze in these few lines from Homer and in the Sophoclean ode might be ascribed to coincidence, as might even the prominence of Lycurgus. However, the verbal echoes, particularly δεινὸν μένος, reduce the probability of chance similarlity to near zero. With the addition of a stepmother hostile to her two stepsons, with Ares close in attendance, it seems virtually impossible that the Sophoclean song and its images could have arisen independently of the Homeric lines. The Diomedes and Aphrodite episode provides the only resolution of the string of apparent improprieties in the ode; recognizing what may have been in part Sophocles' private collusion releases the interpretive tension which has led to condemnation of the stasimon as irrelevant.

What made Sophocles turn to this Homeric passage at this point in *Antigone*? First, there is a reasonable chance that the use of the *Iliad* will be at least partly recognized and therefore make an effective allusion. As an outstanding specimen of the consolation genre, the Homeric reply to Aphrodite (along with its continuation in Diomedes' speech) acts as a foil for the Sophoclean consolation *manqué*. That is, the chorus defies generic expectations by using mortal examples. Yet at the same time that the chorus avoids the inclusion of divine beings in their normal roles as sufferers, it nevertheless refers, implicitly and explicitly, to the three gods – Aphrodite, Dionysus, and Ares – whose roles stem from and in various ways are reinforced by the Homeric model. Here is a second authorial motive: the presence of these gods in *Antigone* has not been determined only by their reference to epic, for they have larger thematic relevance as well. This can be seen from other odes: Ares, as he did in Sophocles' Aeschylean models, clatters and rages through the parodos; Aphrodite triumphs fully and somewhat disturbingly in the third stasimon; and Dionysus' cameo appearance at the end of the parodos is expanded to a major role in the fifth stasimon. There is, moreover, one further reason for the inclusion of these three gods. Jebb's comment on the last lines before the fourth stasimon, where Antigone calls on her ancestral gods (938), reminds us that these must be Ares and Aphrodite, since they are Harmonia's parents, and Dionysus, who is Semele's son.

Ultimately, in this play, the greatest of these is Love. Signaled by allusion to the *Choephori*, the theme of the power of love lies only slightly under the surface of the first stasimon (*Ant.* 332–75). In addition, Creon repeatedly focuses on the threat of women and of their love (*Ant.* 484, 525, 651–2, 678–80, 756). Then the topic is eloquently and fully stated in the third stasimon (*Ant.* 781–801), immediately after which Antigone enters and begins her odd negotiation with the chorus for a consolation, which, in the fourth stasimon (*Ant.* 944–87), they finally grant her. There is something in her of the wounded Aphrodite, which gives the Homeric speech to that goddess added relevance as a model. Sophocles' conversation with Ion about Phrynichus and the light of love turns out to lie at the heart of *Antigone* after all. But the beautiful boy who poured the poets' wine was merely a harmless Eros, whereas Antigone, as great a force for love in reality as in her own self-description (523), could hardly be more dangerous. Her love for her brother leads her to awesome acts, and although φιλία and ἔρως are not identical, the latter is also part of her power. Like Aphrodite, Antigone can be wounded; but even in death, she uses the invincible power of Eros to draw into her destruction not only a man who hates her, but the man who loves her as well.[93]

The climax of the messenger's speech after the last stasimon is his description of Haemon committing suicide over Antigone's corpse. With his last gasps the young man chokes out blood (*Ant.* 1238–9), and the phrases, as Fraenkel confidently affirmed, are closely imitated from Clytemnestra's triumphant description of Agamemnon's final bloody breaths (*Ag.*1389–90). The highly wrought, unforgettable Aeschylean lines attracted Sophocles in the Ajax as well.[94] With Haemon's death, *Antigone*'s allusion to the *Choephori* ode on the dread effects of sexual passion reaches its final chilling note. In whatever ways she is right or wrong, Antigone directs forces of frightening power; although she is seldom seen this way, she has much in common with Aeschylus' Clytemnestra – and with Euripides' Medea, to whom we turn next.

THE DESTRUCTION OF THE NATURAL ORDER:
MEDEA

The *Medea* is a terrifying play of universal catastrophe with the horror inherent in the murder of children made even more horrible by having them die at the hands of their own mother. Jason sets out to consolidate his place in society by making a traditional marriage into power, but the wedding gift his children bring turns the flesh of his fair young bride to streams of bloody pitch. Medea ensures that Jason is deprived not of one family but of two, and in the end he does not even have a decent corpse – from the old family or the new – to bury. It would be a small but welcome consolation to find some order at the root of such violence, and although Euripides' allusions in this play are less extensive than in *Alcestis*, they are significant and point to a reading of the play which rescues it from utter darkness.

At the end of Medea's first confrontation with Jason the chorus sing of the problems of excessive desire, wishing for "soundness of mind, the best gift of the gods" (σωφροσύνα, δώρημα κάλλιστον θεῶν, 635–6). Denys Page suggested that this might be a conscious imitation of a very similar phrase in Aeschylus' *Agamemnon*: "soundness of mind is the greatest gift of god" (τὸ μὴ κακῶς φρονεῖν θεοῦ μέγιστον δῶρον, 927–8). We shall see in the next two chapters what an enormous influence the *Oresteia* had on Euripides, and there are very good reasons why he might have had his eye on these lines from *Agamemnon*. They are spoken by Agamemnon in his great argument with Clytemnestra when she is leading him to his doom over lovely carpets just as surely as Medea ruins Jason. Clytemnestra, like Medea, is jealous of her husband's affections for a new woman,[95] but Clytemnestra takes her revenge by stabbing her husband, whereas Medea stabs her husband's children. At the close of the *Medea* Jason begs for the childrens' bodies, and when he complains to Zeus of her refusal to return them, he calls her "child-murdering" (παιδοφόνου, 1407). The word has appeared once before in poetry, in the last line of Priam's plea to Achilles, where the question was likewise the return of a son's body to a parent (*Il.* 24.506). Medea – it is the verdict reached after comparing her to Clytemnestra, who at least does not murder her children, or to Achilles, who returns Priam's – is monstrous in her unbending cruelty.

This active use of earlier poetry is manifest not only at critical moments in *Medea* but on the way to and from them as well. Euripides' debt to Aeschylus, for example, is certainly evident in Jason's virtual quotation (523) from the *Seven against Thebes* (62) even though the unrelated contexts do not afford opportunities even for collusive comparison or contrast. (The subject in Aeschylus' ὥστε ναὸς κεδνὸς οἰακοστρόφος is merely put into the accusative in Euripides.[96]) The nurse's term δυσκατάπαυστος (109), used of Medea's wounded spirit which cannot be calmed, is very likely to have been borrowed from Aeschylus' *Choephori* 470, the only other place it occurs, where it is also applied to pain. Similarly, Aegeus' striking comment on Medea's "melting complexion" (χρώς τε συντέθηκε, 689), which is how he describes her tears, imitates the only other use of this phrase, which describes Penelope's weeping in the Odyssey (τήκετο δὲ χρώς, 19.204). Even though in both scenes there is a deception in progress – Odysseus' of Penelope and Medea's of Aegeus – the phrase is simply borrowed without allusion. And the same is probably true of two echoes from Hector's final battle in the Iliad which find their way into Euripides' poetry here: παντοίας ἀρετᾶς (*Med.* 845, *Il.* 22.268) and the rare verb κατηφεῖς (*Med.* 1012, *Il.* 22.293: κατήφησας).[97]

Other echoes in the play, however, are more meaningful: in the first brilliant choral song of *Medea* all the elements borrowed from earlier poetry are used to set the complex themes of the play in motion with an elegance which matches the allusive art of the other plays from this period. The first stasimon (410–45) tells of a great upheaval in nature and human society. We shall refer to almost every line before we are done, so it will be useful to have it before us:

ἄνω ποταμῶν ἱερῶν χωροῦσι παγαί,   410
καὶ δίκα καὶ πάντα πάλιν στρέφεται.
ἀνδράσι μὲν δόλιαι βουλαί, θεῶν δ'
οὐκέτι πίστις ἄραρε·
τὰν δ' ἐμὰν εὔκλειαν ἔχειν βιοτὰν στρέψουσι φᾶμαι·
ἔρχεται τιμὰ γυναικείῳ γένει·
οὐκέτι δυσκέλαδος φάμα γυναῖκας ἕξει.

μοῦσαι δὲ παλαιγενέων λήξουσ' ἀοιδῶν   421
τὰν ἐμὰν ὑμνεῦσαι ἀπιστοσύναν.
οὐ γὰρ ἐν ἁμετέρᾳ γνώμᾳ λύρας
ὤπασε θέσπιν ἀοιδὰν
Φοῖβος, ἁγήτωρ μελέων· ἐπεὶ ἀντάχησ' ἂν ὕμνον
ἀρσένων γέννᾳ. μακρὸς δ' αἰὼν ἔχει
πολλὰ μὲν ἁμετέραν ἀνδρῶν τε μοῖραν εἰπεῖν.

σὺ δ' ἐκ μὲν οἴκων πατρίων ἔπλευσας   431
μαινομένᾳ κραδίᾳ, διδύμους ὁρίσασα πόντου
πέτρας· ἐπὶ δὲ ξένᾳ
ναίεις χθονί, τᾶς ἀνάνδρου
κοίτας ὀλέσασα λέκτρον,
τάλαινα, φυγὰς δὲ χώρας
ἄτιμος ἐλαύνῃ.

βέβακε δ' ὅρκων χάρις, οὐδ' ἔτ' αἰδὼς   439
Ἑλλάδι τᾷ μεγάλᾳ μένει, αἰθερία δ' ἀνέπτα.
σοὶ δ' οὔτε πατρὸς δόμοι,
δύστανε, μεθορμίσασθαι
μόχθων πάρα, τῶν τε λέκτρων
ἄλλα βασίλεια κρείσσων
δόμοισιν ἐπέστα.

Men are treacherous, and the bad reputation of women will be
converted to good (410–30). Medea, who left her home out of love
for Jason, has been betrayed and replaced by a new queen
(431–45). On its surface the song has the simplicity and clarity of
structure shared especially by the first three stasima in the play:
generalizations are stated in the first strophe and antistrophe and
then applied to the events of the play in the second.[98] However, the
exact relation of the themes which the chorus raises within this
framework to the events of the play is anything but simple; by
seeing how the issues are grouped around echoes and quotations
from earlier poetry we can at least clarify the complexity.

The power of love, so important in Greek poetry in general and
the explicit theme of the second stasimon in Medea (627–62),
makes a notable appearance here at the opening of the second
strophe. It was the force which originally moved Medea to help
Jason and follow him to Greece. "You set sail with a crazed heart,"
sings the chorus to Medea, and their phrase for her madness,
μαινομένᾳ κραδίᾳ (432), is, like Jason's line noted above, an
exact quotation from Aeschylus' Seven against Thebes (781). There
the chorus is singing of Oedipus and his marriage to Jocasta, with
its unfortunate consequences for the close relatives it joined and the
closer ones it created. A disaster brought on by the madness of love
was perhaps best known in the infamous example of Paris and
Helen, and this seems to be the reason for another borrowing from
Aeschylus.[99] The old men in Agamemnon sing lyrically of Helen's

setting sail from her luxurious curtains (ἐκ τῶν ἁβροπήνων προκαλυμμάτων ἔπλευσεν, 690–1), which for Medea becomes a less baroque embarcation from her father's house: ἐκ μὲν οἴκων πατρίων ἔπλευσας (431). Medea herself provides an additional indication that Euripides had Aeschylus' description of Helen's voyage and marriage in mind: later in this same chorus of *Agamemnon* the old men reflect on the consequences for Troy of the "bitter end of the marriage-rites" of Helen and Paris (γάμου πικρὰς τελευτάς, 745), and Fraenkel was surely right to see Medea's closing description of the bitter results of her marriage for Jason (πικρὰς τελευτὰς τῶν ἐμῶν γάμων, 1388) as a reminiscence of Aeschylus. Euripides' use of two descriptions of Helen from the same Aeschylean song constitutes at least a collusive focus. We must ask whether this is evidence that Helen is in some sense a model or parallel for Medea.

The dangers of women and disastrous love affairs would not be a surprising theme for Greek song. Yet surely that cannot be the true theme here; in fact, the chorus wants to insist on something, if not exactly opposite, at least quite different. The old songs, such as those about Helen and Clytemnestra, which have continuously and unfairly sung of women's faithlessness, are now to be stopped and corrected (421–2). This statement in the opening lines of the first antistrophe responds to the first lines of the stasimon which state more generally that the streams of the sacred rivers are flowing backwards and the natural order is being reversed (410–11). Euripides, as if to give a specific illustration of the general reversal proclaimed, has neatly made his poetic tag flow backwards: the chorus's ποταμῶν ἱερῶν echoes the *Odyssey*'s ἱερῶν ποταμῶν (10.351).[100] In the *Odyssey* the rivers designate the origin of the four helpers of Circe, and, considered in the immediate context, such an allusion does not further the restoration of women's reputations. Circe, dangerously skilled with drugs, recalls the wrong side of Medea. More broadly considered, the opening tag suggests the proper allusive course: the *Odyssey*, as opposed to the *Iliad*, contains the great example of female faithfulness, Penelope.

Epic, to judge by the mention of Muses and ancient songs (421), does seem to be suggested. Moreover, the participle for singing – ὑμνεῦσαι – occurs in an Ionic dialect form characteristic of the Homeric poems and practically non-existent in Euripides except with non-Attic verbs, which this is not.[101] Thus content and diction alike will have readied the audience for one of the most striking exact Homeric quotations in all Greek tragedy. The chorus explain that Phoebus did not grant them the divine voice of the lyre; and, as if to point out the paradox that this disclaimer of poetic talent is couched in such lovely poetry, their words have been taken straight from the *Odyssey*. Perhaps the most important epic reflections on the nature of song and the talents of the singer come at the banquet given for Odysseus by Alcinous. When Odysseus praises Demodocus as the best of mortal singers, he declares that Apollo has given him the divine voice – ὤπασε θέσπιν ἀοιδήν (8.498) – and these are the exact words used by the chorus in *Medea*.[102] If this quotation from the *Odyssey* triggers thoughts of the good Penelope, it furthers the chorus's concern to redeem female reputation. Equally appropriate are the immediate associations with Odysseus in the Demodocus passage. Euripides' chorus opened the stasimon with a denunciation of the crafty plans of men (δόλιαι βουλαί, 412); the disguised Odysseus, as notoriously crafty a planner as any man,[103] couples his praise of Demodocus with a request for the story of one of his greatest deceptions (δόλον, 8.494), the wooden horse. Thus, in this overtly bookish first half of his ode, Euripides gives his singers – even as they disclaim poetic ability – an allusion which points to men's treachery at the same time that it ostensibly flatters their gift of song.

Nevertheless, although it keeps the focus on men who deceive, the statement of Medea's passion follows, and the second half of the song is largely occupied with the dishonor of her certain exile and her lack of recourse. The chorus open by saying everything is being reversed: do they really have anything more in mind than women's reputations? Might not the upset of the world's order involve something more than rumor?

The reputation which is no longer to hold women is called ill-sounding (δυσκέλαδος, 420). The adjective is extremely rare in extant Greek; its only Homeric use, for noise in battle, is not relevant (*Il.* 16.357).[104] However, its only other certain use before *Medea* is not military: it describes envy in Hesiod's *Works and Days* (v.196), in a passage which Euripides has used extensively for this ode:

οὐδέ τις εὐόρκου χάρις ἔσσεται οὐδὲ δικαίου   190
οὐδ' ἀγαθοῦ, μᾶλλον δὲ κακῶν ῥεκτῆρα καὶ ὕβριν
ἀνέρα τιμήσουσι· δίκη δ' ἐν χερσί· καὶ αἰδὼς
οὐκ ἔσται, βλάψει δ' ὁ κακὸς τὸν ἀρείονα φῶτα
μύθοισι σκολιοῖς ἐνέπων, ἐπὶ δ' ὅρκον ὀμεῖται.
ζῆλος δ' ἀνθρώποισιν ὀιζυροῖσιν ἅπασι   195
δυσκέλαδος κακόχαρτος ὁμαρτήσει στυγερώπης.
καὶ τότε δὴ πρὸς Ὄλυμπον ἀπὸ χθονὸς εὐρυοδείης
λευκοῖσιν φάρεσσι καλυψαμένω χρόα καλὸν
ἀθανάτων μετὰ φῦλον ἴτον προλιπόντ' ἀνθρώπους
Αἰδὼς καὶ Νέμεσις· τὰ δὲ λείψεται ἄλγεα λυγρὰ   200
θνητοῖς ἀνθρώποισι· κακοῦ δ' οὐκ ἔσσεται ἀλκή.

There will not be favor for one who keeps his oath or is
just or good; rather they will honor the man who does
evil and outrage. Justice will be violence; there will
be no Reverence. The bad man will harm the better with
slander and will swear an oath. Ill-sounding envy with
hateful face and delight in evil will follow men, all of
them wretched. Then Reverence and Indignation,
cloaking lovely complexion in white robes, will leave
the wide earth for Olympus, abandoning men for the race
of immortals. Bitter pains will be left for mortals,
and there will be no remedy for evil.

These are the conditions which will prevail at the destruction of the
race of iron men, the last generation of mortals: humanity collapses
into violence and the civilized order comes to an end. The darkness
of Hesiod's picture informs the chorus's pessimism about Medea's
future. They too note that the favor of oaths is gone (439). And the
most striking eschatological sign that they recognize is also the
most detailed echo from Hesiod: Reverence (αἰδώς) no longer
exists among men but has flown up on high (439–40).

The allusion to Hesiod explains the seriousness of the events in
the play. A chain of violence has been set in motion, violence that
will culminate in the end of this human community. Hesiod asserts
(182) that not even parents and children will be exempt from the
strife, and so it will be – most horribly – here in Corinth. Medea is
caught in this disintegration of family and humanity, but she is not
the responsible party: Jason, at once disregarding oaths and
faithfulness to the gods, has brought about this particular tragic

world-end. This story, the chorus suggests, could have been a tale about a bad woman, or a disastrous love affair; it could have been like the story of Clytemnestra or of Helen, but it will not be. The borrowings from Aeschylean descriptions of Helen evoke her model, passive or seductive, only so that it may be more pointedly rejected. For once the song will take a different direction. Medea's wrath is a cosmic force. Her play is not a story of sordid jealousy but rather of sacred human bonds which must not be violated. Such a reading may emerge even if one hears no poetic echoes in the text; but having heard them, we can be much more certain that Euripides has not plunged us into chaos.

CONCLUSIONS

The plays of this period exhibit a great range in both the poetry they draw on for allusion and the uses they make of it. Of the Homeric poems both the *Iliad* and the *Odyssey* are important, and Hesiod, Bacchylides, and Aeschylus all have primary roles to play as well. Significant allusions are found most frequently in choral sections, but, as in *Alcestis*, they occur in iambic sections too. Sometimes one poetic source predominates, as the *Iliad* does in *Ajax*; but in the other three plays the important allusions are more wide-ranging.

Despite such variety, or side by side with it, various patterns emerge even in these early decades. Some involve both tragedians: Hector's great scenes, in both life and death, are crucial in the Ajax and in *Alcestis*, and Sophocles and Euripides both seem extremely familiar with Aeschylus' *Seven against Thebes*. Other patterns are those of one writer or the other: Euripides, in both *Alcestis* and *Medea*, uses his allusions to point out specifically the remarkable nature of his female protagonists in contrast to the male heroes of epic song. Sophocles seems particularly drawn to passages in Aeschylus' *Agamemnon* which themselves owe a debt to the Homeric poems. As we have seen, two different passages, widely separated in *Antigone*, may be modeled on the vulture simile from the parodos of the *Agamemnon* (48ff.) which in turn draws on one simile from each of the epics (*Il.* 16.428–9, *Od.* 16. 216–19). And in both the *Ajax* (376) and *Antigone* (1238) Sophocles draws on Clytemnestra's gleeful description of the murder of Agamemnon (*Ag.* 1389–92) which Aeschylus so effectively adapted from a more benign

Homeric simile of simpler joy (*Il.* 23.597–9).

In fact, in these early plays Sophocles' allusive technique seems in many ways more akin to Aeschylus' than does Euripides'. Like Aeschylus, Sophocles is drawn to the Homeric simile when creating an allusion of particular significance: the lion simile makes the height of Ajax's epic glory the brilliant foil for his tragic death. In the Homeric version, Ajax functions as the powerful figure in both tenor and vehicle, the defender of Patroclus' vulnerable body. In Sophocles' variation Ajax is shoved suggestively to the side: a helpless corpse, he is the literal parallel for Patroclus, the needy figure in the Homeric tenor. But technically he cannot even claim this position in the Sophoclean simile. Instead it belongs to his abandoned son. Thus Sophocles' allusive rewriting demotes Ajax not once but twice. The complexity of the treatment resembles but surpasses Aeschylean use of the Homeric simile. Yet another Aeschylean effect can be seen in the *Ajax*: the use of Homeric material for allusion in a story of Homeric heroes allows the connections to take on an added level of implication just as it did in the *Agamemnon*. Resemblances between primary and secondary fields are generally seen to be more than illuminating similarities: they are actually either predictive or confirming, reinforcing the bonds of character and destiny which inform Sophoclean tragedy.

In *Antigone* we find a technique of allusion precisely parallel to that of borrowing a metaphor or simile: in a song which consists of mythological exempla, Sophocles creates an extended allusion to a Homeric passage which also consists of exempla applied to the events of the epic narrative. Event and exempla to be compared create a dynamic which is parallel to that of simile or allusion: the event is the equivalent of the tenor, the exempla form the vehicle. Since the fourth stasimon of *Antigone* and the passage of the *Iliad* to which it alludes both respond to a distraught female by citing past examples of suffering, the relationship between the two texts is the same as that which arises when a simile is borrowed. Both the primary and the secondary field admit a further symmetrical subdivision into tenor and vehicle. As we have seen, Sophocles further complicates his allusion by including a certain amount of overlap between the material in the two texts.

Ultimately the most striking feature of allusion in these early plays is its central importance in the works. Seeming disturbance in the narrative is more than once explainable in terms of Homeric allusion: Admetus' odd speech (*Alc*. 885–8) jars us into thoughts of Priam and Hector. The fourth stasimon of *Antigone*, Sophocles' most maligned choral effort, carefully preserves a host of details from the confrontation of Aphrodite and Diomedes and leads us to reflections which help unify the play's different lyric moments. Most of all, the allusions themselves illuminate the heart of these often dark and difficult plays. The contrast of the fallen Ajax with the active defender of Patroclus' corpse creates a shudder of recognition at the central reversal which divides the play's two worlds. In *Alcestis*, a more delightful change is wrought by contrasting the grim Iliadic allusions to death with the joyous Bacchylidean borrowing for the return to life. In *Antigone* Sophocles' use of an ode from the *Choephori* and its relation to his Homeric parallels gives us insight into the power of Antigone. And the combined set of quotations and references in one song of *Medea* allows us to accept the horrible actions to which a mother may be driven as part of a larger human order.

As we shall see next, in the plays of the middle period Euripides and Sophocles do not always seem to have concerned themselves so much with allusion; but when they did, their meditations on earlier poetry could be quite complex.

4

Sophocles and Euripides: The Middle Plays

INTRODUCTION

The Euripidean plays discussed below very likely appeared between 430 and 415 B.C. The three Sophoclean plays, on the other hand, are notoriously difficult to date. *Oedipus Rex* is perhaps the most certain to fall in this period; the other two are considered here because they illuminate and are illuminated by two of the Euripidean plays confidently placed in these years. First, Sophocles' *Women of Trachis* and Euripides' *Hercules Furens* both depend indirectly on Aeschylus' *Oresteia* – especially the *Agamemnon*: both Sophocles and Euripides tell the story of Heracles' return as a variation on that of Agamemnon. Second, the *Oresteia* has an even more direct influence on the *Electra* plays of both playwrights. Thus the four plays, at once similar in being connected to the *Oresteia* yet different in their manner of connection, form a natural unit.

In the remaining six plays the nature and extent of imitation and allusion vary widely. Some provide little more in the way of allusion than the early Aeschylean plays; others seem closer to the early work of Euripides and Sophocles, although never as extensively allusive as the plays discussed in the last chapter. As a whole, the plays help further to establish patterns of allusion and imitation seen in the earlier plays. In addition, they provide examples of some techniques seen first in this period and then repeated in later plays as well.

HERACLES AND AGAMEMNON: RETURN TO CATASTROPHE

The story of Heracles and Deianeira in Sophocles' *Women of Trachis* is built on a plot pattern familiar from the earliest Greek poetry: a hero long absent returns home to his waiting wife. Epic had focused on two models, Odysseus' return to Penelope and, in explicit contrast, Agamemnon's to Clytemnestra. In the opening scenes of Sophocles' play, situation and allusion alike suggest that Heracles' return will be of the happy variety enjoyed by Odysseus, but ominous undercurrents eventually surface as the story becomes an explicit variation on Agamemnon's disastrous homecoming and death.

As long as Sophocles' text suggests that Heracles, his wife Deianeira, and his son Hyllus are parallel with Odysseus, Penelope, and Telemachus, all the echoes are Homeric. The example of the *Odyssey* arises at the opening of *Trachiniae*, for the nurses' suggestion that Hyllus go in search of his father (54–6) recalls Telemachus' journey to learn of Odysseus' fate.[1] Hyllus' arrival is marked by the first hint of a Homeric echo. He appears, as the nurse notes, as if on cue; the adjective which marks his timely coming is ἀρτίπους (58), "with opportune step." The rare word occurs once in each of the Homeric poems: in the *Iliad* it describes Ruin which rushes on its victims (9.505), and in the *Odyssey* is it a characteristic of Ares in his adulterous misadventure with Aphrodite (8.310). The diction, collusive or not, has an eerie perfection at the opening of a play in which the power of Aphrodite will lead both Heracles and Deianeira, different though they are, to actions culminating in mutual annihilation.

Three Homeric images, two similes and a metaphor, ornament the lines that follow Hyllus' departure to learn more of Heracles. First, the chorus wonders whether Heracles may be at sea somewhere (99–100). Needless to say, being Greeks, they are led by this thought almost inevitably to nautical metaphor; but the simile, comparing Heracles' troubled life to a stormy sea (112–13), is modeled closely on an epic description of the noise and movement of the Greek troops (*Il.* 2.394–7).[2] Their next simile, as they consider how grief and joy revolve through human life, compares fortune with the wheeling of the stars – specifically the constellation of the Great Bear (130–1). This amplifies the Homeric description of Odysseus navigating by the Great Bear on his journey homeward (*Od.* 5.273–5), and if the adaptation of this element of Odysseus' return is not an allusion, the relevance of the epic material at least helps explain why Sophocles used the passage.[3] Finally, Deianeira describes sheltered youth as the growth of a young plant (144–7), a metaphor to which two Homeric passages seem to have contributed: both Thetis' sad memory of her young Achilles (*Il.* 18.56) and the description of the plants in which the shipwrecked Odysseus takes refuge (*Od.* 478–81) seem relevant.[4] At one level, this metaphor and the chorus' similes simply help maintain a Homeric tone. This, in turn, serves the further purpose of keeping alive the allusive suggestion of Odysseus' return from the sea to a happy reunion with his wife.

And yet, other Homeric echoes hint at developing catastrophe. So, for example, Deianeira, having described the happiness of youth, contrasts her own current sorrows. In particular, she is concerned about a tablet left by Heracles at his last departure (153–7), a tablet inscribed with tokens (ξυνθήματα, 158) which, as Jebb notes, recall Bellerophon's deadly tablets with their inscribed signs (σήματα, *Il.* 6.168). Recollection of this sole epic mention of writing may be triggered by the rare tragic use of the epicism ἦμος (155), with which Deianeira introduces her account.[5] Moreover, Deianeira also begins her speech with a verb unique in extant Greek – θυμοφθορεῖν, to consume the heart (142) – a verb which seems to have been coined by Sophocles under the influence of the Homeric θυμοφθόρα (*Il.* 6.169), describing the fatal inscription on Bellerophon's tablets. However, Deianeira's pessimism ends with the arrival of a messenger bringing news of Heracles. A hundred lines later (*Trach.* 258) there will be one more imitative echo of Homer when Heracles' fulfilled boast is described as if it were a Homeric weapon that had reached its target. Otherwise, Homeric echoes cease for a considerable time.

Despite an ode of joy inspired by the messenger's news, the replacement for Homeric echoes is material from the *Oresteia* which further develops the ominous tone suggested by the reminiscence of *Iliad* 6. Heracles' return will increasingly resemble not Odysseus' but rather Agamemnon's.[6] This transformation begins immediately with the arrival of Lichas, who brings a group of captive women, one of whom is Iole, Heracles' new mistress. Iole, entirely silent, even in the face of Deianeira's sympathetic questions (298–313), inevitably suggests Aeschylus' Cassandra who, brought home as a captive from Troy by Agamemnon, remains mute in the face of Clytemnestra's questions (*Ag.* 1035–68).[7] Implications of this allusion are developed over the next five hundred lines in a whole

series of further allusions to the *Agamemnon* and *Choephori*.[8]
Deianeira, then, having learned the truth about Iole, begins to
sound disturbingly like Aeschylus' Clytemnestra. Iole, says Deianeira, has been brought in as a "piece of merchandise destructive to
my heart" (λωβητὸν ἐμπόλημα τῆς ἐμῆς φρενός . . .,
Trach. 538). So Clytemnestra, after murdering Agamemnon and
Cassandra, closes a memorable speech by saying that Cassandra
was brought in as "a relish to my meal of luxury" (παροψώνημα
τῆς ἐμῆς χλιδῆς . . ., *Ag.* 1447). Both Clytemnestra
and Deianeira focus on the sexual insult these captive women
represent, and Sophocles has given Deianeira's bitter metaphor
exactly the same rhythm as Clytemnestra's.[9] No matter how
different Deianeira is from Clytemnestra, no matter how nonviolent
her intentions, the allusion to the *Agamemnon* casts an ominous
shadow over the plan that she goes on to describe to the chorus.

It is worth noting that the allusion to Clytemnestra's description
of Cassandra occurs in an iambic speech of Deianeira's. Usually
significant allusions in tragedy occur in lyric sections, especially at
the beginning – or in Euripides at the end – of a stasimon. In the
Trachiniae, by contrast, most of the allusions come in iambic
trimeter. Jebb noted the unusual number and extent of elaborated
iambic narrative speeches in this play; that Sophocles has worked
his allusions into these speeches provides another specific index to
their importance.[10] By placing allusions to Clytemnestra in
Deianeira's own speech, Sophocles emphasizes the irony in his
heroine's tragedy: she acts and even speaks like Aeschylus'
Clytemnestra without knowing it. Thus, with phrases that bear an
allusive meaning she cannot grasp, she summons up the vehicle or
secondary field which illuminates her fate for us.

In this manner, then, Deianeira's instructions to Lichas about
her message to Heracles (624–32) strongly recall Clytemnestra's
remarks to the herald (*Ag.* 604–14). Both women want their
returning husbands to know that all has been kept safe in the
house; both use similar rhetorical questions to cut short their
conversations with the messengers; and both mention their longing
for the long-absent men. In *Agamemnon*, the herald has just
mentioned Agamemnon's spoils (λάφυρα, 578); in the *Trachiniae* the
chorus immediately sings of Heracles' spoils (λάφυρα, 646). As
the focus on Heracles becomes increasingly fixed, so the allusions
to the *Oresteia* begin to suggest his role as the Agamemnon to

Deianeira's Clytemnestra. As soon as Deianeira has sent Lichas on
his way, the chorus sings the second stasimon (633–62). Deianeira
had referred to Heracles in her last speech as a "sacrificer"
(θυτήρ, 613), and the chorus describes him with the same word,
referring to the sacrifice he is carrying out at Cape Cenaeum (659).
Outside the *Trachiniae* this word is confined to Aeschylus' *Oresteia*,
where it is used only for Agamemnon, and in particular to describe
him as the sacrificer of his own daughter at Aulis (*Ag.* 224).[11] The
word helps bring into sharper focus the similarity between
Heracles sacrificing in Euboea and Agamemnon sacrificing at
Aulis, and it may suggest that before all is done, Heracles will
undertake some brutal action there. At the same time, it hints that
his homecoming may bear comparison with Agamemnon's –
something that Iole's presence has already suggested.

This prospect is further suggested by the next choral allusion.
When Aeschylus' Agamemnon returned, it was not he but
Clytemnestra who made the sacrifices before his arrival; the
Euripidean chorus's words which immediately follow their reference to Heracles as sacrificer are an allusion to Clytemnestra's
sacrifices in the *Agamemnon*. The Sophoclean passage is difficult but
highly suggestive and extremely important, as the closing lines of a
stasimon often are:

> ὅθεν μόλοι πανίμερος,
> τῷ Πειθοῦς παγχρίστῳ συγκραθεὶς
> †ἐπὶ παρφάσει †θηρός.

(660–2)

Whence may he come, full of desire, conjoined with Persuasion's
full-anointed allure.[12]

The chorus is thinking of the anointed robe which Deianeira has
sent to Heracles in order that it may work its erotic charms on him
and return him to her not merely in body but in spirit as well. But
the robe, instead of dissolving Heracles' resistance, will attack his
flesh, and the Heracles they have just called a sacrificer will
become a sacrifice that must be burned on a pyre. The vehicle in
this allusion is the description of Clytemnestra's preliminary
sacrifices in the *Agamemnon* which are a prelude to her sacrifice of
her own husband:

ἄλλη δ' ἄλλοθεν οὐρανομήκης
λαμπὰς ἀνίσχει,
φαρμασσομένη χρίματος ἁγνοῦ
μαλακαῖς ἀδόλοισι παρηγορίαις,
πελάνῳ μυχόθεν βασιλείῳ.

(92–6)

Here and there torches rise as
high as heaven, medicined by
sacred ointment's soft guileless
persuasions, royal unguent from
the heart of the house.

Persuasion in the form of unguent for the husband's return, the
uncomfortable mixture of sacrifice and sexuality, and, on top of
everything else, the dramatic irony which in both plays means that
the returning husband will ultimately be sacrificed – all these
elements show that Sophocles is working closely from the model of
Aeschylus' Clytemnestra.[13] Moreover, as the chorus's last note dies
away, Deianeira enters with disturbing news: the wool with which
she annointed the robe has rotted away, and now her explanation
of the unguent and how she preserved it echoes that same passage
from the *Agamemnon* to which the chorus had just alluded. The
Centaur Nessus, she explains, had ordered her to keep the
unguent, φάρμακον, in the heart of the house, μυχοῖς, until
she should spread it fresh, ἀρτίχριστον (*Trach.* 685–7: cf.
φαρμασσομένη χρίματος . . . μυχόθεν, *Ag.* 92–6). The
danger to Heracles from Deianeira's actions was implicit in the
chorus' ironic lyric allusion in which tenor and vehicle share a
ground with a number of striking details. That allusion in turn acts
as a trigger for the even more explicit echoes in Deianeira's immediately following iambic speech; together the two point to Heracles'
destruction. Although Deianeira acted out of love, the consequences of her scheme will be as murderous as Clytemnestra's.

At this point, Sophocles' allusions turn from the *Agamemnon* to
the *Choephori*. In the course of her speech to the chorus Deianeira
has realized the probable outcome of her actions. In trying to
regain her sexual partner, she has done – the exact words are
important – a terrible deed: ἔργον δεινὸν ἐξειργασμένην
(706). The arrow that has infected her unguent destroys all beasts
it touches: χ᾽ὧνπερ ἂν θίγῃ/ φθείρει τὰ πάντα

105

κνώδαλ' (715–16). The destructive nature of the actions to which love has driven her suggests the great stasimon on this topic from Aeschylus' *Choephori* (585–651), a stasimon Sophocles also used in *Antigone*. In *Choephori* too the chorus is concerned with terrible things, as their memorable opening phrase declares (δεινὰ δειμάτων, 586). Most terrible of all is the erotic force which drives women to do anything (γυναικῶν . . . παντόλμους ἔρωτας, 596–7), love that destroys the unions of men and beasts (ξυζύγους . . . ἔρως παρανικᾷ κνωδάλων τε καὶ βροτῶν, 599–601). Thinking of the love that drove Clytemnestra to murder Agamemnon, Aeschylus' chorus sings of other murderous women. The echoes from this chorus put into the speech of Deianeira herself (again an iambic section) connect her sadly and tragically with Clytemnestra.

Hyllus, arriving after Deianeira's revelations, confirms her worst fears. If Heracles' return could have been like Odysseus', Hyllus would have been a Telemachus; as it is, he must be an Orestes to confront the woman who is both his mother and the destroyer of his father. His blunt accusation immediately suggests the comparison of this family to Agamemnon's: "Your husband – my father – you killed today," he says (*Tr.* 739–40), and the scene threatens to become a repetition of the fatal encounter between Orestes and Clytemnestra (*Cho.* 887ff.) which centers on just this explicit charge (*Cho.* 908ff.). Hyllus explains his accusation by reporting the effects of the robe on Heracles. Put schematically, two liquid elements in Heracles' normal sacrifice first prefigure and then are polluted by two others of ghastly and perverted similarity. The syntax of Hyllus' description grimly imitates the events he describes, so that the blood of the Heracles' sacrifice and the fatty pitch of the burning wood blend with Heracles' own sweat and his sticky flesh, liquified by the robe (765–8). Sacrifice of animal victim replicates itself in the human celebrant with the result that even as the ritual order disintegrates into unparalleled chaos, complex patterns of mythological and literary destiny are assuming their symmetrical shapes. To describe the mordant action of the poison Hyllus employs a simile: it feasts on his father like the venom of a hateful viper (ἐχθρᾶς ἐχίδνης, 771). These images of the robe and the snake will become increasingly significant in the fateful manner of Aeschylean images in the *Oresteia*. Even here, the vehicle of Hyllus' simile is more apt than he realizes, for, in terms of mythology, the robe is smeared with poison from the viperous hydra: what he makes a vehicle is actually a tenor. Likewise, from a literary standpoint, his image has allusive fitness, for when Aeschylus' Orestes describes his father's death in the robe-net provided by Clytemnestra, his metaphor is of death in the coils of a hateful viper (δεινῆς ἐχίδνης, *Cho*. 249). Thus Hyllus' description alludes to a secondary field in which his counterpart, Orestes, has used the same vehicle to describe a remarkably similar tenor. The symmetrical split in the two fields of the allusion is reminiscent of Stesichorus' use of Homeric simile and Sophocles' use of the Homeric consolation of Aphrodite in the fourth stasimon of *Antigone*.

The series of allusions to the *Oresteia* is interrupted by a brief but important use of *Odyssey* 9. This begins as Hyllus follows the description of Heracles' pain with an equally gruesome account of Lichas' death at Heracles' hands. Granted, the earlier reference to Heracles conducting a sacrifice at the Cape with its allusion to Agamemnon sacrificing at Aulis is still relevant here: just as Agamemnon's murder of Iphigeneia is part of the series of events that seals his fate, so Heracles concludes his sacrifice with a brutal murder, one that recalls the murders and battles of his violent past and their connection to his ruinous infatuation with Iole. But Hyllus' account of the murder includes an additional echo from the *Odyssey* to emphasize Heracles' savage nature. Heracles seized Lichas by the ankle and dashed him down so that the brains oozed out his shattered skull (μάρψας ... μυελὸν ἐκραίνει, *Trach*. 779–81); it was the Cyclops' method for slaughtering Odysseus' men (μάρψας ... ἐκ δ' ἐγκέφαλος ... ῥέε ..., *Od*. 9.289–90; cf. ὀστέα μυελόεντα, 9.293).[14] Again, these echoes of the *Odyssey*, like those of the *Choephori*, have been woven into Sophocles' elaborate iambic narrative.

One of the ironies of Sophocles' play is that Heracles, who has labored to rid the world of the monstrous and bestial, is undone by his own animal side, his uncontrolled violence and sexual passion. This allusion to the uncivilized Cyclops underlines the point, and Sophocles reinforces it almost immediately with another reference to this episode of the *Odyssey*, this time in the more common way, with an allusion at the opening of a stasimon (821ff.). The Sophoclean play has reached that stage at which the pattern of fate is becoming clear, and the chorus realizes that Heracles' impending death fulfills the old oracle – τᾶς παλαιφάτου προνοίας (*Trach.* 823). As Jebb saw, this recalls the Cyclops episode again: having learned Odysseus' identity, the blinded Polyphemus realizes that the old prophecy of his fate, παλαίφατα θέσφατα (9.507), has come true.[15] There is a third and final indication that the wild Cyclops is a model for Heracles: Heracles' reaction to the revelation of Nessus' role in his destruction again recalls Polyphemus' dismay at learning Odysseus' name.[16] The allusions help ensure that Heracles' own nature, or at least one part of it, will be remembered as part of what has led to the present. The past is finding its fulfillment in the events of the play.[17] Thus, although the immediate vehicle in these allusions is the *Odyssey*, their more general effect is to further the Aeschylean allusions which surround them: Heracles' violent past has closed in on him just as Agamemnon's did.

This reading is immediately affirmed in the third stasimon: there the second strophe returns to the *Oresteia*, closing with an echo of Clytemnestra's contemptuous dismissal of Agamemnon's moral standing: in speaking of Agamemnon's death Clytemnestra mentioned δολίαν ἄτην (*Ag.* 1523) which is just what Sophocles' chorus of Trachinian women see closing in on Heracles: δολίαν καὶ μεγάλαν ἄταν (*Trach.* 850–1).[18] From this point on all Sophocles' allusions are to the *Oresteia*; they all are placed in iambic trimeter; and the most obvious references, which pave the way for the rest, come at the beginning of Heracles' great speech (1046–111).[19]

Heracles' own description of his painful disintegration surpasses even the horrifying account given by Hyllus. His metaphors for the robe Deianeira sent him are drawn directly from the images of Aeschylus' *Agamemnon*, with complex implications. The vampire-robe, which has taken on a parasitic life of its own, drinking his blood and robbing his lungs of breath (1054–6), is the "Furies' woven net": Ἐρινύων ὑφαντὸν ἀμφίβληστρον (*Trach.* 1051–2). This is the image used by Agamemnon's own enemies: when Clytemnestra first appears triumphant over her husband's corpse, she draws attention to the robe in which she has entrapped him, a "boundless net" (ἄπειρον ἀμφίβληστρον, *Ag.* 1382). Later Aegisthus delights to see Agamemnon "lying in the Furies' woven robes" (ὑφαντοῖς ἐν πέπλοις Ἐρινύων, *Ag.* 1580). In the *Choephori* Electra calls on her father's ghost to remember the fatal net (ἀμφίβληστρον, 492), and Orestes calls it "fetters" (πέδαις, 493), a metaphor which Heracles also uses for the robe destroying him (πέδη, *Trach.* 1057). The most obvious result of these allusions is to emphasize that just as Hyllus did, Heracles sees Deianeira (wrongly) as a murderous Clytemnestra.[20] Even after Heracles has finished his set speech, he continues his attacks on Deianeira with language borrowed from a speech of Orestes' in the *Choephori*. Heracles calls Deianeira πατροφόντου μητρός (1125), Orestes called Clytemnestra μητέρα . . . πατροκτόνον μίασμα (*Cho.* 1027–8).

Once Hyllus explains Deianeira's innocence, she is ignored; Heracles and Hyllus remain. The robe which destroys Heracles is a Furies' net according to Heracles' allusion, but the Furies are not properly Deianeira's, as Heracles' own words will make clear. When, at the end of his long speech, Heracles reconsiders his pitiful disintegration, he reviews his great accomplishments. One was the taming of Cerberus, offspring of hateful Echidna (1099). The phrase δεινῆς 'Εχίδνης echoes Hyllus' simile for the fatal robe, and even more exactly than that first phrase alludes to Orestes' description of Clytemnestra as a hateful viper – δεινῆς ἐχίδνης (*Cho.* 249). The allusions thus cooperate with the play's non-allusive images and plot elements: Heracles' Clytemnestra is not Deianeira after all; if anything, it is himself. He has produced his own Furies.[21] He has captured women and beasts, tamed and killed beasts and men, and the poison of one of his monstrous conquests has blended with the blood of another so that one of his captured women could use it to try and regain him from the latest female prize. The last line of the play says that none of the events is not Zeus; it could just as well have said none of them was not Heracles. Events and the images which describe them have woven themselves into a fateful net which the hero virtually throws around himself. A play full of allusions to Aeschylus' *Oresteia* seems to share not only its poetic method but its vision of human fate as well.

The *Trachiniae* has indeed seemed to more than one a play of "virtually unrelieved darkness."[22] Of all its catastrophes, the death of Deianeira as a mere incidental casualty of Heracles' doom is perhaps the hardest to accept. To be sure, there is nothing to bring Deianeira back from the dead; but she survives in another way. Hyllus, far from being an Orestes, has defended his mother, indeed exonerated her from unjust charges, and she must live on in him.

Hyllus must be Heracles' survivor as well, and another function of Sophocles' allusions is to specify the relationship between the generations. The designation of Heracles as θυτήρ (*Trach.* 659) alluded to Agamemnon's sacrifice of Iphigeneia. At the end of the *Trachiniae*, Hyllus states that he has often been a sacrificer – θυτήρ (1192) – on Mt. Oeta. Now he must carry out a more difficult sacrifice. The unusual word at once links him with his father, whose sacrifice he must now arrange, and signals a variation of the Aeschylean theme. In the *Oresteia*, descendants echo the murderous actions of their ancestors so that one horrible sacrifice leads to another. Hyllus, by contrast, breaks the pattern of his father's uncontrolled violence: Hyllus' piety is exemplary, his father will become immortal. The allusions to the *Odyssey* had first held out false hope of a happy homecoming, then shifted to emphasis of Heracles' violent nature. Allusions to the *Agamemnon* and *Choephori* pointed to the true catastrophe of return. The story needs no allusions to the *Eumenides*, for, as the final allusion shows, Hyllus is the obedient agent of a peaceful resolution to the family's disaster. He will see to it that all that is bestial in Heracles will be burnt away in sacrifice. The world he leaves behind will be more civilized and more human.

Euripides' *Hercules Furens* shares much with Sophocles' *Trachiniae*: it is an unhappy story of Heracles' return; it echoes and alludes to Aeschylus' *Oresteia*; and it even imitates the *Trachiniae* itself. Yet if Sophocles' allusions in the *Trachiniae* work to incorporate the Aeschylean vision of the *Oresteia*, the allusions and imitations of *Agamemnon* in *Hercules* have the opposite effect: Euripides' concerns are far from those of either the *Trachiniae* or the *Oresteia*. His allusions, including echoes of Pindar, the *Prometheus Bound*, and the *Iliad* help establish his distance from Aeschylus and Sophocles. Thus whereas in the *Oresteia* and *Trachiniae* we are invited to contemplate curses and complex series of interrelated causes and actions, in *Hercules* we are not. Instead, Euripides creates a picture of human action and responsibility that is a meditation on human limitations in the midst of disjointed and apparently irrational external forces.

Although there is great concern for the welfare of Heracles at the opening of the *Trachiniae*, his absence is cause for even greater anxiety in the opening scenes of *Hercules*. Despite the leisurely iambic prologue delivered by Heracles' mortal father Amphitryon, the situation is dire. He and Heracles' wife and children face imminent death at the hands of Lycus, and their only hope for salvation lies in the timely arrival of the champion Heracles: Amphitryon and the chorus are too feeble to mount a defense themselves.[23]

The feeble old age of Amphitryon and the chorus provides a foil against which Euripides develops the theme of Heracles' strength, a theme of basic importance for the play.[24] As the chorus of *Hercules* wanders in, the old men sing of their frailty with a repetitive insistence appropriate to their age. Drawing attention to their staffs, they call themselves ancient singers, a mere vision of nighttime dreams (δόκημα . . . ἐννύχων ὀνείρων, 112–13). This first sentence, which fills most of their first strophe, recalls the words of the old men in *Agamemnon*. The Aeschylean chorus describes itself as dream wandering at daybreak: ὄναρ ἡμερόφαντον ἀλαίνει (*Ag.* 82).[25] The old men also sing of their staffs (*Ag.* 74–5), and later, when sufficiently provoked by Aegisthus, they are prepared to use them (1652), just as Euripides' old men are when Lycus later enrages them with threats of slavery (*HF* 254–5).[26]

Opposed to these helpless creatures who have faded away to mere words (*HF* 112) is Heracles, their natural antithesis, presumably capable of any action whatsoever – if only he were present. In this play, Euripides uses Heracles, much as he had in *Alcestis*, as the archetypical victor.[27] Epinician poetry highlighted the victor's brilliance with the dark vision of man as the shadow of a dream, feeble in old age; the old men of the chorus provide just such a foil in *Hercules*. And as in *Alcestis*, Euripides reinforces his contrast of human greatness and human limitations by introducing a combination of echoes and allusions to epinician poetry.

Heracles' greatness is given a complex presentation in the longest extant Euripidean song, an elaborately wrought first stasimon (348–441). In apparent technical and metrical imitation of Aeschylus, Euripides has used a metrical refrain at the end of each strophe and antistrophe, giving the chorus a large number of neat sections in which to list the great deeds of Heracles. The song defies precise classification: it simultaneously resembles a hymn to a god, a victory song for a mortal, and a lament. Such ambiguity is no accident, for the status of Heracles is specifically in question and, as we shall soon see, thematically very important. As far as the chorus knows, he could be either the son of Zeus (353) or of the mortal Amphitryon (354), either alive or dead.

The epinician character of this ode is signaled immediately with an extended imitation of Pindar precisely where such imitations and allusions are so often found – in the first sentence of the first strophe.[28] The chorus says that Apollo sings his song "striking the lovely-sounding lyre with his golden plectrum" – Φοῖβος ἰαχεῖ τὰν καλλίφθογγον κιθάραν ἐλαύνων πλήκτρῳ χρυσέῳ (349–51). Thus Pindar describes Apollo singing and "striking the seven-tongued lyre with his golden plectrum" – φόρμιγγ᾽ Ἀπόλλων ἑπτάγλωσσον χρυσέῳ πλάκτρῳ διώκων ἀγεῖτο παντοίων νόμων (N. 5.24–5). Even if both poets were borrowing the "golden plectrum" from the Hymn to Apollo (185), the synonyms ἐλαύνω and διώκω, which normally mean to "drive," are apparently used only in these two passages for playing the lyre, suggesting that Euripides had this particular ode of Pindar's in mind. Moreover, the strophe ends with a flurry of epinician phrases which, although they seem not to be taken from any particular victory ode, clearly recall the genre.[29] As the chorus narrates the labors of Heracles, their language frequently has the general sound of victory song, and a number of times seems to have been borrowed from specific Pindaric passages. The striking adjective χρυσοκάρηνος ("with head of gold," HF 375) may reflect the influence of Pindar's χρυσοκέρων in his own version of this Heraclean labor (Ol. 3.29); ξεινοδαΐκτης ("stranger-butchering," HF 391) was also used by Pindar as an epithet for one of Heracles' enemies (fr.140a 56); and the noun εὐηνορία ("manliness," HF 407) has its only other classical occurrence in Pindar (Ol. 5.20).

An oddity arises in the epinician atmosphere these imitations produce: the figure who would be the victor, Heracles, also provides all the "mythological" exempla which would normally adorn a mortal victor's song. Yet this oddity is also the point, for the double role which Heracles is given in the song reflects his problematic role in the play. Moreover, from this point on, the play and its allusions will increasingly focus on typical epinician topics – the nature of human excellence and its limits, the relation of the victor to superhuman forces in the world, and the human

112

conditions which put the victor ultimately on a level with all men.

The last feat of Heracles' mentioned in the first stasimon is his descent to Hades (426). The possibility that he is among the defeated and powerless rather than the victorious seems to grow as the play progresses. By the time Megara calls on Heracles' shade to appear (494), he has become virtually indistinguishable from his foils, the old men of the chorus. But Heracles appears almost immediately afterward. He makes it explicit that his status as victor is at stake, using his traditional epinician epithet: unless he defends his family, he will no longer be καλλίνικος (581–2).

However, there seems little doubt that Heracles will succeed, and the second stasimon (637–700) is even more obviously composed as an epinican song than the first.[30] The themes of wealth, time, and human excellence are developed in Pindaric manner, and the close of the song confidently affirms Heracles' divine parentage, making him the mythical example for his own victory ode. The themes and echoes from early poetry first sounded in the openings of both the parodos and the first stasimon are repeated here. Just as the chorus of *Hercules* made an entry recalling the staffs and dreamlike nature of the old men in *Agamemnon*, so here they assert their continued ability to sing (despite old age) just as their Aeschylean counterparts had (*HF* 678, *Ag.* 104).[31] Moreover, they repeat the phrase γέρων ἀοιδός (*HF* 679) from the original echo at the opening of the parodos (*HF* 110) and then underline that emphasis by using the identical words in the responding position of the antistrophe (*HF* 693). And, of course, the topic of song, which had opened the first stasimon in a Pindaric echo (*HF* 348–51), is repeated here as well (*HF* 673–86). Thus Euripides prolongs the notes originally sounded with echoes of Aeschylus and epinician.

In the next scene, Aeschylean echoes predominate. After the second stasimon Lycus makes a brief appearance before entering the house, where he will be murdered by Heracles. After he and Amphitryon are gone, the chorus begins a lyric introduction to the third stasimon in a situation that echoes but neatly reverses the parallel one in the *Agamemnon*. In Aeschylus' play, Agamemnon's disastrous homecoming culminated in his entry into the house, where he was murdered while the chorus listened to his death cries outside (*Ag.* 1343, 1345). In *Heracles* the old men hear instead the death cries of the house's usurper Lycus (*HF* 750, 754), as the victorious Heracles makes an infinitely more successful return.

It may be that Euripides reinforces these parallel situations by making his chorus echo several choral passages from the *Agamemnon*; or else he uses the situation to help trigger the echoes; or perhaps each element contributes something to all the rest. In any case, with the return of the good Heracles and the murder of the wicked Lycus, justice seems to have prevailed, prompting the chorus to ask who it is who has questioned the power of the gods (*HF* 757–9). Similarly, the chorus at *Agamemnon* 369–72 criticizes whoever has claimed that the gods do not care about human wrong-doing. Again, the Euripidean chorus's musings on the ability of wealth and success to make men act unjustly (773–80) parallel the thoughts expressed by the chorus in the *Agamemnon* (381–4, 462–70).[32] And further, the resurrection Amphitryon hinted at (*HF* 719) has taken place, for the "dead" Heracles has returned from Hades to kill the living Lycus (*HF* 769–71) in what seems like an echo of the riddle in the *Choephori* when Orestes finally exacts vengeance for the murder of Agamemnon (*Cho.* 886–7). As the stasimon closes with another Pindaric echo (*N.* 10.54) affirming the divine parentage of Heracles (*HF* 802), the plot seems to have collapsed the first two plays of the *Oresteia* into a more compact action with justice done more directly.[33] And so the chorus' closing lines declare that justice has emerged in this contest of armed vengeance – ξιφηφόρων ἐς ἀγώνων (*HF* 812) – and their phrase is borrowed directly from *Choephori* 584, the last line before the famous stasimon which begins πολλὰ μὲν γᾶ τρέφει.

However, this apparent Aeschylean cadence gives way to the harshest dissonance. As soon as Euripides' chorus finishes their pronouncement about justice and the gods, they are shocked by the appearance of Iris and Lyssa, the goddesses who will arrange for Heracles to slay his own family. Thus entry into the house will lead to great disaster for Heracles as it did for Agamemnon. In this way Euripides introduces a new and horrible parallel for *Agamemnon* that will put all the references to Pindaric victory and Aeschylean justice in a very different light.

This short, arresting scene with the goddesses (*HF* 822–73) recalls the equally unusual prologue of *Prometheus Bound*, suggests comparisons with that situation, and gives the topic of Heracles' status and accomplishments a new urgency and relevance to humankind. The Titan Prometheus, like his divinely fathered counterpart Heracles, struggled to benefit the human race. The violent action to be carried out against Prometheus is debated by Kratos with a rather reluctant Hephaestus, just as Lyssa here has reservations with which Iris is impatient. Both scenes establish the necessity that Prometheus and Heracles suffer in accordance with the directions of Zeus or Hera.[34] Such similarities highlight differences. For one thing, the reduction of Heracles by making him destroy his own loved ones in an insane episode is more pathetic than Prometheus' binding. Even worse, Heracles' fate seems to grow much less logically from his own actions than did Prometheus'. This is a distinction to which we shall return shortly in reference to Aeschylus' Agamemnon and Sophocles' Heracles.

The remainder of Euripides' play treats the aftermath of Heracles' great misfortune during which Theseus arrives and persuades his friend to go on with life. The remaining imitations and allusions are taken largely from Homeric, Sophoclean, and Aeschylean catastrophes. For example, when Theseus arrives he has an exchange with Amphitryon (HF 1185) that echoes similar comments made by Ajax and Tecmessa in Sophocles' Ajax (591). Parallel contexts add to the verbal and structural similarity: both great heroes, in moments of delirium, have used their famed might against disastrously inappropriate opponents.[35] In a shift from tragedy to epic, the description of Heracles as παιδοφόνος ("child-killing," HF 1201) may recall the one Homeric use of the adjective at the close of Priam's speech to Achilles (Il. 24.506).[36] One borrowing comes from a lighter context: the simile of a bird crying for the loss of its young, used in the Odyssey at the reunion of Odysseus and Telemachus (16.216–19), is here used to describe Amphitryon's reaction to the death of the children upon Heracles' quite different return (HF 1039–41). Thus even as the closer parallelism between tenor and vehicle in Euripides' simile corrects the inverted Homeric relationship, it heightens the tragedy of the three generations in Euripides by recalling the happier Homeric model. This would be Laertes if Odysseus had killed Telemachus along with the suitors.

This last simile could just as well be an echo of Aeschylus' Agamemnon 48 with its similar image, and the more significant and suggestive echoes from the closing scenes of Hercules involve Agamemnon and Trachiniae. Heracles describes the destruction he has brought to himself (ἄτας, 1284) with a rare and striking metaphor – he has coped the roof of his house with ills, δῶμα θριγκῶσαι κακοῖς (1280). The image is taken from Cassandra's description of the series of closely interrelated catastrophes which befall the house of Atreus and will culminate in Orestes' murderous return, ἄτας τάσδε θριγκώσων (*Ag.* 1283).[37] This allusion must be considered along with another: later Heracles reflects on all his troubles, bursts into tears, and says, "I have tasted of many ills... but now..." (πόνων δὴ μυρίων ἐγευσάμην... νῦν δ'..., 1353–7). This clearly recalls the Heracles of the *Trachiniae* who cries for the first time (1070–4) and reflects on his fate in near identical verse: μόχθων μυρίων ἐγευσάμην... νῦν δ' (*Trach.* 1101–3).[38] Both allusions serve to distance Euripides' protagonist from those of his fellow tragedians. Orestes returns home to murder a family member, but unlike Heracles he has chosen his act consciously as a matter of vengeance. Agamemnon, like Sophocles' Heracles in *Trachiniae*, is caught in a web of events that he has helped to weave in many ways. The pattern of fate is complex but comprehensible and at some level seems to complete a chain of events in an inevitable if pitiable way. The same can be said of Prometheus in the *Prometheus Bound*.

Euripides' Heracles, by contrast, is involved in a humbling human disaster pointedly different from all the parallels the play alludes to. And this is in line with the epinician tone established in the early stasima. In the second half of Euripides' play Heracles provides his own admonitory foil demonstrating the limits of human excellence which Pindar and Bacchylides warned their own victors about with gnomic and mythic material. Heracles' exploits are here balanced by irrational, unforeseen, and unavoidable external forces which threaten to reduce him to nothingness and which certainly make him the equal of every human being who is subject to the sadness life brings. Euripides' Heracles stands as a corrective to the Heracles of Sophocles and Agamemnon of Aeschylus. The ultimate hero of epinician song and perfect example of the greatest achievements of human excellence, Heracles, in the chaos of his homecoming and fate, becomes the ultimate model for the terror of the unexpected in the face of which human pride must always be tempered by humility.

THE *ELECTRAS*

One afternoon, when much more of Greek tragedy than has survived was still available, Dio Chrysostom amused himself by reading the *Philoctetes* of each of the three great tragedians. Other choices for comparison were presumably available to him as well; for us only one such possibility remains. In Aeschylus' *Choephori* Orestes returns and, with Electra, murders their mother Clytemnestra who had murdered their father Agamemnon. The story is retold both by Sophocles and Euripides in plays titled *Electra*, and a great deal more than Dio's pleasant afternoon has been lavished on the comparison of the three treatments.

The sole point of agreement to emerge is that Sophocles and Euripides have made explicit use of the Aeschylean material. Differing views on the tone of *Electra*, whether Sophocles' or Euripides', in turn affect views of the allusions. Especially in the absence of a consensus it may be worth working experimentally in the opposite direction: the allusions may provide help in interpreting the plays. Inasmuch as it has fewer poetic allusions than Sophocles' *Electra*, Euripides' *Electra* will figure less in the following discussion. Nevertheless, Euripides' recognition scene, as the most infamous case of poetic allusion in Greek tragedy, provides a natural starting point. This is followed by a consideration of Sophocles' treatment of the recognition. Next is a brief comparison of the three tragedians' use of Homeric material. Then the *Oresteia* is examined as a source of images for the two *Electras*. This leads finally to the examination of a set of uniformly dark Sophoclean allusions.

Aeschylus leads his Electra gradually to the recognition of her brother Orestes by means of a series of tokens: a lock of hair at her father's tomb, footprints, and finally her old embroidery work which Orestes himself presents as the conclusive sign (*Cho.* 164–245). The old man who comes to the Euripidean Electra's hut introduces the same tokens in the same order: he has seen the lock, he suggests that there might be a footprint, and he asks whether there was any fancy-work that might provide a sure sign of Orestes' return (*El.* 518–40). That is, the three pieces of real evidence in Aeschylus have been reduced to one in Euripides; the full list is retained by the ostentatious transformation of the second item into a suggestion of possibility, of the third into a hypothetical speculation. As if Euripides had not made the allusion sufficiently obvious, further emphasis results from Electra's impatient dismissal of the old man's suggestions as ridiculous. As an ungrammaticality, a deviation which disrupts the text, this Euripidean material forms the most blatant trigger in all Greek tragedy – so much so that there have been serious attempts to eject the lines altogether.[39] Generally, however, the authenticity of the passage is accepted, and it is taken as sophisticated literary criticism. Whether or not Euripides is parodying Aeschylus, he certainly had his eye on the text of the *Choephori*.[40] The discussion of the lock of hair, for example, reproduces Aeschylean phrasing and imagery alike:

σκέψαι δὲ χαίτην προστιθεῖσα σῇ κόμῃ,

(*El.* 520)

Set the lock beside your own and examine it,

σκέψαι, τομῇ προσθεῖσα βόστρυχον τριχός,

(*Cho.* 229)

Set a lock of your hair by the cutting and examine it,

πολλοῖς δ' ἂν εὕροις βοστρύχους ὁμοπτέρους

(*El.* 530)

For many you might find locks of the same feather. . .

καὶ μὴν ὅδ' ἐστὶ κάρτ' ἰδεῖν ὁμόπτερος–

(*Cho.* 174)

Indeed, to look at it, this is very much of the same feather –

On the surface, this would seem to be our case of "cherries in the grass" – an allusion over too little distance to bridge with profit. In this case, however, the allusion facilitates a dramatic effect. Obviously interested in recognition scenes, Euripides was an inventive master of heightening tension with variations on delayed and failed recognitions which threaten to dissolve the plot.[41] This is the effect in *Helen* of the initially failed recognition between Helen and Menelaus. More complicated and integral to its play is the early scene between Ion and Creousa in *Ion* in which a host of elements suggests that a recognition will occur. It does not – with the further clever consequence that later in *Ion*, when only a recognition between mother and son will prevent matricide, all the possibilities for recognition will seem already to have been used. In

118

the *Electra* Euripides creates the same effect in miniature. Orestes and Electra have already met face to face; if all the Aeschylean means to achieve recognition fail, what will work? Alerted by the allusive rejection of the recognition used in *Choephori*, the Euripidean audience will wonder just what sort of surprising twist the plot may take. In the end, Euripides gives them the old man and the device of the tell-tale scar (*El.* 572–5).[42]

Sophocles' recognition scene is also heavily allusive, but neither the Sophoclean manner of allusion nor the effects it achieves have much in common with Euripides' approach. Aeschylean tokens are brushed politely aside, not because they are ridiculous, but simply because by the time they are reported, Electra has good reason to believe that Orestes is dead. Sophocles delays Electra's recognition of Orestes until very late in the play, which contributes to the stunning success of the scene. In preparation, the play concentrates on the effect Orestes' "death" has on Electra. Thus Chrysothemis' report of the tokens at the tomb has been intentionally and effectively diminished by prefacing it with the vivid account of Orestes' death and then following it with Electra's moving speech with the urn containing – so she thinks – Orestes' ashes. Yet while de-emphasizing allusion to the Aeschylean tokens, Sophocles has invested the scenes before and after the traditional tokens with other imitations and allusions to the *Iliad* and to the *Oresteia*.

The remarkable account of the fictional chariot race delivered by the disguised Paedagogus has been foreshadowed in various ways. First comes the reference to the Paedagogus as a trusty horse (25–7), then the first mention of the deceptive story (49–50), and finally the chorus's ironically appropriate recollection of Pelops' disastrous chariot race (504–12). It has been suggested that the idea for the race and its concomitant imagery grew from Aeschylus' *Choephori*.[43] There the chorus first describes Orestes' misfortune in the loss of his father in terms of the chariot race (*Cho.* 794–8); then Orestes, after murdering Clytemnestra, likens his incipient madness to horses in a chariot race stampeding out of control (*Cho.* 1022–5) – just as they do in the fictional Euripidean account of Orestes' death. Once the Paedagogus begins his narrative, however, Aeschylean echoes are replaced by the imitation of the chariot race in the funeral games of *Iliad* 23, from which both the general course of events and a number of phrases have been borrowed.[44] The fact that there seems to be no special significance in the source from which the details are drawn is, of course, particularly appropriate. The Paedagogus' account is pure fiction, its content as false as its form is entertaining: the tenor is no more real than the vehicle.

What once was Orestes has supposedly been reduced to ashes in an urn, and this urn becomes the prop around which Sophocles stages the recognition following Electra's rejection of the Aeschylean tokens. Just as the chariot race has been introduced in the prologue of *Electra*, so has the deception with the urn. Orestes describes it in his opening speech as a τύπωμα χαλκόπλευρον (54), a "molded thing with bronze sides." The odd phrase echoes the deception speech in Aeschylus' *Choephori* where Orestes describes the urn which supposedly holds his ashes as λέβητος χαλκέου πλευρώματα (*Cho.* 686), "the sides of a bronze urn."

Subsequent mentions of the urn in Sophocles' *Electra* continue to allude to the *Oresteia* but shift from the *Choephori* to a memorable passage from *Agamemnon*:

. . . ἀντὶ δὲ φωτῶν
τεύχη καὶ σποδὸς εἰς ἑκά-   435
στου δόμους ἀφικνεῖται.

ὁ χρυσαμοιβὸς δ' Ἄρης σωμάτων   str. g
καὶ ταλαντοῦχος ἐν μάχῃ δορὸς
πυρωθὲν ἐξ Ἰλίου   440
φίλοισι πέμπει βαρὺ
ψῆγμα δυσδάκρυτον, ἀντ-
ήνορος σποδοῦ γεμί-
ζων λέβητας εὐθέτους.

. . . in place of men,
urns and ashes come
to the homes of each.

Ares the gold-changer, body-changer,
holder of scales in battle of spear,
sends fire's product from Troy
to the relatives, heavy gold-dust,
bitterly wept over,
filling the shapely urns with ashes
in place of men.

So the Paedagogus concludes his account of the race by saying that Orestes' body has been burnt and is being brought in the form of ashes in an urn (*El.* 756–8): πυρᾷ κέαντες . . . ἐν βραχεῖ χαλκῷ μέγιστον σῶμα δειλαίας σποδοῦ. And the image of the man's body reduced by fire to such a small quantity of equivalent dust is repeated just before the recognition both by Orestes as he hands the urn to Electra and by Electra herself as she mourns over it: σμικρὰ λείψαν' ἐν βραχεῖ τεύχει (Orestes 1113–14); σμικρὸς . . . ὄγκος ἐν σμικρῷ κύτει (Electra 1142).[45] Individually, these references seem to have little significance beyond the general relevance of the *Oresteia* to the *Electra*. As a set, however, the passages suggest that Sophocles understood Aeschylean imagery in a way we would find very familiar. That is, Sophocles has taken the urn images from the *Oresteia* – both from *Agamemnon*, where the material is choral and partly metaphorical, and from *Choephori*, where the image is narrative and literal but fictitious – and used them for a series of references to the urn which becomes so important in his own version of the story of Orestes' return. An Aeschylean image which never makes an actual stage appearance has been developed into a vivid focus of attention in Sophocles' play.[46]

Although Sophocles' treatment of allusions is more complex than Euripides' in handling the recognition scene, elsewhere in the *Electra*s the two poets' roles are reversed. Both poets, for example, use Homeric material in ways that recall Aeschylean techniques in the *Oresteia*, but in this case Sophocles takes the simpler approach. Material from the *nekyia* of *Odyssey* 11, including the encounter between Odysseus and the ghost of Agamemnon, had been exploited by Aeschylus both in the *Agamemnon* (1453–7, 1559) and in the *Choephori* (324–6). Whether or not he was following Aeschylus' lead, Sophocles too decided to incorporate echoes of this passage, and so when Electra contrasts her father's inglorious death by murder instead of in battle at Troy (*El.* 95–9), her words and sentiments recall those expressed by Agamemnon himself to Odysseus in Hades (*Od.* 11.406–11).[47]

Euripides also uses a Homeric allusion in connection with the death of Agamemnon, again recalling an Aeschylean practice, but very different from the Sophoclean instance just noticed. Asked about her fate, Electra gives a bitter answer: her father's blood is rotting, his tomb is dishonored, and Aegisthus jumps on it, asking contemptuously "Where is his son Orestes" (*El.* 318–31). In the *Iliad*, Agamemnon, speaking to Menelaus, envisions what it would be like to return home if Menelaus died at Troy. Menelaus' bones would rot in the earth, and someone would jump on his tomb and say contemptuously, "May Agamemnon vent his anger on everyone this way" (4.169–82). Euripides' allusion, at once pathetic and ironic, makes the horrible future Agamemnon envisioned better than the one that actually materialized. Not his brother, but he himself rots in the tomb, and the taunts are directed not only at himself but also at his apparently ineffectual son. The technique recalls that of Aeschylus in borrowing the image of murdering the unborn young from a speech made by Agamemnon to Menelaus in the *Iliad* (6.57–60) and incorporating it into the imagery of the *Agamemnon* with relevant application to the two sons of Atreus (*Ag.* 108–24).[48] In Aeschylus, the omen at Aulis is darkly furthered on the battlefield of the Homeric *Iliad*; in Euripides the Homeric anxiety is sadly realized after Troy's fall. Both playwrights use allusion to juxtapose a moment of myth in their texts with another moment separated both by narrative time and by the gap between the two texts.[49] As with the Sophoclean collection and reuse of urn images from the *Oresteia*, one wonders if this may not provide an indirect look at Euripides' views of Aeschylean technique.

Sometimes the influence of Aeschylus' *Oresteia* on the *Electra* plays seems equally to demand and resist explanation. Some of the detailed verbal echoes of *Choephori* which Euripides incorporated into his recognition scene can be found in Sophocles as well. When Sophocles' Chrysothemis reports the signs at the tomb, she reasons that the lock of hair could have come only from her brother whom she calls φιλτάτου βροτῶν πάντων Ὀρέστου (903–4). Both her words and her reasoning echo the reaction of Electra in the *Choephori* who feels that the lock of hair must come from τοῦ φιλτάτου βροτῶν Ὀρέστου (*Cho.* 193–4). Moreover, both Aeschylus' *Electra* and Sophocles' Chrysothemis call the lock an ἀγλάϊσμα (*Cho.* 193, *El.* 908).[50] The word occurs only here in Sophocles, in Aeschylus never outside the *Oresteia* (cf. *Ag.* 1312) – and Euripides borrowed it for his own *Electra* as well. In a passage in which we have already examined Euripides' Homeric allusion, Electra uses the word in the same context – offerings at the grave – as her Aeschylean and Sophoclean counterparts; but her bitter statement is that her father's tomb never gets such cheerful things (Eur. *El.* 325). She also uses the very similar word ἀγλαΐα to contrast with the squalor of her own condition which she finds equally bitter (175), and the chorus's echo makes the word more emphatic (192, cf. 861). In tragedy the word occurs in only one other place. In her equally bitter and similar introductory scene, Sophocles' Electra hopes that Clytemnestra and Aegisthus will never meet with anything so nice (211). If the echo were limited to the Aeschylean word ἀγλάϊσμα, one might claim that Euripides and Sophocles were drawn – inexplicably, but still possibly independently – to imitate the *Oresteia*. But the additional occurrence of ἀγλαΐα in the *Electra* plays, in similar contexts, a word which does not occur in Aeschylus or in any other extant Greek tragedy, strongly suggests either that Sophocles was imitating Euripides or vice versa. Unfortunately there is no way to rule out either possibility. And the attraction of these two words and their ultimate poetic significance must probably remain mysterious.

Before turning to the more elaborate borrowings from the *Oresteia* which can be traced in the *Electra*s, we may look briefly at some of the smaller ways in which Sophocles followed the example of Aeschylus. First, when his Electra describes the abuse she suffers from Clytemnestra, her speech is made colorful with direct quotes of her mother's remarks. "Impious hateful thing" (δύσθεον μίσημα, *El.* 289) is one insult leveled at Electra, and, as Jebb notes, the adjective is otherwise confined to Aeschylus where it is regularly applied by members of the house of Atreus and Thyestes to other members whom they hate.[51] More than anything else, it is an epithet for Clytemnestra in the *Choephori* used both by Electra (191) and by the chorus .(46, 525). So Sophocles allows Electra's report to make Clytemnestra use the very insult which in the *Choephori* is regularly used of her. On both occasions when the Aeschylean chorus describes Clytemnestra this way, it is telling of the nightmare which has caused her to send the libations it bears, and Sophocles also imitates their description of the nightmare when his Chrysothemis explains her similar mission (410).[52] Clytemnestra's tirade in which she mentions the pain of childbirth (*El.* 530ff.) is commonly seen as a reflection of a similarly angry speech in the *Agamemnon* (1415–18). And lastly, Orestes' description of his sister as in manifest pain (ἐμπρέπουσαν ἄλγεσιν,

El. 1187) echoes his reaction to the sight of her in Aeschylus: πένθει λυγρῷ πρέπουσαν (*Cho.* 17–18). Although none of these echoes is laden with implications, they, and a host of smaller ones, help convey how intensely Sophocles had focused on his predecessor's text.[53]

At times Sophocles, and for that matter Euripides as well, takes an image from the *Oresteia* and expands it for more significant effect in much the same manner as he used the urn in the recognition scene. Let us consider a Euripidean example first. Just before Aegisthus enters in Aeschylus' *Choephori*, the chorus sings a prayer that Orestes, as a slayer, may have the bold heart of Perseus (*Cho.* 831–7). Because Euripides' elaborate way of using this image is seldom understood, it has earned him more blame than praise. First a Euripidean chorus, thinking back in the story to the war at Troy, sings of the arms of Achilles and the emblem of Perseus with the Gorgon's head on his shield (*El.* 458–63). As a way of invoking Perseus, it differs from the libation bearers' prayer, but apparently it is equally effective: when Euripides' Orestes slays Clytemnestra, he is like Perseus, for he must avert his eyes from his victim (*El.* 1221–3).[54] Euripides seems to have done much the same thing with Clytemnestra: another figural ornament of Achilles' arms, as described by Euripides' chorus, is a threatening lioness (*El.* 474); later the chorus describes Clytemnestra as a lioness in her murderous attack on Agamemnon (*El.* 1162). And just as the image of Perseus for Orestes has been taken from *Choephori*, so the image of Clytemnestra as lioness is drawn from the lyric vision of Cassandra at *Agamemnon* 1258.

Sophocles likewise incorporates images from both these plays of the *Oresteia*. His Electra is described by the chorus as melting away in "insatiate lament" (ἀκόρεστον οἰμωγάν, 123); she has inherited the grief for the death of Agamemnon which Cassandra began in *Agamemnon*, where the chorus described her almost identically as ἀκόρετος βοᾶς (1143). This Aeschylean chorus likens Cassandra to a nightingale crying "Itys, Itys" (*Ag.* 1144), and in fact Sophocles' Electra likens herself to the nightingale (*El.* 107) and also recalls the repeated cry of "Itys" (*El.* 148). But this Electra has an active side as well as a passive, which Sophocles brings out by means of daring borrowing from the *Choephori*. In Aeschylus' play, Orestes describes the murder he will commit as the insatiable Fury drinking a third round of undiluted blood (ἄκρατον αἷμα, 577). Sophocles' Clytemnestra quotes the arresting phrase exactly when she complains of Electra endlessly drinking her life's blood (El. 786). Allusion or collusion, the quotation implies that she will become the bloody victim of this Fury-Electra; the implication is correct.[55]

At times Sophocles allusively condenses large stretches of material and great themes of the Choephori into small space. Burton has well shown how a few lines of choral song in Electra (475–9) on the coming of avenging justice concentrate much of the Aeschylean "thought and language" in the great ode which follows the murder in Choephori (935–71), and how a brief choral call for help to Agamemnon in Hades (El. 1066–9) echoes an entire central scene of the Aeschylean version (Cho. 315–509).[56] Elsewhere, the scale of the Sophoclean allusion more nearly matches the Aeschylean original. Such is the case with the solving of a riddle at the climax of both plays. When Aegisthus is being murdered, Clytemnestra's attention is drawn to the servant's disturbed cries that culminate in his riddle that the dead are killing the living (Cho. 886), and, with a jolt, the solution to the Aeschylean enigma comes to her (887). Similarly, Sophocles prepares the paradox with choral comments (El. 1420–1) reminiscent of Aeschylus' lines; then, when Aegisthus is shown Clytemnestra's corpse, Orestes grimly suggests that the roles of the dead and the living are the reverse of what Aegisthus has imagined (El. 1478). Understanding comes to Aegisthus just as it did to Clytemnestra in the Choephori, and his exclamation is nearly an exact quotation of hers:

Clyt: οἴ 'γώ, ξυνῆκα τοὔπος ἐξ αἰνιγμάτων.

(Cho. 887)

Aeg: Οἴμοι, ξυνῆκα τοὔπος·

(El.1479)

Segal has suggested that Sophocles has taken the Aeschylean detail and constructed "a vast metaphor which permeates every part of his drama," a world in which life has in many ways degenerated to a form of death.[57]

Even if death does not reign totally, the world Sophocles has constructed for Orestes to return to is quite grim, as some of the more careful allusions show. Electra, in her first great speech, tells how Aegisthus and Clytemnestra murdered her father, splitting his head "with a murderous axe, as woodcutters do an oak" (*El.* 97–100). The simile at once makes her bitter description more vivid and recalls the work of woodcutters in the Homeric simile (cited by Jebb) that likens the fall of a slain warrior to that of the tall tree cut down by the workers' newly sharpened axes (*Il.* 13.389–91 = 16.482–4). But whereas the Homeric simile remains objective and perhaps confers some nobility and grandeur with the felling of the tall pine, the Sophoclean reworking makes the death degrading and squalid.[58] The allusions based on material from the *Oresteia*, especially a concentrated set of them near the end of the play (*El.* 1415–79), have a similarly somber effect. Sophocles' Electra explains that she waits for Orestes to return, but is losing hope (*El.* 303–4), and that in such conditions it is not possible to be moderate or reverent (οὔτε σωφρονεῖν . . . οὔτ' εὐσε-βεῖν, 307–8). Aeschylus' Electra too prays near the beginning of *Choephori* for the return of Orestes (138–9), and her prayer continues with the hope that she will be more moderate and reverent than her mother (σωφρονεστέραν . . . εὐσεβεστέ-ραν, *Cho.* 140–1). The imitation triggers allusion, promoting a comparison of contexts; Sophocles' world leaves less room for human kindness than did Aeschylus' – at least in the eyes of their Electras.[59]

As the *Choephori* moves to a climax, Aeschylus makes fate close in with seemingly inevitable repetition by echoing phrases and images from the *Agamemnon*; the Sophoclean treatment of the murder of Clytemnestra draws on the *Agamemnon* precisely in this ominous Aeschylean way. The opening signal for Sophocles' series of allusions is the death cry of Clytemnestra, repeating identically that of Aeschylus' Agamemnon. Both victims cry ὤμοι πέπληγ-μαι at the first blow (*Ag.* 1343, *El.* 1415) and ὤμοι μάλ' αὖθις at the second (*Ag.* 1345, *El.* 1416). The unchanged quotation from the original murder demonstrates how exact the exaction of vengenace is.[60] Later, Sophocles' Aegisthus shows himself to be the proper continuation of his original in the *Agamemnon* by repeating his distasteful metaphor for power taken from taming animals (*El.* 1462, *Ag.* 1624, 1632, 1639–40).[61] But perhaps the most significant echo of this sort is the last in the series, in a passage already considered for its echo of the solution of the riddle in *Choephori* – *Electra* 1476–9. Here Aegisthus asks with horror whose nets (ἀρκυστάτοις, 1476) he has fallen into, triggering allusion to *Agamemnon* 1375 and *Eumenides* 112, the only places in tragedy where this word for "net" has occurred. Moreover, by suggesting the Aeschylean secondary field, the allusion evokes the net imagery which pervades the *Oresteia*, thus underlining the whole series of echoes from the *Agamemnon*. The Fates and Furies recoil on their victims as inevitably in Sophocles' *Electra* as they did in the *Oresteia*, indeed as they did in the *Trachiniae*. Sophocles has inherited, or perhaps appropriates, not only Aeschylean images but the entire vision of human fate which they and their patterned use help to convey.

OTHER PLAYS FROM THIS PERIOD

Hippolytus would seem the perfect opportunity for allusions to Bacchylides 17, the song of Theseus' dive. When Euripides' chorus recalls Phaedra's wedding voyage and the boat that sped her from Crete to Athens (*Hipp.* 752–64), her eventual husband's Bacchylidean voyage to Crete would have made a suggestive secondary field. Likewise, the messenger speech reporting Hippolytus' catastrophe (*Hipp.* 1173–254) could have called up a poignant contrast: Theseus (in Bacchylides) called on his father Poseidon and leaped into the sea, was rescued by his father's dolphins, and re-emerged as a joyful wonder; in *Hippolytus* Theseus calls on Poseidon and draws a bull from the sea foam which causes Hippolytus' horses to panic and mangle him. In Bacchylides' poem, Theseus' miracle grew out of his gallant defense of a maiden threatened by sexual advance. In Euripides' play, Theseus' impulse is the same: Phaedra, so he thinks, has been similarly threatened, but the result of his horrible mistake is that he loses his son as well as his wife. Yet Euripides makes none of these allusions; by some irrecoverable artistic logic, Bacchylides 17 is reserved for frequent use in later plays.

Another Bacchylidean ode, however, is used in *Hippolytus*, at least for imitation. In her despair, Phaedra describes what for her must be an erotic scene of the hunt. Her images, barely coherent, confuse the Nurse, as if Euripides had transcribed them from a fragmentary section of the Bacchylides papyrus *before* Jebb supplied the connections. Indeed, the abrupt motion, golden hair, and javelin toss (*Hipp.* 220–2) all may owe something to Bacchylides' description of an athlete whose javelin throw and golden hair are

mentioned in the same passage (Bacchyl. 9.24–43). And the same
Bacchylidean ode may have supplied the Euripidean chorus a little
earlier with the epithet πολυζήλωτος (*Hipp*. 168) which in
Bacchylides (9.45) occurs in a passage on the Amazons, the tribe
that supplied Hippolytus' mother.

The remaining imitations and allusions in *Hippolytus* all have to
do with Phaedra's passion as well. Eventually her disturbed cries
draw a response from the chorus (*Hipp*. 573–4) which, as Fraenkel
has pointed out at *Agamemnon* 1150, almost certainly shows once
again the great influence which the *Oresteia* exerted over Euripides.
The meter, the form of the choruses' questions, the rare word
ἐπίσσυτος which they share, the mention of fear in both
passages, and in particular the fact that the Aeschylean chorus is
responding to Cassandra's disturbed cries all show that Euripides
had the *Agamemnon* in mind.[62] Since the *Oresteia* is so often used by
Euripides, one may wonder whether the phrase γᾶ τρέφει
(*Cho*. 585) has influenced Euripides' use of the identical words at
Hippolytus 1277, but other parallels may be equally important
there.[63] The last Aeschylean imitation comes in a description of the
power of love (*Hipp*. 1274), a repetition of the phrase from
Aeschylus' *Septem* (μαινομένᾳ κραδίᾳ, 781) which Euripides
had already used at *Medea* 433.

Finally, the chorus devotes an entire song (*Hipp*. 525–64)
explicitly to the problem of Eros, and although the stasimon has a
superficial coherence, an authorial collusion provides even greater
unity at a deeper level. Through most of the song love is portrayed
as a violent, military phenomenon. By contrast, the opening
associates love with sweetness. But the apparent contrast is made
an element of formal unity through a final recapitulation which
depicts Cypris as a darting bee (*Hipp*. 563–4), thus framing the
central section. This description of the bee – μέλισσα . . .
πεπόταται – seems to derive from the first extended simile of the
Iliad and the bees (μελισσάων, 2.87) which flutter there
(πεποτήαται, 2.90) in the description of Greek warriors fighting
a war that was waged for love. This collusion with the *Iliad*
achieves two things at once. First, it unifies the images of violence
and sweetness by reference to the secondary field of epic where
they are held together by the simile. Second, the association with
the Trojan War underlines the violent potential of the passion
which in *Hippolytus* leads to the deaths both of the woman it

touches and of the man it does not.

In the *Hecuba*, written just a few years later, it was not Bacchylides but the *Iliad* which offered the most obvious secondary field of reference. This baroque Euripidean creation presents a collection of atrocities as a gruesome, petty coda to the Trojan War. The play opens with a clear Homeric allusion, the phrase δούλειον ἦμαρ (*Hec.* 56), quoted from the closing lines of Hector's gloomy vision of the fall of Troy which he paints for Andromache (*Il.* 6.463). In triggering reference to their original context, the words call up for poignant comparison the time before the fall of Troy, happy in Hector's moment with Andromache and their son, sad in his correct vision of the ultimate outcome of the war.

Aside from this one instance, however, Euripides' poetry in the *Hecuba* shows the pervasive influence of Aeschylus. As so often in Euripides' plays, there are echoes of *Persae*. The first of these is the close of Hecuba's opening prayer to the underworld gods to save her child (*Hec.* 94). Like Hecuba, Aeschylus' Atossa has a dream which has caused her to worry about the welfare of her child, and so she orders the chorus to pray to the gods of the underworld (*Pers.* 619–20). Striking as the similarities are – both great eastern queens have just had great blows dealt to their empires by Greeks – Euripides seems to be imitating rather than alluding. This seems equally true when later the war cry from Aeschylus' *Persians* (ὦ παῖδες Ἑλλάνων, 402) is quoted exactly (*Hec.* 930).

By contrast, the next Aeschylean echo, this time from the *Oresteia*, seems more suggestive. As Fraenkel noted at *Agamemnon* 1461, the description of Helen, the baneful effects of her marriage to Paris, and, most specifically, calling the disaster οἰζύς are all imitated by Euripides' chorus of Trojan captives singing of the same subject (*Hec.* 943–9). In both plays the reflection on Helen comes as a strong, threatening woman is engaged in revenge: in the *Agamemnon*, Clytemnestra has just murdered Agamemnon; in Euripides' play, Hecuba is negotiating with Agamemnon to get what she wants. The similarities between Clytemnestra and Hecuba may have led Euripides to this passage of the *Agamemnon*. Such use of the *Oresteia* seems even more probable in light of the last Aeschylean allusion in *Hecuba*. There, the terrible phenomenon that women represent is summed up in a phrase of Polymestor's that recalls the treatment of that subject in the related *Choephori*

THE MIDDLE PLAYS

stasimon: γένος γὰρ οὔτε πόντος οὔτε γῆ τρέφει τοιόνδ'· (*Hec.* 1181–2) echoes the opening phrase πολλά μὲν γᾶ τρέφει δεινὰ δειμάτων ἄχη, πόντιαί τ' ἀγκάλαι κνωδάλων ἀνταίων βρύουσι (*Cho.* 585–8).[64] Because the *Choephori* passage is so frequently used by Sophocles and Euripides, Polymestor's words may well trigger an allusion to the Aeschylean stasimon; this further suggests that the *Choephori* stasimon was also in Euripides' mind when he wrote *Hippolytus* 1277.

Two suppliant plays, *Children of Heracles* and *Suppliant Women*, contain a fair number of echoes, but in both tragedies the material, even when it can be confidently traced, seems somewhat generically deployed, helping more to create atmosphere than to suggest allusion. In *Heracleidae* the echoes do not always have even this vague function. For example, there is one extensive imitation of Aeschylus' *Persians*: Iolaus speaks of Eurystheus' coming to Athens (ἐς τὰς 'Αθήνας, *Hcld.* 387) and notes that Zeus chastises arrogant thoughts (ἀλλὰ τῶν φρονημάτων/ ὁ Ζεὺς κολαστὴς τῶν ἄγαν ὑπερφρόνων, 387–8). Here Euripides virtually quotes Aeschylus' Darius who, speaking also about Athens (μέμνησθ' 'Αθηνῶν, *Pers.* 824), expresses the same opinion about Zeus (Ζεύς τοι κολαστὴς τῶν ὑπερκόμπων ἄγαν/ φρονημάτων ἔπεστιν, 827–8). But as usual, imitations from *Persians* are just that, with no allusion suggested. Iolaus' opinion that few children are the equal of their fathers (*Hcld.* 326–8) is another simple borrowing, this time from Athena at *Odyssey* 2.276–7.[65]

Such other echoes as can be found in *Heracleidae* are all from the *Iliad* and serve the purpose of heightening the epic martial tone which prevails around the battle in the second half of the play.[66] As Iolaus departs with his servant before the great battle, he tells Alcmene that war is men's work (*Hcld.* 711–12), in what may well be an echo of Hector's last words to Andromache as he leaves to go back to the battle with Paris (*Il.* 6.492–3). Then after the battle the chorus notes the apparent security of their freedom with a phrase which may be an echo from just slightly earlier in the Hector and Andromache scene (ἐλεύθερον . . . ἦμαρ, *Hcld.* 868: ἐλεύθερον ἦμαρ, *Il.* 6.455); the speech and topic are often echoed by Euripides.[67] Between these two echoes, the chorus sings a song which more than once has a Homeric ring.[68] Most notably, the first sentence of the stasimon contains two words, each of which occurs only once in the *Iliad*, and in a key passage. One, λαμπρόταται (*Hec.* 749), occurs in the often-used passage in which Priam begs Hector to come inside the city walls (*Il.* 22.30). The other, φαεσίμβροτοι (*Hec.* 750), is from the last lines of the poem, describing the dawn on which Hector (who had resisted his father's plea) is given his funeral (*Il.* 24.785). If the words could convey ominous implications, they would match the apprehensive feeling of this chorus awaiting the outcome of the battle; if not, they simply help create a Homeric and solemn tone.

Euripides' *Suppliant Women* tells of the aftermath of the expedition of the *Seven against Thebes*, so it is not surprising that the play contains echoes of Aeschylus' *Seven* and, perhaps, of *Antigone*. In addition, the messenger speech that recounts the battle between Athens and Thebes contains an echo of battle in the *Iliad*. And finally – as in most plays – there are the echoes of *Agamemnon*.[69] All of these can be described briefly. Euripides' first echo of *Seven against Thebes*, a description of Capaneus' boast, is a near repetition of the same material in Aeschylus. Compare Aeschylus' θεοῦ τε γὰρ θέλοντος ἐκπέρσειν πόλιν/ καὶ μὴ θέλοντός φησιν (*Septem* 427–8) with Euripides' ὤμοσεν πόλιν/ πέρσειν θεοῦ θέλοντος ἤν τε μὴ θέλῃ (*Supp.* 498–9). Less directly, Theseus' vision of the battle he is preparing for with the image of the horses' foam and the move against Thebes (*Supp.* 584–7) reflects the description of the original battle in the *Seven* (59–61).[70] Both references seem simple imitations.[71]

The report of Theseus' battle against Thebes begins with reference to the sun's bright ray (*Supp.* 650). Thebes' recent victory over the Seven is here notably reversed, and the words might just be intentional repetition from the opening of Sophocles' parodos in the *Antigone* (100) which reported the Theban victory.[72] In a messenger speech full of general Homeric phrases there is one imitation of a specific passage: the Euripidean warriors fall out of chariots like tumblers or divers (691–3) just as the unfortunate Cebriones did in the *Iliad* (16.742–50). The echo is a good illustration of how imitation and allusion tend to formal similarity, making them difficult to distinguish: both the source for this imitation of Homer, a simile, and Euripides' placement of it, a messenger speech, are common signs of allusion (see Appendices C and D).

Later the chorus ends a lyric section with a reference to bitter marriages, and their final word is Ἐρινύς, the Fury (*Supp.* 837).

The passage is remarkably similar to a choral reflection of bitter marriage in Aeschylus' *Agamemnon* where the strophe also ends with the word Ἐρινύς (744–9). Still, Euripides seems more to have drawn on a specific passage for a general tragic effect, just as elsewhere in this play he draws on epic, lament, and public speech in ways which suggest the appropriate genre without making any specific reference.[73] The *Agamemnon* also provides a final echo in the *Suppliants*, at once the most striking and the most interesting one in the play. In the closing scene the sons arrive with the remains from their fathers' pyres to hand over to their mothers (*Supp.* 1123–31). Fraenkel follows Paley in seeing that the whole passage is based closely on a most memorable choral reflection in the *Agamemnon* on the return of warriors' ashes from Troy (434–44). In both passages the bodies have been replaced by ashes, pitifully small remains incommensurate with the weight of the grief they occasion. We have seen to what great effect Sophocles employed this image in his *Electra*; since Euripides seems more than once to have followed Sophocles' technical and/or allusive lead,[74] it is tempting to see again here evidence of Euripides imitating a Sophoclean borrowing. If, in fact, he did, that would give a rough range for the years – say 424–420 B.C. – before which Sophocles' *Electra* would have had to appear. But in such matters there will be no certainty.

Andromache is a characteristically Euripidean sequel set in the aftermath of the *Iliad* and the *Oresteia*: the ashes of Troy are long cold, and Hector, Achilles, Agamemnon, and Clytemnestra have all been slain. Yet the play presents a tumultuous continuation of the lives of Andromache, Neoptolemus, and Orestes that proves poetically that no ending is an end. Such a story provided Euripides with natural opportunities for allusion to the texts whose resolutions he was dissolving, the *Iliad* and the *Oresteia*.

A small but extremely specific amount of allusive attention is devoted to Orestes, connecting him with his Aeschylean namesake first by his own words and then by the messenger's. When Orestes complains of Neoptolemus' unsympathetic reaction to the problem of Clytemnestra's Furies, his mention of the goddesses with their gory faces (*Andr.* 978) echoes the description he had voiced when he first saw them immediately after killing his mother (*Cho.* 1058). Later, recounting the strategem used to kill Neoptolemus, the messenger describes Orestes as "Clytemnestra's child" (*Andr.* 1115), a "stitcher of crafty plans" (μηχανορράφος, *Andr.* 1116).

Although the adjective occurs earlier in the play when Andromache hurls it as an insult to Menelaus and all his fellow Spartans (*Andr.* 447), it is found practically nowhere else in Greek.[75] However it recalls the verb used – and in extant Greek *only* used – by Orestes to describe himself as a schemer: μηχανορραφῶ, he told Electra when he came to kill their mother (*Cho.* 221). Obviously, the murderous plans of Clytemnestra's child did not end then.

However, the play is more Andromache's than Orestes', and the Homeric echoes help remind us that this is the continuation of her story envisioned by Hector before he died.[76] This is especially true in the opening scene as Andromache lists all she has to mourn for (*Andr.* 96–9). The last item on her list is the slavery she has fallen into: she calls it δούλειον ἦμαρ (*Andr.* 99), just as Hector did in the close of his speech which foresaw her future (*Il.* 6.463). It is perhaps Euripides' most poignant use of an often used scene.[77] Andromache closes her reflections on Paris, Helen, and the fate of Troy in elegiac couplets, a meter especially suited to the telling of that story. The epic material is emphasized with striking Homeric formulae such as ἐπὶ θῖνα θαλάσσας (*Andr.* 109), and then as Andromache, in danger of death, wonders why she should remain in the upperworld at all, there is a clear echo from Odysseus' trip to the underworld. She describes the suppliant position in which she clings to the statue, περὶ χεῖρε βαλοῦσα (*Andr.* 115), an imitation of Odysseus' περὶ χεῖρε βαλόντε when he is trying to embrace his mother's ghost (*Od.* 11.211). Again, they are sad words at a sad time, and the allusion makes *Andromache* seem all the closer to death.

Since the characters and chorus in *Andromache* frequently look back to the Trojan War and the events that led to it, there are times when the most natural words to use are Homeric: the reference is directly to the myth rather than to specific Homeric verses. Such, for instance, is the chorus' mention of the old men of Troy as advisers at the time of Paris' birth: to call them δημογέροντες is in one sense to allude to their unforgettable appearance on the walls of Troy (*Il.* 3.149), the only other use of this word (in the plural) in extant Greek of the classical period.[78] In some other sense it is the only proper word to use for the city's elders. The same stasimon has even more general words and phrases such as κεκορυθμένον (*Andr.* 279). Even the phrase ψυχὰς δὲ πολλάς (*Andr.* 611) for all the men who were destroyed in the war for Helen, while an obvious echo of *Iliad* 1.3, comes near to being a simple statement of fact, or rather, insult.[79]

Later in the play, however, Euripides uses a series of Homeric suggestions in an apparently more pointed way. The set of passages is an excellent illustration of a general tendency to use epic materials in messenger speeches. Here the effect from the very outset is perhaps somewhat ironic: the speech recounts the violent death of Achilles' son Neoptolemus, the present husband of Hector's widow Andromache. Thus the relation of Homeric battle to this world and these people is indirect, but suggestively relevant. In the battle with the Delphians at the temple of Apollo Neoptolemus is crushed by missiles falling thick and fast like a snowstorm (*Andr.* 1129). The image is a great poetic success in suggesting the contrast between feathery silent snowfall and the murderous clangor of considerably heavier weapons – and it is famous from its Homeric use at *Iliad* 12.154–60 and 12.278–89. When Neoptolemus collects himself he leaps at the Delphians and they flee like doves at the sight of a hawk, again echoing a simile from the *Iliad* (21.493–6).[80] In these two examples, as with Euripides' imitation of the Homeric simile of the divers in *Suppliants*, both the use of similes and the setting in a messenger speech help to suggest poetic dependence. Besides setting the brilliant Homeric world of Neoptolemus' father Achilles and its more honorable battles in contrast with this squalid Euripidean scheme designed to entrap Hector's young successor, the epic battle images serve as a trigger, preparing the audience to recognize with effective shock an allusion a few lines later. When Neoptolemus is finally slain, all the Delphians gather around to wound the corpse (*Andr.* 1149–54). And so Andromache's present husband is treated in death exactly as her former one: the Greeks had joked cruelly as they gathered round to take turns wounding the helpless corpse of Hector (*Iliad* 22. 367–74).[81] The echoes draw the Homeric world and the Euripidean one close together so that the differences can be clearly seen. The battle arranged against Andromache's new husband by Orestes commands no respect when set beside the ones fought by his father Agamemnon against Hector; the world of the primary field is a diminished vision of that in the secondary one.

The last play to consider from this period is Sophocles' *Oedipus*

Rex. In treating the legend, Sophocles' poetic predecessors were many and varied: there were epic versions of the story of Thebes and specifically of Oedipus, there were lyric narratives, and, finally, there had been other tragedies. All were lost in the collapse of the ancient world, and only the smallest, most tantalizing bits have been recovered.[82]

All, of course, except Aeschylus' *Seven against Thebes*. But even this is merely a fragment, for it is the third play in a connected tetralogy which began the story with *Laius*, continued it with *Oedipus*, and after the *Seven* closed with a satyr play, *Sphinx*. The complex connections of mortals with divine instructions, the echoing of the family story across generations, riddles to be undone in the course of time, and images like the Sphinx all made perfect material for Aeschylean treatment such as we know from the *Oresteia*. And although Sophocles' *Electra* corresponded to the second play of that trilogy, Sophocles also grounded his allusions in its first, the *Agamemnon*, providing poetic depth with references simultaneously to earlier stages of the story and to earlier poetry. Sophocles' *Oedipus* similarly focuses on the Theban myth at the stage of Aeschylus' second play. Moreover, it is obsessed with recovering the events connected with Laius – that is, with Aeschylus' opening play. *Electra* alludes to *Agamemnon* almost three times as often as it does to the *Eumenides* – to say nothing of its allusions to *Choephori*. If *Oedipus Rex* similarly favors *Laius* and *Oedipus* – and it seems logical that it should – much more of Aeschylus' trilogy has come down to us than is usually recognized. But the sieve that can pan the lost Aeschylean nuggets from the surviving Sophoclean stream has not yet been devised.

So we are left with the echoes of the *Seven* that can be identified with relative security. The first involves Eteocles and his father Oedipus: Aeschylus has Eteocles use the verb νωμάω in the very rare sense "to ponder" when referring to the blind seer Teiresias' mental processes (*Septem* 25), and Sophocles makes Oedipus use the same verb in the same rare sense for the same seer's thoughts (*OT* 300). Father and son are also linked by a second echo from Aeschylus' prologue: the messenger in *Septem* addresses Eteocles as φέριστε (39), and the only other occurrence of this vocative in extant tragedy is the servant's address to Oedipus in Sophocles (*OT* 1149).[83] Not surprisingly the remaining echoes of *Septem* are from a stasimon which looks back at the misfortunes of Laius and

Oedipus, bringing together the sequence of disasters which links the Aeschylean trilogy (*Septem* 720–91). The Aeschylean chorus seems to have been famous: Euripides quoted it at both *Medea* 433 and *Hippolytus* 1274, and it generally informs the fourth stasimon of *Oedipus* (1186–222) which also considers these events once they have become horribly clear. In both *Oedipus* and the *Seven*, for example, Oedipus' union with his mother is described in terms of the furrows he has plowed (*Septem* 753, *OT* 1211). To be sure, the image has a traditional basis in the Greek marriage vow, but it is especially pointed and striking in these two songs.[84]

Sophocles' other notable poetic source is, as usual, the Homeric poems.[85] In general the borrowings here do not seem to be used allusively. In a mainly dactylic section of the parodos which has a number of epic phrases, there is a description of fear (*OT* 153) which may ultimately owe something to Andromache's reaction when she fears Hector is dead (*Il.* 22.451–5). It has been suggested that the image of ghosts speeding westward (*OT* 178) is an echo from the *Odyssey* (20.356), but if so, it is faint.[86] More striking is the phrase παλαίφατα θέσφατα (*OT* 906–7) which is quoted from the Cyclops' realization that the oracle has been fulfilled at *Odyssey* 9.507. It is not, apparently, a significant allusion; but we can be reasonably sure that the passage was in Sophocles' mind since he uses it to great effect at *Trachiniae* 822–3. Moreover, just as the episode of *Odyssey* 9 figured in other passages of *Trachiniae* as well (779–82, 931), so here in *Oedipus* the choral description of a wild, wooded, deserted spot, including the Homeric hapax χηρεύει (*OT* 479), seems to owe not only the rare word but the setting as well to *Odyssey* 9.118–24. Again, both verbal echo and details of context connect Oedipus' order to tie the shepherd's hands so that he can be tortured (ἀποστρέψει χέρας, 1154) with the related fate of the evil goatherd Melanthius in the *Odyssey* (χεῖράς τε δέον . . . ἀποστρέψαντε, 22.189–90). But whereas Oedipus' assurance to the chorus that he recognizes them (*OT* 1325) does seem a verbal echo of Achilles speaking to Priam (*Il.* 24.563), the contexts seem unrelated.

Oedipus contains one particularly striking Homeric echo, and Sophocles has placed it at the opening of the fourth stasimon when the chorus has reached full awareness. The fate of Oedipus, the total disaster which has overtaken so great a man, reminds them of the vulnerability and fragility of all mankind in a way which has come to be thought of as the essence of tragedy. It was said of Homer in the ancient world that the most beautiful thing he said was that the steadily passing generations of men, coming and going with time, were like the leaves:

ἓν δὲ τὸ κάλλιστον Χῖος ἔειπεν ἀνήρ·
"οἵη περ φύλλων γενεή, τοίη δὲ καὶ ἀνδρῶν"·

(Simonides 8.1)

So Simonides quotes *Iliad* 6.146, and the lines have remained popular throughout western poetry from century to century in various languages. The Sophoclean chorus begins its sympathetic reflections with the exclamation ἰὼ γενεαὶ βροτῶν (1186), also echoing the famous lines from the *Iliad*.[87] Brief as the verbal recollection is, conventional placement helps trigger the Homeric allusion. Just so in the *Antigone* Sophocles had repeatedly used the first line of prologue and stasimon for allusive poetic tags. And even though the loss of so many of the poetic antecedents of *Oedipus* limits analysis of the play's allusions, we can still see that the first line of the prologue (*OT* 151) has a Homeric hapax (ἡδυεπής), appearing only there in extant tragedy. Moreover, the opening of the first stasimon is written to echo that first line of the prologue – both begin with similar questions about Delphi – and the line of the stasimon itself contains a similar word, θεσπιέπεια (*OT* 463), which Sophocles may have coined for that song. A final additional indication that Sophocles was using the Homeric meditation on leaves and men for his own fourth stasimon is the occurrence of the phrase ἀμαιμακέτου πυρὸς in the prologue (*OT* 176), a phrase which seems derived from the Chimaera of this passage in *Iliad* 6: it both is ἀμαιμακέτην (179) and breathes fire (πυρός, 182).

With its echoes of Aeschylus' *Seven against Thebes*, and very likely of other plays in that trilogy as well, this fourth stasimon of *Oedipus* appears to be carefully ornamented with literary reference. In such highly wrought lines, the chorus recognizes the precarious nature of man's happiness, the ephemeral nature of the generations of mortals. Their use of one of the keynotes of the *Iliad* ties the tragedy broadly to epic, and helps the audience to recognize that the fate of mankind resembles the fates of Achilles and Oedipus. The recognition is terrifying; poetry makes it easier to bear.

CONCLUSIONS

The ten Euripidean and Sophoclean plays considered in this chapter show a great range both in the amount of attention given to allusion and imitation and in the ways that allusion is used. At one end of the scale are plays such as *Heracleidae* and *Oedipus Rex* which are comparable to the early plays of Aeschylus in their sparing use of imitation and allusion. Euripides' *Suppliant Women* is interesting because it may show Euripides following in Sophocles' footsteps. Euripides borrows from the *Agamemnon* the image of the war dead reduced to ashes, men's bodies replaced by pathetically tiny urns, just as Sophocles had used the material in *Electra*. Euripides seemed to have followed Sophocles similarly in the *Alcestis*, using Homeric material Sophocles had borrowed for allusions in *Ajax*. The same pattern will be even more certainly discernible in Euripides' *Orestes* and *Cyclops* in their relation to Sophocles' *Philoctetes* and *Trachiniae*.

Hippolytus, *Hecuba*, and *Andromache* are all interesting in their own right; their allusions are limited in scope, but in each play the borrowings, at least once, are parallel to or serve to emphasize some important aspect of the poetry. In *Hippolytus* the concern with the power of love is encoded at the close of a stasimon on Eros through a collusion with Homeric verse (*Hipp.* 563–4, *Il.* 2.87–90). Here Euripides has drawn on the first extended simile of the *Iliad*, and his use of the darting bee shows the attraction of the Homeric simile which can be observed from Aeschylus' plays on. In *Hecuba* the frightening conversion of Priam's wife from a pathetic old woman to a monster of great power is emphasized through allusion to the disturbing list of dangerous women in Aeschylus' *Choephori* (*Hec.* 1181, *Cho.* 585). And in *Andromache* the technique which dominates the play, the alien presence of grand figures from distant epic in a tawdry, all too familiar world, is summed up in the messenger speech: Neoptolemus' death is reported with a series of Homeric similes and images that show the world of the play to be a squalid imitation of lost nobility.

The most extended use of allusion in this period is to be found in the four plays – two each by Euripides and Sophocles – that most heavily use Aeschylus' *Oresteia*. The two *Electra* plays show that the "strawberries are cherries in the grass" rule is only a rough and ready one: even though these tragedies tell very much the story of

Aeschylus' *Choephori*, both playwrights found ways to exploit the very smallness of the gap between tenor and vehicle in allusions to the Aeschylean material. For Euripides the gain, typically, is chiefly technical: allusion to Aeschylus' recognition allows the brief illusion that recognition may not be possible at all. For Sophocles, the *Agamemnon* and *Choephori* supply a set of images and phrases that are taken as the basis for a series of variations on the original; the Aeschylean minor notes become the basis for more extended adagio treatment of new darkness, as if Sophocles' art were able to convert the minor to an even more melancholy mode.

For the purposes of allusion to the *Oresteia*, the two Heracles plays have an initial advantage over the *Electra*s, for their material lies at a distance from which allusion more easily calls for a substantial interpretive act. Sophocles has combined paradigmatic family similarities with verbal echo to highlight the way he has constructed the story of a good Clytemnestra, a Deianeira who is trapped by fate in an Aeschylean manner just as Heracles is. The *Trachiniae* makes an interesting technical contrast with *Antigone*. The convention of placing allusions in lyric at the beginning of stasimon or at least of strophe, so pervasive in *Antigone*, was obviously only one option: in *Trachiniae* a whole series of critical allusions is worked into the play's important iambic speeches. In another way, however, the *Trachiniae* recalls the technique of *Antigone*: Hyllus' simile of the hateful viper, alluding to Orestes' identical metaphor so similarly applied, created a symmetry of split primary and secondary field comparable only to the use of Aphrodite's consolation exempla for the narrative examples in *Antigone*'s fourth stasimon. Such reduplication of tenor and vehicle in both fields of the allusion is not a part of the surviving technique of Aeschylus or Euripides, unless one counts the image of the bee in *Hippolytus*.

Seen another way, the allusive technique of *Trachiniae* bears the greatest resemblance to that of *Ajax*. Hyllus' simile of the viper's venom, itself an elaborate allusion further complicated by its ironic literal aptness and by later echoes in the play, functions remarkably like Teucer's lion simile. Both allusive comparisons come as the culmination of a long series of images; both set the seal on the destruction of the tragic hero; both are woven into the themes and allusions of their plays as if part of a net which traps the characters in their fates. The simile allows the importation of an image which collects and intensifies the energy of the ambient themes. In Aeschylus, generational patterns seem to suggest the inevitability of destiny. In Sophocles' *Ajax* and even more in the *Trachiniae* the curse is not familial; it is literary. The mythological parallels, evoked by Sophocles' allusions to epic and tragedy, give the impression that the protagonists are caught in poetic patterns of doom. The machinery of Agamemnon's death is invented by his ancestors; that of Heracles' death in the *Trachiniae* by Sophocles' colleagues.

Euripides' *Hercules Furens* is one of those plays which routinely cause interpretive difficulty; its allusions may help to shed light on the problems it seems to pose. The echoes of earlier stories, the *Oresteia*, *Prometheus*, and *Trachiniae*, all seem to point in the same direction: this story of Heracles' madness is not one of fate which the protagonist shapes and draws upon himself. With allusions to other plays Euripides creates distance and alienation for his own; what sounds familiar is seen to be inapplicable in its new setting. The echoes of epinician give the proper direction for Euripides' meaning: Heracles, normally the almost divine victor, is here the lesson in human frailty, the foil of vulnerability for his own ephemeral achievements. This technique of distancing allusions, with similar disturbing effects, will be brought to full perfection in the *Orestes*.

5

Sophocles and Euripides: The Last Plays

INTRODUCTION

The great age of Athenian tragedy ended at the close of the fifth century with the deaths of Euripides and Sophocles. Like the nearly simultaneous end of the Athenian empire with the loss of the Peloponnesian War, the fall of the curtain comes at a comprehensible point: death and defeat in battle are among the most reliable and acceptable historical punctuation marks. There is always a temptation to seek, in the final act, signs of the approaching end; in the matter of allusion there seem to be none. The plays of this period carry no sets of allusions which focus on the troubles of Athens or the profession of poets. In fact, when, for once, in Euripides' *Ion*, Athens is important to the play itself, fewer literary echoes are identifiable than in any other extant tragedy.[1]

However, although there are no signs, at least in poetic echoes, that Sophocles and Euripides were brooding over the fate of Athens or were increasingly anxious about the influence of earlier verse, the practice of allusion and imitation in these late plays differs from that in earlier ones. Particularly notable is the paucity of Sophoclean material. *Oedipus at Colonus* arouses the same suspicions as *Oedipus Tyrannus*: the apparent differences may be partly due to lost sources. Still, little use is made of the opportunities in the latter play for allusion to Aeschylus' *Seven*. And while the discovery of Aeschylus' or even of Euripides' *Philoctetes* might reveal a certain amount of imitation in Sophocles' play of this title, the contrast it provides with *Ajax* in its relation to the *Iliad* could hardly be greater: opportunity has been deliberately neglected.

By default, then, this final chapter becomes largely an examination of late Euripidean practice. His plays here considered span the decade from 415 to his death in 406. For once, tradition

141

has been kind. We have, apparently, two plays produced immediately after Sophocles' *Philoctetes*, the *Orestes* and *Cyclops*, and they allow yet another glimpse at the younger poet closely following the older. In addition, there is a range of plays dealing with the House of Atreus and with the beginning and end of the story of the Trojan War, making it possible to see further how the Homeric poems and Aeschylus' *Oresteia* continued to exert their influence right up to the death of Euripides.

Two Euripidean practices can be dealt with at the outset: in the first, one old habit seems merely continued; in the second, another seems to show further development. The simpler phenomenon is the steady appearance of unmistakable echoes of Aeschylus' *Persae*. Twice in the *Cyclops* and once each in *Iphigeneia in Tauris*, *Orestes*, and the *Bacchae* Euripides has incorporated phrases which, considered singly, are generally taken as echoes from the *Persae*.[2] The case for each seems strengthened by the existence of all the others, including those noted earlier in *Alcestis*, *Hecuba*, *Heracleidae*, and *Hercules*. Although none of these later instances seems more than a reuse of what has been made the poet's compositional stock, one might ask why the *Persae* was important enough to be used so repeatedly in Euripides' (and sometimes Sophocles') lines. The answer may simply be the historic importance of the Aeschylean play and the event it had commemorated for the Athenian empire. Poetry of such political interest may have been learned especially thoroughly by Euripides and indeed other Athenians as well.

Athenian political pride also seems the most likely factor to help explain a more important feature common to a number of Euripidean plays – his use of Bacchylides. Most of the Bacchylidean odes used by Euripides are echoed not once but twice in the extant plays: Euripides had made a speech of Apollo's from Bacchylides' third ode one of the central elements of *Alcestis*, and then used the lines again in *Andromache*; *Hippolytus* hints at acquaintance with the ninth ode at two different points; the simile of the gamboling fawn from Ode 13 used in *Electra* seems to make another appearance in the *Bacchae* (862–72).[3] Finally, the long-necked birds of *Helen* 1487 and the long-necked swan of *Iphigeneia at Aulis* 793 may well both be derived from Bacchylides 16.6. For one thing, the adjective δολιχαύχην occurs only in these three passages. Moreover, as we shall immediately see, Euripides was otherwise concerned with Bacchylides in the *Helen*. And last, the

Iphigeneia passage is particularly bookish: the chorus refers to the story of the swan in poems which it calls "the tablets of Pieria" (*IA* 797), and Pieria, in Ode 16, is the stated source of Bacchylides' store of songs (Bacchyl. 16.3). The Bacchylidean ode is a tearful tale of the captive Iole, and the chorus of *Iphigeneia* mentions in this song that they are tearful captive maidens too (*IA* 790–1).

There is one exception to this set of twice-echoed odes: Bacchylides 17 figures in three plays from this last decade. While the Bacchylidean imitation does not rest in the heart of these plays as it does in *Alcestis*, in two of them – *Helen* and the *Iphigeneia in Tauris* – it is perhaps even more extensive, and its explanation has implications for Athenian politics and Athenian education from the 470s to the end of the century. The seventeenth ode tells the story of Theseus' miraculous dive to the bottom of the sea. This outrageous act was required by the tyrannical Minos, who had been enraged when Theseus saved the maiden Eriboia from his rude advances. The argument takes place aboard the ship which is speeding Theseus and a group of Athenians to Crete where the young men and women are to become victims for the Minotaur. Not a small part of the miracle of Theseus' trip is that he resurfaces precisely at the spot the ship has reached even though, as Bacchylides emphasizes, the winds have sped it swiftly along the whole time that the great Athenian has been under the thundering waves. The rescue of women threatened by foreign tyrants, and exciting scenes aboard ship – and speeding ships at that – were all used by Euripides for *Iphigeneia Taurica*: Orestes saves Iphigeneia from the barbarian Thoas with a plan to speed away by sail. And the scheme, which there dramatically threatens to fail, goes without a hitch in *Helen* when Menelaus rescues his wife from the villainous Egyptian prince Theoclymenos. The same charming optimism informs all three romantic incidents, making lusty adventure glow with playfulness and wonder and, ultimately, a sense of divine protection.

Bacchylides' brilliant creation, the miracles which take place on and under the speeding ship, directly inspired Euripides; the proof of this immediate influence lies not in the remarkable similarities in plot and tone outlined above, but rather in the words and phrases Euripides has taken from the ode to use in his two plays. One of the critical moments in Bacchylides occurs at the moment of the dive when Minos orders the ship to continue on what he believes will be a fatally distancing course. Fortunately for Theseus, divine forces are with him:

μοῖρα δ' ἑτέραν ἐπόρσυν' ὁδόν.
ἴετο δ' ὠκύπομπον δόρυ·

(Bacchyl. 17.89–90)

Fate intended a different path.
And the swift-going keel rushed on.

Bacchylides almost certainly coined this adjective for "swift-going" for his song. It recurs in Greek apparently only in *Iphigeneia in Tauris*, where it describes first the ship which is to whisk Orestes and his sister to safety (1137) and then the oars of the tyrant who intends to pursue and destroy them (1427). Moreover, the tyrant refers to the ship which will further his own threatening designs as a δόρυ – the same somewhat unusual designation used of Minos' ship in Bacchylides' ode ("keel," above).[4]

The same two lines of Bacchylides are slightly reworked in a chorus in *Helen* which, in a very Bacchylidean manner, tells the story of Persephone and Demeter. There Euripides describes the divine plan thus: Ζεὺς . . . ἄλλαν μοῖραν ἔκραινε (1317–18). The same chorus twice (*Hel.* 1305, 1351) uses the adjective βαρύβρομος ("deep-thundering") which Minos had used (Bacchyl. 17.77) to describe the sea he ordered Theseus to dive into. True, this Euripidean stasimon tells a different story than that of Helen's sea-escape; but when the chorus takes up that subject, Bacchylides 17 figures there as well. They sing of the flight of Helen and Menelaus; and the sea, the dolphins playing in it, and the winds blowing over it (*Hel.* 1455–6) all echo exactly the vocabulary of the Bacchylidean setting.[5] As a final coda, we may add that the opening of *Trojan Women* (1–3), with its description of the Nereids' dancing feet at the bottom of the ocean, also recalls the Bacchylidean marvel (Bacchyl. 17.100–8).

Even though the Bacchylidean narrative seems virtually composed with a view to reuse in Euripidean romance, there may be other, more basic, factors behind these imitations. John Barron has demonstrated in great detail that Bacchylides 16 and 17, both devoted to Theseus, allude programmatically to the family of Kimon and Miltiades and its supposed descent from Theseus through Ajax. Certainly Kimon placed great importance on the

early Athenian hero, bringing his remains back to Athens and
having the Thesion decorated with narratives from Theseus' life –
all contemporary with the Bacchylidean compositions. As Pausa-
nias relates, one of the walls of the Thesion depicted part of the
story of Theseus' dive told in Bacchylides 17; and, as Barron
acutely points out, beyond the propagandistic genealogical ties of
Kimon and Miltiades to Theseus, there were flattering analogical
ones in Theseus' Bacchylidean trip to Crete. Theseus' frustration of
the plans of Minos the thalassocrat could be seen as prefiguring
Kimon's blows to the Persian fleet.[6]

Thus, in their possible reflection of old civic pride, the allusions
to Bacchylides 17 seem very like the frequent allusions to
Aeschylus' *Persae*. It would seem that Bacchylides' odes on Theseus
were composed with, among other things, an eye to pleasing
Athenian aristocratic pride, particularly pride in Athenian political
achievement. Perhaps the story on the walls of the Thesion
encouraged the teaching of the Bacchylidean ode to Athenian boys
in the days of Euripides' youth and in subsequent decades as well.
In that case the echoes incorporated by Euripides would reflect
not only his own poetic training and preference but the education,
and therefore the poetic competence, of his audience as well. Such
familiarity would also lend more power to the echoes of this
Bacchylidean ode in the *Prometheus Bound*.[7] Certainly at the time
Iphigeneia Taurica and *Helen* were produced the audience would have
appreciated any reminder that Athenians with their swift-going
ships might expect miraculous salvation on the deep-thundering
sea.

PHILOCTETES, ORESTES, AND CYCLOPS

After a few easy turns around the track in his chariot, Dio
Chrysostom, on a hot day somewhere near the beginning of the
second century A.D., decided to distract himself with a tragic
competition in the library: he would read and compare the plays
on Philoctetes by all three of the great tragedians. He was even
industrious enough to produce an essay on the plays, from which
we learn that the earlier plays by Aeschylus and Euripides were far
more rhetorical than Sophocles' version. They featured a disguised
Odysseus whose speeches were apparently showy set pieces

persuading Philoctetes to end his long, lonely stay on the island of Lemnos and bring his bow to Troy so that the Greeks could win the war.

In 409 B.C., after decades of war and political upheaval in Athens, Sophocles, nearer to 90 years of age than to 80, chose to write a very different sort of play. The style does not encourage imitation of earlier verse. For one thing, the role of the chorus has been very much changed. By convention, significant allusions more often than not were placed in the highly wrought, less colloquial choral stasima; yet this play has only one formal stasimon. Instead of making lyric meditations, these sailors engage in much more prosaic interchange with Odysseus, Neoptolemus, and Philoctetes. The tragedy is a series of attempts at communication, practical and painful, more fractured than extended, more colloquial than rhetorical; the elaborate iambic speeches of *Trachiniae*, an alternative location for allusive phrases, have no place here. Instead of delivering speeches with poetic allusions to the epic world of the *Iliad* and its heroes, Philoctetes makes direct staccato inquiry, then comments with bitter terseness on the blunt news that the great men have died and taken the great world with them. What remains is a desperate time in which the community's survival can only just be achieved through the cooperation of the idealistic young and the embittered old, embodied respectively in Neoptolemus and Philoctetes. And even the meeting of young and old depends precariously on the cynical manipulations of the practical, experienced, middle-aged Odysseus.

The few allusions and imitations in *Philoctetes* stem from the fact that even though this story is told in a new way, its elements are very old indeed. Texts of Aeschylus' or Euripides' *Philoctetes*, of course, might reveal some contributions to Sophocles; certainly he repeated a near quotation from Aeschylus' *Philoctetes* that he had already adapted for *Ajax* 854. Here the Aeschylean ὦ θάνατε παιὼν μή μ' ἀτιμάσῃς μολεῖν (fr. 255R) appears as ὦ θάνατε θάνατε πῶς... οὐ δύνα μολεῖν (797).[8] But there are other less direct parallels to the story of this isolated, uncooperative hero. Philoctetes is a member of the community who has been removed to its periphery and who refuses reintegration when the embassy finally comes with a compromise which offers and asks for help. The magic bow makes him a defiant Prometheus chained with his secret to the rock or a sulking Achilles who has taken off his armor and nurses his wounded pride to the sounds of his lyre and the waves breaking on the beach. The comparison is implied by Neoptolemus' response to the Emporos' deceptive report that Diomedes and Odysseus are soon to come for Philoctetes.[9] Pretending not to know what the Atreidae want, Neoptolemus asks, "What desire reached them?" (τίς ὁ πόθος αὐτοὺς ἵκετο, 601). The combination of subject and verb is practically non-existent, but it occurs once in the *Iliad* at the beginning of Achilles' and Agamemnon's quarrel. Achilles is withdrawing himself from action, and he warns that sometime "Desire for Achilles will reach the sons of the Achaeans" (1.240) – ἦ ποτ' 'Αχιλλῆος ποθὴ ἵξεται υἷας 'Αχαιῶν. The explicit verb parallel reinforces the extensive contextual one.[10] But Sophocles takes this suggested comparison no further. Nor does he take advantage of other obvious possibilities: for example, the lame Philoctetes (486) who both asks about Thersites (442ff.) and himself reviles Odysseus could easily have been made, with allusions, a pointed variation on the ugliest of Greeks – but he has not been.[11]

Instead Philoctotes is likened to an even less human monster. Sophocles had alluded to the story of Odysseus and the Cyclops from *Odyssey* 9 before – once in *Oedipus Rex*, but more significantly and frequently in *Trachiniae*. However, of his surviving plays the *Philoctetes* is best suited by its subject matter to accommodate references to the Homeric episode. Philoctetes' isolated life in his island cave parallels the rustic existence of the Cyclops Polyphemus. But even here Sophocles has been sparing: no striking hapax word, for example, which might be associated specifically with the Cyclops episode, occurs in *Philoctetes* – not even such a promising candidate as φαρμάσσω.[12] Instead Sophocles has used a small group of somewhat more common Homeric words, all taken from *Odyssey* 9, in the introduction to Philoctetes' life alone in the cave at the edge of the island. First there is the description of this site on the shore as ἐσχατιαῖς (*Phil.* 144), just like Polyphemus' cave (*Od.* 9.182).[13] Next, the chorus refers to Philoctetes' distress in this primitive life in the cave with the verb ἀλύει (*Phil.* 175), the word used to describe Polyphemus' suffering when he is blinded by Odysseus (*Od.* 9.398). Both are accompanied with a participial form of ἵσταμαι (*Phil.* 176, *Od.* 9.402), and it seems likely that the epic scene with the gruesome account of Polyphemus' disfigurement was studied by Sophocles when he decided to include graphic descriptions of Philoctetes' bloody wound. Finally in this opening, the chorus notes that Philoctetes lives not with men but with shaggy (λασίων) beasts (183). In its only occurrence in the *Odyssey*, the adjective notably describes the ram Odysseus hides under to escape from the blinded Polyphemus (9.433).[14] But the elliptic style Sophocles has chosen for *Philoctetes* provides nothing beyond these early hints at comparisons with Polyphemus. As with the reference to Achilles, Sophocles merely drops the allusion into the surface of his play and allows the implications to ripple, if they will, across the following scenes.

Mythical tradition connected Philoctetes and Heracles: mysterious fate bound the two men with their monstrous pain and a magic bow. This relationship may be partly what suggested another of the play's Homeric allusions to Sophocles. Philoctetes suffers a horrible attack while Neoptolemus is with him, screaming as the blood throbs from his open wound. As the pain subsides he loses consciousness, and instead of a stasimon the chorus delivers a kommos which is a paian to Sleep (827–64). When, in the *Iliad*, Hera had needed Sleep to carry out her famous deception of Zeus, she went to Lemnos to secure his help (*Il.* 14.230).[15] The Sophoclean chorus's call to Sleep and his power, Ὕπν' ὀδύνας ἀδαής, Ὕπνε δ' ἀλγέων (827), recalls Hera's opening words to him on Lemnos – Ὕπνε, ἄναξ πάντων . . . (*Il.* 14.233), and their allusion is secured by conventional placement in the first line of their song. The allusion directly rewards interpretive attention with the perception that Hera's mission of deceit resembles that in which Neoptolemus and the chorus are engaged. Moreover, in both cases Sleep's victim is the deceived party. There is a further indirect relevance in this reference: Sleep reminds Hera (*Il.* 14.243–62) that previously he had helped her to thwart Heracles. If this last point seems no more than collusive, the interweaving of Heracles' and Philoctetes' fates is nevertheless addressed directly with the appearance of Heracles at the end of the play. And the spectacle on stage of Philoctetes in excruciating pain, his appeals to death, and the care not to wake him all seem to recall Sophocles' picture of the dying Heracles in *Trachiniae*. Once again, however, the comparison to Heracles is very much like those to Achilles and Polyphemus earlier: the content of Sophocles' story, its setting, the points of tension, and the motives of action suggest rich relationships between Philoctetes and these three models; but the verbal texture of Sophocles' play gives only the initial suggestions. It is as if Sophocles, calculating the intensity needed to keep attention totally fixed on the struggle between his two creatures, found that allusive comparison and contrast would be superfluous or even distracting, and so presented the encounter of Neoptolemus and Philoctetes with near perfect economy.

Euripides' *Orestes*, produced the next year, proceeds from an artistic decision similar in one way to Sophocles' for *Philoctetes*: it is a highly innovative play presenting a world more immediate and familiar than the heroic world of conventional tragedy. But whereas Sophocles chose a broken, almost colloquial texture for his play, largely avoiding poetic echo and choral song, Euripides typically chose a more paradoxical method for making his play new. His poetry imitates the *Odyssey*, it closely uses *Philoctetes*, and most of all it rings with tragic phrases of Aeschylus and Sophocles taken from, and usually alluding to, the *Oresteia* and *Electra*.[16] Thus, as the actions in Euripides' *Orestes* become steadily more bizarre and less predictable – indeed, unlike anything else we know of in tragedy – the poetic texture is often eerily familiar, forcing the comparison to earlier plays and heightening our perception of Euripides' invention to great effect.

As *Orestes* begins its title character is asleep on his sick-bed; Electra provides the prologue, she and Helen have a brief exchange, and, then, since the protagonist must not be wakened, the chorus performs its parodos on tiptoe (140–207). Repeatedly Euripides echoes his own scene in *Hercules Furens* in which Amphitryon tries to keep silence so that the unfortunate mad Heracles may sleep as long as possible before learning that he has slaughtered his own family (*HF* 1042ff.).[17] But the scene also recalls the more recent one in which Sophocles' *Philoctetes* has finally fallen into an exhausted sleep after an attack of his own disease – a scene which in turn seemed to glance at Sophocles' own picture of Heracles in *Trachiniae*.[18]

Granted, the similar situations of Orestes and Philoctetes have other parallels as well; yet a host of explicit references shows Euripides closely using the Sophoclean *Philoctetes* of the year before. Of all the sets of echoes in Greek tragedy, these from *Philoctetes* in *Orestes* most stubbornly resist classification either as mere imitation or as more significant allusion. On the one hand, the phrases are all taken from iambic trimeter and, except for one which Euripides has modified to fit trochaic tetrameter, they have all been reused in iambic trimeter as well. As we have seen, with the exception of *Trachiniae*, it is unusual to find many pointed allusions in iambic verse. On the other hand, however, each passage deals with some topic of significance for the two plays: disease, its dehumanizing effects on Philoctetes and Orestes, friendship, betrayal, nobility.[19]

The imitations begin just after the parodos ends. Electra asks Orestes, even though his sickness makes him almost untouchable, if he would like for her to touch him. It could as easily be Neoptolemus talking to Philoctetes:

βούλη θίγω σου κἀνακουφίσω δέμας;

(*Or.* 218)

Should I touch you and ease your body?

βούλη λάβωμαι δῆτα καὶ θίγω τί σου;

(*Phil.* 761)

Should I take hold, then, and touch you?

A few lines later Electra's remark to Orestes that he has grown wild (ὡς ἠγρίωσαι, 226) again echoes Neoptolemus speaking to Philoctetes (σὺ δ' ἠγρίωσαι, 1321, cf. 226), words Menelaus repeats exactly (*Or.* 387). Then Orestes makes a request of Menelaus like Odysseus' request to Neoptolemus in the opening of *Philoctetes*; the petitioners emphasize that they just need one day's cooperation for their somewhat questionable causes (*Or.* 656–7, *Phil.* 83–4). When it has become apparent that the help Menelaus is willing to give is lukewarm at best, Orestes exclaims, οἴμοι προδέδομαι (722), and the only other tragic occurrence of this verb form is Philoctetes' cry when he learns that Neoptolemus has betrayed him (*Phil.* 923).[20] When Philoctetes is still convinced of Neoptolemus' good will, the young man explains that despite Philoctetes' illness, their bond of friendship means that he will not hesitate to help the old man (*Phil.* 887). Pylades makes a very similar statement to Orestes, even repeating the noun ὄκνος (*Or.* 794). Pylades' generosity moves Orestes to reflect on the value of a friend (806) and this too, though in some ways a commonplace, seems to reflect Neoptolemus' sentiment (*Phil.* 673). Finally, a similar gnomic expression about noble children of noble parents

seems to find its way from Philoctetes' approval of Neoptolemus
(εὐγενὴς . . . κἀξ εὐγενῶν, 874) to Menelaus' final
commendation of himself and Orestes as he gives him Hermione to
wed (εὐγενὴς δ' ἀπ' εὐγενοῦς, Or. 1676). This last echo
provides a good example of Euripides' technique of subversion in
Orestes: the expression of traditional nobility in traditional tragic
language takes on a very different tone after so many scenes which
have put the nobility of Menelaus and Orestes in doubt.[21]

In addition to these verbal echoes, Orestes shows traces of
technical borrowing from Philoctetes. One feature is admittedly
slight: Euripides' only tetrameter line with two speaker changes,
Orestes 1525, has a precedent in Philoctetes 1407, the last line of
Sophocles' play before the spectacular appearance of Heracles. Yet
the other technical imitation both involves more lines and is
backed up by an accompanying verbal echo: in Orestes Euripides
has put considerable distance between a strophe (1353–65) and its
corresponding antistrophe (1537–48), something which is rarely
done in tragedy, and for which the closest parallel is in Philoctetes
(391–402, 507–18).[22] Moreover, Euripides' strophe contains the
unusual phrase θεῶν νέμεσις (1361–2), a phrase which
occurs twice in Philoctetes, the first time in the final clause of the
antistrophe which is so distant from its strophe (Phil. 518).[23] In
general, while such technical imitations are themselves neither
allusions nor ungrammaticalities signaling them, they confirm –
without helping to explain or interpret – the verbal echoes of
Philoctetes in Orestes. In particular, by inscribing his technical
imitation of strophic split with a phrase from the very Sophoclean
strophic structure which provided the model, Euripides would
seem to indicate that the poetic source holds some clue to the
importance of his use of it. Yet no interpretive solution is apparent.
Perhaps even the allusive signpost is a bit of Euripidean mischief,
inviting an answer to a riddle which has none.

By contrast, Euripides' allusions to other plays on the House of
Atreus are, despite some complexity, easier to analyze. By the time
Orestes was written there had been a sufficient number of plays
about Agamemnon and his family to make echoes and imitations
quite a complicated matter. Some of the words and images from
the Oresteia in particular must have become practically traditional.
For example, the opening reference to Clytemnestra's net as
ἀπείρῳ . . . ὑφάσματι (Or. 25) combines two Aeschylean

phrases – ἄπειρον ἀμφίβληστρον (*Ag.* 1382) and πατροκτόνον γ' ὕφασμα (*Cho.* 1015) – to recall the image so dominant
in the *Oresteia*. And when Electra recalls a "father-killing mother"
(*Or.* 193), it is difficult to say in what sense this is an echo of the
"mother, . . . a father-killing pollution" of *Choephori* 1027–8. The
nature of the problem can be seen in the disagreement over the
reading of the text at *Orestes* 119: in this reference to libations at the
tomb, should we accept πρευμενῆ with Willink because it
would be an Aeschylean word in an Aeschylean context, or, with
Di Benedetto, retain the manuscripts' εὐμενῆ as an echo of
Sophocles' *Electra* 453?[24]

Even when the echoes are not assignable to a single original
passage, Euripides can derive striking effects from the associations
they bring up. For example, the scene in which Orestes, Pylades,
and Electra invoke Agamemnon's help in carrying out their violent
conspiracy (*Or.* 1225–45) clearly recalls and is modeled on the
similar scenes in Aeschylus' *Choephori* (479–509) and Euripides'
own *Electra* (671–84), as West has pointed out.[25] The allusion helps
emphasize the horrifying development that the violent vengeance
slayings have not come to their traditional and expected end after
the slaying of Clytemnestra, the event which is here echoed.
Euripides has put on the old record of trouble in the House of
Atreus, and it is scratched – or rather, he has gouged it – so that
the needle, instead of advancing to the cadence, skips back to
repeat the theme of family murder. Perhaps the best example of
this suggestive allusion with traditional phrase is the Phrygian
slave's reference to the plot against Helen as a contrivance "of
nets" (ἀρκυστάταν, *Or.* 1421). The adjective had been used in
identical metaphorical fashion by Aeschylus and Sophocles for the
family murders of Agamemnon and Clytemnestra and for the
Furies' attempt to catch Orestes (*Ag.* 1375, *Eum.* 112, Soph. *El.*
1476). In fact, it only occurs in these four tragic scenes. Its
recurrence in *Orestes* implies that the familial hunt and kill will
continue.

Of the echoes which can be securely associated with a specific
passage from the *Oresteia* or Sophocles' *Electra*, some merely help to
maintain the continuity of reference to the earlier plays. Such is the
choral description of Helen (*Or.* 1385–9) which, as Willink has well
pointed out, with its lyric images for Helen, ranges through words
compounded with δυσ- and culminates in ἐρινύν, just as the

lines of the chorus's description of her do at *Agamemnon* 738–49.[26] From the same passage, the chorus's striking adjective for the fawning look (φαιδρωπόν, *Ag.* 725) of the temporarily benign lion-cub has worked its way into the description of a flatterer in Euripides' messenger speech (*Or.* 894). Similarly, Electra's affectionate words to her brother (*Or.* 1045–6) are a near quotation of her greeting of the old servant in Sophocles' play (*El.* 1357–8). And Orestes' defiant call to the Sun to witness his bloody deed (*Cho.* 983–90) is explicitly condemned by Euripides' chorus (*Or.* 821–2).

These echoes all serve the overall effect in *Orestes* – to begin with something which seems related to the end of *Choephori* and to the *Eumenides* while moving steadily further from anything recognizable at all. The tone is set in this way particularly in the scene after the parodos when Orestes wakes. This long distichomythic passage (217–54) formally resembles the lines in *Choephori* (1051–64) when Clytemnestra's Furies arrive to torture Orestes.[27] The first mention of the Furies' effects on Orestes' mental clarity and the description of their bloody faces all recall that Aeschylean passage (respectively: *Or.* 237–8, *Cho.* 1026; *Or.* 253–4, *Cho.* 1056; *Or.* 255–6, *Cho.* 1058).[28] When they actually arrive in Euripides' play (*Or.* 272–4), the language becomes a concentration of phrases from Apollo's encounters with them in the *Eumenides* (180–90, 628). As *Orestes* continues, however, the familiar echoes are used with increasingly disturbing implications.

The technique is the same as with some of the general echoes considered above: once the plot to murder Helen takes shape and the plot of *Orestes* largely considered begins to spin out into baroque improvisation, Euripides repeatedly alludes to the *Electra* of Sophocles and to the *Oresteia*, making them foils for his grotesque variations. As Pylades affirms his determination to go through with the murder plan, he echoes the words of Sophocles' *Electra* who was equally determined to be nobly saved or nobly die (*Or.* 1151, *El.* 1320–1).[29] Not to be outdone, Euripides' Electra comes up with the additional plan for taking Hermione hostage, moving Orestes to compliment her for her man's mind in a woman's body (*Or.* 1204–5). His careful antithetical phrasing makes her, in a scant two lines, ominously like the Clytemnestra of the *Agamemnon* and of the *Odyssey*. As to the *Agamemnon*, Aeschylus' watchman had marveled at Clytemnestra's "man-planning heart" (*Ag.* 11); and Euripides' odd pleonastic phrase γυναιξὶ θηλείαις (*Or.*

153

1205) was most regularly associated in Homeric verse with reports given in Hades about Clytemnestra's shameful and wicked deeds (*Od.* 11.434, 24.202).[30] Soon, however, the allusions in *Orestes* revert to Sophocles' *Electra*, as the cries of Helen are heard within the house: Electra stands at the door, urging the murderers on (*Or.* 1297–310), presiding now at the slaughter of her aunt just as she had at the murder of her mother in Sophocles' play (*El.* 1398ff.).[31]

The Phrygian slave's lyric description of the attempted murder of Helen contains some of the traditional images listed above. It also includes the final specific allusions to the *Oresteia*; both refer to the third stasimon of the *Choephori*, sung after Clytemnestra and Aegisthus are dead. The word used so memorably by Aeschylus for the stricken House of Atreus, χαμαιπετεῖς (*Cho.* 964) is used by the Phrygian for the fallen Helen (*Or.* 1491). His description of Hermione's entry into the house is somewhat like a phrase from that stasimon (*Or.* 1490, *Cho.* 935–6); it closely echoes his earlier report of the entry of Orestes and Pylades as two lions: ἦλθον ἐς δόμους . . . λέοντες . . . δύο (*Or.* 1400–2). This, however, is nearly identical to the chorus' statement in Aeschylus: ἔμολε δ' ἐς δόμον . . . διπλοῦς λέων (*Cho.* 937–8) – the *Oresteia* has become so well-known that even a barbarian can quote from it.[32] Ultimately the tone of *Orestes* is maddeningly difficult to ascertain; whatever it is, it derives from Euripides' relentless mixture of dramatic tradition with wild innovations, and that art has been furthered and emphasized with a host of allusions and imitations to plays his audience would have found more familiar, and, one must think, more comprehensible than *Orestes*.

Dating Euripides' *Cyclops* depends partly on deciding whether or not it, like his *Orestes*, echoes the *Philoctetes*. Metrical criteria encourage the possibility: judiciously applied, they suggest a late date.[33] Now in the final line of *Cyclops*, before the chorus's closing couplet, the Cyclops pointedly notes that his cave has two entrances (707). As Paley noted, the adjective which means "open at both ends," ἀμφιτρής, occurs elsewhere in Greek only at *Philoctetes* 19 where it describes a cave of similar formation. The coincidence seems too involved to be coincidental, the description too carefully – almost obtrusively – placed to be accidental. It may even have been prepared for in the play's opening by referring to the cave as ἀμφίθυρον (*Cyc.* 60), another less exotic designation for the double opening also used for Philoctetes' cave (*Phil.* 159).[34]

In any case, the closing reference seems to create the ungrammaticality needed to spark the recognition of the allusion. Although this matter of the cave has not convinced everyone that *Cyclops* follows *Philoctetes*, there are other possible approaches. No one of them alone is conclusive; together they provide considerable support.[35]

First let us consider another of Euripides' borrowings in the *Cyclops* that has unquestionably been taken from Sophocles. It has always been recognized that the description of Cyclops eating two of Odysseus' men (*Cyc.* 396–405) is taken largely from *Odyssey* 9.289–92 where the Cyclops Polyphemus makes a similar meal. In both passages the Cyclops snatches two men and dashes their skulls open so that the brains flow out. Compare particularly the Homeric σὺν δὲ δύω μάρψας ὥς τε σκύλακας ποτὶ γαίη κόπτ'· ἐκ δ' ἐγκέφαλος χαμάδις ῥέε (*Od.* 9.289–90) with Euripides' φῶτε συμμάρψας δύο . . . παιὼν . . . ἐγκέφαλον ἐξέρρανε (*Cyc.* 397–402). Despite striking similarity, the passages differ in small details. In Euripides one of the unfortunate victims is dashed against a rock instead of the ground (401), and he has been snatched up by the ankle (400), something not mentioned at all in the *Odyssey*. Finally, the brains ooze out with a much rarer and more vivid verb in Euripides – ἐξέρρανε as opposed to the Homeric ἐκ . . . ῥέε. The only other certain occurrence of the Euripidean verb in all of extant Greek describes the oozing of Lichas' brains in Sophocles' *Trachiniae* (781). Like Odysseus' companion in *Cyclops*, he has been snatched at the ankle (779) – by Heracles of course, not a Cyclops – and dashed on a rock (780).

Euripides obviously owes these details to Sophocles. What is most interesting is that Sophocles himself was clearly using the Cyclops episode from *Odyssey* 9 in writing his passage on the fate of Lichas, as he in fact used it elsewhere in *Trachiniae*.[36] Euripides, it would seem, while writing an account in which he used *Odyssey* 9, thought of a Sophoclean use of that passage as well; we have found an audience of at least one Athenian who caught Sophocles' allusion. We have seen that *Philoctetes* also borrows from *Odyssey* 9, both in its general setting and with specific verbal echoes; and we have seen that Euripides, in the *Orestes*, uses the *Philoctetes*. Would it not be like Euripides to allude to both of these Sophoclean plays which use the very episode from the *Odyssey* that his entire play is based on? It cannot be proved, but combined with the arguments produced by others, the case for putting *Cyclops* in 408 B.C. and for hearing echoes of *Philoctetes* is quite strong.

Whenever *Cyclops* was produced, there is no argument about its frequent use of *Odyssey* 9.[37] Since Euripides follows the Homeric plot fairly closely, there are many inevitable parallels – the same objects must be named, the same events recounted. So words for flocks and goats and drinking cups (as well as many others) which occur only once in the Homeric poems recur here; there is the joke about Odysseus' name (*Cyc.* 548–51, *Od.* 9.355–70), which the Cyclops thinks is No One; and there is the realization that the old oracle has been fulfilled (*Cyc.* 696–700, *Od.* 9.507–21), another passage used by Sophocles in *Trachiniae*. There is not space here to consider all the details: more than one detailed study of the relationship between the two texts has been done. However, it is worth looking in detail at a few of Euripides' more significant adaptations.[38]

Sometimes, perhaps in the light spirit of the satyr play, Euripides seems to be joking with his allusions.[39] As Seaford points out, Odysseus' prediction of the Cyclops' disgusting belching in his sleep (*Cyc.* 591–2) is based on the actual event in the *Odyssey* (9.372–4) – as if Odysseus had read (or heard) the poem and knew it would happen. The most elegant and extended instance of such Euripidean adaptation centers on the similes in *Odyssey* 9 which describe the blinding of Polyphemus. The first simile likens the twirling of the stake in Polyphemus' eye to the work of shipwrights with their drill (*Od.* 9.383–6). Euripides repeats the simile, retaining the Homeric vocabulary, but as with the Cyclops' belch, we have Odysseus' rather poetic – and so perhaps even intentionally jarring – description of the future, of what he will do, rather than a narrative account of the blinding in progress (*Cyc.* 460–3). As with the final reference to the cave, the oddity here creates a gap, bridged by recalling the original narrative in the *Odyssey*. The next Homeric simile compares the sizzling of the eye to the sound of a smith tempering a hot iron ax or adze in cold water (*Od.* 9.391–4). But Euripides replaces that, as the chorus offers its help, with a related but different image; if Seaford is correct, the new image is of dipping a fire-brand in water at sacrifice. In any case, the second simile from the *Odyssey* has been incorporated not here with the first one, but later in *Cyclops*, when the satyrs gleefully anticipate the blinding and describe it as if the smith from the Homeric simile were going to do the blinding with his tongs (*Cyc.* 608–10). Finally, when at first the satyrs are bravely offering to help Odysseus with the drilling of the Cyclops' eye, they avow their readiness to lift a stake that would weigh as much as a hundred carts (*Cyc.* 473). This image has been given to them from an earlier point in the Homeric narrative: it would have taken twenty-two carts to move the rock Polyphemus used to seal his cave (*Od.* 9.241–2).

The nature of allusion and imitation in *Cyclops* is different from that in tragedy; it tends more to parody and satire, coming close to the art of Aristophanes at times. Still, it provides an important look at the way Euripides could take verse and rework it for his own ends. Moreover, with his borrowing from *Trachiniae*, it shows a tragic playwright aware, first, that another poet too has effectively used a specific scene from earlier poetry and, second, that Sophocles' allusive creation in turn could be drawn on in combination with the original. The work is deliberate, careful, complicated, and detailed – in short, what one would expect of an Athenian poet.

THEBAN TALES: *PHOENICIAN WOMEN*, *BACCHAE*, AND *OEDIPUS AT COLONUS*

These three plays form a less unified group than the heading they have been collected under might imply. Still, they are all connected with Thebes, they represent some of the last work of Euripides and Sophocles, and the Sophoclean play seems to contain at least passing echoes of both the Euripidean ones. There are no extended programs of allusions in these plays, but even the scattered examples reward examination. Euripides remains clever; Sophocles, in his allusions, achieves a graceful melancholy which seems both a continuation of the technique of the *Philoctetes* and a farewell to writing.

Critics have long seen *Phoenician Women* as Euripides' answer to Aeschylus' *Seven*, which tells much the same story. Some years earlier, Euripides had staged the sequel to these events in *Suppliant Women*, and the range of poetic imitations in that play and the *Phoenician Women* is very much the same. Besides predictable references to Aeschylus' *Seven* both Euripidean plays echo the

Agamemnon and perhaps Sophocles' Theban play *Antigone*. Further-more, both *Phoenician Women* and *Suppliant Women* use the same detail from a battle in the *Iliad*. The choruses in *Phoenician Women* elaborately cover the mythical history of Thebes with a scope suggestive of an Aeschylean tetralogy; however, just as with Sophocles' *Oedipus* plays, the most likely poetry for Euripides to have imitated in his lyrics is lost.[40] It is tempting to speculate that if we had the epic poems on Thebes or – especially since the influence of the *Seven* is so pervasive – Aeschylus' *Laius* and *Oedipus*, we could find significant allusions particularly in some of the play's striking strophic openings. As it is, out of the five choral songs in the play, a parodos and four stasima, only the first stasimon produces any echoes at all.[41] Otherwise virtually all the imitations in *Phoenician Women* occur in iambic trimeter, which would make it very like *Trachiniae*, except that there the echoes are generally more suggestive.

Just as with verbal coincidence in *Odyssey* 9 and *Cyclops*, it is sometimes difficult to determine which shared features of Aeschy-lus' *Seven* are pointedly repeated in *Phoenician Women* and which are merely a necessary consequence of retelling the same story. This, of course, is always a problem when tenor and vehicle are so nearly identical, when the ground is so massive that there is no perceptible gap. Capaneus' boast, for example, is probably a traditional element in the attack against Thebes (*Septem* 427–31, *Pho.* 1175–6).[42] So may be the city's towers, πυργώματα (*Septem* 30, 251, 469; *Pho.* 287).[43] Sometimes the rhythm of two lines seems close enough to suggest influence, as in παῦσαι πόνων με καὶ σὲ καὶ πᾶσαν πόλιν (*Pho.* 437) and αὐτὴ σὲ δουλοῖς κἀμὲ καὶ πᾶσαν πόλιν (*Septem* 254).[44] Eteocles' statement that it would be too tedious to list the opposing generals by name (*Pho.* 751) was seen by Didymus (if the scholiast is correct) as a direct criticism of the great catalogue in Aeschylus' *Seven* (375–652). Critics have by and large followed Didymus: after all, this is the sort of thing most people expect from Euripides.[45] Jebb, at least, commenting on *Oedipus at Colonus* 1116, saw the criticism here as one instance of a more widespread dramatic phenomenon, detecting in Sophocles' *Electra* (1289) and *Oedipus at Colonus* (1116) similar hits at earlier poetic verbosity.

More likely, Euripides alludes to the catalogue in the *Seven* to confuse his audience and achieve a greater effect later. Eteocles' words will be taken as a rejection of the catalogue, perhaps to the disappointment of an audience eagerly expecting a sequel that would surpass its original; this enables Euripides to give what he seemed to have taken away by including, in a later messenger speech, the very list Eteocles scorned (*Pho.* 1104ff.). Thus, this criticism of Aeschylus evaporates in exactly the same way as that in *Electra*, where the supposed criticism of the recognition scene in the *Choephori* was in fact merely a tactical move: it allowed Euripides to make the recognition seem to fail so that the audience would wonder what was going to happen instead.

Other parts of Aeschylus' *Seven* are adapted by Euripides without any suggestion of criticism whatsoever. For example, even as Eteocles declines to recite the Aeschylean catalogue, he declares that he will position himself opposite his own brother, closely paraphrasing his expression of the identical intention in Aeschylus' play (*Pho.* 755, *Septem* 672–3). Moreover, at the close of his speech in Euripides' play (*Pho.* 779–80) he again echoes his speech in Aeschylus' (*Septem* 675–6) with the call to bring his armor so that he can prepare for battle.

In *Phoenician Women* these references, Eteocles' echoes of his earlier role in the *Seven*, may be partially prepared for by the immediately preceding stasimon. Sophocles had made extensive use of the second stasimon from the *Seven* in his own second stasimon of *Antigone*, and he referred to it again in *Oedipus Rex*.[46] Likewise, Euripides chose to use the *Seven*'s second stasimon in his first stasimon of *Phoenician Women* (638–89): both his ode and Aeschylus' look back into the troubled past of the Theban royal family, and although Euripides' chorus dwells on more remote events, it takes image and phrase from the chorus of the *Seven*. Cadmus, Euripides' chorus sings, came and slew a dragon described as ὠμόφρων (*Pho.* 658). Then they call the killing in the first battle at Thebes (fought among the Spartoi when the dragon's teeth were sown) σιδαρόφρων (*Pho.* 672). Aeschylus' chorus, considering the Theban curse and the violence which threatened the city, had sung of ὠμόφρων σίδαρος (*Septem* 730). Moreover, they immediately describe Theban soil drinking the murderously spilt blood: γαῖα κόνις πίῃ μελαμπαγὲς αἷμα φοίνιον (*Septem* 736–7). Euripides' chorus, too, in speaking of iron-hearted slaughter, notes that the murder wets the Theban earth with blood: σιδαρόφρων δέ νιν φόνος πάλιν ξυνῆψε γᾷ φίλᾳ. αἵματος δ' ἔδευσε γαῖαν (*Pho.* 672–4). The adjective σιδηρόφρων was obviously suggested from earlier in the *Seven* (52); but the combination of vocabulary and content points to the passage from the second stasimon.[47] However, as with the borrowings in iambics, the lines seem more imitative than allusive.[48]

The echoes of Sophocles are similarly bland and sometimes additionally troubling in that they occur in passages which may not be genuine. In any case, they include a mention of the gold brooches with which Oedipus blinded himself (*Pho.* 61–2, *OT* 1268–9); the assurance to Oedipus that the speaker – Antigone in *Phoenician Women* (1555–6), Creon in *Oedipus Rex* (1422–3) – has no intention of mocking or chiding him in the midst of his sorrows; a series of small echoes and quotations from the prologue of *Antigone* (*Pho.* 1603, 1629–34; *Ant.* 26–30) on Polyneices' corpse; and finally, the moralizing trochaic tetrameter lines which sum up the catastrophe for Oedipus at the end of *Oedipus Rex* (1524–5) and of *Phoenician Women* (1758–9). These echoes, like those of Aeschylus' *Seven*, are all drawn from vehicles too similar to the tenor to provide any enrichment through comparison of contexts.

Three Homeric echoes deserve notice. The deaths of Eteocles and Polyneices are described at the close of the messenger's longer speech with a phrase borrowed from the *Iliad*: his γαῖαν δ' ὀδὰξ ἑλόντες (*Pho.* 1423) nearly repeats Achilles' γαῖαν ὀδὰξ εἷλον (*Il.* 22.17). The opening of *Iliad* 22 is one of the two parts of the Homeric poems most frequently alluded to in Greek poetry; even if it is not intended as an allusion here, it likely occurred to Euripides because Hecuba there sees her son die in a duel before the walls of the city, just as Jocasta has seen both her sons die at Thebes. An earlier messenger speech had described Thebans who fell in battle like tumblers diving headlong (*Pho.* 1148–52). This detail is the same one used by Euripides in the account of a battle in the closely related *Suppliants* (691–3) where, as here, it is taken from a simile at *Iliad* 16.742–50. The subsequent messenger speech again uses the language of the *Iliad* passage to describe a rock used as a missile, exactly repeating the phrase μάρμαρον πέτρον (*Pho.* 1401, *Il.* 16.734–5) which appears to occur nowhere else in extant Greek.[49] This added detail shows that Euripides was not simply reintroducing the tumblers from *Suppliants* without reference to the original source; he must have consulted the Homeric passage again, this time coming away with an additional phrase.

Despite its formal archaizing, the *Bacchae* has even fewer echoes of earlier poetry than does *Phoenician Women*. The imitations of Bacchylides and *Persians* were mentioned above. Virtually all the other echoes are concentrated in one messenger speech. The one exception combines two common tendencies in Euripidean and Sophoclean allusion: it is an echo of the *Oresteia*, and it has been placed at the beginning of a metrical refrain (similar to the placement at the beginning of strophe or antistrophe).[50] The refrain for the fourth stasimon is a call for Justice to come with its sword to slash the neck of the lawless and godless Pentheus:

ἴτω δίκα φανερός, ἴτω ξιφηφόρος
φονεύουσα λαιμῶν διαμπὰξ
τὸν ἄθεον ἄνομον ἄδικον Ἐχίονος
γόνον γηγενῆ.

(991–6)

The adjective "sword-bearing" may well have been coined by Aeschylus to describe the justice Orestes brought to Clytemnestra (*Cho.* 584). Certainly Euripides had used the Aeschylean line before in *Hercules Furens* (812, cf.730). Although Euripides uses the adjective elsewhere, there are two additional reasons for seeing direct influence of the *Oresteia* here. First, the vengeance in *Choephori* is exacted on the mother by her son, and in *Bacchae* it will be Pentheus' mother who, unwittingly, carries out the justice. Second, as the chorus of *Bacchae* continues it gives as the reason for Pentheus' outrageous behavior παρακόπῳ . . . λήματι (1000), his "frenzied will." The adjective παράκοπος is extremely rare, but it is used to describe madness in the refrain of the Furies' Binding Song in the *Eumenides* (329, 342). Moreover, Euripides may have been influenced by the use of the noun παρακοπή to describe the state of mind which led Agamemnon to sacrifice Iphigeneia (*Ag.* 223). The opening of the refrain, then, implies both by allusion and by collusion (with the fitting parallel of *Agamemnon* 223) that the justice called for in this stasimon may well be the savage familial sort found in the *Choephori*.

Like so many tragic messenger speeches (see Appendix D), the one in *Bacchae* which reports Pentheus' dismemberment (*Bacch.* 1043–152) has been highly wrought and ornamented with echoes of earlier poetry. As Dodds noted, Pentheus' pine tree reaching to heaven (1064–5) seems a reminiscence of an equally tall pine at *Odyssey* 5.239. A more important epic model for Pentheus' spying in the pine tree, also noted by Dodds, is the deception of Zeus in the *Iliad* during which Sleep climbs into a pine tree. Pentheus' ascent, his sitting down on the branches, and the extreme height of the tree all recall specific phrases from the Homeric passage (*Bacch.* 1061, 1070, 1073; *Il.* 14.286–91). Euripides has obviously modeled one carefully prepared deception on another. Yet another echo in this narrative recalls the defiant speech made by Clytemnestra just after murdering Agamemnon (Aesch. *Ag.* 1372–98), a speech alluded to by Euripides in *Orestes* and by Sophocles in *Ajax*, *Antigone*, *Trachiniae*, and *Electra*. The Euripidean messenger chooses an odd phrase to say that Pentheus was sitting out of reach of the women who wanted to destroy him: κρεῖσσον γὰρ ὕψος τῆς προθυμίας ἔχων καθῆσθ' ὁ τλήμων (1101–2). The awkward expression triggers the allusion to its more appropriate use in a vivid metaphor (one of the trilogy's many net images) with which Clytemnestra explains her entrapment of Agamemnon: how else, she asks, could one fence harm's nets to a height too great to jump over (πῶς γάρ τις . . . πημονῆς ἀρκύστατ' ἂν φράξειεν ὕψος κρεῖσσον ἐκπηδή-ματος, *Ag.* 1374–6)? Dodds thought the echo might be unconscious; it seems more likely that the situation of Pentheus, entrapped and doomed to die at the hands of a female relative, led Euripides to think of Clytemnestra's often-used words and appropriate them, at the very least, for collusion.

The final Theban play to consider is Sophocles' last, *Oedipus at Colonus*. For all its length, it contains few poetic echoes, perhaps partly as a function of its style, which is often similar to that of *Philoctetes*. However, the play stands out somewhat because for once there are a number of apparent borrowings from plays of the recently deceased Euripides, as if Sophocles, grieving for his fellow poet, inscribed this play on death and old age with commemorative phrases composed by Euripides himself. Two of these echoes are from *Phoenician Women*, which, after all, shares much the same cast of characters and events with this *Oedipus*. Thus, when Polyneices enters with the cry of what to do and who to grieve for, his words nearly repeat those of Creon in Euripides' play. Compare:

οἴμοι, τί δράσω; πότερ' ἐμαυτὸν ἢ πόλιν
στένω δακρύσας . . .

Pho. 1310–11

Alas, what should I do? Should I weep and
bewail myself or the city . . .

οἴμοι, τί δράσω; πότερα τἀμαυτοῦ κακὰ
πρόσθεν δακρύσω . . .

OC 1254–5

Alas, what should I do? Should I weep
for my own ills first . . .

Once this disastrous meeting with Oedipus is over, Polyneices, now under his father's fatal curse, departs for Thebes to meet certain death, προῦπτον "Αιδην (OC 1440). The only other time the phrase is voiced in extant Greek is by Hippolytus, who sees the certain death which has come from his own father's curse (προῦπτον ἐς "Αιδην, Hipp. 1366).[51] Antigone's attempt to keep her brother from returning to Thebes begins just as does Jocasta's plea to Eteocles not to enter the same battle in *Phoenician Women*: μὴ σύ γε, the women say to these brothers (Pho. 532, OC 1441).

Sophocles' most extensive use of Euripides, as Dodds saw, was to take material from a messenger speech in the *Bacchae* and incorporate it into a messenger speech in *Oedipus at Colonus*. Sophocles' model is precisely that messenger speech in *Bacchae* which contains so many poetic echoes itself, and the lines Sophocles chose to imitate come immediately after Euripides' extensive imitation of the Deception of Zeus in *Iliad* 14 (*Bacch.* 1061–73). Both passages (*Bacch.* 1078–90, OC 1621–9) come at the moment when the fates of the plays' main figures, Pentheus and Oedipus, are determined. Both concentrate on details of sound and silence: stillness (*Bacch.* 1084, σίγησε δ' αἰθήρ; OC 1623, ἦν μὲν σιωπή), a voice (*Bacch.* 1078, φωνή τις; OC 1623, φθέγμα . . . τινός), and an unvoiced cry (*Bacch.* 1085, οὐκ ἂν ἤκουσας βοήν; OC 1622, οὐδ' ἔτ' ὠρώρει βοή). Both have the instant of sudden recognition of the supernatural – ὡς δ' ἐγνώρισαν σαφῆ κελευσμὸν Βακχίου (*Bacch.* 1088–9), ὁ δ' ὡς ἐπήσθετ' ἐκ θεοῦ καλούμενος (OC 1629). And, as Dodds pointed out, the greatest indication that

Sophocles has used the *Bacchae* is an echo that has nothing to do with sense or the situation: ἔστησαν ὀρθαί (*Bacch.* 1087) in Euripides is the women of Thebes; in Sophocles ὀρθίας στῆσαι (*OC* 1624–5) is the hair of the astounded witnesses. The miracle of Oedipus' death echoes the miracle of Pentheus'; Sophocles' messenger speech alludes to the Euripidean messenger speech which itself had carefully used epic and Aeschylus; it is the compliment of one old poet to another who reached death's threshold first.

Echoes of Aeschylus' *Seven against Thebes* are to be expected in a Theban play. Polyneices' list of the seven generals includes the adjective δορυσσός (*OC* 1313) just as the mention of them did in Aeschylus (*Septem* 125). Calling Thebes ὠγύγιοι (*OC* 1770) might be a nod at Aeschylus' use of that word for Thebes at *Septem* 321. But the most likely borrowing is the figurative use of γῆρας in speaking of "anger's old age" (*OC* 954–5) much as Aeschylus had used it to speak of "this pollution's old age" (*Septem* 681–2). The aged Sophocles may have paid special attention to Aeschylus' unusual use of the word.

None of the echoes cited so far is from a lyric section of *Oedipus at Colonus*. There are, however, two, both concerned with death, both placed at the beginning of strophic sections. In the first, at the opening of the antistrophe in the third stasimon (1224–8), the chorus says that the best thing is never to have been born (μὴ φῦναι), but once born, the second best thing by far is to return to where one came from as quickly as possible (ὡς τάχιστα). Bacchylides wrote some very similar lines (5.160), but, as Jebb noted, they only express the first of this Sophoclean chorus's thoughts. The full maxim, however familiar it may have been, occurs elsewhere only at Theognis 425–8. Best not to have been born (μὴ φῦναι), he says, and after birth to pass through the gates of Hades as soon as possible (ὅπως ὤκιστα). At this point in *Oedipus at Colonus* the scholiast quoted the lines from Theognis, and Jebb thought that the Sophoclean form indicated "that Sophocles was thinking of the verses" (*ad OC* 1225). This echo may even linger on into Sophocles' next imitation at the opening of the fourth stasimon. There the chorus opens with an invocation of Persephone and Hades (*OC* 1556–60), their call to the latter, ἐννυχίων ἄναξ Αἰδωνεῦ, modeled on the Homeric ἄναξ ἐνέρων Ἀϊδωνεύς (*Il.* 20.61) where the God of the Underworld actually fears that Poseidon's earthquake will rend the earth and expose the dank destination of every mortal.[52] In these final Sophoclean echoes and imitations of earlier poetry, the somber tone seems to reflect the thoughts of the aged tragedian as he approached the time when he would finally stop writing and join Homer, Theognis, Aeschylus, and Euripides for all time.

TROY AND THE HOUSE OF ATREUS

Four Euripidean plays remain to be considered – *Trojan Women*, *Helen, Iphigeneia among the Taurians*, and *Iphigeneia at Aulis*. All deal in some way with Agamemnon, Menelaus, Iphigeneia, and Helen. All, as discussed above, have reference to Bacchylides' poetry. However, the single most frequent source of imitation for these plays is *Agamemnon*. As in the case of Euripides' *Orestes*, it is often difficult to distinguish between specific allusions and general reference to what have become traditional elements of the legend or traditional images associated with it. Some additional features linking some of these plays have long been noticed, such as the extensive similarities in both plot and diction between *Helen* and *Iphigeneia among the Taurians*. These two plays also show a persistent tendency to place allusions and echoes at strophic beginnings or ends, a technique seen frequently in earlier plays, and also used, though less often, in *Trojan Women* and *Iphigeneia at Aulis*.

The epic phrase which served as Euripides' emblem for the fall of Troy and the fate of its women was δούλιον ἦμαρ, the day of slavery which Hector envisioned for Andromache (*Il.* 6.463). Euripides had included it in both *Andromache* (99) and *Hecuba* (56), and in *Trojan Women* Hecuba laments this fate as well with the slightly varied δούλειον ἀμέραν (1330).[53] However Euripides' main efforts in allusion are concentrated on the Cassandra scene in Aeschylus' *Agamemnon*. In particular he has taken two of her speeches (*Ag.* 1214–41 and 1256–94) to use as models for both Hecuba and Cassandra in the early parts of *Trojan Women*. Paley claimed that Cassandra's first long speech (*Tro.* 353–405) was "composed with reference" to the scene in *Agamemnon*, and its continuation (*Tro.* 424–61) also reflects Aeschylean influence. Among other things, Euripides' Cassandra predicts many of the events of *Agamemnon* and *Choephori*, including some that Aeschylus' Cassandra had foreseen in her speeches. But since much of the story was common property of Greek legend, not all the details in *Trojan Women* can be taken as echoes of the speeches in *Agamemnon*. So, for example, although Paley took the Euripidean Cassandra's statement that she would not sing of the axe (*Tro.* 361) as a criticism of mentions of the axe and chopping-block in *Agamemnon* (e.g. 1277), the reference is probably more general. Not only is the axe a feature of the murder of Clytemnestra in *Choephori* (889), it is recalled vividly by Sophocles' Electra (*El.* 99) and mentioned most frequently of all in Euripides' *Electra* (*El.* 160, 279, 1160).

Some details from the lines of Aeschylus' Cassandra, however, certainly appear in *Trojan Women*. The news that she will be carried off as Agamemnon's possession means to Euripides' Cassandra that any meaningful service as Apollo's priestess is at an end. So, for example, both her action of discarding the clothing associated with her religious office and the words she uses as she does so have been modeled on the gesture and speech of her Aeschylean counterpart. In *Agamemnon* Cassandra disrobes with the dismissive ἴτ' ἐς φθόρον (*Ag.* 1267); in *Trojan Women* the accompanying words are ἴτ' ἀπ' ἐμοῦ χρωτός (*Tro.* 453). Euripides has even prepared for this allusive moment, having Hecuba react to the news of Cassandra's fate by exclaiming that her daughter should rip off her priestly tokens (*Tro.* 256–8).[54] Yet another feature of the Aeschylean speech shows up when Euripides' Hecuba lists her misfortunes. The last, she says, is that she will go to Greece as a slave, and this is the copestone of the evils (*Tro.* 489–90). Euripides had borrowed the rare metaphor from *Agamemnon* for use in *Hercules Furens* (1280–4). Here in *Trojan Women* the context of the original model is more relevant: Aeschylus' Cassandra follows the list of evils she and Agamemnon must endure with the assurance that Orestes will give the copestone of ruin to it all (*Ag.* 1283).[55] As soon as Hecuba has finished the speech in which she lists her woes (*Tro.* 466–510), the chorus sings, and the final words of their first strophe are yet another echo of *Agamemnon*. They call the ruin of Troy achieved with the Wooden Horse δόλιον . . . ἄταν (*Tro.* 530), a phrase used by Aeschylus' Clytemnestra (δόλιαν ἄτην, *Ag.* 1523) shortly after carrying out the murder of Agamemnon and Cassandra just as Cassandra foresaw.[56] For Paley, the comparison of Euripides' Cassandra to Aeschylus' Cassandra, suggested by the echoes in *Trojan Women*, worked to the disadvantage of the younger playwright: Cassandra's scene in *Agamemnon* was far more brilliant.

But the judgement is based on incomplete evidence, for Cassandra's scene in *Trojan Women* could only be evaluated artistically in light of the trilogy's first two plays, *Alexander* and *Palamedes*. If we could read those two plays first, the scope of the tragedy of Troy and the impact of Cassandra might compete better with Aeschylus' conception.[57]

Helen is a more playful look at the legends of Troy. Willink has recently drawn attention to Euripides' long fascination with Helen, apparent even with only a fraction of his plays surviving. In *Helen* Euripides tells a story which exonerates Helen from charges of frivolous adultery with Paris: she has been in Egypt throughout the war, the Helen at Troy a mere phantom. This was not a Euripidean innovation introduced for the purpose of clearing Helen's name: Stesichorus had done something like this long before. Thus, Whitman saw a natural allusion to a Stesichorean palinode in the Euripidean Helen's lament.[58] She calls to the Sirens, winged maidens – πτεροφόροι νεάνιδες, παρθένοι (*Hel.* 167–8) – with words that echo Stesichorus' opening vocative χρυσόπτερε παρθένε (*PMG* 193). Moreover, Euripides has placed the echo in the first and second lines of the strophe, the expected place. If we had Stesichorus' full description of the wedding of Helen and Menelaus (cf. *PMG* 187), we might well see it connected with the references to that ceremony by Euripides' Menelaus (*Hel.* 639–41) and the messenger (*Hel.* 725), as Dale suspected.[59] In addition to the Stesichorean opening of Helen's lament, her mention of plains sounding with horses' hoofs, ἱππόκροτα (*Hel.* 207), may reflect a recent Euripidean reading of Pindar's *Pythia* 5, where a road is ἱππόκροτος (5.92), and Helen is in North Africa with Menelaus on his wanderings after the war.[60] But Helen's most obvious allusion to earlier poems about her comes in her prologue with the reference to the many souls who died on her account at Troy, a repetition of the opening of the *Iliad* (ψυχαὶ δὲ πολλαί, *Hel.* 52; πολλὰς . . . ψυχάς, *Il.* 1.3).

When Menelaus and Helen plan their escape from Egypt, the poetic imitations and references begin to have, as they will for the remainder of the play, more varied sources. Helen's scheme calls for an announcement of Menelaus' death, an ominous thing to put in words but worth doing for the gain it will bring (*Hel.* 1049–52). The plan itself and Menelaus' evaluation of the bad and good in it recall the plan for Orestes' feigned death and his willingness to die in words for the sake of gain in Sophocles' *Electra* (cf. *Hel.* 1050–1, κερδανῶ . . . θανὼν λόγῳ; *El.* 59–61, λόγῳ θανὼν . . . κέρδει). And just in case the audience might miss the fact that the plan is no tragic innovation, Euripides' Menelaus calls attention to the fact by commenting that the whole thing seems a bit stale (*Hel.* 1056).[61] The scene closes with Helen's prayer, a typical Euripidean mixture of elements, sophistic in its preoccupation with the contrast between ὄνομα and σῶμα (1100), then immediately traditional with a request to Aphrodite modeled on a prayer of Ajax's in the *Iliad*. In the battle for Helen at Troy, Ajax had prayed to Zeus at least to give the Greeks light to die in if he intended to destroy them (*Il.* 17.645–7); Helen echoes this by asking Aphrodite to let her die in her native land if the goddess intends to kill her (1101–2).[62]

The remaining poetic imitations in *Helen*, all contained in the play's three stasima, reflect a remarkable range of sources, from epic and epinician to tragedy and even, for once, comedy. Helen's prayer is immediately followed by the long delayed first stasimon (1107–64). If Helen opened her monody with a call for a group of winged Sirens to help her mourn, the chorus, conversely, now calls for only a single co-mourner, the proverbial tearful nightingale. Paley declared that their description of the bird was "so familiarly applied" and Dale that it was "so much of a cliché" that the similarity of *Helen* 1110–11 to Aristophanes' *Birds* 213–14 was not remarkable. But the verb ἐλελίζω occurs nowhere else in extant Greek either with the word used for the nightingale's throat (γένυς, "jaw") or with the adjective "trilling" (ξουθός), much less with both together. So Euripides' ξουθᾶν γενύων ἐλελιζομένα must be modeled directly on Aristophanes' ἐλελιζομένη . . . γένυος ξουθῆς, particularly since both are dramatic invocations of the mournful nightingale; Aristophanes' poetry need not be too low to imitate simply because it occurs in comedy. To be sure, the tone of the first stasimon is serious, even – given the general tone of *Helen* – surprisingly somber. The chorus reflects on Helen, her marriage to Paris, and the deaths caused by the Trojan War, and both the general tone and the specific phrasing of their thoughts recall portions of the first and second stasima in the *Agamemnon*. The last lines of the first strophe (1117–21) tell of Paris and Helen sailing to Troy and the grief Paris brought to his city, repeating many of the images of *Agamemnon* 681ff., especially 700–16. And even if Euripides' Πάρις αἰνόγαμος (*Hel.* 1120) and Aeschylus' Πάριν τὸν αἰνόλεκτρον (*Ag.* 712) stem from a common tradition of compounds in αἰνο- used for Paris and Helen, the last words of Euripides' strophe, as Fraenkel saw, are a variation of the end of Aeschylus' third strophe.[63] Compare Πριαμίδαισιν πομπᾷ Διὸς ξενίου (*Ag.* 747–8) and Πριαμίδαις . . . πομπαῖσιν ᾿Αφροδίτας (*Hel.* 1118–21). The antistrophe continues with a list of ways the Greeks involved with Troy have perished, considering too the wives' grief (*Hel.* 1122–36). The content is much like that of *Agamemnon* 437ff. where Ares the Exchanger sends ashes back to Greek women in place of their husbands' bodies. The resemblance is more specific when the Euripidean chorus, in their final antistrophe, summon up the cost of war with mention of those Greeks who rest at Troy. As Dale says, Πριαμίδος γᾶς ἔλαχον θαλάμους (*Hel.* 1158) is "probably a direct reminiscence of the unforgettable" words of Aeschylus' chorus: οἱ δ᾿ αὐτοῦ περὶ τεῖχος θήκας ᾿Ιλιάδος γᾶς εὔμορφοι κατέχουσιν· ἐχθρὰ δ᾿ ἔχοντας ἔκρυψεν (*Ag.* 453–5). With this the darkness of *Helen* ends.

In the second and third stasima of *Helen*, the Homeric poems and Bacchylides provide all the echoes.[64] The Bacchylidean echoes have been examined above in the introduction to the chapter, but there is another remarkable feature to note about them. An echo of *Agamemnon* in the last stasimon was placed at strophe end. Likewise, the most striking of the three Bacchylidean phrases in this ode – "Zeus decreed another fate" – occurs at the end of the first strophe (*Hel.* 1318), and another comes at the end of the second strophe (1351–2). Since the Homeric phrase πένθει . . . ἀλάστῳ has been placed at the close of the first antistrophe (1337), only the second antistrophe lacks a poetic echo at its close, and there the text is quite corrupt.[65] If the "unforgettable grief" (1337) refers to its only occurrence in the *Iliad* (πένθος ἄλαστον, 24.105), it may help make the reference in *Helen* clearer. At *Iliad* 24.105, Thetis grieves for her child Achilles; in this ode Demeter sorrows for the loss of her daughter. The echo of the *Iliad* will help reinforce one of the themes which ties this difficult ode to the play: Helen is concerned with her child Hermione, who is mentioned before and after this ode (*Hel.* 688, 1476).

Finally, the placement of poetic echo at strophe beginning or end, so pervasive in *Helen*, can be detected in the third stasimon as well. Again, the Bacchylidean echoes have been discussed earlier. But the opening of the second strophe contains a description of the cranes of Libya modeled on the great simile at the beginning of *Iliad* 3 where it described the noise of the Trojan army readying for battle, an army to which the image no longer could apply since the Greeks had destroyed it (*Hel.* 1478ff., *Il.* 3.3ff.).

Both *Helen* and *Iphigeneia among the Taurians* are set in exotic places with foreign customs, both reunite loved ones long parted, and in both, a woman who before the Trojan War was whisked away from Greece by divine translation engineers an escape from a barbarian ruler. Many verbal similarities link the plays, even in minute detail such as drawing on the same passage from Bacchylides 17 for echoes to place at strophe end.[66] If *Helen* provided occasion to glance at Aeschylus' *Agamemnon*, this *Iphigeneia*, written a year or two earlier, repeatedly demands comparison with the *Oresteia*. Verrall saw a Euripides engaged here in literary battle with Aeschylus, but the younger tragedian is rather more engaged in cat and mouse.[67]

Just as Euripides alluded to Aeschylus' *Choephori* in his own *Electra* and to *Seven against Thebes* in *Phoenician Women* not so much to satirize or criticize as to create suspense, so in this *Iphigeneia* the references to the *Oresteia*, especially *Agamemnon*, trigger a series of associations which heighten the tension of the plot. This is most true in the opening scene, where Euripides achieves his effect with statements made first by Iphigeneia, then Orestes, and finally the chorus. Iphigeneia's opening speech explains her presence at the gruesome Tauric temple of Artemis. Detailing her duties, she hesitates at explicit mention of human sacrifice and, fearing the goddess (as she explains), simply says: τὰ δ' ἄλλα σιγῶ (*IT* 37). The words are an exact quotation from the Watchman's prologue in *Agamemnon* (36). He has well-founded misgivings about the management of the house; his mistress will require the death of her returning husband. Will Artemis, in Euripides' play, require her servant Iphigeneia to kill her brother Orestes? The daughter would indeed be like the mother.

The danger to Orestes is made to seem more real by allusions which liken him to his father Agamemnon. Clytemnestra, in a speech which at once greeted her husband and chastized his long absence, had called him the pillar of the roof, στέγης στῦλον (*Ag.* 897–8), one of a series of images for the salvation of the house. The only other occurrence of στῦλος in this metaphor in classical Greek is in Iphigeneia's prologue (*IT* 50–7). After explaining her identity and occupation, she relates a dream she has just had: living again in Argos she was awakened by an earthquake, ran outside, and saw the house fall with only a pillar remaining. In her interpretation of the dream the pillar must be Orestes, for male children are the pillars of the house.[68] This metaphor is not the only image which connects Orestes and Agamemnon across the separate plays: at the sight of the temple, Orestes exclaims in shock at the "net" Apollo has led him into (*IT* 77), recalling the Aeschylean nets which so famously describe the death of Agamemnon.

To make matters more ominous, Euripides has also set the events of this *Iphigeneia* in motion in ways which associate Iphigeneia with Clytemnestra. First there is her dream (*IT* 42–60) which raises questions of Orestes and causes her to want to give libations. The circumstance and her response both seem contrived with special reference to Clytemnestra's dream and reaction at the opening of the *Choephori*. And further, the chorus, coming at Iphigeneia's call, speaks in ways which have been suggested by the arrival of the chorus in *Agamemnon*. In Aeschylus' play the old men ask what is wrong and what Clytemnestra has seen or heard: τί χρέος; τί νέον; τί δ᾽ ἐπαισθομένη (*Ag.* 85). Likewise in *Iphigeneia* the chorus asks, τί νέον; τίνα φροντίδ᾽ ἔχεις (*IT* 137). Moreover, in identifying Iphigeneia as Agamemnon's daughter, they refer to his fleet with the same word used by Aeschylus' old men on their arrival – and used nowhere else (χιλιοναύτης, *Ag.* 45, *IT* 141).

As so often, further echoes are delivered in a messenger speech; in *Iphigeneia* the speaker is the herdsman, who brings the first report of Orestes and Pylades (*IT* 260–339). He quotes Orestes who described the Furies to Pylades as "terrible vipers" – δειναῖς ἐχίδναις (*IT* 287). The direct reference is to Aeschylus' *Choephori*, for δεινῆς ἐχίδνης is exactly what Orestes called Clytemnestra there (*Cho.* 249). This allusion has further interest because Sophocles had effectively referred to the same Aeschylean passage with one of his many echoes of *Choephori* in the *Trachiniae*. Moreover, Euripides had noticed Sophocles' borrowing from Aeschylus when he borrowed a different phrase from the same passage of *Trachiniae* to use in his *Hercules Furens* (see above pp. 106–7, 109 and 116). Finally, this allusion matches the procedure Euripides would follow a few years later when, in his *Cyclops*, he would borrow both from *Odyssey* 9 and from the passage of Sophocles' *Trachiniae* which was modeled on *Odyssey* 9.

The herdsman's next echo comes from the *Eumenides*. As he continues with his direct quotation of the conversation he has heard between Orestes and Pylades there is more description of the Furies. This time it is their fiery bloody breath (*IT* 288), and this time the image has been taken from the words of Clytemnestra's ghost, urging the same Furies to pursue her son (*Eum.* 137–8).[69] Finally, the herdsman reports Orestes' insane attack on the cattle he mistakes for Furies and the bloodying of the ocean by the shore. It was as if the sea bloomed out in blood, he says (*IT* 300); the puzzling over-poetic exaggeration triggers the recognition that it has been imported from the *Agamemnon* where it more naturally described the corpse-filled sea which faced Orestes' father after the wreck of the fleet (*Ag.* 659). The herdsman's allusions are not as concertedly ominous as those in the opening, but after all, the play is to take a very positive turn eventually. Orestes will not die at his sister's hands, and as the threat of a grotesque variation of a family bloodbath disappears, the allusions to the *Oresteia* do as well.

The story of *Iphigeneia at Aulis*, as told by Euripides, covers one of the great crises in Greek mythological history. The Greeks are gathered at Aulis, but unless their fleet sets sail, there will be no Trojan War; unless Agamemnon sacrifices his daughter Iphigeneia, there will be no setting forth from Aulis. And so the death of Iphigeneia is the prerequisite without which none of the events of the *Iliad* or the *Oresteia* could take place. Writing at the end of the fifth century, Euripides was able to exploit a long established tradition of dramatic composition: the *Iliad*, known by every educated Athenian, had long been used as a source for the poetry of tragedy; the *Oresteia* had been more alluded to by Sophocles and Euripides over the decades than any other dramatic work we know of. Almost certain to be recognized, Euripides' allusions to the *Iliad* and *Oresteia* in *Iphigeneia at Aulis* create a dizzying double movement, simultaneously looking backward to the masterworks of the epic and tragic poetic traditions and forward to events which would stem from the actions of the play. True, the technique had

been used at least as long ago as Aeschylus' *Agamemnon*, where the
omen reported from before the Trojan War is so constructed as to
be fulfilled by a passage in the *Iliad*. But Euripides expands this
technique so that phrase after phrase borrowed from earlier Greek
poetry becomes an omen certain of fulfillment thanks to Euripides'
position at the end of the poetic tradition.

The earlier echoes in *Iphigeneia* look forward to its immediate
sequel, the Trojan War as told in the *Iliad*.[70] For example, the old
servant's opening description of Agamemnon crying, θαλερὸν
κατὰ δάκρυ χέων (*IA* 39–40), pairs the Greek general with
Hector's wife Andromache, whose tears (θαλερὸν κατὰ
δάκρυ χέουσα, *Il.* 6.496) are a direct result of the war
Agamemnon and Menelaus bring to Troy.[71] The parodos provides
excellent opportunity for epic tone as the chorus describes the
Greek army which has assembled for Troy. There are general
echoes of the catalogue in the second book of the *Iliad*, such as
Ἄρεος ὄζον (*IA* 201–2; cf. ὄζος Ἄρηος, *Il.* 2.540, 704,
745, and 842). And there is one specific borrowing, almost a
"correct reference" to information from that catalogue: Nireus is
the fairest of the Greeks (*IA* 204–5, *Il.* 2.673). Even such a simple
borrowing is placed at the end of the strophe where more evocative
ones would often go. Later in the play Achilles makes a confident
declaration of the ease with which he can acquire a wife, a boast
which he will have occasion to repeat later at Troy. He is not
concerned, he explains to Clytemnestra, that Agamemnon's
dishonesty is robbing him of the promised wedding to Iphigeneia,
for countless girls seek his bed (*IA* 959–60). In the *Iliad*, when the
embassy brings Achilles what would seem to be a more sincere
offer from Agamemnon of one of his daughters to marry, Achilles
will again explain that he can have any he wishes of many Greek
girls (*Il.* 9.395).[72] In light of the Euripidean echo, the rejection of
the offer in the *Iliad* is not surprising – after the events at Aulis it
would be enough to anger a calmer man than Achilles. That
passage of the *Iliad* which has figured in every chapter of this book,
Hector's last scene before the walls of Troy in *Iliad* 22, may be used
here as well. *Iphigeneia*'s request to her father to pity her
(αἴδεσαι μέ, *IA* 1246) might just recall Hecuba's plea to her
son (αἴδεο καὶ μ' ἐλέησον, *Il.* 22.82): no lines are more
frequently alluded to in extant tragedy. There is, however, an even
more likely model in the *Oresteia*. Having come to the end of epic

allusions in *Iphigeneia*, we can now turn to Euripides' exploitation of Aeschylus.

The chorus in *Agamemnon* looks back to the events leading to the sacrifice of Iphigeneia, from the initial omen up to the last moment before her death at the altar (*Ag.* 104–59, 184–249). This account provided the logical beginning for Euripides' series of allusions to the *Oresteia*. Euripides' Agamemnon makes the initial reference, speaking of the yoke of necessity (ἀνάγκης ζεύγματα, *IA* 443), and then simply the necessity (*IA* 511), which requires him to sacrifice his daughter. Aeschylus' chorus described Agamemnon's decision with just the same image – ἀνάγκας . . . λέπαδνον (*Ag.* 218). They describe the preliminary rites for the sacrifice as προτέλεια (*Ag.* 227), and before Euripides' Clytemnestra understands exactly what the ritual will be, she too refers to it this way (*IA* 718). Once she learns of Agamemnon's plan, however, she speaks of his savagery and willingness to dare anything, echoing the same lines from *Agamemnon* which describe Agamemnon's state of mind (πάντολμα, *IA* 913; παντότολμον, *Ag.* 221).[73] Since these echoes, all four deriving from a few lines of *Agamemnon*, all describe the same events in both plays, the original context neither adds to nor changes their tone in Euripides. Instead they serve to point toward the *Agamemnon* so that further echoes can do more complicated work.

The remaining allusions in *Iphigeneia* all look forward in the story of Agamemnon's family to events which will take place after the Trojan War in Aeschylus' *Agamemnon*, *Choephori*, and *Eumenides*. Twice in Euripides' play when Agamemnon is addressing Clytemnestra on the subject of Iphigeneia, once before and once after his true intentions are known, he calls his wife Λήδας γένεθλον (*IA* 686 and 1106). These are the first two words he will speak directly to her when he returns from the war years later, just moments before she avenges her daughter's death by murdering him (*Ag.* 914). The allusion makes his words in *Iphigeneia* a signal of the death he will bring on himself by going through with his plan. In similar fashion Achilles describes Clytemnestra even at this early date as "suffering at the hands of those dearest to her" (παθοῦσα πρὸς τῶν φιλτάτων, *IA* 932) – the very thing Clytemnestra's ghost will say of itself after considerable further family trouble (παθοῦσα . . . πρὸς τῶν φιλτάτων, *Eum.* 100).[74]

Next come two short speeches with phrasing which will be repeated at Agamemnon's return from Troy. The first is Clytemnestra's thanks to Achilles. She wonders how to praise him without exceeding or falling short of the mark in χάρις (*IA* 977ff.), commenting on general human custom. All these features are repeated in the chorus' address to Agamemnon in Aeschylus (*Ag.* 787ff.).[75] Again, Clytemnestra, revealing to Agamemnon that she knows of his plans to sacrifice Iphigeneia, says she will reveal her own meaning and no longer speak in riddles (*IA* 1146–7); her language is echoed closely by Cassandra, shortly before Clytemnestra kills her, when she removes the veils from her own statements and speaks, like Clytemnestra, no longer in riddles (*Ag.* 1178–83).[76] Iphigeneia's plea to Agamemnon (*IA* 1246, quoted above) finds its future fulfillment not in the *Agamemnon* but in *Choephori* when, instead of daughter pleading with father for life, mother pleads with son, using the same imperative – since Euripides has allusively borrowed it (αἴδεσαι, *Cho.* 896). Once again, Iphigeneia's plea in Euripides becomes the pregnant hint at the long series of family murders to follow.

Iphigeneia at Aulis contains one more allusion to the *Agamemnon*, emphasized by being placed not once but twice at the beginning of a long lyric period, in the words first of Iphigeneia and then of the chorus (*IA* 1476, 1511). Both times Iphigeneia is called ἑλέπτολις because her sacrifice will lead to the taking of Troy. The use of the word is jarring: armies of men take cities; Iphigeneia is a helpless girl. This apparently deviant usage triggers the recognition of the proper vehicle, a much more powerful woman – Helen; for so Aeschylus had more naturally described her in the memorable stasimon which began with the reflections on her name ('Ελέναν . . . πρεπόντως ἑλένας, ἕλανδρος, ἑλέπτολις, *Ag.* 687–90), a passage Euripides had imitated much earlier in his career in describing Medea. In *Iphigeneia* this is Euripides' last reminder of the way this action leads to that of the *Iliad* and of the *Oresteia*. But from our perspective it is a final emblem of the poetic interconnections which make the reading of Greek poetry so complicated and so rich.

The echo may lead us to reflect on the causes of the war, of war in general, and all causality. In some sense, Troy is sacked by Iphigeneia, as the poetry says. Each person, each person's actions, have ramifications which may extend and magnify almost infinitely. One deed leads to others, each bound up with those which came before. So the words of the Homeric poems, like *Iphigeneia*, stand at the beginning of a great poetic web. Verses and phrases are repeated and varied, regrouped and reheard. Sometimes we are able to trace them back and to know what forces shaped a new poetic phrase. No doubt, as with events, one's standpoint makes all the difference in one's understanding. Euripides' art contrives to make *Iphigeneia* the absolute center: all the words of the poetic past, all the deeds of the heroic future, are concentrated in her as she stands trembling before the altar. From this smallest point the whole can be reconstructed. Such is the art of allusion.

CONCLUSIONS

The diversity of allusive techniques and effects in Greek drama continued undiminished as long as Sophocles and Euripides were writing plays. In its ominous and prophetic use of Aeschylus and the *Iliad*, *Iphigeneia at Aulis* shows us Euripides in his most serious and Sophoclean allusive mode. Yet from the same period we have *Orestes*, a tragedy that uses allusions to the *Oresteia* in an entirely different spirit. Here fragments of past poetry collide with phrases in an alien environment with the result that everything is shattered or flattened. The allusions do not suggest added levels of significance; if anything, they question the possibility of meaning.

Between these two extremes, conservative complexity and cynical nihilism, lies the playful and clever Euripides. The allusions of *Cyclops* create an airy and whimsical effect. Euripides' Odysseus repeatedly describes future events with absolute accuracy: he is allowed, as it were, to look ahead in and use phrases from the "script" of *Odyssey* 9. Similarly, the final reference to Philoctetes' cave is tossed off at the very end of *Cyclops* like a throw-away line, a parting joke at the end which is not intended to hold any deeper meaning. A similar – if more carefully constructed – lightness pervades the allusions of *Iphigeneia among the Taurians*. The constant early echoes of the *Oresteia* have gloomy implications, but they do not in fact signal the relentless approach of Atreid doom. Rather they increase tension so that it can be released to maximum effect in the joyful, brilliant recognition scene of Orestes and Iphigeneia where, for once, the reunion of brother and sister will not lead immediately to another family murder.

Both Euripides and Sophocles allude to Polyphemus' slaughter of Odysseus' men in *Odyssey* 9 and to Aeschylus' image of the terrible viper in the *Oresteia*. But whereas Sophocles uses these images for the darkest and most savage elements in the *Trachiniae*, in Euripides' hands they are turned into mere grotesquerie in the *Cyclops* and the engine of stage suspense in *Iphigeneia among the Taurians*. The one exception to the generally greater sobriety of Sophoclean allusion persuasively confirms the rule: Sophocles' *Oedipus at Colonus* contains a set of allusions created in a lighter spirit – as a nod of respect to Euripides' own allusive practice. Sophocles' messenger speech (*OC* 1621–9) includes a collection of echoes of a messenger speech from Euripides' *Bacchae* (1078–90), a Euripidean speech which itself alludes to earlier poetry.

The seriousness of Sophoclean allusion seen first in *Ajax* and *Antigone* still informs *Philoctetes*, but in a form stripped bare, making great demands on the interpreter. The play takes place in a setting which suggests the Cyclops of the *Odyssey* and along a plot line which suggests the isolation and resistance of Achilles. Into this general atmosphere Sophocles introduces specific but tiny allusive hints. The texture of *Philoctetes* permits a larger interpretive structure based on these synecdochic foundations, but, in keeping with the atmosphere of the play, these allusions are ultimately more mysterious, their full implications less specific. One allusive parallel, Heracles, is more carefully organized across the surface of the play. The early hints at Heracles perhaps make even greater interpretive demands than the allusions to Achilles and Polyphemus. The full implications of the chorus's invocation to Sleep (*Phil.* 827) appear only when all the details of Sleep, Lemnos, Hera, and Heracles are retrieved from the secondary field of *Iliad* 14. This initial suggestion of Heracles sets up a significant thematic anticipation, for the actual arrival of Heracles later in the play saves the plot just as it seems in danger of taking a direction which would derail much of traditional mythology.[77] Heracles picks up the pieces of the shattered deception and ensures the taking of Troy. The interpretive energy required for such a reading is so great, the process so cerebral, that the initial reference to Heracles must be seen as deeply collusive. Fortunately for the Greeks, it is the textual or dramatic destiny of Heracles to appear and save the situation whether or not anyone – in the play or outside it – notices the allusive sign of his coming.

6

Generations of Leaves

THE BACKGROUND OF ALLUSION

When Pindar or Bacchylides juxtaposes a victor with a moment of myth, a gap is simultaneously created and closed. The past is brought to bear on the present and colors it with the more than mortal power inherent in the figures of the poetic tradition. Thus epinician technique imitates metaphor on a large scale: the primary field or tenor is the victor himself; the secondary field, the mythic narrative chosen by the poet to give meaning to the present. Like vehicles in metaphor, the exempla may apply in a complex variety of ways, but exempla they are. In this sense, then, epinician allusions to myth are merely an outgrowth, albeit luxuriant and exotic in the extreme, of a phenomenon present in the earliest Greek poetry – the example of the past adduced for comparison with the present. Dione tells Aphrodite of Ares' hardships; Diomedes tells Glaukos of the madness of Lycurgus; Phoenix tells Achilles of Meleager's stubbornness; Achilles tells Priam of Niobe's grief. Granted, in that such examples call for explicit comparison, they are more like simile than metaphor or allusion, for the latter two create tension by remaining implicit. Still, just as in epinician, the Homeric examples are summoned up to apply – at least within the narrative framework of the poems – to an immediate non-fictional situation.

Literary allusion in Greek tragedy necessarily implies more self-conscious artifice than epinician or epic exemplum. The secondary field is applied not to a living person (as in epinician), but to some figure already part of mythic narrative; the interpretive comparison is suggested not by a character in the poetry, who explicitly calls on past history (as in epic), but by the author, who triggers the

allusion with echoes of earlier verse. This complex authorial move
heightens some of the tense ambiguities inherent in Greek tragedy.
Tragedy is part of a religious festival, part, that is, of ritual and
tradition. But whereas ritual must be entirely unvarying in order to
be efficacious, each tragedy is a new variation, a departure from
the sum total of past poetic narrative. By alluding to earlier poetry,
the poet calls attention to the creative aspect of this annual
performance. The illusion that the performance is a window into
the past is dispelled. Instead, allusion emphasizes convention; it
reminds the audience not only that this is an artificial poetic
presentation, but that it is like or unlike earlier, equally artifical
narratives composed by other poets. The play requires interpretation because it is not merely a transparent cultural artifact, an
undigested celebration of the treasures of Greek mythology, but
rather the creation of an individual, signed not just once, but each
time the poet points to a personal choice or decision. Allusions
make for some of the most obvious poetic signatures.

Besides baring part of the mechanism of poetic composition,
allusions may provide an index to the poets' audience. The
references to *Persae* and Bacchylides 17 seem to point to Athenian
political pride and recall the civic side of the tragic festivals. Such
allusions would only be effective if the audience recognized them,
of course. And so the material may suggest some generalizations
about Athenian education. Poetic texts of political relevance are
likely to have been learned by Athenian youth. Similarly, the
general distribution of allusions may be at least partially an
indication of what poetry was most popular and likely to be
recognized as the vehicle of allusion. Aeschylus' *Oresteia*, especially
the *Agamemnon* and *Choephori* would seem to have been especially
well known. The *Odyssey* appears altogether less often than its
companion poem. As for the *Iliad*, Books 6 and 22 again and again
provide material for allusion and imitation of all sorts; no other
books of the *Iliad* are used as frequently. Granted, these parts of the
poem have an innate thematic weight: they depict the family facing
the burdens of community obligation and two great heroes locked
in fatal combat. Nevertheless, the passages are exploited for many
purposes besides larger thematic allusions, giving the impression
that Homeric texts were well thumbed at these points. Or, if it is a
better model for education in this society, that these were the boys'
recitation passages that would come to mind most readily. Other

179

guesses can be made; Homeric similes, for example, seem to be drawn on with particular confidence. Perhaps they also figured large in the poetry lessons of palaestra and gymnasium. All such suggestions will be speculative. But Athenian citizens had been taught *some* Homer as boys, and they are unlikely to have learned it all equally well. I suspect their teachers are even less likely to have filled the hours of instruction with random selections: teachers tend to teach what they find congenial, and, for better or worse, they tend to teach it over and over again. Thus distribution of Homeric allusions seems likely to provide some key to the use of Homer in the pedagogy of fifth-century Athens.

THE PRACTITIONERS OF ALLUSION

Although practised by artists, allusion was an art, a τέχνη, and so even three tragedians as different as Aeschylus, Sophocles, and Euripides show some common tendencies. All, for example, make use of Homeric similes (see Appendix D), and each playwright, at least once in the extant works, has composed in such a way that the allusion to the simile can bear considerable interpretive weight. In Aeschylus there is the innocent Homeric joy in the morning dew which becomes Clytemnestra's delight in her husband's blood (*Ag.* 1390–2; *Il.* 23.597–9). In Sophocles there is the simile of the lion and its cubs transferred from Ajax's moment of great glory to the scene of his shameful suicide (*Aj.* 985ff.; *Il.* 17.133–5). Euripides transforms the splendor of Homeric battle into the squalor of Neoptolemus' death with a pair of borrowed comparisons (*Andr.* 1129–41, *Il.* 12.154–60, 21.493–6). Aeschylus drew on the first extended simile from the *Odyssey* (*Ag.* 1224–5), Euripides from the first in the *Iliad* (*Hipp.* 563–4); both men used the Homeric image of birds crying for their lost young (*Od.* 16.216–19; *Ag.* 40–54, *HF* 1039–41). In Aristophanes' *Frogs* neither Aeschylus nor Euripides comments on this aspect of their craft, perhaps because their practices are quite similar.

Another feature found in all three tragedians is the placement of allusion and imitation in messenger speeches (see Appendix C). The Homeric nature of such speeches has long been noted; it is even adduced as one explanation for the peculiarity that the syllabic augment may be omitted from the verb in these narratives. But the echoes are not confined to epic. These speeches bring to the poetry of the play not only events which occur outside the action on stage, but words and phrases which originate outside the text of the play and enrich the interpretation of events on stage and off.

The most pervasive tragic convention for literary allusion is the placement of imitation or allusion at the beginning of a strophe, antistrophe, or comparable metrical unit (see Appendix A), or – somewhat less commonly – at the end of a lyric run (Appendix B). These opening and closing positions seem to some extent to have served as triggers in and of themselves, although they obviously could be (and were) combined with other devices to effect the allusive interpretation. Sophocles seems to have been particularly fond of this device.

The loss of so much of Greek tragedy may mean that the list of allusive techniques shared by all three playwrights is artificially small. Similarly, since the surviving plays form a precariously small sample from the complete output of Aeschylus, Sophocles, and Euripides, the list of individual differences may include distinctions which would blur or even disappear if more plays could be examined. Still, some of these apparent distinctions bear re-emphasizing. Already in Aeschylus' *Agamemnon* two widely separated points in time are juxtaposed by alluding to the Homeric poems: his chorus, for example, looks back to an omen at Aulis (*Ag.* 108–20) which is specifically echoed by events later in the battlefield at Troy (*Il.* 6.57–60). Or, reversing the temporal direction of the Homeric allusion, the chorus describes the fall of Troy in words which echo Sarpedon's angry prediction of that event (*Ag.* 357–61, *Il.* 5.485–9). The technique coincides with Aeschylus' method of tying together his own trilogy with similar internal echoes; it may well have been learned from epinician poets who, in a much shorter poetic genre, had brought the complex collection of different points in time to a dazzling perfection.[1] On the one hand, this method unites Aeschylus with the other tragedians: they continue to use it, often alluding to the *Oresteia* itself when dealing with the House of Atreus. On the other hand, however, Aeschylus uses this technique and all the other techniques of allusion much more sparingly than either Sophocles or Euripides. The one Aeschylean exception, if it is Aeschylean, is *Prometheus Bound.*

Sophocles' works, by contrast, present an abundance of

181

invention. In the *Ajax*, the great series of allusions to the Hector
and Ajax of the *Iliad* constantly reinforces the themes Sophocles
has introduced by more direct means. Moreoever, the allusions are
arranged to build to a shock of recognition at the transformation of
a powerful to a powerless Ajax. A Homeric simile is reapplied: the
raging lion that was the epic Ajax is now a useless corpse; the lion
cub of Sophocles' play, Eurysakes, is left without defense (*Aj.*
985ff., *Il.* 17. 133–5). In *Electra*, Sophocles experiments with
expanding a borrowed image; the funerary urns mentioned in
Aeschylus' *Agamemnon* and *Choephori* are alluded to and then used
as a major element for the scene between Electra and Orestes. The
Trachiniae depends on a combination of Homeric and Aeschylean
allusions. The most notable is perhaps Hyllus' simile which echoes
a metaphor of Aeschylus' Orestes. Both tenor and vehicle in the
Sophoclean lines have more relevance than Hyllus can know; the
importance is compounded by Heracles' subsequent repetition of
the image; and the Aeschylean echoes serve to underline Sophocles'
extended parallel which contrasts and compares Deianeira and
Heracles with Clytemnestra and Agamemnon. Alluding to a simile
or metaphor, as Hyllus does, necessarily multiplies the possibilities
for applying vehicle to tenor or secondary field to primary, since
there are two of each instead of one. In *Antigone* Sophocles
developed this possibility to the fullest by making a whole set of
exempla in the fourth stasimon, meant to illuminate Antigone's
situation, allude to another set of exempla in the *Iliad*, used for
comparison to Aphrodite's misfortune.

Sophocles' complex variety of allusions are set in apparently
intentionally varied larger frameworks. The *Antigone* concentrates
allusions in the choral sections, especially at the openings of the
stasima. *Trachiniae*, by contrast, sends the audience to other texts
with echoes triggered in elaborate iambic speeches. In *Ajax*
Homeric parallels are suggested and then programmatically
developed with further allusions. In *Philoctetes* the epic material is
hinted at and then dropped from the verbal texture of the play.

The surviving tragedies encourage the impression that Euripides
admired and imitated Sophocles' allusive creativity. This is
different from the matter of his allusions to Sophoclean plays
themselves. For example, Sophocles' use of the Homeric Hector
seems to have influenced Euripides' use of the *Iliad* in *Alcestis* just a
few years later. Similarly, when Euripides was modeling *Cyclops* on

Odyssey 9 and making his allusions to the Homeric material, he consulted and reproduced some of the Sophoclean treatment of that episode in the *Trachiniae*. The *Hercules Furens* may also be following the *Trachiniae* at one level in its concern with Aeschylus' *Agamemnon*. And, although this must remain speculative, it seems that Euripides, in his *Electra*, followed Sophocles' *Electra* in the matter of some verbal echoes from Aeschylus, especially with the words ἀγλάϊσμα and ἀγλαΐα.

Euripides had his own uses for allusion as well. What have often been seen as criticisms of Aeschylus are generally devices for creating suspension and surprise in plotting, especially in *Electra* and *Phoenician Women*. And Euripides' talent for making the familiar seem strange found a convenient support in allusion to earlier dramatic treatments of myth: this technique becomes almost the basis for the presentation of *Orestes*. Finally, Euripides seems to have had a special fondness for using epinician poetry in his plays. There are small Bacchylidean references sprinkled throughout his works, and the allusions to and imitations of Pindar and Bacchylides in *Alcestis* and *Hercules Furens* are central to their plays.

THE ANATOMY OF ALLUSION RECONSIDERED

The art of allusion in classical Athens is very different from that practised in Alexandria. It is less precious, less focused on rare words and obscure variation, more likely to suggest a substantive interpretive response which enriches the play in which the allusion has been placed.[2] But the cerebral demands of the Alexandrian librarians are nonetheless present, and to the initial anatomical analysis of allusion offered above in Chapter 1 certain details and complexities can now be added.

For all the similarity between metaphor and allusion, the interpretive integration of an allusion to another text is a far more complicated process. The initial stages most resemble those involved in metaphor: a gap is perceived, the vehicle identified, and tenor and vehicle are connected through some relatively direct similarity. If Euripides' Admetus calls to Alcestis as Achilles did to Patroclus in the *Iliad*, we see that Alcestis and Patroclus are alike because both died for men they loved. But this is only the beginning of the solution, for the gap bridged in poetic allusion is always one between two texts. Thus the complexity of both tenor and vehicle, primary and secondary fields, invites a further, more metonymic or synecdochic stage of interpretation. Once the two texts are made contiguous, any number of elements in the extended primary and secondary fields may resonate or interact. This partly explains why the Stesichorean example in the introduction, the battle of Heracles and Geryon with its allusion to the battle in the *Iliad*, sets up a more intricate process than do the allusions of Mimnermus and Tyrtaeus examined there: the primary field in lyric poems is usually simpler, limited to fewer elements. In the Stesichorus fragment, as in Attic tragedy, the primary field is narrative, equal – or nearly so – in complexity to the narrative epic field to which it alludes.

The Stesichorean fragment makes its allusion with the reuse of a Homeric simile. Since the simile itself involves a split field, the Stesichorean and Homeric texts share a formal, symmetrical complication. Somewhat paradoxically, this makes the final reading of the allusion more manageable. The very complexity of a metaphor or simile as the tenor for an allusion provides a specificity that frames – or at least gives the impression of framing – a more clearly defined portion of the two texts involved in the poetic allusion. Interpretive energy must be so focused on comparing the relationships in these select sections that the primary and secondary fields seem more sharply defined, the way to integrate them more clearly indicated. Ultimately such limits are illusory: there is nothing to prevent a continued interpretive expansion beyond the borrowed simile or metaphor: they are parts of a whole text, and synecdoche begins with a complex part as well as with a simple one. Nevertheless, successful recognition of the relation between two comparisons in two texts brings with it a certain sense of closure.

Opposed to these elaborately specific figures are allusions which seem to direct the poetic audience in a much more nebulous way. As allusions, of course, they send one to a specific place, but when one opens the door, one finds a room at once atmospheric and yet vast. Most such allusions in Attic tragedy are to the *Iliad*. They tap into the heroic world and its associations by means of a Homeric allusion which works by calling on an identifiable passage but does this in order to draw on the epic as a whole – the least limited secondary field. For such purposes, of course, a clearly identifiable imitation will do as well as an allusion, and both may work much the same as the ostentatious use of a Homeric formula. The world of Achilles and Hector is called up for the reader, sometimes to lend splendor to the primary field, sometimes, as in *Andromache*, to provide a backdrop against which the tragic props seem shabby and cheap. Nor are such allusions always Homeric: Euripides frequently uses Aeschylus' *Oresteia* for much the same effect in *Orestes*.

Between these allusions of greatest and least specificity lie all the rest. In some, the allusion brings a thematic or paradigmatic parallel to bear on the tenor in the primary text. So in *Prometheus Bound* Achilles is summoned from the secondary field of the *Iliad* as a parallel to Prometheus. Aeschylus' Agamemnon and his return to Mycenae are alluded to as an ominous model for Heracles in *Trachiniae*. The Homeric Patroclus becomes a double for Euripides' Alcestis, and the contiguity of the *Iliad* and the *Alcestis* encourages further interpretation along the same lines – Admetus as Achilles. Such allusive and collusive parallels adduced by the playwrights provide incomparable commentary, as if scholiasts with perfect poetic taste and certain knowledge had incorporated their notes into the verses themselves.

In another type of allusion important in Greek tragedy, closing the gap between the texts of tenor and vehicle results in a collapse or folding of time, the juxtaposition of two moments from what can be seen as a continuous narrative. If the early poetry which treated the tales of Thebes had survived, this type of allusion might well be even more fully represented. In the extant plays it appears most often in conjunction with tales of the Trojan War and the House of Atreus with the *Iliad* and the *Oresteia* generally serving as the vehicles of allusion. Even in the *Oresteia* Aeschylus achieves this effect – the allusive equivalent of omen and prophecy – with echoes of the *Iliad*; Sophocles sets the events of the *Ajax* in relation to the role of his hero in epic; Euripides plays fantastic chronological tricks in *Iphigeneia at Aulis*, prophesying past literature with eerie effects; and so on.

Often these formal types and the range of effects they bring are combined. A simile, a paradigm, or an allusion to a character's future or past can bring the general atmosphere of the secondary field along as well. Coinciding chronological and typological parallels or connections are often emphasized through allusion: the story of Achilles resembles the story of Prometheus and is

185

chronologically connected. Similarly, the plot which connects the deaths of Iphigeneia, Agamemnon, and Clytemnestra is full of parallels, and Sophocles and Euripides emphasize them with allusions to Aeschylus' *Agamemnon*. Any allusion based on the content of paradigmatic or temporal reference can include the formal mechanics of simile, metaphor, or exempla. Thus, Sophocles brings out the similarities in Heracles and Agamemnon by allowing Hyllus to turn Orestes' metaphor into a simile. Again, Sophocles makes Aphrodite work as a model for Antigone partly by supplying details from Homeric exempla adduced for Aphrodite in the exempla offered for Antigone.

Because these complicated processes make such intense interpretive demands, the distinction between allusion and collusion is, at the most rewarding interpretive level, relatively insignificant. No Attic tragedy depends on allusion for dramatic success; nearly every play is enriched through the analysis of its allusive relation to other Greek poetry. Moreover, as presented in this study, the allusions always coincide with the tones and textures peculiar to their plays. If this harmony is a near inevitable result of the overall interpretive process, it may well represent not a defect but rather a merit of this poetic device. The flexibility possible in interpreting textual allusions, the multiplicity of solutions possible in such a complicated problem, is no cause for alarm. Once we decide that Euripides has created an allusion that invites us to compare his Admetus with the Achilles of the *Iliad*, who will tell us what this means? What human will see Achilles – his pride, his grief, his friendship with Patroclus, his feelings for his father – the same way every year, or even in every season of one year? And can Admetus' feelings about death or for his wife Alcestis always look the same? We will read many different *Iliad*s, many different *Alcestis*es in the course of our lives, and the relationship between the two texts, and between Achilles and Admetus, will change accordingly. Sometimes it is difficult to distinguish between ourselves and the poetry, or our reading of it. But of course the words on the page are always the same; it is we who change a little each year, just like the tree outside our library window. Thus it happens that as we examine ourselves in the poetry on the page, its allusions to us may change from time to time. But when the buds ripen in spring, the tree brings forth leaves like the ones that the wind blew away in the fall.

APPENDICES

A: ECHOES AT THE BEGINNING OF STROPHE, ANTISTROPHE, OR LYRIC SECTION

* Indicates beginning of song.

Aeschylus

Sept. 322	*Il.* 1.1–5
Agam. 403–8	Sappho 16.9, 17
Agam. 1453–7	*Il.* 1.1–5
Cho. 324–6	*Od.* 11.219–22
Cho. 345–53	*Od.* 1.234–44, 24.30–4
*Cho. 585	H. Hymn Aph.
Cho. 946	*Il.* 1.542, 6.161

Sophocles

Aj. 706	*Il.* 17.83
*Ant. 100	Pind. Paean 9.1*
Ant. 134	A. *Sept.* 343–4
*Ant. 332	A. *Cho.* 585ff.*
Ant. 615	Pind. *Ol.* 12.6ff.
*Ant. 944	*Il.* 5.382ff.
Trach. 112–13	*Il.* 2.394–7
*Trach. 821ff.	*Od.* 9.507
*OT 151	*Il.* 1.248
*OT 1186	*Il.* 6.146
*Phil. 827	*Il.* 14.231ff.
*OC 1224	Theognis 425ff.

Euripides

*Alc. 436	Il. 23.19
*Med. 410	Od. 10.331
Med. 431	A. Ag. 690–1
Med. 635	A. Ag. 927–8
Med. 846	Od. 10.331
Hcld. 75	Il. 22.310
Hcld. 608	Il. 6.487–93, 24.524–51
Hcld. 748	Il. 22.26–31
El. 860–1	Bacchyl. 13.84–90
El. 1221–3	A. Cho. 830–6
*HF 107–13	Ag. 74–82
*HF 349–51	Pind. N. 5.24–5
*Hel. 167	Stesich. 193 PMG
Hel. 1478	Il. 3.3
Ba. 862–72	Bacchyl. 13.84–90
Ba. 991ff.	A. Ag. 223, Cho. 584, Eum. 329–42
IA 204–5	Il. 2.673
IA 1476	A. Ag. 690
IA 1511	A. Ag. 690
Cyc. 608–10	Od. 9.391–3

B: ECHO AT THE END OF STROPHE, ANTISTROPHE, OR LYRIC SECTION

Sophocles

Trach. 661–2	A. Ag. 94–6
Trach. 850	A. Ag. 1523
OT 1105–9	Anacreon 357 PMG

Euripides

Med. 845	Il. 22.268
Hipp. 168	Bacchyl. 9.45
Hipp. 563–4	Il. 2.87–90
HF 530	A. Ag. 1523
Supp. 837	A. Ag. 749
IT 1136	Bacchyl. 17.89–90
Hel. 118–21	A. Ag. 713ff., 748
Hel. 1318	Bacchyl. 17.89

Hel. 1337	*Il.* 24.105, *Od.* 1.342
Hel. 1351	Bacchyl. 17.77
Cyc. 360	*Od.* 9.425

C: MESSENGER SPEECHES WITH IMITATION OR ALLUSION

Aeschylus
  Pers. 302–30

Sophocles
  Ant. 1586–666
  OC 1192–243

Euripides
  Andr. 1085–165
  Supp. 650–730
  Pho. 1090–199
  Pho. 1356–424
  Or. 866–956
  Bacch. 1043–152

D: USES OF HOMERIC SIMILES

Stesichorus P. Oxy. 2617	*Il.* 8.300–9
Simonides 8.1–2	*Il.* 6.146–9
Mimnermus 2.1–5	*Il.* 6.146–9

Aeschylus

Pers. 314–17	*Il.* 4.141–7
Supp. 223–4	*Il.* 22.139–40 (cf. *PV* 857)
Supp. 734	*Il.* 13.62
Agam. 40–54	*Od.* 16.216–19
	(cf. Eur. *HF* 1039–41)
Agam. 40–54	*Il.* 16.428–9
Agam. 1224–5	*Od.* 4.334
	(1st Extended Sim. In *Od.*)
Agam. 1390–2	*Il.* 23.597–9

Sophocles

Ajax 137	*Il.* 14.414
Ajax 175	*Il.* 23.846
Ajax 985ff.	*Il.* 17.133–5
Trach. 112–13	*Il.* 2.394–7
OT 1186	*Il.* 6.146–9
El. 97–100	*Il.* 13.389–91 = 16.482–5

Euripides

Hipp. 563–4	*Il.* 2.87–90
	(1st Extended Sim. In *Il.*)
Andr. 1129	*Il.* 12.154–60, 278–89
Andr. 1140–1	*Il.* 21.493–6
Supp. 691–3	*Il.* 16.742–50
Hel. 1478ff.	*Il.* 3.3ff.
Pho. 1148–52	*Il.* 16.742–50
Cyc. 460–3	*Od.* 9.383–6
Cyc. 608–10	*Od.* 9.391–4

E: PASSAGES USED
BY POETS

Passage alluded to: Allusion/echo in:

Iliad

1.3	Aesch. *Ag.* 1456–7
1.3	Aesch. *Septem* 322
1.3	Eur. *Alc.* 462
1.3	Eur. *Andr.* 611
1.3	Eur. *Hel.* 52
1.4–5	Aesch. *Supp.* 800–1
1.4–5	Soph. *Ajax* 830
1.4–5	Eur. *Ion* 505
1.194ff.	Soph. *Ajax* 729ff.
1.234–45	[Aesch.] *PV* 167–76
1.240	Soph. *Phil.* 601

1.542	Aesch. *Cho.* 946
1.597–600	Eur. *Ion* 1171–3
2.38–40	Aesch. *Ag.* 66–7
2.87–90	Eur. *Hipp.* 563–4
2.111	Soph. *OC* 525
2.213	Soph. *Ant.* 660
2.394–7	Soph. *Trach.* 112–13
2.673	Eur. *IA* 204–5
3.3	Eur. *Hel.* 1478ff.
3.64	Mimn. 1W.1–4
3.64	Sappho 16.17
3.276–8	[Aesch.] *PV* 88–92
3.351	Aesch. *Cho.* 18–19
3.397	Eur. *Ion* 888
4.141–7	Aesch. Pers. 316
4.169–82	Eur. *El.* 318–31
4.171	Eur. *Alc.* 560
4.247–8	Bacchyl. 13.149–50
4.518	Aesch. *Septem* 300
5.93–6	Mimn. 13.3–4
5.153	Soph. *Ajax* 506–7
5.367	Sappho 1.13ff.
5.382	Panyassis *Her.* fr. 16K
5.382–97	Soph. *Ant.* 944–5
5.385–91	Soph. *Ant.* 970–6
5.487–9	Aesch. *Ag.* 357–61
6.57–60	Aesch. *Ag.* 108–20
6.130–7	Soph. *Ant.* 955–65
6.143	Bacchyl. 5.63ff.
6.143	Pind. P. Oxy. 2622
6.143	Simonides 8W
6.143	Arist. Birds 685ff.
6.143	Mimn. 2.1
6.146	Soph. *OT* 1186

6.161	Mimn. 1.3
6.161	Aesch. *Cho.* 946
6.168–9	Soph. *Trach.* 142, 157–8
6.179	Soph. *OT* 176
6.182	Soph. *Ant.* 959–60
6.206ff.	Tyrt. 10W.9
6.400	Soph. *Ajax* 559
6.415–32	Soph. *Ajax* 510–24
6.429	Aesch. *Cho.* 238–43
6.429	Eur. *Alc.* 646–7
6.455	Eur. *Hcld.* 868
6.458	Soph. *Ajax* 485
6.462–3	Soph. *Ajax* 499–504
6.463	Eur. *Androm.* 99
6.463	Eur. *Hec.* 56
6.464	Eur. *Tro.* 1330
6.466–70	Soph. *Ajax* 545–7
6.476–81	Soph. *Ajax* 550–1
6.487–93	Eur. *Hcld.* 608ff.
6.490–1	Soph. *Ajax* 293
6.490–3	Aesch. *Septem* 200–1
6.492–3	Eur. *Hcld.* 711–12
6.496	Eur. *IA* 39–40
7.84–91	Eur. *Alc.* 1000–4
7.235–7	Aesch. *Ag.* 1401–6
7.222 = 16.107	Soph. *Ajax* 1025
7.302	[Aesch.] *PV* 191
7.301–2	Aesch. *Septem* 934–6
7.301–2	Soph. *Ajax* 661–5
7.301–2	Soph. *Ajax* 817ff.
8.16	[Aesch.] *PV* 152
8.485–6	Soph. *El.* 17–19
9.322	Soph. *Ajax* 1269ff.
9.395	Eur. *IA* 959–60
9.410	[Aesch.] *PV* 874
9.410–16	Mimn. 2.5–7

9.413	Sappho 44.4
9.413	Bacchyl. 13.65
9.413	Ibycus 151.47 SLG
9.485–95	Aesch. *Cho.* 751–3
9.593	Aesch. *Ag.* 824
9.593	Aesch. *Eum.* 937
9.640–2	Soph. *Ajax* 506
11.527–30	Soph. *Ajax* 340
11.532	Soph. *Ajax* 242
12.375	Soph. *Ajax* 376
13.53	Soph. *Ajax* 452
13.62	Aesch. *Supp.* 734
13.389ff.	Soph. *El.* 98–100
14.231ff.	Soph. *Phil.* 827
14.286–91	Eur. *Bacch.* 1061, 1070, 1073
14.414	Soph. *Ajax* 137
15.19–20	Sem. 7.116
15.207	Pind. *P.* 4.277
15.668–70	Aesch. *Septem* 226–9
16.33–5	[Aesch.] *PV* 242
16.428–9	Aesch. *Ag.* 48
16.645ff.	Eur. *Hel.* 1101–2
16.734–5	Eur. *Pho.* 1401
16.737	Soph. *Trach.* 258
16.742–50	Eur. *Supp.* 691–3
16.742–50	Eur. *Pho.* 1148–52
17.42	[Aesch.] *PV* 105
17.75	[Aesch.] *PV* 184
17.83	Soph. *Ajax* 706
17.128–39	Soph. *Ajax* 985–9
17.139	Soph. *Ajax* 615

18.35–64	[Aesch.] *PV* 127–35
18.56	Soph. *Trach*. 144–7
18.132ff.	Archil. fr. 5W
18.477	[Aesch.] *PV* 56
19.97	Soph. *Trach*. 1062
20.61	Soph. *OC* 1558–60
21.123–5	Bacchyl. 13.164–5
21.493–6	Eur. *Andr*. 1140–1
22.17	Eur. *Pho*. 1423
22.26–31	Eur. *Hcld*. 748ff.
22.38ff., 82ff.	Soph. *Ajax* 506ff.
22.44	Aesch. *Pers*. 286–9
22.51	Sem. 7.87
22.60–4	Eur. *Alc*. 885–8
22.68	Eur. *HF* 1205
22.68	Soph. *Ant*. 529
22.71ff.	Tyrt. 10W.23–7
22.79–83	Aesch. *Cho*. 896–8
22.82	Eur. *IA* 1246
22.87, 94, 146	*Hym. Dem*. 38ff.
22.104–7	Aesch. *Supp*. 400–1
22.110	Aesch. *Ag*. 1304–5
22.139–40	Aesch. *Supp*. 223–4
22.212	Sappho 44.43–4
22.268	Eur. *Med*. 845
22.293	Eur. *Med*. 1012
22.310	Eur. *Hcld*. 75
22.362	Eur. *HF* 1205
22.371	Eur. *Andr*. 1153
22.401	*Hym. Dem*. 38ff.
22.451–5	Soph. *OT* 153
23.19	Eur. *Alc*. 436
23.19	Pind. *I*. 2.48
23.257–70	Eur. *Alc*. 1031

23.336–40	Soph. *El.* 721–2
23.352–3	Soph. *El.* 710
23.363–4	Soph. *El.* 711–12
23.454, 471	Soph. *El.* 705
23.597–9	Aesch. *Ag.* 1390–2
23.714–17	Soph. *Ajax* 772
23.846	Soph. *Ajax* 175
24.5	Bacchyl. 13.205
24.40–1	[Aesch.] *PV* 164a
24.105	Eur. *Hel.* 1337 (see *Od.* 1.342)
24.205	[Aesch.] *PV* 242
24.211	Soph. *Ajax* 237
24.506	Eur. *Med.* 1407
24.506	Eur. *HF* 1201
24.524–51	Eur. *Hcld.* 608ff.
24.703	Soph. *Ajax* 851
24.785	Bacchyl. 13.128
24.785	Eur. *Hcld.* 750
24.797	Soph. *Ajax* 1165
24.797	Soph. *Ajax* 1403
24.797	Eur. *Alc.* 898

Odyssey

1.32–43	[Aesch.] *PV* 1072–3
1.234–44	Aesch. *Cho.* 345–53
1.237	Aesch. *Cho.* 365
1.242	Aesch. *Eum.* 565
1.342	Eur. *Hel.* 1337 (see *Il.* 24.105)
2.276–7	Eur. *Hcld.* 326–8
3.261	Aesch. *Ag.* 1101
3.262ff.	Aesch. *Ag.* 1625–7
4.121–36	Eur. *Or.* 1426–40
4.180	Bacchyl. 13.63–4
4.182	Eur. *HF* 431

4.333ff.	Aesch. *Ag.* 1224
5.33 = 7.264	Aesch. *Pers.* 68
5.239	Eur. *Bacch.* 1064–5
5.270	Aesch. *Septem* 3
5.273–5	Soph. *Trach.* 130–1
5.478ff.	Soph. *Trach.* 144–7
6.119	Soph. *Trach.* 984–5
8.498	Eur. *Med.* 425
8.498	Pind. O.6
9.124	Soph. *OT* 479
9.132	Eur. *Cy.* 88
9.176	Eur. *Cy.* 125
9.182	Soph. *Phil.* 144
9.241–2	Eur. *Cy.* 473
9.288–93	Soph. *Trach.* 779–82
9.289–92	Eur. *Cy.* 395–400
9.301	Soph. *Trach.* 931
9.355–70	Eur. *Cy.* 548–51
9.372–4	Eur. *Cy.* 591–2
9.383–6	Eur. *Cy.* 460–1
9.391–4	Eur. *Cy.* 469–71, 608–10
9.398–402	Soph. *Phil.* 175–6
9.425	Eur. *Cy.* 360
9.433	Soph. *Phil.* 183
9.433	Archil. fr. 112
9.507	Soph. *Trach.* 822–3, 828
9.507	Soph. *OT* 906–7
9.507–10	Eur. *Cy.* 696–700
9.515–16	[Aesch.] *PV* 548–50
10.351	Eur. *Med.* 410, 846
10.521 = 36 = 11.29 = 49	Eur. *Tro.* 193
11.211	
11.211	Aesch. *Ag.* 1559
	Eur. *Andr.* 115

11.219ff.	Aesch. *Cho.* 324–6
11.287	Eur. *IA* 202
11.386, 434	Eur. *Or.* 1205
11.406–11	Soph. *El.* 95–9
11.418–24	Soph. *El.* 193–6
11.436ff.	Aesch. *Ag.* 1453–5
11.543	Soph. *Ajax* 865
12.37	Soph. *Trach.* 581
14.68–71	Aesch. *Ag.* 60–7
15.245	Soph. *El.* 134
15.329 = 17.569	Soph. *Ajax* 195–8
16.216–19	Aesch. *Ag.* 48
16.216–19	Eur. *HF* 1039–41
19.204	Eur. *Med.* 689
19.390ff.	Eur. *El.* 572–5
19.515ff.	Aesch. *Ag.* 889–94
19.518–22	Aesch. *Ag.* 1141ff.
20.356	Soph *OT* 178
21.85	Aesch. fr. 399
22.190	Soph. *OT* 1154
23.187–8	Aesch. *Cho.* 878–9
23.296	Soph. *Ant.* 799–800
24.30ff.	Aesch. *Cho.* 345ff.
24.202	Eur. *Or.* 1205

Aeschylus

Persians
122	Eur. *Alc.* 951–2

164	Eur. *Bacch.* 764
250	Eur. *Or.* 1077
307	Soph. *Ajax* 597
378	Eur. *Cyc.* 86
386	Soph. *Ajax* 672–3
402	Eur. *Hec.* 930
428	Eur. *IT* 110
462–3	Eur. *Cyc.* 359
464	Soph. *Trach.* 713
619–20	Eur. *Hec.* 94
805	Eur. *HF* 1163–4
824–8	Eur. *Hcld.* 386–9
840	Eur. *HF* 247, 503–5

Septem

25	Soph. *OT* 300
30 (251, 469)	Eur. *Pho.* 287
60ff.	Eur. *Supp.* 586ff.
62	Eur. *Med.* 523
80–92	Soph. *Ant.* 106–9
103–5	Soph. *Ant.* 126
125	Soph. *OC* 1313
254	Eur. *Pho.* 437
269	Soph. *Ant.* 1019
321	Soph. *OC* 1770
340–4	Soph. *Ant.* 134–40
369ff.	Eur. *Pho.* 1104ff.
378ff.	Eur. *Phoen.* 751
427–8	Eur. *Supp.* 498
427–31	Eur. *Pho.* 1175–6
488	Eur. *Pho.* 1130
582–3	Soph. *Ant.* 199–201
652	Soph. *Ant.* 994
671	Soph. *Ajax* 445
672–3	Eur. *Pho.* 755
675–6	Eur. *Pho.* 779–80
681–2	Soph. *OC* 954–5

720–65	Soph. *Ant.* 582–625
727–41	Eur. *Pho.* 656–75
753	Soph. *OT* 1211
772ff.	Soph. *OT* 1186ff.
781	Eur. *Med.* 433

Supp.

223–4	[Aesch.] *PV* 857
380	Eur. *IA* 56

Agamemnon

11	Eur. *Or.* 1204–5
36	Eur. *IT* 37
45	Eur. *IT* 141
74	Eur. *HF* 254–5
82	Eur. *HF* 111–13
85	Eur. *IT* 137–8
94–6	Soph. *Trach.* 661–2, 685–7
104	Eur. *HF* 678
218	Eur. *IA* 443, 511
218	[Aesc.] *PV* 108
218–21	Eur. *IA* 912–13
223	Eur. *Bacch.* 991ff.
224	Soph. *Trach.* 659, 1192
226	Eur. *IA* 718
279–81	Soph. *El.* 17–19
335	Soph. *Ant.* 356–7
367–72	Eur. *HF* 755–9
381–4	Eur. *HF* 773–80
383–4	Soph. *Ant.* 853–6
434–44	Soph. *El.* 1139ff.
434–44	Eur. *Supp.* 1123–31
440ff.	Soph. *El.* 756–8
449–60	Soph. *Ant.* 692–700
453	Eur. *Hel.* 1158 (1122–5, 1130)
462–70	Eur. *HF* 773–80
495	Soph. *Ant.* 246–7, 429
526	Soph. fr. 727P
526	Arist. *Birds* 1240
559	Soph. *Ajax* 600–5
560–2	Soph. *Ajax* 1206–10

604–14	Soph. *Trach*. 624–32
659	Eur. *IT* 300
682–91	Eur. *Pho*. 636–7
690	Eur. *IA* 1476 = 1511
690–1	Eur. *Med*. 431
713ff.	Eur. *Helen* 1118–21
725	Eur. *Or*. 894
738–49	Eur. *Or*. 1385–9
744–9	Eur. *Supp*. 832–7
745	Eur. *Med*. 1388
748	Eur. *Helen* 1118–21
750	Eur. *HF* 26
787	Eur. *IA* 977ff.
897–8	Eur. *IT* 50–4
914	Eur. *IA* 686 = 1106
927–8	Eur. *Med*. 635
943	Soph. *Ajax* 1353
1143	Soph. *El*. 123
1150	Eur. *Hipp*. 574
1178–83	Eur. *IA* 1146–7
1227ff.	Eur. *Tro*. 353–405
1258	Eur. *El*. 1162
1264–7	Eur. *Tro*. 256ff., 453
1283	Eur. *HF* 1280, *Tro*. 488–9
1293	Soph. *Ajax* 833–4
1343–5	Soph. *El*. 1415–21
1348–71	Eur. *HF* 252–74
1375	Soph. *El*. 1476–8
1375	Eur. *Or*. 1421
1376	Eur. *Bacch*. 1101–2
1382	Soph. *Trach*. 1051–2
1389–92	Soph. *Ant*. 1238–9
1390	Soph. *Ajax* 376
1405	Eur. *HF* 1139
1415–18	Soph. *El*. 530ff.
1446–7	Soph. *Trach*. 536–8
1461	Eur. *Hec*. 946ff.
1523	Soph. *Trach*. 850–1
1523	Eur. *Tro*. 530
1580	Soph. *Trach*. 1051ff.

1611	Soph. *El.* 1476–8
1624, 1632, 1639–40	Soph. *El.* 1462
1652	Eur. *HF* 254–5
Choephoroi	
3a/5a	Eur. *El.* 534
11	Eur. *El.* 513
17–18	Soph. *El.* 1187
46, 191, 525	Soph. *El.* 289
140–1	Soph. *El.* 307–8
164–245	Eur. *El.* 520–84
174	Eur. *El.* 530
185–6	Eur. *Alc.* 184
193	Eur. *El.* 325
193ff.	Soph. *El.* 903–8
221	Soph. *OT* 387
221	Eur. *Andr.* 1116
230	Eur. *El.* 520
248–9	Soph. *Trach.* 769–71, 1099
248–9	Eur. *IT* 287
315–509	Soph. *El.* 1066–9
318	Soph. *El.* 436
360	Soph. *El.* 225
439	Soph. *El.* 445
470	Eur. *Med.* 109
479–509	Eur. *Or.* 1225–45
493	Soph. *Trach.* 1057
523	Soph. *El.* 410
577	Soph. *El.* 786
584	Eur. *HF* 812
584	Eur. *Bacch.* 991ff.
585ff.	Soph. *Ant.* 332ff.
585ff.	Eur. fr. 1059
585ff.	Eur. *Hec.* 1181ff.
586, 600–1	Soph. *Trach.* 716
600	Soph. *Ant.* 792, 795
686	Soph. *El.* 54
794	Soph. *El.* 49–50
830–6	Eur. *El.* 462, 1221–3
886–7	Soph. *El.* 1476–8

896	Eur. *IA* 1246
908ff.	Soph. *Trach.* 739–40
935–6	Eur. *Or.* 1490
935–8	Soph. *El.* 475–9
937–8	Eur. *Or.* 1400–2
940	Soph. *El.* 70
946–52	Soph. *El.* 475–9
964	Eur. *Or.* 1491
982	Soph. *Trach.* 1057
983–90	Eur. *Or.* 821–2
1022–3	Soph. *El.* 49–50
1025–6	Eur. *Or.* 193
1027–8	Soph. *Trach.* 1125
1051–64	Eur. *Or.* 217–54
1058	Eur. *Andr.* 978
1058	Eur. *Or.* 256
1063–4	Soph. *OT* 1478–9

Eumenides

36	Soph. *El.* 112, 119–20
100	Eur. *IA* 932
112	Soph. *El.* 1476–8
112	Eur. *Or.* 1421
137–8	Eur. *IT* 288
180–90	Eur. *Or.* 272–4
329 = 342	Eur. *Bacch.* 991ff.
539–42	Soph. *Ant.* 853–6
628	Eur. *Or.* 272–4

Fragments

255 Radt	Soph. *Ajax* 854
255	Soph. *Phil.* 797
399	Pindar *P.* 8.95–6
399	Soph. *Ant.* 1170
399	Soph. *Phil.* 946–7

Sophocles

Ajax

591	Eur. *HF* 1185

Antigone

26–30	[Eur. *Pho.* 1629–34]
100	Eur. *Supp.* 650
523	Eur. *IA* 407

Trachiniae

779–82	Eur. *Cy.* 400
1012	Eur. *HF* 225
1070	Eur. *HF* 1353–7
1075	Eur. *HF* 1412
1101	Eur. *HF* 1353–7

Oedipus Tyrannus

1268–9	Eur. *Pho.* 61–2
1422–3	Eur. *Pho.* 1555–6
1524–5	[Eur. *Pho.* 1758–9]

Philoctetes

19	Eur. *Cy.* 707
83–4	Eur. *Or.* 656–7
159	Eur. *Cy.* 60
188	Eur. *Or.* 903
391–402 = 507–18	Eur. *Or.* 1353–65 = 1537–48
518, 601–2	Eur. *Or.* 1361–2
673	Eur. *Or.* 806
761	Eur. *Or.* 217–18
874	Eur. *Or.* 1676–7
923	Eur. *Or.* 722
1290	Eur. *Cy.* 140
1321	Eur. *Or.* 225–6
1407	Eur. *Or.* 1525

Electra

56–64	Eur. *Hel.* 1049–56
211	Eur. *El.* 175, 192, 861
1357–8	Eur. *Or.* 1045–6

Euripides

Hipp. 1366	Soph. *OC* 1439
Pho. 532	Soph. *OC* 1441
Pho. 1310–11	Soph. *OC* 1254–5

Bacch. 1078–88	Soph. *OC* 1622–9

Alcaeus

6V	Aesc. *Pers.* 87–92
208V	[Aesc.] *PV* 1085–8

Anacreon

357 *PMG*	Soph. *OT* 1105–9

Archilochus

fr. 13W.5–7	Alcaeus 335.3
114W	Eur. *Or.* 1532
121W	Soph. *Ajax* 648–9
177W	Aesc. *Cho.* 246–59
fr. 213	Aesc. *Cho.* 587
fr. 227W	Aesc. *Pers.* 763

Aristophanes

Aves 210ff.	Eur. *Hel.* 1110–11

Bacchylides

3.78–84	Eur. *Alc.* 779–802
3.78–84	Eur. *Andr.* 480
9.24–34	Eur. *Hipp.* 220–2
9.45	Eur. *Hipp.* 168
13.84–90	Eur. *El.* 860–1
13.84–90	Eur. *Bacch.* 862–72
13.204ff.	Simonides 531 *PMG*
16 *passim*	Eur. *IA* 790–1
16.3	Eur. *IA* 797
16.6	Eur. *Hel.* 1487, *IA* 793
17.26–7	[Aesc.] *PV* 103–4
17.77	Eur. *Hel.* 1305, 1351
17.80	Eur. *IT* 132
17.89	Eur. *Hel.* 1318
17.89–90	Eur. *IT* 1136–7, 1427
17.90	Eur. *IT* 1326
17.96–111	[Aesc.] *PV* 127–35
17.97 (17.4, 6, 77)	Eur. *Hel.* 1454–9
17.100–15	Eur. *Tro.* 1–3

Cypria
VII.1 (Allen)   Eur. *IA* 202

Hesiod
Works and Days
  190–201   Eur. *Med.* 410–45
  582–8   Alcaeus fr. 347
  701   Sem. 7.110f.
  702–3   Sem. 6.1–2
  707ff.   Aesc. *Cho.* 266

  Theog.
  55   Soph. *Ant.* 151
  521–2   [Aesc.] *PV* 64–5

Homeric Hymns
Aphrodite
  4ff.   Aesc. *Cho.* 585ff.
  264   Eur. *Pho.* 1515
  Apollo 203   Bacchyl. 3.17

Phrynichus
  Phoen. 1   Aesc. *Pers.* 1
  fr. 13N   Soph. *Ant.* 783–4

Pindar
  Ol. 2.36   [Aesc.] *PV* 765
  Ol. 4.7–8   [Aesc.] *PV* 365
  Ol. 5.20   Eur. *HF* 407
  Ol. 12.6ff.   Soph. *Ant.* 615–17
  P. 1.15–28   [Aesc.] *PV* 349–73
  P. 4.70   Eur. *Andr.* 795
  P. 8.55   Eur. *Bacch.* 87
  N. 5.24–5   Eur. *HF* 349–51
  N. 10.54   Eur. *HF* 802ff.
  I. 8.34–5   [Aesc.] *PV* 921–5
  I. 8.35   [Aesc.] *PV* 768
  Paean 9.1   Soph. *Ant.* 100
  fr. 140a56   Eur. *HF* 391

Sappho
  16   Aesc. *Ag.* 403–6
  96.6   Bacchyl. 9.27

Sappho or Alcaeus
  fr. 10 V   Soph. *Ajax* 168–71

Solon
  27.6W   [Aesc.] *PV* 23

Stesichorus
  187 *PMG*   Eur. *Hel.* 639–41, 725
  193 *PMG*   Eur. *Hel.* 167ff.

Theognis
  425–8   Soph. *OC* 1225–8
  1183–4   Bacchyl. 13.202–3

F: POETS' ALLUSIONS BY WORK

Note: In the following index the tragedians are indicated with the following abbreviations: Aeschylus – A., Sophocles – S., and Euripides – E. For complete plays the type of reference is tentatively classified as allusion (a), collusion (c), or imitation (i).

Primary work:	Work referred to:	Type of reference:

Aeschylus and Author of *Prometheus Bound*

Persae

1	Phrynicus *Phoen.* 1	a
68	*Od.* 5.33, 7.264	i
87–92	Alcaeus 6V	i?
286–9	*Iliad* 22.44	c
316	*Iliad* 4.141–7	c
763	Archilochus 227W	i

Supplices

223–4	*Iliad* 22.139–40	i
400–1	*Iliad* 22.104–7	i?

| 734 | *Iliad* 13.62 | i |
| 800–1 | *Iliad* 1.4–5 | i |

Septem
3	*Od.* 5.270	i?
200–1	*Iliad* 6.490–3	i?
226–9	*Iliad* 15.668–70	i?
300	*Iliad* 4.518	i
322	*Iliad* 1.1–5	a
934–6	*Iliad* 7.301–2	c

Agamemnon
48	*Iliad* 16.428–9	a/c
48	*Od.* 16.216–19	a/c
60–7	*Od.* 14.68–71	c
66–7	*Iliad* 2.38–40	c
108–20	*Iliad* 6.57–60	a/c
357–61	*Iliad* 5.487–9	a/c
403–8	Sappho 16.9, 17	i
824	*Iliad* 9.593	i
889–94	*Od.* 19.515ff.	c
1101	*Od.* 3.261	i
1141–6	*Od.* 19.518–23	c
1224	*Od.* 4.333–40	i/c?
1304–5	*Iliad* 22.110	i/c?
1390–2	*Iliad* 23.597–9	c
1401–6	*Iliad* 7.235–7	c
1453–7	*Od.* 11.436–9	i
1456–7	*Iliad* 1.3	i
1559	*Od.* 11.211	i
1625–7	*Od.* 3.262–4	i

Choephori
18–19	*Iliad* 3.351	i
238–43	*Iliad* 6.429–30	i
244–61	Archilochus fr. 177	i?
266	Hesiod *Op.* 707ff.	i?
324–6	*Od.* 11.219–22	i
345–53	*Od.* 1.234–44	c
345–53	*Od.* 24.30–4	i
585ff.	Hom. Hymn Aph. 4ff.	i

587	Archilochus fr. 213	i?
751–3	*Iliad* 9.485–95	i?
878–9	*Od.* 23.187–8	c
896–8	*Iliad* 22.79–83	a
946	*Iliad* 1.542, 6.161	c

Eumenides

565	*Od.* 1.242	c
937	*Iliad* 9.593	i?

Prometheus Bound

23	Solon 27.6W	a/c
56	*Iliad* 18.477	c
64–5	Hes. *Theog.* 521–2	i
88–92	*Iliad* 3.276–8	i?
103–4	Bacchyl. 17.26–7	i
105	*Iliad* 17.42	i
108	A. *Ag.* 218	i
127–35	*Iliad* 18.35–64	a
127–35	Bacchyl. 17.96–111	i
152	*Iliad* 8.16	i
152	Hes. *Theog.* 717ff.	i
164a	*Iliad* 24.40–1	a/c
167–76	*Iliad* 1.234–45	c
184	*Iliad* 17.75	i
191	*Iliad* 7.302	i/c?
242	*Iliad* 16.33–5, 24.205	c
349–73	Pind. *Pyth.* 1.15–28	c
365	Pind. *Ol.* 4.7–8	i
548–50	*Od.* 9.515–16	c
765	Pind. *Ol.* 2.36	i
768	Pind. *Isth.* 8.35	i
857	A. *Supp.* 223–4	i
874	*Iliad* 9.410	a
921–5	Pind. *Isth.* 8.34–5	i
1072–3	*Od.* 1.32–43	i
1085–8	Alcaeus 326 LP/208V	c/i

Fragments

399	*Od.* 21.85

Sophocles

Ajax

137	*Iliad* 14.414	i/c
168–71	Sap. or Alc. fr. 10V	i?
175	*Iliad* 23.846	c
195–8	*Od.* 15.329 = 17.569	i
237	*Iliad* 24.211	c
242	*Iliad* 11.532	c
293	*Iliad* 6.490–1	i?
340	*Iliad* 11.527–30	c
376	A. *Ag.* 1390	i
376	*Iliad* 12.375	c?
445	A. *Septem* 671	c
452	*Iliad* 13.53	c
485	*Iliad* 6.458	a
499–504	*Iliad* 6.462–3	a
506	*Iliad* 9.640–2	c
506–7	*Iliad* 5.153	i
506ff.	*Iliad* 22.38ff., 82ff.	a
510–24	*Iliad* 6.415–32	a
545–7	*Iliad* 6.466–70	a
550–1	*Iliad* 6.476–81	a
559	*Iliad* 6.400	i?
597	A. *Pers.* 307	i?
600–5	A. *Ag.* 559	i
615	*Iliad* 17.139	c
648–9	Archil. 121.1W	i?
661–5	*Iliad* 7.303–10	a
672–3	A. *Pers.* 386	i/c
706	*Iliad* 17.83	c
729ff.	*Iliad* 1.194ff.	i?
772	*Iliad* 23.714–17	i/c?
817–20	*Iliad* 7.303–10	a
830	*Iliad* 1.4–5	a
833–4	A. *Ag.* 1293	c
851	*Iliad* 24.703	c
854	A. *Phil.* fr. 244 Radt	i
865	*Od.* 11.543	a?
985–9	*Iliad* 17.128–39	a

1025	*Iliad* 7.222 = 16.107	a/c
1165	*Iliad* 24.797	a
1206–10	A. *Ag.* 560–2	i
1269ff.	*Iliad* 9.322	i
1353	A. *Ag.* 943	c
1403	*Iliad* 24.797	a

Antigone

100	Pind. *Paean* 9.1	c
106–9	A. *Septem* 80–92	i
126	A. *Septem* 103–5	i
134–40	A. *Septem* 340–4	i
151	Hes. *Theog.* 55	i
199–201	A. *Septem* 582–3	i
246–7	A. *Ag.* 495	i
332ff.	A. *Ch.* 585ff.	a/c
356–7	A. *Ag.* 335	i
429	A. *Ag.* 495	i
582–625	A. *Septem* 720–65	i
615–17	Pind. *Ol.* 12.6ff.	i
660	*Iliad* 2.213	i
692–700	A. *Ag.* 449–60	i
783–4	Phrynichus fr. 13N	i
792, 795	A. *Ch.* 600	i
799–800	*Od.* 23.296	i/c/a?
853–6	A. *Ag.* 383–4, *Eum.* 539–42	i
944	*Iliad* 5.382–97	a/c
955–65	*Iliad* 6.130–7	i
959–60	*Iliad* 6.182	i
970–6	*Iliad* 5.385–91	a/c
994	A. *Septem* 652	i
1019	A. *Septem* 269	i
1170	Aesc. fr. 399	i?
1238–9	A. *Ag.* 1389–92	c

Trachiniae

112–13	*Iliad* 2.394–7	i
130–1	*Od.* 5.273–5	i/c
142	*Iliad* 6.168–9	i/c
144–7	*Iliad* 18.56, *Od.* 5.478ff.	i
157–8	*Iliad* 6.168–9	c

258	*Iliad* 16.737	i
536–8	A. *Ag.* 1446–7	a/c
581	*Od.* 12.37	i
624–32	A. *Ag.* 604–14	a/c
659	A. *Ag.* 224	a/c
661–2	A. *Ag.* 94–6	a/c
685–7	A. *Ag.* 94–6	a/c
713	A. *Pers.* 464	i
716	A. *Ch.* 586, 600–1	a/c
739–40	A. *Ch.* 908ff.	a/c
769–71	A. *Ch.* 248–9	a/c
779–82	*Od.* 9.288–93	a/c
822–3, 828	*Od.* 9.507–8	a/c
850–1	A. *Ag.* 1523	c
931	*Od.* 9.301	i
984–5	*Od.* 6.119	i
1051–2	A. *Ag.* 1382, 1580	a/c
1057	A. *Ch.* 493, 982	a/c
1062	*Iliad* 19.97	c?
1125	A. *Ch.* 1027–8	a/c
1192	A. *Ag.* 224	c
Oed. Tyr.		
151	*Iliad* 1.248	i
153	*Iliad* 22.451–5	i
176	*Iliad* 6.179	i
178	*Od.* 20.356	i?
300	A. *Septem* 25	c
387	A. *Ch.* 221	i?
479	*Od.* 9.124	i
906–7	*Od.* 9.507	i
1105–9	Anacreon 357 *PMG*	i?
1149	A. *Septem* 39	c
1154	*Od.* 22.190	i
1186	*Iliad* 6.146	a
1186ff.	A. *Septem* 772ff.	i
1211	A. *Septem* 753	c
1325	*Iliad* 24.563	i
1478–9	A. *Ch.* 1063–4	i?

Electra

17–19	*Iliad* 8.485–6	i
17–19	A. *Ag.* 279–81	i/c?
49–50	A. *Ch.* 794, 1022–3	c
54	A. *Ch.* 686	c
70	A. *Ch.* 940	i
95–9	*Od.* 11.406–11	c
98–100	*Iliad* 13.389–91, 16.482–4	c
112	A. *Eum.* 36	i
119–20	A. *Eum.* 36	i
123	A. *Ag.* 1143	c
134	*Od.* 15.245	i
193–6	*Od.* 11.418–24	i
225	A. *Ch.* 360	i
289	A. *Ch.* 46, 191, 525	c
307–8	A. *Ch.* 140–1	a/c
410	A. *Ch.* 523	i
436	A. *Ch.* 318	i
445	A. *Ch.* 439	i
475–9	A. *Ch.* 935–8, 946–52	c
530ff.	A. *Ag.* 1415–18	i
705	*Iliad* 23.454, 471	i
710	*Iliad* 23.352–3	i
711–12	*Iliad* 23.363–4	i
721–2	*Iliad* 23.336–40	i
756–8	A. *Ag.* 440ff.	c
786	A. *Ch.* 577	c
903–8	A. *Ch.* 193–4	i
1066–9	A. *Ch.* 315–509	i/c?
1139ff.	A. *Ag.* 434–44	c
1187	A. *Ch.* 17–18	i
1415–21	A. *Ag.* 1343–5	a
1462	A. *Ag.* 1624, 1632, 1639–40	c
1476–8	A. *Ag.* 1611	c
1476–8	A. *Ag.* 1375, *Eum.* 112	a
1476–9	A. *Ch.* 886–7	c/a

Philoctetes

144	*Od.* 9.182	a/c
175–6	*Od.* 9.398–402	a/c

183	*Od.* 9.433	a/c
601	*Iliad* 1.240	c
797	A. fr. 255 Radt	a/c/i?
827	*Iliad* 14.231ff.	a/c
946–7	A. fr. 399	i?

Oedipus Coloneus

525	*Iliad* 2.111 = 9.18	i
954–5	A. *Septem* 681–2	i
1224–8	Theognis 425–8	i
1254–5	E. *Pho.* 1310–11	i
1313	A. *Septem* 125	i
1440	E. *Hipp.* 1366	i
1441	E. *Pho.* 532	i?
1558–60	*Iliad* 20.61	i
1622–9	E. *Bacch.* 1078–88	i
1770	A. *Septem* 321	i

| fr. 727P | A. *Ag.* 526 | |

Euripides

Alcestis

184	A. *Ch.* 185–6	i
436	*Iliad* 23.19	a
464	*Iliad* 1.1ff.	c
560	*Iliad* 4.171	c
646–7	*Iliad* 6.429	c/a
779–802	Bacchyl. 3.78–84	a
885–8	*Iliad* 22.60–4	c/a
898	*Iliad* 24.797	a
951–2	A. *Pers.* 122	i
1000–4	*Iliad* 7.84–91	c
1031	*Iliad* 23.257–70	c/a

Medea

109	A. *Ch.* 470	i
410	*Od.* 10.351	c/a
410–45	Hesiod *Op.* 190–201	a
425	*Od.* 8.498	a
431	A. *Ag.* 690–1	c
433	A. *Septem* 781	i/c?

213

523	A. *Septem* 62	i
635	A. *Ag.* 927–8	i
689	*Od.* 19.204	i
845	*Iliad* 22.268	i
846	*Od.* 10.351	i
1012	*Iliad* 22.293	i
1388	A. *Ag.* 745	c
1407	*Iliad* 24.506	i/c

Heracleidae
75	*Iliad* 22.310	i?
326–8	*Od.* 2.276–7	i
386–9	A. *Pers.* 824–8	i
608ff.	*Iliad* 6.487–93	i?
608ff.	*Iliad* 24.524–51	i?
711–12	*Iliad* 6.492–3	i
748–9	*Iliad* 22.26–31	i
750	*Iliad* 24.785	i
868	*Iliad* 6.455	i

Hippolytus
168	Bacchyl. 9.45	i
220–2	Bacchyl. 9.24–34	i
563–4	*Iliad* 2.87–90	c
574	A. *Ag.* 1150	i

Andromache
99	*Iliad* 6.463	a
115	*Od.* 11.211	a/c
480	Bacchyl. 3.78–84	i
611	*Iliad* 1.1ff.	a
795	Pind. *P.* 4.70	i
978	A. *Ch.* 1058	i/c
1116	A. *Ch.* 221	c
1140–1	*Iliad* 21.493–6	i
1153	*Iliad* 22.371	a/c

Hecuba
56	*Iliad* 6.463	a
94	A. *Pers.* 619–20	i
930	A. *Pers.* 402	i
946ff.	A. *Ag.* 1461	i/c

| 1181ff. | A. *Ch.* 585–8 | a/c |

Supplices

498	A. *Septem* 427–8	i
584–7	A. *Septem* 59–61	i
650	S. *Ant.* 100	c
691–3	*Iliad* 16.742–50	i
832–7	A. *Ag.* 744–9	i
1123–31	A. *Ag.* 434–44	i/c

Electra

175	S. *El.* 211	i
318–31	*Iliad* 4.169–82	a
325	A. *Ch.* 193	i
513	A. *Ch.* 11	c
520	A. *Ch.* 229	a
520–84	A. *Ch.* 164–245	a
530	A. *Ch.* 174	a
534	A. *Ch.* 3a/5a	i/a
572–5	*Od.* 19.390ff.	i
860–1	Bacchyl. 13.84–90	i
1162	A. *Ag.* 1258	a/c
1221–3	A. *Ch.* 830–6	a/c

Hercules Furens

26	A. *Ag.* 750	i
111–13	A. *Ag.* 82	i
225	S. *Trach.* 1012	i
247	A. *Pers.* 840	i
252–74	A. *Ag.* 1348–71	i
254–5	A. *Ag.* 74, 1652	i
349–51	Pind. *N.* 5.24–5	i
391	Pind. fr. 140a56	i
407	Pind. *O.* 5.20	i
431	*Od.* 4.182	i/c
503–5	A. *Pers.* 840	i
678	A. *Ag.* 104	i
755–9	A. *Ag.* 367–72	i
773–80	A. *Ag.* 381–4, 462–70	i
802–4	Pind. *N.* 10.54	i
812	A. *Ch.* 584	c

938	A. *Ag.* 1405–6, *Ch.* 231	i
1039–41	*Od.* 16.216–19	c
1139	A. *Ag.* 1405–6, *Ch.* 231	i
1163–4	A. *Pers.* 805	i
1185	S. *Ajax* 591	i/c
1201	*Iliad* 24.506	i/c
1204	*Iliad* 22.362	i?
1205	*Iliad* 22.68	i?
1280	A. *Ag.* 1283	c
1353–7	S. *Trach.* 1070–4, 1101	c
1412	S. *Trach.* 1075	c

Troades

1–3	Bacchyl. 17.100–15	i
193	*Od.* 10.521, 536, 11.29, 49	i
256–8	A. *Ag.* 1264–7	c/a
353–405	A. *Ag.* 1227ff.	c/a
453	A. *Ag.* 1264–7	c/a
488–9	A. *Ag.* 1283	c
530	A. *Ag.* 1523	c
1330	*Iliad* 6.463	a

Iphigeneia Taurica

37	A. *Ag.* 36	c/a
50–4	A. *Ag.* 897–8	c/a
110	A. *Pers.* 428	i
132	Bacchyl. 17.80	a
137–8	A. *Ag.* 85	c/a
141	A. *Ag.* 45	c/a
287	A. *Ch.* 248–9	c/a
287	S. *Trach.* 1099	c
288	A. *Eum.* 137–8	c/a
300	A. *Ag.* 659	c/a
1136–7	Bacchyl. 17.89–90	a
1326	Bacchyl. 17.90	a
1427	Bacchyl. 17.89–90	a

Ion

505	*Iliad* 1.1–4	a
888	*Iliad* 3.397	c?
1171–3	*Iliad* 1.597–600	i

Helen

52	*Iliad* 1.1ff.	a
167ff.	Stesichorus 193 *PMG*	a?
207	Pind. *P.* 5.92	i
639–41	Stesichorus 187 *PMG*	a?
725	Stesichorus 187 *PMG*	a?
1049–56	S. *El.* 56–64	a
1101–2	*Iliad* 16.645ff.	i
1110–11	Arist. *Aves* 210ff.	i
1118–21	A. *Ag.* 713ff., 748	c/a
1158	A. *Ag.* 453	a
1305	Bacchyl. 17.77	a
1318	Bacchyl. 17.89	a
1337	*Iliad* 24.105 ? *Od.* 1.342	c
1351	Bacchyl. 17.77	a
1454–9	Bacchyl. 17.97 (17.4, 6, 77)	a
1478ff.	*Iliad* 3.3	c/a
1487	Bacchyl. 16.6	i

Phoenissae

61–2	S. *OT* 1268–9	i
287	A. *Septem* 30, 251, 469	i?
437	A. *Septem* 254	i
636–7	A. *Ag.* 682–91	i?
656–75	A. *Septem* 727–41	i
751	A. *Septem* 378ff.	a
755	A. *Septem* 672–3	i
779–80	A. *Septem* 675–6	i
1104ff.	A. *Septem* 369ff.	i
1148–52	*Iliad* 16.742–50	i
1175–6	A. *Septem* 427–31	i?
1130	A. *Septem* 488	i
1401	*Iliad* 16.734–5	i
1423	*Iliad* 22.17	i/c?
1515	Hom. *Hymn Aph.* 264	i
1555–6	S. *OT* 1422–3	i
1629–34	S. *Ant.* 26–30	i
1758–9	S. *OT* 1524–5	i

Orestes

193	A. *Ch.* 1027–8	i

217–18	S. *Phil.* 761	i
217–54	A. *Ch.* 1051–64	a
225–6	S. *Phil.* 1321	i
256	A. *Ch.* 1058	a
272–4	A. *Eum.* 180–90, 628	a
656–7	S. *Phil.* 83–4	i
722	S. *Phil.* 923	i
806	S. *Phil.* 673	i?
821–2	A. *Ch.* 983–90	c/a
894	A. *Ag.* 725	i
903	S. *Phil.* 188	i?
1045–6	S. *El.* 1357–8	i
1077	A. *Pers.* 250	i
1204–5	A. *Ag.* 11	c/a
1205	*Od.* 11.386, 434	c/a
1205	*Od.* 24.202	c/a
1225–45	A. *Ch.* 479–509	a
1353–65 = 1537–48	S. *Phil.* 391–402 = 507–18	i
1361–2	S. *Phil.* 518, 601–2	i
1385–9	A. *Ag.* 738–49	a/i
1400–2	A. *Ch.* 937–8	a/i
1421	A. *Ag.* 1375	a
1421	A. *Eum.* 112	a
1426–40	*Od.* 4.121–36	c
1490	A. *Ch.* 935–6	a/i
1491	A. *Ch.* 964	i/c/a
1525	S. *Phil.* 1407	i?
1532	Archilochus 114W	c
1676–7	S. *Phil.* 874	i
Bacchae		
87	Pindar *P.* 8.55	i
764	A. *Pers.* 164	i
862–72	Bacchyl. 13.84–90	i
991ff.	A. *Ag.* 223, *Ch.* 584,	
	Eum. 239 = 42	c
1061	*Iliad* 14.286–91	i/c
1064–5	*Od.* 5.239	i
1070	*Iliad* 14.286–91	i/c
1073	*Iliad* 14.286–91	i/c
1101–2	A. *Ag.* 1376	c/a?

Iphigeneia Aulidensis

39–40	*Iliad* 6.496	c/a
56	A. *Supp.* 380	i
202	*Od.* 11.287	i
202	*Cypria* VII.1 (Allen)	i
204–5	*Iliad* 2.673	i/c
407	S. *Ant.* 523	i
443	A. *Ag.* 218	c
511	A. *Ag.* 218	c
686 = 1106	A. *Ag.* 914	c
718	A. *Ag.* 226	c
790–1	Bacchyl. 16 *passim*	c
793	Bacchyl. 16.6	c
797	Bacchyl. 16.3	c
913	A. *Ag.* 218–21	c
932	A. *Eum.* 100	c
959–60	*Iliad* 9.395	c/a
977ff.	A. *Ag.* 787	c
1146–7	A. *Ag.* 1178–83	c
1246	A. *Ch.* 896	c
1246	*Iliad* 22.82	c
1476 = 1511	A. *Ag.* 690	c

Cyclops

60	S. *Phil.* 159	i/a?
86	A. *Pers.* 378	i
88	*Od.* 9.132	i
125	*Od.* 9.176	i
140	S. *Phil.* 1290	i/c
359	A. *Pers.* 462–3	i
360	*Od.* 9.425	i
395–405	*Od.* 9.289–92	i(a)
400	S. *Trach.* 779–82	i/c
460–3	*Od.* 9.383–6	c/a
469–71	*Od.* 9.391–4	c/a
473	*Od.* 9.241–2	c/a
548–51	*Od.* 9.355–70	i(a)
591–2	*Od.* 9.372–4	c/a
608–10	*Od.* 9.391–3	c/a
696–700	*Od.* 9.507–21	i(a)

707	S. *Phil.* 19	i/a?
fr. 1059	A. *Ch.* 585ff.	

Miscellaneous

Alcaeus
335.3	Archilochus fr. 13W.5–7
347	Hesiod *Op.* 582–8

Archilochus
5W	*Iliad* 18.132ff.
112	*Od.* 9.433

Aristophanes
Birds 1240	A. *Ag.* 526, *Pers.* 811

Bacchylides
3.17	Hom. Hymn Ap. 203
5.63ff.	*Iliad* 6.143
9.27	Sappho 96.6
13.63–4	*Od.* 4.180
13.65	*Iliad* 9.413
13.128	*Iliad* 24.785
13.149–50	*Iliad* 4.247–8
13.164–5	*Iliad* 21.123–5
13.202–3	Theognis 1183–4
13.205	*Iliad* 24.5

Homeric Hymns
Demeter
38ff.	*Iliad* 22.87, 94, 146
38ff.	*Iliad* 22.401

Ibycus
151.47 SLG	*Iliad* 9.413

Mimnermus
1W.1–4	*Iliad* 3.64
1.3	*Iliad* 6.161
2.1	*Iliad* 6.143
2.5–7	*Iliad* 9.410–16
13.3–4	*Iliad* 5.93–6

Panyassis
  Herakleia fr. 16K   *Iliad* 5.382

Pindar
  P. Oxy. 2622   *Iliad* 6.143
  O. 6   *Od.* 8.498
  P. 4.277   *Iliad* 15.207
  P. 8.95–6   A. fr. 399
  I. 2.48   *Iliad* 23.19

Sappho
  1.13ff.   *Iliad* 5.367
  16.17   *Iliad* 3.64
  44.4   *Iliad* 9.413
  44.43–4   *Iliad* 22.212

Semonides
  6.1–2   Hesiod *Op.* 702–3
  7.87   *Iliad* 22.51
  7.110ff.   Hesiod *Op.* 701
  7.116   *Iliad* 15.19–20

Simonides
  8W   *Iliad* 6.143
  531 *PMG*   Bacchyl. 13.204ff.

Tyrtaeus
  10W.9   *Iliad* 6.206ff.
  10W.23–7   *Iliad* 22.71ff.

ABBREVIATIONS

The following abbreviations are used in references in the Notes.

AJP   *American Journal of Philology*
BICS   *Bulletin of the Institute of Classical Studies*
CJ   *Classical Journal*
CP   *Classical Philology*
CQ   *Classical Quarterly*
CR   *Classical Review*
CSCA   *California Studies in Classical Antiquity*
GRBS   *Greek, Roman, and Byzantine Studies*
HSCP   *Harvard Studies in Classical Philology*
JHS   *Journal of Hellenic Studies*
LCM   *Liverpool Classical Monthly*
LSJ   *A Greek–English Lexicon*, compiled by George Liddell
        and Robert Scott, rev. by H. S. Jones with the assistance
        of R. McKenzie, Oxford, Oxford University Press, 1968
PCPS   *Proceedings of the Cambridge Philological Society*
PMG   *Poetae Melici Graeci*, edited by D. L. Page, Oxford,
        Oxford University Press, 1962
QUCC   *Quaderni urbinati di cultura classica*
TAPA   *Transactions of the American Philological Association*

NOTES

1 INTRODUCTION: THE LYRIC BACKGROUND

1 M. Kumpf makes the case for precisely these two words as significant thematic allusions in Euripides' *Cyclops* in his dissertation, "The Homeric Hapax Legomena and their Literary Use by Later Authors," (Columbus, 1974). The dissertation is discussed further below, Chapter 5, notes 12 and 38.

2 The allusions considered here are discussed at greater length in C.M. Dawson, "Σπουδογέλοιον: Random Thoughts on Occasional Poems," *YCS*, 19 (1966), pp. 42–7 and Mark Griffith, "Man and the Leaves: A Study of Mimnermus fr. 2," *CSCA*, 8 (1975), pp. 73–88, especially, pp. 77–8.

3 The similarity in function of metaphor and allusion is discussed by G. Conte in *The Rhetoric of Imitation* (Ithaca and London, 1986), pp. 38 and 53–5.

4 The terms "tenor," "vehicle," and "ground" were developed by I.A. Richards in his discussion of metaphor in Chapters 5 and 6 of *The Philosophy of Rhetoric* (New York, 1936) pp. 89–138. M.S. Silk retains the terms "tenor" and "vehicle" and substitutes the phrase "neutral term" for "ground." His usage is slightly different from Richards', but is applied with great precision to much Greek poetry. See M.S. Silk, *Interaction in Poetic Imagery* (London and New York, 1974), especially pp. 9–26.

5 This discussion is a pastiche of many excellent analyses. In addition to Conte, *The Rhetoric*, I have found especially helpful and stimulating P. Ricouer, *The Rule of Metaphor* (Toronto, 1977), M. Riffaterre, *Semiotics of Poetry* (Bloomington, 1978), and the collection of essays in *On Metaphor* edited by S. Sacks (Chicago and London, 1979).

6 P. Pucci's analysis of allusion, or intertextuality, is similar. He calls ungrammaticalities or deviations "infelicities" (pp. 134–5) which are an invitation to interpretation (p. 237) which in turn effaces inconsistencies or fills gaps (p. 241). These terms are employed in the service of a stimulating treatment of epic, *Odysseus Polutropos: Intertextual Readings in the Odyssey and the Iliad* (Ithaca and London, 1987).

7 The term "trigger" is used by Arthur Adkins in *Poetic Craft in the Early*

Greek Elegists (Chicago and London, 1985). See especially p. 25.

8 Notable passages which use these Homeric lines are [Semonides] 8 West, Mimnermus 2 West, Bacchyl. 5.63ff., Pind. P. Oxy. 2622, Soph. *OT* 1186 (see Dawe, *ad loc.*), Aristophanes *Frogs* 685, Aristotle *NE* v. 9.1136b9. See Hugh Lloyd-Jones, "Heracles at Eleusis: P. Oxy. 2622 and P.S.I. 1391," *Maia*, 19 (1967), pp. 206–29. Most of these passages and some later ones are reproduced in the dedication at the front of the book.

9 Wayne Booth notes the importance of context for the interpretation of metaphor and the general tendency to underinterpret. See "Ten Literal 'Theses,'" in Sacks (ed.) *On Metaphor*, pp. 173–4. Compare Pucci, *Odysseus Polutropos*, on the impossibility of specifying the limits of meaning (p. 240) and implications for interpretation (pp. 51–2).

10 The most rewarding discussion of all these complexities, difficult in its own right but well worth effort, is in Gordon Williams, *Figures of Thought in Roman Poetry* (New Haven, 1980), especially pp. 20–188. He brings out, among other things, the ways in which the final reintegrating interpretation depends on processes of metonymy and synechdoche. Much of what follows is indebted to his explanations which here are greatly simplified.

11 Adkins, *Poetic Craft*, p. 24.

12 This is one of the least disputed instances of Homeric allusion in Greek poetry before the Hellenistic period. It has been discussed in detail by Dawson, "Random Thoughts," pp. 50–8, and by A.W.H. Adkins, "Callinus 1 and Tyrtaeus 10 as Poetry," *HSCP*, 81 (1977), pp. 91–3. Other allusions to *Iliad* 22 in lyric and tragedy are listed in Appendix E. In the following chapters, there are frequent discussions of this scene from the *Iliad*, for it more frequently serves as the vehicle for allusion than any other single passage of poetry. As David Konstan has pointed out to me, it even serves as a model for and is quoted in one of the odder scenes of Chariton's *Chaereas and Callirhoe* 3.5.4–6. R.L. Fowler entertains the possibility, in *The Nature of Early Greek Lyric* (Toronto, 1987), p. 31, that "Homer" may be imitating Tyrtaeus 10W rather than the other way around. It seems more likely that Tyrtaeus called on the same spot of the *Iliad* which others found so striking than that the composer of *Iliad* 22 adapted a section of Tyrtaeus so successfully that later poets then took it up. In general, Fowler denies the possibility of allusion in early Greek poetry. From the promising passages, he admits a few exceptions, argues against some others, but fails to mention a great number. See especially his pp. 20–39.

13 Adkins, "Callinus 1," p. 93, gives a careful estimation of the effects of this phrase. Dawson, "Random Thoughts," pp. 57–8, selected two occurrences and suggested more specific allusive force. I prefer Adkins' more conservative claim. The instances are *Il.* 17.271, *Od.* 22.177; and, line initial, *Il.* 2.699, 17.153, 17.478, 17.672, 22.436, *Od.*11.156.

14 See especially L. Rissman, *Love as War: Homeric Allusion in the Poetry of Sappho* (Königstein, 1983). Rissman discusses the contributions of the Homeric passage to Sappho fr. 1.13ff. on p. 10 and to fr. 13 on pp.

83–5. The allusion in fragment 1 is also discussed by J. Svenbro, "Sappho and Diomedes: Some Notes on Sappho 1 LP and the Epic," *Museum Philologum Londiniense*, 1 (1975), pp. 37–49, by K. Stanley, "The Rôle of Aphrodite in Sappho Fr. 1," *GRBS*, 17 (1976), pp. 305–21, and by J.D. Marry, "Sappho and the Heroic Ideal: ἔρωτος ἀρετή," *Arethusa*, 12 (1979), pp. 71–92. Particularly good is J. Winkler, "Gardens of Nymphs: Public and Private in Sappho's Lyrics," *Women's Studies*, 8 (1981), pp. 65–91 (pp. 68–72 for Sappho 1).

15 Winkler is especially good on this aspect of Sappho 1, "Gardens," pp. 70–2.

16 In the spring of 1986 I worked on the *Geryoneïs* with Marty Hipsky in such close collaboration that I can no longer separate my ideas on this poem from his. Many of the following points are made in an unpublished paper of his, Marty A. Hipsky, Jr., "Imagery in Stesichorus' *Geryoneïs*," 1986. Whatever is persuasive in this discussion should be credited to him.

17 That the fight continues after the elimination of the first head can be seen from the fragments which continue the narrative and from the vases. For a full discussion of the *Geryoneïs* see D. Page, "Stesichorus: The *Geryoneïs*," *JHS*, 93 (1973), pp. 138–54. The evidence from vases is collected in M. Robertson, "*Geryoneïs*: Stesichorus and the Vase-Painters," *CQ*, 63 (1969), pp. 207–21. For a much earlier treatment – in bronze – of the same narrative see P. Brize, "Samos und Stesichoros: Zu einem Früharchaischen Bronzeblech," *Athenische Mitteilungen*, 100 (1985), pp. 53–90.

18 Cf. Virgil, *Aeneid* 9.436.

19 Page, "*The Geryoneïs*," p. 153.

20 The scholiasts refer to relevant passages of Homer in their commentaries on tragic lines, but it could be argued that their viewpoint is the product of the age of Hellenistic poetry and is anachronistically applied. Furthermore, the level of expertise found in the scholia does not encourage taking them as legitimating authority. Callimachus uses the verb ἀπομάττεσθαι to describe Aratus' use of Hesiod as a model (Epigr. 27.3), but there are only the faintest traces of earlier usage along these lines: see Arist. *Frogs* 1040 and Aristotle *NE* 1172a12.

21 See *Clouds* 1364ff. This observation is made by Hutchinson in his commentary to Aeschylus' *Seven against Thebes*, p. xli.

22 Some of these factors are outlined and considered by M. Griffith in "The Vocabulary of *Prometheus Bound*," *CQ*, 34 (1984), p. 286. Griffith recognizes the difficulties, and the possibility of proceeding to study allusion in tragedy – always with informed caution. P. Easterling also outlines the problems in identifying allusions between tragedies in the introduction to her edition of Sophocles' *Trachiniae*, p. 21.

2 SLICES FROM THE BANQUET: THE TRAGEDIES OF AESCHYLUS

1 It is beyond the scope of this book to examine borrowed formulae or repeated phrases which, however precise, could not clearly be associated with a particular passage in epic. For Aeschylus such phrases have been collected by Alexander Sideras in his *Aeschylus Homericus* (Göttingen, 1971). This is supplemented by R.W. Garson, "Aspects of Aeschylus' Homeric Usages," *Phoenix*, 39 (1985), pp. 1–5. For a sober reduction to more certain examples see G.O. Hutchinson in his commentary, *Septem contra Thebas* (Oxford, 1985), pp. 89–90.

2 For the importance of opening lines of works as signatures or as significant initial declarations and the implications this has for allusion, see G.B. Conte, *The Rhetoric of Imitation* (Ithaca and London, 1986), pp. 35, 70.

3 J.B. Bury suggested that the echo was a compliment acknowledging literary debt: "Two Literary Compliments," *CR*, 19 (1905), p. 10. But J.T. Sheppard suggested that the quotation with its change was designed for sinister effect: "Notes on Aeschylus' *Persae*," *CR*, 29 (1915), pp. 33–4. More recently Broadhead has doubted the significance of Aeschylus' choice of words (*ad loc.*), but R.P. Winnington-Ingram agrees with Sheppard: *Studies in Aeschylus* (Cambridge, 1983), pp. 198–9.

4 Eduard Fraenkel, *Aeschylus Agamemnon* (Oxford, 1950), vol. 2, p. 50.

5 Broadhead notes the Homeric phrase without comment. Sidgwick said, "Aeschylus is clearly echoing the Homeric phrase."

6 See the treatment of Tyrtaeus 10W in Chapter 1. The claim for Aeschylus was made by A.H. Coxon in the remarkable article "Persica," *CQ*, 52 (1958), pp. 45–53. Some of his claims are based on combinations of passages which seem to me rather complex even to consider as echoes; but this article, along with comments of his reported by others, show a fine sense for the art of allusion and imitation in Greek tragedy.

7 Some may object to considerations of author's intent and effort. In this matter I agree with the comments of M.L. West. He has recently noted that some scholars feel "that it is not our business to pry into the stages by which [the author] arrived at [his or her text]. I disagree. The creative process is a legitimate object of scholarly interest.": "Problems in Euripides' *Orestes*," *CQ*, 37 (1987), p. 285.

8 Conradt makes the reference to the simile (*ad loc.*).

9 The phrase "full of Ares" to describe the *Septem* occurs in Aristophanes *Frogs* 1021 and Plutarch's *Quaestiones convivales* 715e (a quotation from Gorgias).

10 *Od.* 5.270–1 is cited by Isaac Flagg in his commentary (Boston, 1886) and by more recently by Liana Lupaş and Zoe Petre in their commentary (Paris, 1981).

11 So G.O. Hutchinson, *ad loc.*

12 For allusions at strophic opening, see Appendix A. Other allusions to

Il. 1.1 can be found in Appendix E. See Fraenkel on *Ag.* 1455ff. and Stevens at *Andr.* 611. For a late use which derives its unparalleled lightness of tone from the criticisms eternally leveled at doctors see *Anthologia Graeca* 11.401.

13 For a more general discussion of the tradition of the fall of Troy and the effects of Homeric echoes in this chorus see Hutchinson, *ad loc.*

14 The connection between the two passages seems to have been suggested first by A.H. Coxon. It is reported in print by Hutchinson, *ad loc.*

15 In addition to the three instances discussed below there are two passages which may have the Iliad as their ultimate poetic source. Pelasgus' concern lest someone declare he has brought ruin upon his city is expressed with a direct quote of the hypothetical criticism (*Supp.* 400–1). The passage may owe something to the similar criticism Hector imagines also in the form of direct speech in his final scene before the walls of Troy (*Il.* 22.104–7), as H. Friis Johansen has suggested, *ad loc.* Certainly, of all passages in Greek literature this scene of the *Iliad* seems the most alluded to. A less certain echo is Pelasgus' reflection that unlike stolen goods life cannot be replaced (444ff.) which bears some resemblance to Achilles' thoughts in another famous passage, his rejection of the embassy (*Il.* 9.406–9). However, either or both of these may be more general rhetorical topoi than imitations.

16 As H. Friis Johansen notes, *ad loc.*, Aeschylus must have had the reading δαῖτα (a feast) rather than πᾶσι ((all) here).

17 These parallels were first developed by M.L. West, "The Parodos of the *Agamemnon*," *CQ,* 73 (1979), pp. 1–6.

18 The *Choephori* passage which supports West's claim about *Agamemnon* was adduced by R. Janko, "Aeschylus' *Oresteia* and Archilochus," *CQ,* 74 (1980), pp. 291–3.

19 That Aeschylus was using Archilochus has been questioned by M. Davies, "Aeschylus and the Fable," *Hermes,* 109 (1981), pp. 248–51, who suggests more generic influence is at work. H. Lloyd-Jones connects the image of the net and its catch at *Agamemnon* 355–61 with an early version of a fable which survives in Babrius fr. 4: "Agamemnonea," *HSCP,* 73 (1969), pp. 98–9.

20 In his commentary to the *Choephori* Garvie notes both the Pindar parallels, *ad loc.* R.W.B. Burton suggests that the cork simile appears in both passages as a common figure of speech, *Pindar's Pythian Odes* (Oxford, 1962), p. 129.

21 In his note to *Agamemnon* 79.

22 Garvie calls the *Choephori* phrase an imitation of Archilochus, *ad loc.*

23 A. Burnett hints at the relevance of Sappho 16 to this *Agamemnon* passage: *Three Archaic Poets* (Cambridge, Mass., 1983), p. 288. More similarities are outlined in William Calder's "An Echo of Sappho Fragment 16 L-P at Aeschylus, *Agamemnon* 403–19?," *Estudios clasicos,* 26 (1984), pp. 215–18.

24 The relations of these two mother–father–son trios are considered by Simon Goldhill in *Language, Sexuality, Narrative: The Oresteia* (Cambridge,

1984), pp. 183–95, with particular attention to the *Odyssey*. His observations are interesting but depend on a broad notion of intertextuality not limited to specific allusions from one passage to another.

25 Fraenkel notes the close dependence on these two epic passages, *ad loc.*

26 The connection between *Agamemnon* 120–2 and *Iliad* 6.57–60 was outlined long ago by Henry S. Dawson, "On *Agamemnon* 108–120," *CR*, 41 (1927), pp. 213–14.

27 Fraenkel, *ad loc.*

28 Fraenkel (*ad loc.*) is certain that Aeschylus has used the *Iliad* as his model. Like so many things in the *Oresteia*, this image is repeated (with the Homeric verb recurring) at *Eumenides* 937.

29 Fraenkel is particularly good on the effect of Clytemnestra's imagery.

30 Headlam suggests (*ad loc.*) the possiblility of Homeric reminiscence.

31 See Fraenkel, *ad loc.* The chorus's phrase "having destroyed many souls at Troy" (1456–7) also recalls the often-quoted *Iliad* 1.3.

32 Fraenkel points out that ἀνάλκις is also used of Aegisthus in the *Odyssey* (3.310) which helps put the connection between Menelaus' cowardly suitors and Cassandra's cowardly Aegisthus beyond doubt.

33 The text partly depends on a conjecture of Stanley's, but it is universally and rightly accepted. See Garvie, *ad loc.*

34 Garvie (*ad loc.*) says "Aeschylus may have had" the Homeric passage in mind. I think it certain.

35 So Goldhill, *Language, Sexuality, Narrative*, p. 196.

36 Most notable are *PV* 64–5: *Theog.* 521–2 and *PV* 152: *Theog.* 717ff. This later passage also recalls the similarly relevant *Iliad* 8.16.

37 The poet has apparently made extensive use of Pindar in this play. (Some have argued the opposite – that Pindar imitates Aeschylus – but this seems less likely. For bibliography see Griffith's commentary at *PV* 351–72.) The description of Typhus owes something to Hesiod's *Theogony* as does Prometheus' story in general. But more specifically the Typhus passage (vv. 349–73) repeatedly echoes Pindar *Pythia* 1.15–28 on the same topic, with *PV* 365 also recalling Pindar *Olympia* 4.7–8. Pindar's use of the rare word θέορτον (*Ol.* 2.36) may have influenced the poet at *PV* 765.

38 The connection between these two mother-son pairs seems to have gone unnoticed. This is particularly odd in S. Saïd's *Sophiste et tyran ou le problème du Prométhée enchaîné* (Paris, 1985). There is an entire chapter devoted to prophetic knowledge (pp. 187–229) which makes no mention of Prometheus' debt to his mother, of Achilles' debt to his mother, or of any connection between the knowledgeable god and mortal. Thetis and Achilles are mentioned in passing, but not in this connection, on pp. 241–50 and 289.

39 The particle θην which makes its sole appearance in Greek tragedy at *PV* 928 may well derive from a memory of Achilles' use at *Iliad* 9.394 (one of thirteen in the *Iliad*). At any rate, it indicates the importance of epic for this play.

40 Note the mention of the repayment (or lack of it) in terms of honor –

ποινάς τε τίνειν (*PV* 176): οὐδὲν ἔτεισας (*Il.* 1.244); and the importance of the scepter as a symbol of power – *PV* 171, *Il.* 234, 245.

41 For the confusion of Nereids and Oceanids see M.L. West on the two similar sets of cousins at Hesiod *Theogony* 241.

42 This poem of Bacchylides' with its interest in Theseus is likely to have been very well known at Athens. The possible reasons for this and Euripides' frequent and extensive use of the poem are discussed below in Chapter 5, pp. 142–5.

43 Agostino Masaracchia sees the Prometheus–Zeus conflict as modeled on the Achilles–Agamemnon conflict in the *Iliad*. He insists on a strict equivalence whereby Achilles has Zeus' role and Agamemnon Prometheus', but this ignores the much more striking and fundamental parallels between Prometheus and Achilles: "Per l'interpretazione del *Prometeo*. I," *QUCC*, 20 (1985), pp. 46–8.

44 Aeschylus seems to have used it in *Seven against Thebes* (934–6). Sophocles certainly used it as a moment of central importance for *Ajax*: see *Ajax* 661–5, 817ff., and the discussion below, Chapter 3, pp. 53–4, 62–4.

45 Prometheus' description of himself as yoked by necessity (v. 108) may owe something to Aeschylus' *Agamemnon* 218 where Agamemnon puts on the yoke of necessity. It would be like this poet – or at least this play – to take a metaphor and make it more literal. But the image may be common enough not to have been borrowed from a specific passage.

46 For an excellent treatment of some of the aspects of this tantalizing subject see Laura M. Slatkin, "The Wrath of Thetis," *TAPA*, 116 (1986), pp. 1–24.

47 Aristophanes would later borrow this description for one of his most beautiful passages (*Birds* 685ff.).

3 SOPHOCLES AND EURIPIDES: THE EARLY PLAYS

1 *Vita* 20. Although there have been some articles and a passing comment here and there, this aspect of Sophocles' poetic craft has been relatively neglected. One very careful study is J.F. Davidson, "The Parodos of the *Antigone*: A Poetic Study," *BICS*, 30 (1983), pp. 41–51.

2 None of the proposed imitations and echoes of lyric in Ajax seem convincing to me. The image of fearful birds (168–71), which Jebb found a conscious imitation of Sappho or Alcaeus (fr. 10V inc. auct.), seems likely to be a common image taken from life. Ajax's declaration that nothing lies beyond human expectation (648–9) could echo an Archilochan opening line (fr. 122.1W) as Stanford suggests, but it is more likely to be a topos. And the phrase "famous Athens" (861), which Stanford suspects may echo the same words in Pindar fr. 76Sn, seems most likely of all to have been a common set phrase.

3 Noted by Stanford, *ad loc*. Sophocles would borrow the cry again for his own *Philoctetes*. See the discussion below, Chapter 5, p. 146.

4 In his introduction to *Ajax* Jebb reproduces the list included in

G. Wolff's 1887 edition: *Aj.* 56–*Pers.* 426; *Aj.* 412–*Pers.* 367; *Aj.* 673–*Pers.* 386; *Aj.* 740–*Pers.* 489; *Aj.* 172,954–*Pers.* 633; *Aj.* 1404–*Pers.* 584. Jebb adds *Aj.* 789ff.–*Pers.* 248 and *Aj.* 769–*Pers.* 477. Stanford also suggests *Aj.* 597 may be a paraphrase of *Pers.* 307. All recent editors of *Ajax* and *Persae* seem to agree on the close relationship of *Aj.* 673–*Pers.* 386.

5 When Ajax describes a dark (ἐρεμνόν) stream of blood (376) Jebb says that the adjective was "doubtless suggested by Aesch. *Ag.* 1390" where Clytemnestra uses the same adjective for the shower of blood which comes from Agamemnon as she murders him. The rare word also describes a dark storm to which Ajax is likened in the midst of his rage at *Iliad* 12.375. Each passage is suggestive. Sophocles may be imitating one or both.

6 Diog. Laert. 4.20; *Vita* 20. For Sophoclean Homerisms in morphology and dialect, a type of borrowing not considered in this book, see A. Colonna, "De Genetivi in -οιο Usus apud Tragicos Scriptores," *Sileno*, 3 (1977), pp. 207–9, especially p. 209.

7 *Due seminari di Eduard Fraenkel*, ed. L.E. Rossi *et al.* (Rome, 1977), p.15. Of course there are ways of being Homeric without imitating or alluding to specific Homeric passages, some of which can be well illustrated from *Ajax*. A passage may be loaded with general Homeric epithets (cf. *Aj.* 372–6). Homeric epithets can be used with irony, as Jebb and Stanford suggest is done with Odysseus' πολύτλας at 865. Or Homeric narrative may be pointedly referred to or corrected as perhaps the vision of an Ajax speaking in Hades (865), contrasts with the strikingly silent one of *Od.* 11.543 (so Stanford, *ad loc.*).

8 These are *Aj.* 499–*Il.* 6.432; *Aj.* 501–*Il.* 6.460; *Aj.* 514–*Il.* 6.413, 429; *Aj.* 545–*Il.* 6.264 (this is the meeting of Hector with his mother; the scholiast sees what to my mind is a very doubtful if not comic similarity in the question of whether or not to bring a given item – wine or Eurysakes – to the hero. But the oddity of the attempt to connect the two passages is all the more interesting as a reflection of the scholiast's way of working); *Aj.* 550–*Il.* 6.476; and *Aj.* 574–*Il.* 6.418 (also unlikely and equally interesting). The earlier reference is *Aj.* 292–*Il.* 6.490.

9 Other points of influence have been pointed out. For example, Jebb suggests that the description of Astyanax as ἀταλάφρονα (*Il.* 6.400) is reflected in Sophocles' use of the verb ἀτάλλων ("cherishing") in Ajax's speech to Eurysakes (559).

10 P.E. Easterling, "The Tragic Homer," *BICS*, 31 (1984), pp. 1–8.

11 See the discussion in Chapter 1, pages 8–12 along with note 12.

12 An exception is W. Edward Brown, who has paid some attention to the Homeric Ajax in "Sophocles' Ajax and Homer's Hector," *CJ*, 61 (1965–6), pp. 118–21.

13 A different form, ἀργιπόδης, occurs once in the *Greek Anthology* 6.299.8. Commentators, of course, repeat the word in discussions of *Il.* 24.211.

14 The adjective ὠμηστής is rare in Homer. It occurs only in the *Iliad* and only four times there. The first three uses in the poem are all of animals – birds (11.454), dogs (22.67), and fish (24.82) – always in the

plural. Hecuba's use, then, in the singular and of a man should be extremely vivid and memorable.

15 Fraenkel (ad *Ag*. 1293ff.) felt that Sophocles' use of ἀσφάδαστος proved that he had this passage of Aeschylus in mind. Oddly enough, just a few lines later (*Ag*. 1304–5) Aeschylus uses an adverb which occurs only once in the Homeric poems (εὐκλεῶς/ἐϋκλεῶς); the oddity is that the Homeric passage is *Il*. 22.110 – Hector's so frequently used scene before the walls. Like his sister Cassandra, Hector is contemplating his death at the hands of a Greek.

16 There are fewer than twenty instances of the word in any sense in all extant Greek.

17 Of the more than seventy passages in the *Iliad* in which Ajax figures, half are simply bare or very brief mentions. In the following thirty-seven, he appears for more than five lines: 4.272–91, 4.473–500, 5.607–27, 6.5–11, 7.170–330, 8.261–334, 9.620–55, 11.463–501, 11.521–74, 11.580–94, 12.265–90, 12.329–415, 13.47–84, 13.188–205, 13.312–30, 13.701–11, 13.809–37, 14.402–39, 14.468–74, 15.415–516, 15.559–69, 16.101–29, 16.358–64, 16.553–69, 17.91–139, 17.228–315, 17.352–65, 17.507–15, 17.529–37, 17.626–55, 17.706–24, 17.742–61, 18.148–67, 23.707–38, 23.811–25, 23.836–49. There are, of course, echoes or imitations in Ajax of specific passages from the Homeric poems which are not tied to Hector or Ajax. One of the many Greek echoes of the proem to the *Iliad* occurs at *Aj*. 830. Stanford has pointed out that Sophocles seems to have borrowed both a phrase for wretched old age and its application to fathers deprived of sons (ἐν λυγρῷ γήρᾳ, *Aj*. 506–7; γήραϊ λυγρῷ, *Il*. 5.153), and that a passage on hybris seems related to a marked Homeric line (*Aj*. 195–8, *Od*. 15.329 = 17.569).

18 The contest in the funeral games which most seems to foreshadow *Ajax* is the wrestling match between Ajax and Odysseus which Achilles declares a draw (23.707–37), for in the play Odysseus is first Ajax's victorious enemy and then his defender. It may be mere coincidence, but at *Ajax* 772 there is reference to Ajax's bloody hand – χεῖρα φοινίαν; and this root for "bloody" (φοιν) and the word "hand" occur together in the *Iliad* neither when Greek and Trojan are hacking away at each other nor when Nestor or Phoenix are telling tales of great battles in bygone days, but rather only in this struggle which ends in a tie (23.714–17).

19 The verb is used seventeen times in the *Iliad*, five times in Ajax passages: 4.497, 8.269, 11.546, 12.333, and 17.115. A sixth instance occurs just three lines after an extended Ajax passage – 17.674.

20 It is an intriguing passage in its own right. The word ἐντροπαλιζόμενος, for example, is only used four times in the whole *Iliad*. It once describes the goddess Artemis (21.492); but the other three uses all describe someone moving away from Hector – Andromache at the end of the family scene (6.496), Ajax here, and Menelaos in 17.109.

21 Stanford gives the following list of passages with metaphorical

language which echoes this theme: 271–7, 360, 369, 611, 614–15, 735–6, 1253–4. The language in some of these is probably too common to count for much, but some are quite vivid. Stanford, in his commentary, has a few general comments, pp. 274–5.

22 Especially vv. 25–7, 51–65, 141–7, 218–20, 233–44, 295–311, 324–5, 364–6, 373–6, 452–5, and 1061.

23 So Stanford in his appendix on the style of Sophocles, especially pp. 273–5. However, he exaggerates the extent to which these images occur in *Ajax*: the metaphors of the yoke and even more of "driving" are too commonplace to stand out as particularly significant.

24 It will occur once more in extant Greek literature: Euripides' *Bacchae* 981.

25 Aeschylus used the imperative for Clytemnestra's desperate plea at the climax of the *Choephori* (896) and then echoed it at *Eumenides* 539. The sole occurrence in Euripides at *Iphigeneia at Aulis* 1246 is likely to reflect Aeschylean influence.

26 Following the scholiast, Jebb indicated that the scene described in *Ajax* 729ff. was suggested by the quarrel between Achilles and Agamemnon in *Iliad* 1.194ff. Again, later at 1269ff. Jebb hears Teucer's complaints about how frequently Ajax risked his life for the Greeks as echoing Achilles' similar words in his rejection of the embassy (*Il.* 9.322).

27 Most notably in the second stasimon of *Antigone*, which, as even cautious critics recognize, contains extensive echoes of *Septem* 720–61. See, for example, R.W.B. Burton, *The Chorus in Sophocles' Tragedies* (Oxford, 1980), p.106, and the discussion below, pp. 80–1, 235 note 60.

28 A view contrary to mine can be found in "Homer and Sophocles' Ajax," in M.J. Anderson (ed.), *Classical Drama and its Influence* (London, 1965), p. 65, where G.M. Kirkwood claims that Sophocles made no use of the passage on Ajax from *Iliad* 17.

29 In his note to vv. 986–7 and in a discussion of metaphor and simile (p. 276) Stanford notes this Iliadic simile but lists another as well and simply describes the effect in *Ajax* as "epic colouring." "epic ring," and general "Homeric echoes."

30 *Il.* 1.254, 4.417, 7.124, and 17.139.

31 By an odd coincidence it is used in the phrase αἰόλῳ ψεύδει at *Nem.* 8.25, where Pindar has just referred to Ajax's death.

32 Bernard M.W. Knox, "New Perspectives in Euripidean Criticism," *CP*, 67 (1972), pp. 270–9; see there p. 272.

33 Knox, "New Perspectives," p. 70.

34 K. von Fritz analyzed the play as a parody in which Euripides presents characters who are disenchanted and ultimately disenchanting as the harsh reality they embody clashes with the optimism of the original folk-tale: "Euripides' *Alkestis* und ihre modernen Nachahmer und Kritiker," *Antike und Abendland*, 5 (1956), pp. 27–69. Wesley D. Smith reached similar conclusions about the tone of the play emphasizing formal structure more than character in the frequently cited "The Ironic Structure in *Alcestis*," *Phoenix*, 14 (1960), pp. 127–45. In Wolfgang Kullman's analysis, the characters of *Alcestis* engage in

foolish actions with absurd consequences which he sees as the earliest of Euripides' alleged attacks on Apollo and the old religion: "Zum Sinngehalt der euripideischen Alcestis," *Antike und Abendland*, 13 (1967), pp. 127–49.

35 The most influential work in this line has been Anne Burnett's "The Virtues of Admetus," *CP*, 60 (1965), pp. 240–55, along with her chapter on *Alcestis* in *Catastrophe Survived* (Oxford, 1971), pp. 22–46. Wolf Steidle has defended the sincerity of the play largely by examining its elements in the context of structural conventions and social tradition: "Die Alkestis des Euripides," in his *Studien zum Antiken Drama* (Munich, 1968), pp. 132–51. More recently, André Rivier has combatted charges of Euripidean irony and frivolity both by citing dramatic conventions and by presenting psychological explanations for the actions of the characters: "En marge d'Alceste et de quelques interprétations récentes," *Museum Helveticum*, 29 (1972), pp. 124–40.

36 The importance of the theme of life and death has been especially well brought out by Justina Gregory, "Euripides' *Alcestis*," *Hermes*, 107 (1979), pp. 259–70; see especially 259–60, and 268–70.

37 Cedric H. Whitman, *Homer and the Heroic Tradition* (Cambridge, Mass., 1958), p. 131, points out the importance of Patroclus' pyre as one of two climaxes in the funeral motif, the other being Hector's.

38 The epithet is Patroclus' at *Il.* 18.10. It is thrown at Hector as an insult at *Il.* 17.142, but elsewhere is meant as true praise (21.279, 24.242).

39 Placement of allusion at strophe opening is a tragic convention. For a full collection of such allusions see Appendix A.

40 Monk (Cambridge, 1816) may have been the first to declare that these lines of *Alc.* imitate the later lines, *Il.* 23.179. At any rate, his claim has remained the standard one. See F.A. Paley, *Euripides* (London, 1857), W.S. Hadley, *The Alcestis* (Cambridge, 1896), and A.M. Dale, *Alcestis* (Oxford, 1954), all *ad loc.*

41 The parallel was cited at least as early as Blomfield and then repeated. See, for example, Hadley. *ad loc.*

42 See the index and the discussion in Chapter 1, pp. 8–12, along with note 12.

43 Dale, *ad loc.*

44 Burnett, *Catastrophe Survived*, p.29, has pointed out the special emphasis this scene is given. Pheres is dragged in especially: he would not normally appear, for his decision was given long in the past.

45 Admetus' requests have been characterized as the typical sort addressed to self-sacrifice victims with *Hec.* 438ff. and *IA* 1465–6 cited as parallels; see Burnett, *Catastrophe Survived*, p. 27. Hers seems a less compelling comparison than the one suggested here; note especially that the tone of lines 250 and 275 (which she does not cite) seems strikingly like that of Andromache to Hector and, in Sophocles' close imitation, Tecmessa to Ajax – that is, of wife to husband.

46 See the discussion of *Ajax*, pp. 51–2, 58–9 and notes 8–10 above, for the scholiasts' comments and recent scholarship.

47 The phrase πολυδίψιον Ἄργος occurred at least once elsewhere,

as the first line of the *Thebaïs* (fr. 1 Kinkel), Ἄργος ἄειδε θεὰ
πολυδίψιον ἔνθεν ἄνακτες (not cited by *LSJ* or by commentators
on *Alcestis*).

48 Paley, Jerram, Hadley, and Tate all compare the Homeric passage.
Dale actually labels the Euripidean lines a reminiscence of the Homeric
list.

49 The correspondence is not exact, but the impression is one of great
similarity. For a detailed examination see Michael Poliakoff, "Euripides'
Alcestis 1029–32," *Mnemosyne*, 35 (1982), pp. 141–3.

50 This is emphasized in the introduction to Hugh Lloyd-Jones, "Pindar
and the After-Life," *Pindare: Entretiens*, 31 (1985), p. 245.

51 Though she calls Heracles' speech the product of an "elegiac mood,"
Burnett has noted that it is "remarkably close" to Apollo's in
Bacchylides 3: "The Virtues," p. 253.

52 The wealth βαθύπλουταν (Bacchyl. 3.82) has been put into the ode
in honor of Admetus (*Alc.* 588–96); and the gain κερδέων (Bacchyl.
3.84) works its way into Heracles' final speech (*Alc.* 1033), so that
practically nothing from this Bacchylidean speech of Apollo's fails to
make its way into one or another of these three epinician sections in
Alcestis.

53 See the careful analysis of Victor Castellani, "Notes on the Structure of
Euripides' *Alcestis*," *AJP*, 100 (1979), pp. 487–96.

54 The possibility of a direct connection between Ion fr. 745 *PMG* and
Ant. 100–17 is raised very cautiously by J.F. Davidson, "The Parodos of
the *Antigone*: A Poetic Study," *BICS*, 30 (1983), p. 45. The resemblance
is remarkable: Ion's entire phrase ἀελίου λευκᾷ πτέρυγι
πρόδρομον can be constructed from the *Antigone* lines, and the
invocation of a heavenly body at the opening of a song is noteworthy as
well. See G. Huxley, "Ion of Chios," *GRBS*, 6 (1965), p. 34.

55 Jebb notes Ion's anecdote about Sophocles with the Phrynicus passage
in his note to *Ant.* 783ff., and Burton discusses the borrowing briefly in
The Chorus, p. 114.

56 For suggestions of echoes in some non-lyric sections see, for example,
C.R. Haines, "Note on the Parallelism between the *Prometheus Vinctus* of
Aeschylus and the *Antigone* of Sophocles," *CR*, 29 (1915), pp. 8–10. I
find his claims unconvincing, but they are accepted by Valdis Leinieks,
The Plays of Sophocles (Amsterdam, 1962), p. 85. Other borrowings in
the episodes will be examined in the following discussion.

57 Burton, *The Chorus*, notes the echo and insists that it is "purely verbal,"
p. 91. Davidson, "The Parodos," while aware of the parallel, seems to
deny that it is even an echo, pp.41–2.

58 Of course the paean must have been composed *after* the eclipse – in
which case its "apotropaic" function and therefore any arguments
based on the distinction are further vitiated.

59 As Aeschylean echoes in the description of the battle in the parodos we
may note with near certainty 106–9: *Septem* 80–9; and 134–40: *Septem*
343–4. Possible but less significant is 126: *Septem* 103–5. For a much
more extensive treatment of these echoes and their possible significance

for interpreting *Antigone* see Gerald F. Else, *The Madness of Antigone* (Heidelberg, 1976), pp. 35–41. From later in the play ναυκληρεῖς πόλιν (994) is nearly identical with *Septem* 652, and θυστάδας (1019) may reflect the use of the same rare word at *Septem* 269. Another adaptation from the *Seven* follows the parodos: Creon gives a disapproving description of what Polyneices had hoped to accomplish in his attack (*Ant.* 199–201) in lines closely modeled on Amphiaraus' ironic description of the possible outcome of the same battle in the *Seven* (582–3). Such an echo can be dressed up by saying that what was the uncertain future for the seer in Aeschylus has become the certain past for the ruler in Sophocles, but this does not seem to be the way Sophocles is using the material from the *Seven*.

60 There is some discussion of the echoes at Burton, *The Chorus*, p. 106 and even P.E. Easterling (always cautious about such matters) recognizes the subject, "The Second Stasimon of *Antigone*," in R.D. Dawe, J. Diggle, and P.E. Easterling (eds), *Dionysiaca* (Cambridge, 1978), pp. 142, 145. I would list the following similarities: the simile of the wave (*Ant.* 586, *Sept.* 758), the woes of the house and their ancient standing (*Ant.* 594–5, *Sept.* 740–2), those perishing (*Ant.* 595, *Sept.* 732), the sequence of generations (*Ant.* 596, *Sept.* 744), root and blood (*Ant.* 600–1, *Sept.* 755,736), madness (*Ant.* 603, *Sept.* 756), the Fury (*Ant.* 603, *Sept.* 723), transgression (*Ant.* 605, *Sept.* 743), and perhaps the image of falling (*Ant.* 595, *Sept.* 759). In a number of these the Greek roots or full words are notably identical.

61 Jebb cites the *Oresteia* passages; Burton, *The Chorus*, has an excellent discussion (pp. 120–2) and endorses the restoration of ποδί suggested so long ago. Other echoes of *Agamemnon* have been proposed. Fraenkel suspected that the anonymous grumbling of the citizens reported by Haemon (*Ant.* 692–700) owed something to *Ag.* 449–60. He also suggested that in Antigone's reaction to seeing Polyneices' corpse, the simile comparing her to a bird finding its nest empty was influenced by the simile of the vultures who have lost their young at *Agamemnon* 48ff. This same image from *Agamemnon* is considered as possibly connected to the image of the eagle in the parodos of *Antigone* (110–16): Davidson, "The Parodos," p. 44. Perhaps. In any case, these will be borrowings rather than allusions. I would add to these the detailed and extensive echo of Aeschylus' description of the discomforts of the natural elements (*Ag.* 335 and *Ant.* 356–7), and the references to a rocky cave home and metic status in *Antigone* 852, 868, and 890, and *Eum.* 805ff., 1012, 1017, 1023, and 1036.

62 See, for example, Paul Friedländer, "ΠΟΛΛΑ ΤΑ ΔΕΙΝΑ," *Hermes*, 69 (1934), pp. 61–3; R. Coleman, "The Role of the Chorus in Sophocles' *Antigone*," *PCPS*, n.s. 18 (1972), p. 10; C. Segal, *Tragedy and Civilization: An Interpretation of Sophocles* (Cambridge, Mass., and London, 1981), p. 153. And more recently, Garvie in his note to *Cho.* 585–93 (p. 204), and J. Pinsent, "Sophocles, *Antigone* 332–375," *LCM*, 8 (1983), pp. 2–4.

63 Bernard M.W. Knox suggests, indirectly, a much deeper thematic

connection between the themes of this Aeschylean song and that of *Antigone: The Heroic Temper: Studies in Sophoclean Tragedy* (Berkeley and Los Angeles, 1964), pp. 78–9.

64 The influence of the three examples from the *Choephoroi* is assumed by Gennaro Perrotta, *Sofocle* (Milan, 1935), p. 80.

65 *P*. 1456a25ff.

66 H.D.F.Kitto, *Greek Tragedy: A Literary Study* (London, 1950), p. 162, and *Form and Meaning in Drama* (London, 1956), p. 173. Even Burton, *The Chorus*, finds that the song "looks forward to what is so familiar in Euripides, the use of ballad-like lyrics in which there is at times only a very tenuous connection with the plot" (p. 132).

67 Respectively, A.J.A. Waldock, *Sophocles the Dramatist* (Cambridge, 1966), p. 118, and G.F. Else, *The Madness*, p. 69. Very similar charges of irrelevance have been leveled against the first stasimon. Moreover, the various lines of defense and the ways they diverge from each other are much like those described below for the fourth stasimon. For a helpful summary see A.T. von S. Bradshaw, "The Watchman Scenes in the *Antigone*," *CQ*, 56 (1962), pp. 204–5.

68 Many would stop with one or both of these. See Jebb, *ad loc*. Also, for example, G.M. Kirkwood, *A Study of Sophoclean Drama* (Ithaca, 1958), p. 211, and Burton, *The Chorus*, p. 128.

69 Robert Coleman, "The Role," p. 10.

70 Ignacio Errandonea, "El Estásimo Cuarto de Antigona," *Emerita*, 20 (1952), p. 113.

71 Gerhard Müller, *Antigone* (Heidelberg, 1967), p. 220.

72 So Robert F. Goheen, *The Imagery of Sophocles' Antigone: A Study of Poetic Language and Structure* (Princeton, 1951), pp. 68–71; Errandonea, "El Estásimo," pp. 115–18; and most recently R.P. Winnington-Ingram, *Sophocles: An Interpretation* (Cambridge, 1980), pp. 100–4. All three differ on various points, but all concentrate mainly on Danaë and Lycurgus, leaving Cleopatra as problematic or explaining her in some other fashion.

73 Thus C.M. Bowra, *Sophoclean Tragedy* (Oxford, 1944), pp. 105. J.C. Kamerbeek combines the two approaches: the chorus wavers not about which example of imprisonment to apply to Antigone, but, rather, about to whom to apply it – Antigone or Creon. See his commentary, pp. 23–4.

74 Coleman, "The Role," p. 4.

75 Winnington-Ingram, *Sophocles*, pp. 91–116; Segal, *Tragedy and Civilization*, pp. 197–9: and to some extent, Coleman, "The Role," pp. 4–27. Contextual and thematic relevance are, in the end, merely rough divisions for the material in the odes, some of which stubbornly resists classification. Consider, for example, the image of blinding at the end of the fourth stasimon, and the father and sons who figure there. Are these contextually or thematically relevant? Are they relevant at all? For conflicting answers, both well expressed, see S.M. Adams, *Sophocles the Playwright* (Toronto, 1957), p. 55, and Winnington-Ingram, *Sophocles*, p. 108.

76 Winnington-Ingram, *Sophocles*, pp. 108–9; Coleman, "The Role," p. 21.

77 Σ955.

78 For the term see Menander Rhetor 413.5ff. The standard treatment for the genre is by Rudolf Kassel, *Untersuchungen zur Griechischen und Römischen Konsolationsliteratur* (Munich, 1958). However, this monograph, focused on later development, is sometimes incomplete in its citation of early examples. For this study I have collected additional references and developed a somewhat different organization of them.

79 Burton, *The Chorus*, p. 127, mentions both the model and the genre in his discussion of this ode. However, as often in this book, he does not develop at any length the material he so suggestively cites.

80 So Timocles declared that the suffering figures in tragedy fulfilled this function for spectators with similar but lesser misfortunes: fr. 6 Kock.

81 Archil. 13.7 West, Thgn. 991–2, Sol. 13.75–6 West; cf. *Od.* 4.236–7. This formula was also used for other aspects of life which vary with passing time, most notably wealth: Sol. 15 West, Thgn. 155–8, 315–18.

82 *Od.* 4.353–5; Telemachus, as often, is rather harsh with his mother. Cf. *Il.* 24.525–30. This is Euripides' favorite form for expressing this sentiment: *Alc.* 416–19, *Med.* 1017–18, *Hipp.* 834–5, *Andr.* 1037–42, fr. 456; Soph. *El.* 153, 289–90 (the latter rather like *Od.* 4.353, but even less sympathetic).

83 Eur. *Hipp.* 437–9, *Andr.* 851–2, fr. 757; Soph. *El.* 1172.

84 *Il.* 9.632ff.; cf. 24.46ff.; Eur. fr. 1075.

85 Although he does not discuss this statement as a departure from convention, Seth Benardete has at least noted that it is a poor attempt at comfort: "A Reading of Sophocles' *Antigone*," *Interpretation*, 5.1 (1975), p. 49.

86 Cf. Soph. *El.* 150. Cedric H. Whitman, *Sophocles: A Study of Heroic Humanism* (Cambridge, 1951), p. 93, says, "the whole point of the Niobe story was that Niobe was a mortal," and he is therefore moved to ask, "Why does Sophocles in two places make her a goddess?" Convention is surely partly why, as well as the fact that she is Zeus' granddaughter. Gods are the exempla in *Il.* 5.382ff., Panyassis fr. 16 Kinkel; Eur. *Hipp.* 451–61, *HF* 1314–22. The deified or immortalized are featured in Aesch. *Ag.* 1040–1 (Heracles); Pind. *Ol.* 2.18ff. (Semele and Ino); and Soph. *El.* 832–48 (Amphiaraus). Peleus in *Il.* 24.534–40 might seem an exception, but he, like Niobe, is Zeus' grandchild, even if Achilles (and/or Homeric tradition) does not know he is to be immortalized (Eur. *Andr.* 1253ff.).

87 See the discussion of Sappho 1 LP, Chapter 1, pp. 12–14.

88 Fr.16 Kinkel. The assignment of the fragment to a consolation of Heracles was suggested by C.O. Müller, *The History and Antiquities of the Doric Race*, 2nd ed. rev. (London, 1839), vol. 1, p. 429.

89 *Il.* 5.407, 6.131, 6.139–40.

90 See Chapter 1, pp. 3–8.

91 Creon is opposed to Antigone's expression of her love for Polyneices. I know of no rhetorical term by which to designate the way in which

the Iliadic prototype supports the erotic element here.

92 The phrase δεινὸν μένος which in early poetry occurs only here at *Iliad* 6.182 (and in an interpolation in the *Theogony* at 324) appears in no other extant author except Sophocles who used it here in *Antigone* and, at about the same time, in *Ajax* 1066.

93 For the importance of Haemon's love for Antigone and the recognition of the existence of hers for him see R. Scodel, *Sophocles* (Boston, 1984), p. 50.

94 See the discussion on *Ajax* earlier in this chapter, note 5.

95 It is possible that the phrase ἑτέροις ἐπὶ λέκτροις ("about another bed/sexual relationship," 639) is a further sign that Euripides has Clytemnestra in mind here: the phrase could echo ἑτέρῳ λέχεϊ used of Clytemnestra and Aegisthus by Pindar at Pythia 11.24.

96 Verrall (*ad loc.*) claimed that Jason "quoted" the high-sounding line to give a mock-tragic effect. Hutchinson (*ad Septem* 62) suggests an unconscious recollection. We may assume that Euripides was conscious, I think, since he made use of the *Septem* lines again in his play *Suppliants* 586ff. (see below, Chapter 4, p. 131).

97 The verb occurs only here in the *Iliad*, once in the *Odyssey*. As has been noted before, this passage of the *Iliad* supplies more quotations, borrowings, and allusions for extant Greek tragedy than any other passage in epic.

98 See Page's excellent analysis in the metrical appendix of his edition, pp. 188–9.

99 Verrall suggested at *Agamemnon* 690–1 (quoted in the text – it is line 695 in his edition) that Euripides imitated this passage from Aeschylus.

100 The phrase recurs in unreversed form in the third stasimon (*Med.* 846) where it describes the rivers of Athens.

101 Barrett (*ad Hipp.* 166–8) examines all the occurrences of this Ionic contraction in Euripides and finds that non-Attic verbs account for all the examples except for this one in *Medea* and one at *Iphigeneia at Aulis* 789.

102 This episode of the *Odyssey* with its discussion of song must have been a favorite with the singers of epic and the lyric and dramatic poets who followed them. Pindar used the passage for a complicated allusion in *Olympia* 6, vv. 50–1, 64–5. I hope to treat this in a separate study.

103 Helen specifically identifies him in the *Iliad* as one who knows all deceptions (3.202), and, of course, the *Odyssey* is a great exploration of this topic. His crafty thoughts are often explicitly dwelt on: see, for example, *Od.* 21.274.

104 Aside from one use each in Homer and Hesiod, the only occurrence outside of Euripides is in spurious lines of Aeschylus' *Septem* (867–8) and a fragment from some Prometheus play, perhaps one of Aeschylus', in the phrase "ill-sounding strife" (fr. 337M, fr. XX in Griffith's edition of *Prometheus Bound*).

4 SOPHOCLES AND EURIPIDES: THE MIDDLE PLAYS

1 This has been noted frequently. See, for example, F. Stoessl, *Der Tod des Herakles* (Zurich, 1945), p. 35; C. Segal, *Tragedy and Civilization* (Cambridge, 1981), p. 82; and R. Scodel, *Sophocles* (Boston, 1984), p. 31.

2 Jebb (*ad loc.*) notes the detailed resemblance in both words and structure which make him certain "that Sophocles had that passage [*Il.* 2.394–7] in mind."

3 The description of the Great Bear occurs twice in the Homeric poems. Jebb (*ad loc.*) cited the lines from the *Iliad* (18.487ff.), and that reference is repeated both by R.W.B. Burton, *The Chorus in Sophocles' Tragedies* (Oxford, 1980), p. 48, and by Easterling (*ad loc.*). But the lines also occur in the *Odyssey* for Odysseus' commencement of his return, and Sophocles must surely have had Odysseus' return in mind in writing the opening of his play.

4 Both Easterling and Jebb cite both these passages. Easterling also adds *Od.* 4.566 and *Od.* 6.43–4 to the list.

5 As Jebb notes at *OT* 1134 it occurs only at *Trach.* 155, 531, *Aj.* 935, *OT* 1134, and Eur. *Hec.* 915 – never in Aeschylus or comedy.

6 Sophocles' phrase κοὐχ ἡλίωσε τοὔπος (258) is closely modeled on the Homeric οὐδ᾽ ἁλίωσε βέλος (*Il.* 16.737) as Jebb and Easterling note. Jebb also hears a reminiscence of *Iliad* 24.92: οὐδ᾽ ἅλιον ἔπος ἔσσεται.

7 The resemblance is noted by T.B.L. Webster, "Sophocles' *Trachiniae*," in C. Bailey *et al.*, *Greek Poetry and Life* (Oxford, 1936), p. 168; S. Kapsomenos, *Sophokles' Trachinierinnen und ihr Vorbild* (Athens, 1963), p. 39, with references to earlier scholarship; C. Segal, "Sophocles' *Trachiniae*: Myth, Poetry, and Heroic Values," *YCS*, 25 (1977), p. 120; and R. Scodel, *Sophocles*, p. 31. Easterling ("a distant echo" *ad loc.*) is characteristically cautious.

8 The possible exception is the occurrence of the verb ἐξαποφθείρω at *Trach.* 713 which Sidgwick (*ad Pers.* 464) thought an imitation of Aesch. *Pers.* 464. (The verb seems to occur only in these two places.) It is a curiosity of the plays of Euripides and Sophocles that there seem to be a significant number of echoes from *Persians* which have no allusive force. See the discussion Chapter 5, pp. 142, 145.

Kapsomenos, *Sophokles' Trachinierinnen*, pp. 39–107, makes an exhaustive comparison of *Trachiniae* and the *Oresteia*, including situational as well as verbal parallels. He includes a number of the passages I treat here, plus many others which I would consider commonplaces of the poetic tradition such as the mixture of pain and joy in life (p. 92, *Trach.* 126ff.: *Ag.* 551ff.) and wishes for good fortune (p. 96, *Trach.* 300ff.: *Ag.* 462ff.).

9 Fraenkel (*ad Agam.* 1446f.) has an excellent note on this Sophoclean imitation of Aeschylus. Note also that the language in both passages indicates that in some sense Cassandra and Iole are simply side-issues: Clytemnestra's "side-dish" is the more obvious, but Deianeira's

παρεισδέδεγμαι has the same force (537).

10 See Jebb's introduction in his edition, pp. xlvii–xlviii.

11 At *Agamemnon* 224 θυτήρ describes him as sacrificer of Iphigeneia; at *Agamemnon* 241 it includes his helpers in the slaughter; at *Choephori* 255 he is called "sacrificer" without explicit reference to the death of his daughter.

12 The text is wretchedly corrupt. I accept Paley's παρφάσει and leave ἐπὶ and θηρός untranslated, hoping, like Burton (*The Chorus*, p. 63), that they are part of an intrusive gloss.

13 Burton, *The Chorus*, p. 62, compares the *Agamemnon* passage as an example of a familiar type of phrase. I suggest that it is much more than that.

14 This echo of the *Odyssey* is noted by Easterling, *ad loc.* and by Segal, *Tragedy and Civilization*, p. 72.

15 Sophocles used the phrase from *Od.* 9.507–8 without change in *Oedipus Rex* 906–7, if, with Jebb and Dawe, one accepts Hermann's emendation. See the discussion below, p. 136.

16 So Easterling at *Trach.* 1141–2, although she neither calls the resemblance an allusion nor comments on the earlier echo from the third stasimon (823).

17 There are two further echoes of the *Odyssey* in *Trachiniae*. The next uses the Cyclops episode one more time. The description of Deianeira's suicide (931) is modeled on a phrase that describes how Odysseus would have liked to kill Polyphemus (*Od.* 9.301). The echo was identified by the scholiast, repeated by Jebb and Easterling. It is not, of course, an allusion; but it does indicate the way the passage that Sophocles had alluded to twice earlier in the play continued to influence his composition. In the other instance Sophocles has taken the model of Odysseus being awakened by the girls' shout in Nausicaa's ball game (*Od.* 6.119) and used it for Heracles being awakened by Hyllus' shout. Upon awakening both Odysseus and Heracles ask to "what men's land" they have come (*Trach.* 984–5). Easterling credits K. Reinhardt with the connection to *Odyssey* 6, but he actually cites the formula from a later, and less suggestive occurrence at *Od.* 13.200: *Sophokles* (Frankfurt am Main, 1933), p. 256 (third ed., 1947, p. 259). Kamerbeek (*ad loc.*), who sees a probable reminiscence, notes both the Odyssean lines.

18 Burton, *The Chorus*, p. 68, suggests that a few lines earlier the image of death enveloping Heracles as a φονία νεφέλα may imply a net, and so be an additional echo of the net imagery from the *Oresteia*. In any case there will be more certain examples of this in the scenes to follow.

19 There is one more Homeric echo that, as Easterling notes, is modeled on a description of Hera from Agamemnon's retelling of the deception of Zeus in the matter of the birth of Heracles (*Il.* 19.97). The phrase, θῆλυς οὖσα (*Trach.* 1062), describes Deianeira as the unlikely female destroyer of Heracles. The collusive appropriateness of the *Iliad* context, combining Agamemnon, ruin in the form of infatuation with a woman, and, of course Heracles, is unusually complex.

20 So, for example, Webster, "Sophocles' *Trachiniae*," p. 178.

21 For the importance of the Furies in the *Trachiniae* and Heracles' responsibility for his own fate see R.P. Winnington-Ingram, *Sophocles: An Interpretation* (Cambridge, 1980), pp. 212–15.

22 The phrase is Marsh McCall's, from his examination of the complementary characters of *Heracles* and Deianeira in "The *Trachiniae*: Structure, Focus, and Heracles," *AJP*, 93 (1972), p. 162.

23 The play's first echo of *Trachiniae* seems to come in Amphitryon's review of Heracles' accomplishments for which Greece is showing no gratitude. Bond, at least, hears "probably a conscious echo" of the similarly bitter and ironic review by the agonized Heracles, especially in the clearing of the seas: ποντίων καθαρμάτων (*HF* 225), πολλὰ μὲν ἐν πόντῳ . . . καθαίρων (*Trach*. 1012). Bond notes that *Trachiniae* 1014 may also have influenced *Hercules* 224.

24 The importance of this pervasive motif in *Hercules* was well described by J.T. Sheppard, "The Formal Beauty of the *Hercules Furens*," *CQ*, 10 (1916), pp. 72–9. On page 74 he mentions Euripides' debt to the chorus in *Agamemnon*.

25 For other allusions in opening lines of song or strophe see Appendix A. The chorus's reference to itself as an ancient singer echoes Amphitryon's earlier mention of an ancient tale, γέρων . . . λόγος (26), which itself is an imitation of the identical phrase at *Agamemnon* 750.

26 As Bond notes. Fraenkel thought that the Aeschylean chorus produced real swords at the end of *Agamemnon*, but this is dramatically quite difficult. Perhaps even if in the original staging there had been swords they were not envisioned by Aeschylus' later readers or seen by audiences of revivals. As Bond points out in his note to *Hercules* 252–74, the chorus' encounter with Lycus provides an example of another more technical type of borrowing from Aeschylus' *Agamemnon*: the old men are given an unusually large number of iambic trimeter lines and, just as the chorus in *Agamemnon* 1348–71, they use them to declare plans for action which never, in fact, materialize. We will encounter similar technical imitation again in Euripides' *Orestes*.

Bond notes another Aeschylean echo at this point in *Hercules*: Lycus' address to the old men of the chorus (*HF* 247) recalls Darius' to the Persian elders at *Persae* 840, a passage Bond feels is echoed again at *HF* 503–5. Imitations (rather than allusions) of *Persae* pervade the works of Sophocles and Euripides. Later in *Hercules* the mention of the stream of Asopus (*HF* 1163–4) may echo *Persae* 805. For a general discussion of echoes from *Persae* see Chapter 5, p. 142.

27 See above pp. 74–7. In *Hercules* Euripides has repeatedly used the word καλλίνικος which is used in the refrain of Archilochus' famous victory hymn as the epithet of Heracles.

28 See Appendix A.

29 The numerous parallels from epinician are conveniently collected in Bond's note to lines 355–8.

30 See H. Parry, "The Second Stasimon of Euripides' *Heracles* (637–700)," *AJP*, 86 (1965), pp. 363–74, and Bond's comments on the stasimon, *ad loc.*

31 Both Wilamowitz and Fraenkel saw this as an echo of *Agamemnon*. Bond suspects that throughout *Heracles* Euripides is imitating a text which has been lost. But the extensive echoes of *Agamemnon* elsewhere in *Heracles* are a strong argument that Euripides has the Aeschylean chorus in mind here as well.

32 These echoes have been discussed by many. The first suggestions may be found in Walter Headlam, "Emendations and Explanations," *Journal of Philology*, 30 (1909), pp. 293–7, and in his commentary to *Agamemnon*. These were developed further by J.T. Sheppard, "Note on Euripides, *Hercules Furens*, 773–800," *CR*, 29 (1915), pp. 68–9. More recently they have been affirmed by A. Burnett, *Catastrophe Survived* (Oxford; 1971), p. 167, and Bond, *ad loc.*

33 Bond, *ad loc.*, tentatively approves the suggestion of H. Strohm, "Trug und Täuschung," *Würzburger Jahrbuch*, 4 (1949–50), pp. 148ff., that the chorus's πιστόν . . . λέχος echoes Pindar's θεῶν πιστὸν γένος in a passage which mentions *Heracles* (*Nem.* 10. 54).

34 Bond notes some of the similarities between these two scenes. Burnett, *Catastrophe Survived*, p. 169, gives a more detailed list of the resemblances including a number of verbal echoes, and suggests some of the comparisons the allusion may lead the audience to make.

35 Both Jebb and Bond note that the broken lines which in each case begin with the imperative εὔφημα φώνει indicate a Euripidean echo of Sophocles. The descriptions of Heracles' madness may owe something to the descriptions of Ajax's as well.

36 The situations are similar – aftermath of disaster, aged fathers, dead children. Moreover, Euripides seems to have used the word for significant allusive effect at the end of *Medea* (1407) – see the note above. Finally, Amphitryon's use of the rare word ῥέθος (1204) suggests borrowing from Priam's earlier (and extremely frequently used) speech to Hector (*Il.* 22.68), even though the word is here used in a meaning which may be borrowed from Aeolic. See Jebb's note to *Antigone* 529.

37 There may be other minor echoes which show Euripides' interest in the *Oresteia*. Bond suggests that the phrase ἔργον μιᾶς . . . χειρὸς (938) owes something to *Ag.* 1405. I would suggest, if anything, *Cho.* 231. Bond hears further reference at line 995 to Clytemnestra's speech at *Ag.*1386.

38 Bond, who says "a conscious recollection is beyond question," sees further use of *Trachiniae* at *Hercules* 1412 (compare the reference to feminine behavior at *Trach.* 1075).

39 The most thorough case for excising Eur. *El.* 518–44 was made by Fraenkel in Appendix D to his commentary on *Agamemnon*, pp. 821–6, supporting the earlier suggestion of Mau. The lines have been defended by many scholars. See, in particular, G.W. Bond, "Euripides' Parody of Aeschylus," *Hermathena*, 118 (1974), pp. 1–14.

40 There is a helpful collection of bibliography in Garvie's note to *Choephori* 164–245. Several of the items listed in this note are cited below. In addition to echoes from this scene, the prologue of *Choephori*

seems to have been used. M.L. West has ingeniously suggested that Electra's reason for rejecting even the possibility of footprints at the tomb, the rocky ground there (κραταιλέῳ πέδῳ, 534), has been taken over from Orestes' appearance at Agamemnon's grave in the opening lines of *Choephori* – West suggests line 3a or 5a. The rare adjective for "stony" occurs at *Agamemnon* 666, and it would be like Aeschylus to have repeated it in *Choephori*. West gives other arguments as well: "Tragica IV," *BICS*, 27 (1980), pp. 17–21. Moreover, the opening lines of *Choephori* also seem to have provided Euripides with the word μελάγχιμος (*Cho.* 11, *El.* 513).

41 F. Solmsen saw that Euripides' treatment of the Aeschylean tokens was a typical Euripidean device to delay recognition. See his excellent discussion in *Electra and Orestes: Three Recognitions in Greek Tragedy* (Amsterdam, 1967), pp. 12–17. Bond, "Euripides' Parody," also notes Euripides' fondness for punctuating his recognitions with hitches and temporary failures, p. 9.

42 This itself has been seen as an allusion or at least imitation of the scar-motif in *Od.* 19.390ff. by J. Dingel, "Der 24. Gesang der *Odyssee* und die *Elektra* des Euripides," *RhM*, 112 (1969), p. 103. For Dingel this is related to an extended adaptation of Odysseus' homecoming for use in *Electra*: he emphasizes especially Odysseus' encounter with Laertes as a model for Orestes' with Electra. Both men, returning after long absence from home, find family members leading a simple life in rags, etc. (pp. 104–6).

43 So C. Segal in "The *Electra* of Sophocles," *TAPA*, 97 (1966), p. 482.

44 The following are notable: Jebb suggests that the chestnut color of the mares (705) may reflect a similarly colored Anatolian team (*Il.* 23.454, 471); the casting of lots for position is shared (*El.* 710, *Il.* 23.352–3); as Kells notes, the verb ὁμοκλεῖν occurs in tragedy only at *El.* 711–12 and doubtless reflects a similar moment at *Il.* 23.363–4 where the verb is also used; finally the tactics for negotiating the turning post and handling the horse on the right are found at *El.* 721–2 and *Il.* 23.336– 40.

45 Jebb and Garvie (*ad Cho.* 686) note the parallel between *El.* 54 and *Cho.* 686, though both are oddly tentative. Jebb also cites *Ag.* 440ff. at *El.* 758 as does Kells, and they cross-reference 1113–14 and 1139–42. None of the commentators discusses the relationship of all these references.

46 Sheppard, acute as ever, calls Orestes' entry with the urn an "astonishing development of the Aeschylean image," in "*Electra*: A Defence of Sophocles," *CR*, 41 (1927), p. 7.

47 We may perhaps note here two other simple echoes or imitations of Homeric poetry in Sophocles' *Electra*. His juxtaposition of day and night with the phrases λαμπρὸν ἡλίου σέλας and μέλαινα . . . εὐφρόνη (17–19) recalls the one occurrence of the formula λαμπρὸν φάος ἠελίοιο with νύκτα μέλαιναν (*Il.* 8.485–6). This was pointed out by J.T.Sheppard in "The Tragedy of Electra According to Sophocles," *CQ*, 12 (1918), p. 81. Similarly, as Jebb

suggests, παντοίας φιλότητος (*El.* 134) seems a reminiscence of παντοίην φιλότητα (*Od.* 15.246).

48 See the discussion above page 34.

49 This technique of juxtaposing different stages or moments in one extended myth is noted by R. Eisner, "Euripides' Use of Myth," *Arethusa*, 12 (1979), p. 158. He is more concerned with allusions to mythic material than to specific texts, but he does note one literary allusion in *Iphigeneia at Aulis*; see Chapter 5, p. 175.

50 These echoes in similar contexts are noted by Jebb *ad loc.* and discussed at greater length by Solmsen, *Electra and Orestes*, p. 23. Solmsen sees the Sophoclean treatment of the lock as a possible defense of Aeschylus in the face of Euripides' unfair criticism.

51 It is used by Aegisthus of Atreus himself at *Ag.* 1590. It also occurs at *Supp.* 421.

52 Compare ἐκ . . . νυκτιπλάγκτων δειμάτων (*Cho.* 523–4) and ἐκ δείματος τοῦ νυκτέρου (*El.* 410). Jebb says that δεῖμα is "often used of a terrifying dream" but his other instances, Eur. *Hec.* 69 and Lycophron 225, are both very likely imitations of *Choephori* as well. Moreover, δεῖμα is also prominent in the context of *Choephori* as an important word in the opening of the stasimon which begins at 585 and which Sophocles so beautifully used in *Antigone*.

53 Influence of the *Oresteia* can be seen throughout Sophocles' *Electra*. Indeed W. Headlam said that "there is hardly any touch" in the Sophoclean play which could not "be found in Aeschylus," in "Some Passages of Aeschylus and Others," *CR*, 17 (1903), p. 248. He saw *El.* 17–19 as a reflection of the general theme in *Choephori* of the movement from darkness to light (*ibid.*), and Sheppard heard these lines specifically as an echo of *Ag.* 276–81, *CQ* 12 (1918), p. 81. Orestes' description of himself as driven by the gods, θεῶν ὡρμημένος (*El.* 70), echoes the chorus's description of him at *Cho.* 940 as θεόθεν . . . ὡρμημένος. As Woolsey saw, *ad loc.*, Electra's language and invocation of the Furies (*El.* 112, 119–20) show borrowing from *Eumenides* 36. As Jebb noted, Sophocles' sole use of ὄφρα (*El.* 225) has as its parallels uses at *Cho.* 360 and *Eum.* 340. There is very similar language in passages which are concerned with contacting Agamemnon in Hades (*El.* 436, *Cho.* 318). And finally, the existence of the verb μασχαλίζω is limited to a single form found only at *Cho.* 439 and *El.* 445 where it describes the mutilation of Agamemnon's corpse.

54 Denniston, *ad El.* 1221–3, notes that Orestes is like Perseus, but he makes no mention there of the description of Perseus in the earlier stasimon. Garvie, *ad Cho.* 831, refers to the Perseus of *El.* 462, but does not mention the echo at the actual murder. Sheppard, "The *Electra* of Euripides," *CR*, 32 (1918), p. 140, defending the relevance of the Euripidean stasimon, connected *El.* 462 with 1221, and he even cited *Cho.* 831 as well. However, he adduced the Aeschylean passage as evidence of the traditional association of Orestes and Perseus rather

than as Aeschylean influence on Euripides.

55 Jebb cited the parallel passage. Winnington-Ingram notes that Sophocles "may well have had [it] in mind," *Sophocles*, p. 233. Segal, "The *Electra*," *TAPA*, (1966), pp. 486–7, speaks of the boldness of the transferred application.

56 Burton, *The Chorus*, pp. 200, 210.

57 Segal, "The *Electra*," pp. 473–545, but especially 482–3. The relation of the two riddles is discussed by G.A. Longman, "Sophocles *Electra* 1478," *CR*, 68 (1954), pp. 193–4 and Winnington-Ingram, *Sophocles*, p. 237.

58 Segal would see the woodcutting as culture invading nature in the forest, the murder as savage nature invading culture in the house. The application of the simile inverts the invasion and converts the Homeric original resulting in a subversion of heroic values. See his discussion in *Tragedy and Civilization*, p. 257.

59 As usual Jebb had cited the lines from *Choephori*. Sheppard talked of Sophocles recalling Aeschylean themes in a fairly pointed way in his article on Sophocles' *Electra* in *CQ*, 12 (1918), p. 84, and in an article on Euripides' *Electra*, *CR*, 32 (1918), p. 137 stated that Sophocles' use of the Aeschylean material indicated that Electra's moderation and reverence "had become proverbial." Segal sees the reworking of the material as significant as well: *Tragedy and Civilization*, p. 466.

60 The differences in the surrounding lines are pushed rather far for significance by Segal, *Tragedy and Civilization*, p. 255.

61 The parallels were pointed out by Kamerbeek, *ad loc.*

62 As Fraenkel notes, the adjective ἐπίσσυτος occurs only at *Ag.* 887 and 1150, *Eum.* 923, and *Hipp.* 574.

63 Barrett lists many poetic parallels *ad loc.*, and cf. even Hdt. 3.111 for γῇ τρέφουσα.

64 The Lemnian women who figure importantly later in the Aeschylean chorus (*Cho.* 631ff.) have appeared earlier in *Hecuba* at 886–7.

65 The sentiment may have been simply a commonplace, however. It seems to have occurred in very similar form in Hesiod as well (fr. 384), and *Il.* 1.404 and 4.404–5 are closely related.

66 Two passages which might show Iliadic influence are not particularly military. First there is the chorus's description of Iolaus as ἀμαλόν (75), notable because the word occurs only here in classical poetry outside the Homeric poems. In its only occurrence in the *Iliad* Hector, threatened like Iolaus with imminent death, is compared to a tender lamb (*Il.* 22.310); but this may be coincidence. Second, the dactylic chorus at *Hcld.* 608ff. begins both strophe and antistrophe with notably Homeric tags: οὔτινά φημι (608): *Il.* 6.488, 23.579, 24.256, 494; θεῶν ἄτερ (608): *Il.* 5.753; ἀλλὰ σὺ μή (619): *Il.* 9.600. The first is a formula, but the last two are unique. While these do not seem to be specific imitations, they are interesting – especially the phrases which open the strophe – as yet another example of the use of the first line of a choral song for borrowed poetic tags and phrases.

67 In addition to the example from *Hecuba* just discussed above, see below on *Andromache* 99.

68 Note, for example, ἀνεμόεντι at 781 for Athens, a word which in the *Iliad* is a standing epithet for Troy.

69 Collard claims (*ad loc.*) that the prayer to Zeus at *Supp.* 628ff. is modeled on a similar prayer at Aeschylus' *Supp.* 524ff., but the resemblance seems too general to me to justify seeing the Aeschylean passage as a model. Jebb suggested at *Ajax* 728 that Euripides imitated the phrase πέτροισι πᾶς καταξανθείς with his own πέτροις καταξανθέντες at *Supp.* 503. However, Stanford suggested that Sophocles in turn had been imitating Aeschylus, citing fragment 225.2: πέτροις καταξανθέντα. There seems little to help choose among various possibilities for the resemblance of these phrases.

70 So Hutchinson at *Septem* 60ff. and Collard on the Euripidean lines.

71 Bond has suggested that at *Supp.* 846ff. Euripides criticizes Aeschylus for an improbable messenger speech. See "Euripides' Parody," p. 3. I agree with Collard that this is improbable.

72 For a suggestion of how this pointed reversal of the original context would fit in the legalistic debates and repeatedly undermining arguments of the play see R. Garner, *Law and Society in Classical Athens* (London and New York, 1987), pp. 112–13.

73 Collard, who notes the resemblance to the lines from *Agamemnon*, also notes, for example, that all the tragedians use the device of placing Ἐρινύς in emphatic final position: *Cho.* 651, *Septem* 791, *Trach.* 895, *Ant.* 603, *Pho.* 1306, etc.

74 See the matter of allusions to Hector in the early plays. There is also the imitation of *Trachiniae* in *Hercules*, and in the next chapter we will see instances both technical and verbal of Euripides following a Sophoclean lead.

75 The only other occurrence is at Soph. *OT* 387.

76 Aside from the imitations of Aeschylus and the Homeric poems, there are two other poetic borrowings that can be identified in *Andromache*, both from epinician, neither apparently very significant. The first, an echo of Bacchylides 3.78–9 (δίδυμαι πραπίδων γνῶμαι, *Andr.* 480: διδύμους ἀέξειν γνῶμας, Bacchyl.), is interesting for two reasons. It occurs in the first sentence of a strophe, as so many poetic tags do; and it was used by Euripides, with much greater significance, a few years earlier in *Alcestis*: see above, pp. 76–8. The second echo occurs in the third stasimon: ναυστολία (795), describing the voyage of the Argonauts, seems a reminiscence of ναυτιλία for the same voyage at Pind. *Pyth.* 4.70, as Stevens suggests, *ad loc.* Both words are quite rare.

77 See especially *Hec.* 56 and *Tro.* 1330. For additional passages see Appendix E, *Iliad* 6.

78 In the singular at *Il.* 11.372 it refers to the deceased Ilus. Aristotle's use at *EN* 1109b.9 is a direct reference to the scene in *Iliad* 3, as are most of the other uses in extant Greek. Post-classical Greek offers a handful of other usages.

79 The phrase was used similarly, of course, by Aeschylus at *Agamemnon* 1453–5, a passage which we have seen Euripides imitated at *Hecuba*

943–9. To be sure, Euripides did not need Aeschylus' lead here. But it is worth noting that the phrase from *Odyssey* 11.211 that Euripides used at *Andromache* 115 was used by Aeschylus at *Agamemnon* 1559. See above, p. 36.

80 The simile at *Iliad* 22.139–43 is quite similar, and was used, as we have seen, by Aeschylus at *Supp.* 223–4, and by the author of *Prometheus Bound* (in imitation of *Supplices*) at *PV* 857. But that simile involves the κίρκος, the one at *Iliad* 21 the ἴρηξ or, as in Euripides, the ἱέραξ.

81 The reminiscence is noted by Stevens, *ad loc.*

82 Epic produced a *Thebais* and an *Oedipodeia* and there were references, apparently fuller than those in the *Iliad* or *Odyssey*, in the *Kypria* and perhaps elsewhere. The materials which could be recovered were explored by C. Robert, *Oidipus* (Berlin, 1915). The recent discovery of an extensive lyric fragment apparently by Stesichorus has encouraged a review of all the poetic sources. For tragedy see below.

83 Both these parallels are cited by Jebb, and Dawe notes the rarity of the vocative.

84 The formula spoken when handing over a daughter in marriage specified that she was given for the plowing or sowing of legitimate children. Tragedy reflects this indirectly, as in Creon's words at *Antigone* 569, but it can be seen most frequently in Menander: *Dysc.* 842, *Mis.* 444, *Pk.* 1013, *Sam.* 727, etc.

85 Other possibilities are minor. At *OT* 1105–9 Jebb cited Anacreon 357 *PMG*, and Dawe points out that both speak of Dionysus, the mountain tops, and dark-eyed nymphs, and that both have the verb συμπαίζω. Still, the language may be traditional. The possibility of echoes from the *Oresteia* always exists. The adjective μηχανόρραφος used so effectively by Euripides at *Andromache* 1116 to echo *Cho.* 221 makes its only other appearance here at *OT* 387. And Oedipus' final blessing of Creon (*OT* 1478–9) is so similar to the chorus' farewell at *Cho.* 1063–4 that Jebb suggested that Sophocles may have been thinking of Aeschylus: compare ἀλλ' εὐτυχοίης, καί σ' . . . θεὸς φυλάττοι (*Cho.*) with ἀλλ' εὐτυχοίης, καί σε . . . δαίμων . . . φρουρήσας τύχοι (*OT*). Garvie sees simply a stereotyped parting formula.

86 So Burton, *The Chorus*, p. 148.

87 Dawe sees the line as very likely a deliberate echo of *Iliad* 6.146.

5 SOPHOCLES AND EURIPIDES: THE LAST PLAYS

1 In *Ion*, one of Euripides' greatest and most original achievements, no echoes of Aeschylus, Sophocles, or any other historical poet can be found. From the Homeric poems there is almost nothing: perhaps the feast for birds and beasts (505) echoes the proem to the *Iliad* (1.4–5); Apollo μαρμαίρων (888) in his sexual encounter with Creousa may recall the eyes of Aphrodite (ὄμματα μαρμαίροντα) as she appears to Helen (*Il.* 3.397); and there is an echo of Homeric feasting with the bustling old servant making banqueters laugh just as Hephaestus did for the gods (*Ion* 1170–3; *Il.* 1.597–600). But this, in 1,622 lines, is all.

2 The phrases are as follows: *Cyc.* 86, κώπης τ' ἄνακτας: *Pers.* 378, κώπης ἄναξ; *Cyc.* 359, κρεοκοπεῖν μέλη ξένων: *Pers.* 462–3, κρεοκοποῦσι δυστήνων μέλη; *IT* 110, νυκτὸς ὄμμα λυγαίας; *Pers.* 428, κελαινὸν νυκτὸς ὄμμα; Or. 1077, μέγας πλούτου λιμήν; *Pers.* 250, πολὺς πλούτου λιμήν (Nauck conjectured μέγας here too); and *Bacch.* 764, οὐκ ἄνευ θεῶν τινός, identical to *Pers.* 164. The first phrase from *Cyclops* may be tragic parody; the last from *Bacchae* may be thought too general even to be an imitation. The others, however, are striking.

3 For *Alcestis*, *Andromache*, and *Hippolytus* see the earlier discussions on those plays. The resemblance of Bacchyl. 13.84–90 to *El.* 860–1 and *Bacch.* 862–72 was noted as soon as Bacchylides was discovered. See H. van Herwerden, "Euripidea," *Mnemosyne*, 27 (1899), p. 231 and Jebb *ad loc.*

4 A few lines earlier in Ode 17 Minos has called the earth "well-forested" – ἠΰδενδρον – and although Pindar was fond of the word, it is rare: its only tragic appearance is *IT* 132.

5 The dolphins, of course, escort Theseus to the depths – 17.97. The sea – πέλαγος – occurs with the epithet "deep-thundering" at 17.77 and earlier at 17.4. And the winds, which blow throughout the ode, are verbally identical (αὖραι) at 17.6.

6 See the whole of John P. Barron's fascinating "Bakchylides, Theseus, and a Woolly Cloak," *BICS*, 27 (1980), pp. 1–8.

7 See above, pp. 43–4.

8 G. Most, *The Measure of Praise* (Göttingen, 1985), p. 13, mentions that Soph. *Phil.* 946–7, especially the words καπνοῦ σκιάν, resemble Pind. *Pyth.* 8.95–6. But they echo, if anything, Aeschylus: fr. 399, καπνοῦ σκιά. The phrase may simply be proverbial.

9 This lie about a non-existent embassy of Diomedes and Odysseus, if it is given maximum interpretive significance, reduces Euripides' *Philoctetes* to mere sham, for in his version, like the Emporos', it was that team from *Iliad* 10 who were sent out for the old man.

10 Jebb cites the *Iliad* passage, as usual, without comment. Webster calls it a reminiscence. As far as I can determine the only other time in extant Greek poetry or prose where πόθος or ποθή occurs as the subject of ἱκνέομαι is in the *Greek Anthology* 9.57.

11 Other reminiscences of the *Iliad* have been suggested, mainly by Webster. He sees the Homeric ἀστεροπητής (*Il.* 1.580, 609, 12.275) combined with the determination to dare even Zeus' thunder (*Phil.* 1198) as an echo of Ares' determination at *Il.* 15.117; the appearance of Heracles to Philoctetes (1409ff.) as a possible remembrance of Athena's appearance to Achilles (*Il.* 1.194ff.); and the image of two lions (*Phil.* 1436, which Jebb recognized as basically Homeric) as a possible imitation of *Il.* 10.297. The first seems to me too complicated a combination; the second too general; the third too common – see *Il.* 5.548, 16.756, 18.579; Aesch. *Cho.* 934, etc. In favor of *Iliad* 10 is the prominence of Odysseus and Diomedes there and in Euripides' *Philoctetes*. If it were an allusion to *Iliad* 10, it would be the

only one in extant Greek tragedy outside the *Rhesus*. I discuss one other echo of the *Iliad* below.

12 There are, of course, other hapax words from the *Odyssey*, and M.M. Kumpf in his dissertation – "The Homeric Hapax Legomena and their Literary Use by Later Authors, Especially Euripides and Apollonius Rhodius" (Columbus, 1974) – has laid a great deal of significance on the use of some of them: for example, περίρρυτος (*Phil.* 1, 239: *Od.* 19.173) supposedly signals the theme of lies and deception (p. 100–1); ῥόθιος (*Phil.* 688: *Od.* 5.412) marks the theme of trying to reach or leave an island (pp. 101–2). I find these suggestions unconvincing; for one thing, ῥόθιος is used twelve times in Euripides alone. Webster thought that the phrase ἀνέρες ἀλφησταί (*Phil.* 709) showed Sophocles remembering *Od.* 6.8, but Jebb inclined toward *Od.* 13.261 and 9.89. Yet as Jebb also noted, Aesch. *Sept.* 770 is similar, and we have seen that Sophocles used that passage at *OT* 1186ff. Perhaps the phrase is too common to be a specific reminiscence. If there are any pointed contrasts with Odysseus, I would suggest the use of ἀμφίαλος (1464) to describe Lemnos: in the *Odyssey* it occurs fairly frequently, always of Odysseus' Ithaca. Elsewhere in Greek poetry it remained very rare (Pind. *Ol.* 13.40 and Apoll. Rh. 4.425). But this, if significant, is a different sort of reference – the reuse of a common epithet, something like Alexandrian *oppositio in imitando*.

13 Both Jebb and Webster felt Sophocles was remembering the Homeric passage here.

14 The incident must have been famous. Archilochus, of course, had alluded to the line with great skill (fr. 112W). See M.S. Silk, *Interaction in Poetic Imagery* (London and New York, 1974), p. 131.

15 The scholiast, completely unhampered by time, mythological or historical, explains that Hera finds Sleep on Lemnos because Philoctetes had called him there. Many of the points in the discussion of this allusion to *Iliad* 14.231ff., including the citation of the scholiast and the connections between Philoctetes and Heracles, are made by D.M. Jones, "The Sleep of Philoctetes," *CR*, 63 (1949), pp. 83–5.

16 "Literary allusions . . . constitute one of the most important strands in the fabric of the play," says Sir Charles Willink in his excellent commentary (p. lv). Our lists of allusions do not always coincide: for example, he is much more confident than I am in identifying uses of Stesichorus. But his comments are an invaluable aid.

17 The parallels are conveniently detailed by Bond, *ad HF* 1042ff. In this late period Sophocles sometimes and Euripides often can be seen echoing their own earlier work, as discussion below shows. As for *Orestes*, at 1536 there is a direct quotation of his *Hecuba* 45–6, and *Or.* 66 and 1280 respectively reuse *Hec.* 279 and 748, as Willink points out.

18 The resemblance of the parodos in *Orestes* to the sleep scene in *Philoctetes* is noted by C.F. Fuqua, as are some of the other allusions and imitations which are discussed below. See his "Studies in the Use of Myth in Sophocles' *Philoctetes* and the *Orestes* of Euripides," *Traditio*

32 (1976), pp. 29–95. He sometimes hears echoes where I do not, often based on thematic connections between the two plays about which I am less certain than he is.

19 One possible echo is the odd man out all the way around. At *Orestes* 903 the messenger describes an anonymous speaker at the trial as ἀθυρόγλωσσος, perhaps influenced by the chorus's description of Echo at *Philoctetes* 188 as ἀθυρόστομος. But the *Philoctetes* context is lyric rather than iambic, and neither passage deals with the topics listed above, or indeed, with anything which might be called a theme of either play.

20 Willink, p. xxxii, notes the parallel.

21 Although Orestes' opinion is not unbiased, his description of Menelaus as βοστρύχοις γαυρούμενος (*Or.* 1532) is convincing and is bolstered by allusive support from Archilochus' undesirable general who is βοστρύχοισι γαῦρον (114W).

22 As Burton points out, the example from *Philoctetes* is unique in extant Sophocles, and aside from *Orestes* the only other similar instance is *Hipp.* 362ff., 669ff., which is less close because only the strophe is sung by the chorus.

23 Willink says that the phrase first occurs at *Phil.* 518, but it may have occurred in Hesiod, fr. 70.27. Certainly it seems to have occurred nowhere else in the classical period except for there, *Philoctetes*, and *Orestes*. There is one instance in Hellenistic poetry (Apol. Rh. 4.1043) and a few in later prose. The only similar parallel is Pindar *Ol.* 6 which combines allusion with strophic responsion. I hope to treat that ode in a separate study.

24 General Aeschylean influence is very often a factor in Sophocles and Euripides. The mention of παράνοια by the chorus at *Or.* 824 in the context of a son and a horrible crime which involves his mother may owe something to the Aeschylean passage choral on the παράνοια which led Oedipus to marry his mother (*Sept.*756).

25 M.L. West, "Problems in Euripides' *Orestes*," *CQ*, 37 (1987), p. 284.

26 Greek poetry's fascination with Helen is elsewhere reflected in *Orestes*. The Phrygian's description of her spinning owes some of its details to a striking description of her in the *Odyssey* (4.121–36) as well as to other passages from the epic (*Od.* 6.53, 306). Similarly, Electra's condemning epithets for Helen, λιποπάτορα and λιπογάμετον (*Or.* 1305–6), derive ultimately from Stesichorus' description of Helen and Clytemnestra as λιπεσάνορες (*PMG* 223), as Willink notes.

27 This is noted by Willink, who also notes the verbal parallels cited in this paragraph.

28 Willink (following DiBenedetto) thinks that Orestes' plea that the Furies not be "shaken" against him (*Or.* 255–6) may be "an allusive reminiscence" of *Il.* 4.167 where Zeus shakes the aegis (the verb is the same) with its Fury-like Gorgon device. This seems unlikely to me.

29 Jebb notes Euripides' use of these lines.

30 Willink cites the phrase in its only occurrence in the *Iliad* at 8.520, but that nominative is less similar than the datives from the *Odyssey*. In the

Odyssey it also occurs at 11.386 (introduction to Clytemnestra), 15.422, and 23.166 (Penelope's clever test of Odysseus).

31 The similarity is noted, with unnecessary hesitation, by Jebb and by R.W.B. Burton, *The Chorus in Sophocles' Tragedies* (Oxford, 1980), p. 219.

32 Garvie notes both echoes at *Cho.* 964 and 937–8. For the puzzle as to what exactly is meant by the double lion in Aeschylus see Garvie's excellent note.

33 For this and other arguments about chronology, see Richard Seaford, "The Date of Euripides' *Cyclops*," *JHS*, 102 (1982), pp. 161–72.

34 Seaford suggests the reading *ad Cyc.* 60, noting that it may help prepare for the allusion at *Cyc.* 707. I think that the best candidate for an additional specific echo of *Philoctetes* is the exclamation of delight from Silenus when he learns that Odysseus has brought wine: ὦ φίλτατ' εἰπών (140). It would be an exact quotation of Philoctetes' happy words to Neoptolemus (*Phil.* 1290). Both exclamations come from creatures trapped on an island longing to escape and are delivered to men they see as their saviors. To be sure, there is a close variation at *Ion* 1488; but I do not think it significantly affects these two passages.

35 A.M. Dale had suggested that *Cyc.* 707 alluded to *Phil.* 19 in 1956 (available in *Collected Papers*, London, 1969, p. 129). Robert Ussher remains unconvinced: *Cyclops* (Rome, 1978), pp. 201–2.

36 Compare *Trach.* 931 and *Od.* 9.301. See the discussion above, pp. 107–8, 240 note 17. Easterling notes both echoes from *Od.* 9, and C.P. Segal, *Tragedy and Civilization: An Interpretation of Sophocles* (Cambridge, Mass., and London, 1981), p. 72, notes the Lichas episode.

37 The parallels have been repeated in commentary after commentary, but Seaford, who will be cited again, has made more suggestive use of the material than have others. It may have been traditional, or at least quite common, to write plays based on this episode: Cratinus' *Odysseus* seems to have made extensive use of *Odyssey* 9; Epicharmus wrote a comic *Cyclops*; and Aristias had written a satyric *Cyclops*. See Rollin H. Tanner, "The *Odysseus* of Cratinus and the *Cyclops* of Euripides," *TAPA*, 46 (1915), pp. 173–206, and Seaford's introduction to his edition, p. 52.

38 There is a comparison in Seaford's introduction, pp. 51–9. For an extensive comparison see G. Wetzel, *De Euripidis Fabula Satyrica quae Cyclops inscribitur, cum Homerico comparata exemplo* (Wiesbaden, 1965). More recently, Kumpf has examined the use of Homeric hapax legomena in *Cyclops* in his dissertation, "The Homeric Hapax Legomena and their Literary Use by Later Authors." He makes the case that significant thematic associations are reinforced through the use of these words, pp. 120–38. Many of them help convey Homeric atmosphere, and some are almost certainly significant. But I doubt, for example, whether the use of πλήν contributes measurably to the contrast of the Cyclops' barbarity with the Greeks' civilization. This is perhaps his most extreme case, but there are others in his study similarly doubtful due to the great frequency with which the words occur outside the Homeric texts.

39 All the examples in this paragraph receive excellent detailed treatment from Seaford in his commentary on the various lines of *Cyclops* in question.

40 The odes are discussed as a group by M.B. Arthur, "The Curse of Civilization: The Choral Odes of the *Phoenissae*," *HSCP*, 81 (1977), pp. 163–85.

41 Euripides has chosen not only not to echo Homeric epic in his odes, but actively to avoid Homeric echo even where the poetry seems to move toward it. The second stasimon (784–832) has almost exclusively dactylic rhythms perfectly suited for including striking Homeric words. Instead Euripides has filled the lines with seventeen weighty Homeric-sounding compound words (some of them are even repeated in the ode), not one of which occurs in the Homeric poems.

42 Both Paley and Powell feel that Euripides has closely copied Aeschylus here. I am much less certain.

43 The word is used elsewhere by Euripides, but never by Sophocles, and by Aeschylus only in the *Seven*.

44 Cf. the details in the descriptions of armor in *Sept*. 488 and *Pho*. 1130. Verrall considered the Euripidean passage a close imitation of and direct reference to the Aeschylean one.

45 R.P. Winnington-Ingram, "Euripides: *Poiêtês Sophos*," *Arethusa*, 2 (1969), p. 129, notes *Pho*. 751ff. along with the recognition scene in *Electra* and perhaps Eur. *Supp*. 846–56 as Euripidean criticisms of Aeschylus. He credits Euripides' cleverness and playful wit, but gives less credit than I would for the positive effects Euripides gains with these allusions.

46 See the discussion in Chapter 3 pp. 80–1 and above, p. 136. See also P.E. Easterling, "The Second Stasimon of *Antigone*," in R.D. Dawe, J. Diggle, and P.E. Easterling (eds), *Dionysiaca* (Cambridge, 1978).

47 In tragedy, ὠμόφρων is relatively common, occurring in all three major tragedians three or four times. However, σιδηρόφρων occurs elsewhere only at [Aesch.] *PV* 242 (and Eustathius' discussion of that line) and once in Athanasius. In all Greek φόνος or φοίνιος and mention of the earth (γαῖα) wetted with blood (αἷμα) seem to occur only in these lines of Aeschylus and Euripides.

48 A similar borrowing from Aeschylean lyric may be Eteocles' immediately preceding assertion of the etymological appropriateness of his brother's name – the very contentious Polyneices (*Pho*. 636–7). Fraenkel thought it imitative of the choral meditation on Helen's name at *Ag*. 682ff. where, just as here, the etymological appropriateness is taken as a sign of forethought, προνοία.

49 The only similar passage is Strabo *Geog*. 5.2.6 – τὴν ἐν Πάρῳ πέτραν τὴν μάρμαρον. Normally μάρμαρος is a noun.

50 There may be two other imitations of earlier poetry. The reference to the broad streets of Greece, εὐρυχόρους ἀγυιάς, is identical with a phrase from a speech made at Thebes in Pindar's *Pythia* 8.55, but this could be a traditional phrase. Later in the parodos the phrase

δρυὸς ἢ ἐλάτας (110 = *Pho.* 1515) may be modeled on the ἐλάται ἠὲ δρύες of the Homeric Hymn to Aphrodite (264), but if so it is merely imitation, not allusion.

51 From Thucydides on, πρόϋπτος was regularly combined with a small set of near synonyms: κίνδυνος, κακόν, ὄλεθρος, and θάνατος. These combinations all occur many times; the use of "Hades" in the phrase is confined to Euripides and Sophocles.

52 Fraenkel (*ad Ag.* 1565ff.) approvingly notes the suggestion of another Homeric echo in *Oedipus at Colonus*. This would make Oedipus' claim that Thebes had bound him in evil ruin (*OC* 525ff.) a "word for word" use of Agamemnon's claim that Zeus had bound him in weighty ruin (*Il.* 2.111, 9.18). The binding force of destruction seems too common to hear an echo here.

53 The other possible Homeric reminiscence in *Trojan Women* involves what seems to have been a phrase taught at school as one of the Ὁμήρου γλῶτται. In the *nekuia* episode of the *Odyssey* there occurs four times the phrase νεκύων ἀμενηνὰ κάρηνα (*Od.* 10.521, 536; 11.29, 49), and the phrase is the point of discussion in a scene of Aristophanes' *Daitales*: τί καλοῦσ' "ἀμενηνὰ κάρηνα" is the question (fr. 222). Athenian children so trained should, as members of the audience, have recognized this as the model for Euripides' νεκύων ἀμενηνὸν ἄγαλμα (*Tro.* 193).

54 Paley points this out. Fraenkel notes (*ad Ag.* 1264–7) that Canter had seen that *Agamemnon* had served as the model for both passages in *Trojan Women*.

55 The image of a copestone of ruin or anything bad does not seem to appear anywhere in extant Greek except for the three plays mentioned above.

56 Sophocles had used the phrase δόλιαν . . . ἄταν in *Trachiniae* (850–1). It occurs nowhere else in extant Greek.

57 For an excellent treatment which does much to make up for our loss of the companion plays see Ruth Scodel, *The Trojan Trilogy of Euripides* (Göttingen, 1980).

58 C. Whitman, *Euripides and the Full Circle of Myth* (Cambridge, Mass., 1974), p. 42.

59 A.M. Dale, *ad Hel.* 725: "the whole is quite likely to be a deliberate reminiscence of Stesichorus."

60 Euripides had used the adjective at *Hippolytus* 229, but it may well be imitated from Pindar. There are no other early occurrences of the word. Its next appearance in Posidippus looks like an imitation of Euripides (*Anth. Gr.* 12.131.1). After that it occurs once in Aelius Aristides (13.128.10) and finally in Eunapius (*Vit. Soph.* 7.3.5.1).

61 Dale, *ad Hel.* 1049–56, says: "It seems scarcely possible that the two passages [*Hel.* 1049–56 and S. *El.* 56–64] should be independent of each other."

62 Whitman connected the two prayers: *Euripides*, p. 66.

63 Kannicht, *ad Hel.* 1118, gives an impressive list of αἰνο- compounds,

including Alcman's Ἀινόπαρις (*PMG* 77).

64 Because the second stasimon tells the story of Demeter's sorrow at the loss of her daughter, it is related to the Homeric Hymn to Demeter, but the echoes are more general. See Richardson's commentary on the *Hymn to Demeter*, p. 168.

65 This reading of *Helen* 1337 takes L. Dindorf's emendation of ἀλάστωρ to ἀλάστῳ which Dale accepted.

66 Compare *IT* 1136–7 and *Helen* 1318, both of which echo Bacchyl. 17.89–90. It is interesting that Euripides has chosen different phrases from the lines to use in each play.

67 A.W. Verrall, *Euripides the Rationalist* (Cambridge, 1895), pp. 184ff.

68 The maxim recurs in the Sententiae ascribed to Menander once word for word and once with "pillar" and "house" singular rather than plural (*s.v.* στῦλος).

69 This was noted by Verrall in his commentary at *Eum.* 138.

70 Besides the allusions to the *Iliad* and *Oresteia* there is a handful of less significant poetic echoes in *Iphigeneia at Aulis*. Bacchylides has been noted in the introduction to this chapter. One line may be modeled on a line from Aeschylus' *Supplices*. Compare δοῦναί τε μὴ δοῦναί τε, τῆς τύχης ὅπως (*IA* 56) and δρᾶσαί τε μὴ δρᾶσαί τε καὶ τύχην ἑλεῖν (*Supp.* 380). Likewise, if Jebb is right in accepting the text of *IA* 407 as it appears in Plutarch, συνσωφρονεῖν γὰρ οὐχὶ συννοσεῖν ἔφυν may be an imitation of *Ant.* 523 – οὔτοι συνέχθειν, ἀλλὰ συμφιλεῖν ἔφυν. Finally, the phrase θαῦμα βροτοῖσιν (*IA* 202) could have been borrowed either from *Odyssey* 11.287, the often-used *nekyia* scene, or from the *Cypria* (Allen VII.1) where it refers to Helen. Either source would be generally appropriate in the Euripidean context which surveys the Greek troops. More likely, however, the words convey epic tone without specific reference.

71 England, objecting that the tragedians did "not reproduce such undigested morsels" as near quotation, declared the words in *Iphigeneia* not authentic, but *Medea* 425 reproduces *Odyssey* 8.498. This Homeric phrase for weeping occurs once again at *Odyssey* 4.556, but the scene of Hector and Andromache in *Iliad* 6 is a more likely model because of its popularity, and because of the frequency with which Euripides alludes to it.

72 Paley acknowledged Hermann's connection of Achilles' two explanations that he needed no daughter of Agamemnon's to wed.

73 Fraenkel called the reference to the yoke of necessity in *Iphigeneia* a "quote" from *Agamemnon*. England noted that the description of Agamemnon's decision as "all-daring" in both plays was commented on as early as Monk.

74 Again England, seeing that the lines came from Aeschylus' *Eumenides*, denied they could be genuine. By now it should be clear that they are entirely in Euripides' manner.

75 Fraenkel called Clytemnestra's speech "obviously . . . a direct reminiscence of the *Agamemnon*," *ad Ag.* 787.

76 In a general way, of course, this whole speech of Clytemnestra's looks forward to the events of *Agamemnon*, especially *IA* 1171–6, as noted by R. Eisner, "Euripides' Use of Myth," *Arethusa*, 12 (1979), p. 161.

77 For the idea of "thematic anticipation" as a poetic device, and especially for this type of thematic anticipation by synecdoche (though not allusive *per se*) see Gordon Williams, *Figures of Thought in Roman Poetry* (New Haven and London, 1980), pp. 102–22.

6 GENERATIONS OF LEAVES

1 See, for example, the prophecy in Bacchylides 13.44ff. and the discussion by A. Burnett, *The Art of Bacchylides* (Cambridge, Mass., and London, 1985), p. 90.

2 P. Pucci, *Odysseus Polutropos* (Ithaca and London, 1987), p. 29, notes that allusion calls for a comparison and results in "either a controversy or a gesture of admiration." This describes well the straightforward side of much allusion in Greek poetry.

BIBLIOGRAPHY

EDITIONS OF CLASSICAL WORKS:
TEXTS AND COMMENTARIES

Collections and Anthologies

Page, D.L., *Poetae Melici Graeci*, Oxford, Oxford University Press , 1962.
——, *Supplementum Lyricis Graecis*, Oxford, Oxford University Press, 1974.
West, M.L., *Iambi et Elegi Graeci*, 2 vols, Oxford, Oxford University Press, 1971.

Individuals

Aeschylus

Oresteia, edited by George Thomson including the work of Walter
    Headlam, 2 vols, Cambridge, Cambridge University Press, 1938.
Agamemnon, edited by A.W. Verrall, London, Macmillan, 1904.
Agamemnon, edited by Eduard Fraenkel, 3 vols, Oxford, Oxford
    University Press, 1950.
Choephori, edited by A.F. Garvie, Oxford, Oxford University Press, 1986.
Eumenides, edited by A.W. Verrall, London, Macmillan, 1908.
Perser, edited by C. Conradt, revised ed. of L. Schiller, Berlin, Weidmann,
    1888.
Persae, edited by A. Sidgwick, Oxford, Oxford University Press, 1903.
Persae, edited by H.D. Broadhead, Cambridge, Cambridge University
    Press, 1960.
Prometheus Bound, edited by Mark Griffith, Cambridge, Cambridge
    University Press, 1983.
Septem contra Thebas, edited by G.O. Hutchinson, Oxford, Oxford
    University Press, 1985.
The Suppliants, edited by H. Friis Johansen and Edward W. Whittle, 3 vols,
    Copenhagen, I Kommission hos, Gyldendalske Boghandel, Nordisk
    Forlag, 1980.

Euripides

Euripides: with an English Commentary, edited by F.A. Paley, 3 vols, London, Whittaker, 1857, 1858, 1860.

Alcestis, edited by W.S. Hadley, Cambridge, Cambridge University Press, 1896.

Alcestis, edited by C.S. Jerram, Oxford, Oxford University Press, 1884.

Alcestis, edited by A.J. Tate, London, Blackie's Illustrated Greek Series, 1903.

Alcestis, edited by A.M. Dale, Oxford, Oxford University Press, 1954.

Andromache, edited by P.T. Stevens, Oxford, Oxford University Press, 1971.

Bacchae, edited by E.R. Dodds, 2nd ed., Oxford, Oxford University Press, 1960.

Cyclops, edited by R.G. Ussher, Rome, Ateneo & Bizzarri, 1978.

Cyclops, edited by Richard Seaford, Oxford, Oxford University Press, 1984.

Electra, edited by J.D. Denniston, Oxford, Oxford University Press, 1939.

Helen, edited by A.M. Dale, Oxford, Oxford University Press, 1967.

Euripides Helena, edited by Richard Kannicht, Heidelberg, Carl Winter, 1969.

Herakles, edited by Ulrich von Wilamowitz-Moellendorff, 2nd ed., Berlin, Weidmann, 1895.

Heracles, edited by Godfrey W. Bond, Oxford, Oxford University Press, 1981.

Hippolytos, edited by W.S. Barrett, Oxford, Oxford University Press, 1966.

Iphigeneia at Aulis, edited by E.B. England, London and New York, Macmillan, 1891.

Medea, edited by A.W. Verrall, London, Macmillan, 1881.

Medea, edited by D.L. Page, Oxford, Oxford University Press, 1938 (corrected edition 1952).

Orestes, edited by Charles Willink, Oxford, Oxford University Press, 1986.

The Phoenissae of Euripides, edited by John U. Powell, London, Constable, 1911.

Supplices, edited by C. Collard, Groningen, Bouma's Boekhuis, 1975.

Hesiod

Theogony, edited by M.L. West, Oxford, Oxford University Press, 1971.

Homeric Hymns

The Homeric Hymn to Demeter, edited by N.J. Richardson, Oxford, Oxford University Press, 1974.

Sophocles

Ajax, edited by Sir Richard C. Jebb, Cambridge, Cambridge University Press, 1907.

Ajax, edited by W.B. Stanford, Bristol, Bristol Classical Press, 1981.

Antigone, edited by Sir Richard Jebb, Cambridge, Cambridge University Press, 1906.

Antigone, commentary by J.C. Kamerbeek, Leiden, E.J. Brill, 1968.

Antigone, edited by G. Müller, Heidelberg, Carl Winter, 1967.

Electra, edited by R.C. Jebb, Cambridge, Cambridge University Press, 1894.

Electra, edited by J.H. Kells, Cambridge, Cambridge University Press, 1973.

Oedipus Coloneus, edited by R.C. Jebb, Cambridge, Cambridge University Press, 1889.

Oedipus Rex, edited by R.D. Dawe, Cambridge, Cambridge University Press, 1982.

Oedipus Tyrannus, edited by R.C. Jebb, Cambridge, Cambridge University Press, 1893.

Philoctetes, edited by Sir Richard C. Jebb, Cambridge, Cambridge University Press, 1908.

Philoctetes, edited by T.B.L. Webster, Cambridge, Cambridge University Press, 1970.

Trachiniae, edited by R.C. Jebb, Cambridge, Cambridge University Press, 1892.

Trachiniae, edited by J.C. Kamerbeek, Leiden, E.J. Brill, 1959.

Trachiniae, edited by P.E. Easterling, Cambridge, Cambridge University Press, 1982.

BOOKS AND ARTICLES

Adams, S.M., *Sophocles the Playwright*, Toronto, Universtiy of Toronto Press, 1957.

Adkins, A.W.H., "Callinus 1 and Tyrtaeus 10 as Poetry," *Harvard Studies in Classical Philology*, 81 (1977), pp. 59–97.

——, *Poetic Craft in the Early Greek Elegists*, Chicago, Chicago University Press, 1985.

Arthur, Marylin B., "The Curse of Civilization: The Choral Odes of the *Phoenissae*," *Harvard Studies in Classical Philology*, 81 (1977), pp. 163–85.

Barron, John P., "Bakchylides, Theseus and a Woolly Cloak," *Bulletin of the Institute of Classical Studies*, 27 (1980), pp. 1–8.

Benardete, Seth, "A Reading of Sophocles' *Antigone*," *Interpretation: A Journal of Political Philosophy*, 5.1 (1975), pp. 1–55.

Bond, G.W., "Euripides' Parody of Aeschylus," *Hermathena*, 118 (1974), pp. 1–14.

Booth, Wayne, "Ten Literal 'Theses,'" in S. Sacks (ed.) *On Metaphor*, Chicago and London, University of Chicago Press, 1979, pp. 173–4.

Bowra, C.M., *Sophoclean Tragedy*, Oxford, Oxford University Press, 1944.

Bradshaw, A.T. von S., "The Watchman Scenes in the *Antigone*," *Classical Quarterly*, 56 (1962), pp. 204–11.

Brize, Philip, "Samos und Stesichoros: Zu einem Früharchaischen Bronzeblech," *Athenische Mitteilungen*, 100 (1985), pp. 53–90.

Brown, W. Edward, "Sophocles' Ajax and Homer's Hector," *Classical Journal*, 61 (1965–6), pp. 118–21.

Burnett, Anne Pippin, "The Virtues of Admetus," *Classical Philology*, 60 (1965), pp. 240–55.

——, *Catastrophe Survived*, Oxford, Oxford University Press, 1971.
——, *Three Archaic Poets: Archilochus, Alcaeus, and Sappho*, Cambridge, Mass., Harvard University Press, 1983.
——, *The Art of Bacchylides*, Cambridge, Mass., and London, Harvard University Press, 1985.
Burton, R.W.B., *Pindar's Pythian Odes*, Oxford, Oxford University Press, 1962.
——, *The Chorus in Sophocles' Tragedies*, Oxford, Oxford University Press, 1980.
Bury, J.B., "Two Literary Compliments," *Classical Review*, 19 (1905), pp. 10–11.
Calder, W., "An Echo of Sappho Fragment 16 L-P at Aeschylus, *Agamemnon* 403–19?", *Estudios clasicos*, 26 (1984), pp. 215–18.
Castellani, Victor, "Notes on the Structure of Euripides' *Alcestis*," *American Journal of Philology*, 100 (1979), pp. 487–96.
Coleman, Robert, "The Role of the Chorus in Sophocles' *Antigone*," *Proceedings of the Cambridge Philological Society*, n.s. 18 (1972), pp. 4–27.
Colonna, Aristide, "De Genetivi in -οιο Usu apud Tragicos Scriptores," *Sileno*, 3 (1977), pp. 207–9.
Conte, Gian Biagio, *The Rhetoric of Imitation: Generic and Poetic Memory in Virgil and Other Latin Poets*, trans. from the Italian, edited by Charles Segal, Ithaca and London, Cornell University Press, 1986.
Coxon, A.H., "Persica," *Classical Quarterly*, 52 (1958), pp. 45–53.
Dale, A.M. *Collected Papers*, London, Cambridge University Press, 1969.
Davidson, J.F., "The Parodos of the Antigone: A Poetic Study," *Bulletin of the Institute of Classical Studies*, 30 (1983), pp. 41–51.
Davies, M., "Aeschylus and the Fable," *Hermes*, 109 (1981), pp. 248–51.
Dawson, Christopher M., "Σπουδαιογέλοιον: Random Thoughts on Occasional Poems," *Yale Classical Studies*, 19 (1966), pp. 50–1.
Dawson, Henry S., "On *Agamemnon* 108–120," *Classical Review*, 41 (1927), pp. 213–14.
Dingel, Joachim, "Der 24. Gesang der *Odyssee* und die *Elektra* des Euripides," *Rheinisches Museum*, 112 (1969), pp. 103–9.
Easterling, P.E., "The Tragic Homer," *Bulletin of the Institute of Classical Studies*, 31 (1984), pp. 1–8.
—— "The Second Stasimon of *Antigone*," in R.D. Dawe, J. Diggle, and P.E. Easterling (eds), *Dionysiaca*, Cambridge, The Editors, 1978, pp. 141–58.
Eisner, Robert, "Euripides' Use of Myth," *Arethusa*, 12 (1979), pp. 153–74.
Else, Gerald F., *The Madness of Antigone*, Heidelberg, Carl Winter, 1976.
Errandonea, Ignacio, "El Estásimo Cuarto de Antigona," *Emerita*, 20 (1952), pp. 108–21.
Fowler, R.L., *The Nature of Early Greek Lyric*, Toronto, University of Toronto Press, 1987.
Friedländer, Paul, "ΠΟΛΛΑ ΤΑ ΔΕΙΝΑ," *Hermes*, 69 (1934), pp. 61–3.
Fuqua, C.F., "Studies in the Use of Myth in Sophocles' *Philoctetes* and the *Orestes* of Euripides," *Traditio*, 32 (1976), pp. 29–95.
Garner, Richard, *Law and Society in Classical Athens*, London, Croom Helm,

and New York, St. Martin's, 1987.

Garson, R.W., "Aspects of Aeschylus' Homeric Usages," *Phoenix*, 39 (1985), pp. 1–5.

Goheen, Robert F., *The Imagery of Sophocles' Antigone: A Study of Poetic Language and Structure*, Princeton, Princeton University Press, 1951.

Goldhill, Simon, *Language, Sexuality, Narrative: The Oresteia*, Cambridge, Cambridge University Press, 1984.

Gregory, Justina, "Euripides' *Alcestis*," *Hermes*, 107 (1979), pp. 259–70.

Griffith, Mark, "Man and the Leaves: A Study of Mimnermus fr. 2," *California Studies in Classical Antiquity*, 8 (1975), pp. 73–88.

——, "The Vocabulary of *Prometheus Bound*," *Classical Quarterly*, 34 (1984), pp. 282–91.

Haines, C.R., "Note on the Parallelism between the *Prometheus Vinctus* of Aeschylus and the *Antigone* of Sophocles," *Classical Review*, 29 (1915), pp. 8–10.

Headlam, Walter, "Some Passages in Aeschylus and Others," *Classical Review*, 17 (1903), pp. 240–9.

——, "Emendations and Explanations," *Journal of Philology*, 30 (1909), pp. 293–7.

Herwerden, H. van, "Euripidea," *Mnemosyne*, 27 (1899), pp. 225–45.

Hipsky, Marty A., Jr., "Imagery in Stesichorus' *Geryoneïs*," unpublished paper, 1986.

Huxley, G., "Ion of Chios," *Greek, Roman, and Byzantine Studies*, 6 (1965), pp. 29–46.

Janko, R., "Aeschylus' *Oresteia* and Archilochus," *Classical Antiquity*, 74 (1980), pp. 291–3.

Jones, D.M., "The Sleep of Philoctetes," *Classical Review*, 63 (1949), pp. 83–5.

Kapsomenos, S., *Sophokles' Trachinierinnen und ihr Vorbild*, Athens, Greek Humanistic Society, 1963.

Kassel, Rudolf, *Untersuchungen zur Griechischen und Römischen Konsolationsliteratur*, Munich, Beck, 1958.

Kirkwood, G.M., *A Study of Sophoclean Drama*, Ithaca, Cornell University Press, 1958.

——, "Homer and Sophocles' Ajax," in M.J. Anderson (ed.), *Classical Drama and its Influence*, London, Methuen, 1965, pp. 51–70.

Kitto, H.D.F., *Greek Tragedy: A Literary Study*, 2nd ed., London, Methuen, 1950.

——, *Form and Meaning in Drama*, London, Methuen, 1956.

Knox, Bernard, M.W., *The Heroic Temper: Studies in Sophoclean Tragedy*, Berkeley and Los Angeles, University of California Press, 1964.

——, "New Perspectives in Euripidean Criticism," *Classical Philology*, 67 (1972), pp. 270–9.

Kullman, Wolfgang, "Zum Sinngehalt der euripideischen Alcestis," *Antike und Abendland*, 13 (1967), pp. 127–49.

Kumpf, Michael Martin, "The Homeric Hapax Legomena and their Literary Use by Later Authors, Especially Euripides and Apollonius

Rhodius," unpublished Ph.D. dissertation, Columbus, Ohio State University, 1974.

Leinieks, Valdis, *The Plays of Sophocles*, Amsterdam, B.R. Grüner, 1962.

Lloyd-Jones, H., "Heracles at Eleusis: P. Oxy. 2622 and P.S.I. 1391," *Maia*, 19 (1967), pp. 206–29.

——, "Agememnonea," *Harvard Studies in Classical Philology*, 73 (1969), pp. 97–104.

——, "The Electras," *Classical Review*, 83 (1969), pp. 36–8.

——, "Pindar and the After-Life," *Pindare: Entretiens*, 31 (1985), p. 245.

Longman, G.A., "Sophocles *Electra* 1478," *Classical Review*, 68 (1954), pp. 193–4.

McCall, Marsh, "The *Trachiniae*: Structure, Focus, and Heracles," *American Journal of Philology*, 93 (1972), 142–63.

Marry, J.D., "Sappho and the Heroic Ideal: ἔρωτος ἀρετή," *Arethusa*, 12 (1979), pp. 71–92.

Masaracchia, Agostino, "Per l'interpretazione del *Promoteo*. I," *Quaderni urbinati di cultura classica*, 20 (1985), pp. 43–59.

Most, Glenn, W., *The Measures of Praise*, Göttingen, Vandenhoeck & Ruprecht, 1985.

Müller, C.O., *The History and Antiquities of the Doric Race*, 2nd ed. rev., London, J. Murray, 1839.

Page, D., "Stesichorus: The *Geryoneïs*," *Journal of Hellenic Studies*, 93 (1973), pp. 138–54.

Parry, H., "The Second Stasimon of Euripides' *Heracles* (637–700)," *American Journal of Philology*, 86 (1965), pp. 363–74.

Perrotta, Gennaro, *Sofocle*, Milan, 1935; repr. Rome, "L'Erma" di Bretschneider, 1963.

Pinsent, J., "Sophocles, *Antigone* 332–375," *Liverpool Classical Monthly*, 8 (1983), pp. 2–4.

Poliakoff, Michael, "Euripides' *Alcestis* 1029–32," *Mnemosyne*, 35 (1982), pp. 141–3.

Pope, Maurice, "A Nonce–Word in the *Iliad*," *Classical Quarterly*, 35 (1985), pp. 1–8.

Pucci, Pietro, *Odysseus Polutropos: Intertextual Readings in the Odyssey and the Iliad*, Ithaca and London, Cornell University Press, 1987.

Reinhardt, K., *Sophokles*, Frankfurt am Main, V. Klostermann, 1933.

Richards, I.A., *The Philosophy of Rhetoric*, New York, Oxford University Press, 1936.

Ricoeur, P., *The Rule of Metaphor*, Toronto, University of Toronto Press, 1977.

Riffaterre, Michael, *Semiotics of Poetry*, Bloomington, Indiana University Press, 1984; originally published 1978.

Rissman, Leah, *Love as War: Homeric Allusion in the Poetry of Sappho* Königstein, Hain, 1983.

Rivier, André, "En marge d'Alceste et de quelques interprétations récentes," *Museum Helveticum*, 29 (1972), pp. 124–40.

Robert, C., *Oidipus*, Berlin, Weidmann, 1915.

Robertson, Martin, "*Geryoneïs*: Stesichorus and the Vase–Painters," *Classical Quarterly*, 63 (1969), pp. 207–21.

Rossi, L.E. (ed.), *Due seminari di Eduard Fraenkel*, Rome, Edizioni di storia e litteratura, 1977 (= *Sussidi eruditi*, 28, 1977).

Sacks, S. (ed.), *On Metaphor*, Chicago and London, University of Chicago Press, 1979.

Saïd, Suzanne, *Sophiste et tyran ou le problemè du Prométhée enchaîné*, Paris, Klincksieck, 1985.

Scodel, Ruth, *The Trojan Trilogy of Euripides*, Göttingen, Vandenhoeck & Ruprecht, 1980.

——, *Sophocles*, Boston, Twayne Publishers, 1984.

Seaford, Richard, "The Date of Euripides' *Cyclops*," *Journal of Hellenic Studies*, 102 (1982), pp. 161–72.

Segal, Charles Paul, "The *Electra* of Sophocles," *Transactions of the American Philological Association*, 97 (1966), pp. 473–545.

——, "Sophocles' *Trachiniae*: Myth, Poetry, and Heroic Values," *Yale Classical Studies*, 25 (1977), pp. 99–158.

——, *Tragedy and Civilization: An Interpretation of Sophocles*, Cambridge, Mass., and London, Harvard University Press, 1981.

Sheppard, J.T., "Note on Euripides, *Hercules Furens*, 773–800," *Classical Review*, 29 (1915), pp. 68–9.

——, "Notes on Aeschylus' *Persae*, *Classical Review*, 29 (1915), pp. 33–5.

——, "The Formal Beauty of the *Hercules Furens*," *Classical Quarterly*, 10 (1916), pp. 72–9.

——, "The *Electra* of Euripides," *Classical Review*, 32 (1918), pp. 137–41.

——, "The Tragedy of Electra, According to Sophocles," *Classical Quarterly*, 12 (1918), pp. 80–8.

——, "*Electra*: A Defence of Sophocles," *Classical Review*, 41 (1927), pp. 2–9.

——, "*Electra* Again," *Classical Review*, 41 (1927), pp. 163–5.

Sideras, Alexander, *Aeschylus Homericus*, Göttingen, Vandenhoeck & Ruprecht, 1971.

Silk, M.S., *Interaction in Poetic Imagery*, London and New York, Cambridge University Press, 1974.

Slatkin, Laura M., "The Wrath of Thetis," *Transactions of the American Philological Association*, 116 (1986), pp. 1–24.

Solmsen, F., *Electra and Orestes: Three Recognitions in Greek Tragedy*, Amsterdam, N.V. Noord-Hollandsche Uitgevers Maatschappij, 1967.

Smith, Wesley D., "The Ironic Structure in *Alcestis*," *Phoenix*, 14 (1960), pp. 127–45.

Stanley, K., "The Rôle of Aphrodite in Sappho Fr. 1," *Greek, Roman, and Byzantine Studies*, 17 (1976), pp. 305–21.

Steidle, Wolf, *Studien zum Antiken Drama*, Munich, W. Fink, 1968.

Stoessl, Franz, *Der Tod des Herakles*, Zürich, Rhein–Verlag, 1945.

Strohm, H., "Trug und Täuschung," *Würzburger Jahrbuch*, 4 (1949–50), pp. 140–56.

Svenbro, J., "Sappho and Diomedes: Some Notes on Sappho 1 LP and the Epic," *Museum Philologum Londiniense*, 1 (1975), pp. 37–49.

Tanner, Rollin H., "The *Odysseus* of Cratinus and the *Cyclops* of Euripides," *Transactions of the American Philological Association*, 46 (1915), pp. 173–206.

Verrall, A.W., *Euripides the Rationalist*, Cambridge, Cambridge University Press, 1895.

von Fritz, K., "Euripides' *Alkestis* und ihre modernen Nachahmer und Kritiker," *Antike und Abendland*, 5 (1956), pp. 27–69.

Waldock, A.J.A., *Sophocles the Dramatist*, Cambridge, Cambridge University Press, 1966.

Webster, T.B.L., "Sophocles' *Trachiniae*," in C. Bailey, E.A. Barber, C.M. Bowra, J.D. Denniston, and D.L. Page (eds), *Greek Poetry and Life*, Oxford, Oxford University Press, 1936, pp. 164–80.

West, M.L., "The Parodos of the *Agamemnon*," *Classical Antiquity*, 73 (1979), pp. 1–6.

——, "Tragica IV," *Bulletin of the Institute of Classical Studies*, 27 (1980), pp. 9–22.

——, "Problems in Euripides' *Orestes*," *Classical Quarterly*, 37 (1987), pp. 281–93.

Wetzel, G., *De Euripidis Fabula Satyrica quae Cyclops inscribitur, cum Homerico comparata exemplo*, Wiesbaden, O. Harrassowitz, 1965.

Whitman, Cedric H., *Sophocles: A Study of Heroic Humanism*, Cambridge, Mass., Harvard University Press, 1951.

——, *Homer and the Homeric Tradition*, Cambridge, Mass., Harvard University Press, 1958.

——, *Euripides and the Full Circle of Myth*, Cambridge, Mass., Harvard University Press, 1974.

Williams, Gordon, *Figures of Thought in Roman Poetry*, New Haven and London, Yale University Press, 1980.

Winkler, J., "Gardens of Nymphs: Public and Private in Sappho's Lyrics," *Women's Studies*, 8 (1981), pp. 65–91.

Winnington–Ingram, R.P., "Euripides: *Poiêtês Sophos*," *Arethusa* 2 (1969), pp. 127–42.

——, *Sophocles: An Interpretation*, Cambridge , Cambridge University Press, 1980.

——, *Studies in Aeschylus*, Cambridge, Cambridge University Press, 1983.

INDEX

A number of the topics and works below (particularly *allusion* and the *Iliad* and *Odyssey*) are of general concern throughout the book. In such cases only the most important discussions have been indexed. For each play or topic the page numbers of the *main* discussion will be found in italics. For allusions to or in particular passages, the reader is directed to Appendices E and F. The discussion of a particular allusion will generally be found in the *main* discussion of the relevant play.

As a rule, references to modern scholars are indexed only if the reference is made in the text itself. Endnotes have been indexed only when they contain important additional information. Endnote numbers are in parentheses after the number of the page on which the endnote will be found.